The Social Setting
of Jesus and the Gospels

The Social Setting
of Jesus and the Gospels

Edited by

Wolfgang Stegemann
Bruce J. Malina
Gerd Theissen

Fortress Press
Minneapolis

THE SOCIAL SETTING OF JESUS AND THE GOSPELS

Cover images: Capital from Herod's palace at Masada. Photo by Ann Delgehausen. Used by permission.
Sea of Galilee. Photo by Douglas E. Oakman. Used by permission.
Wheat stalks. Getty Images. Copyright © 2002. Used by permission.
Roman coin. Albert J. Copley/Getty Images. Copyright © 2002. Used by permission.
Roman relief. Albert J. Copley/Getty Images. Copyright © 2002. Used by permission.

Cover design: Eric Lecy Design/Michelle Cook/Ann Delgehausen

Book design: Ann Delgehausen

0-8006-3452-7

Manufactured in the U.S.A.
06   05   04   03   02   1   2   3   4   5   6   7   8   9   10

Contents

Social-Boundary Concerns

Politics and Political Religion

Politics and Political Economy

An Overview of the Task

Dedication

The essays in this volume were written for and presented at the fourth international meeting of the Context Group, held in Tutzing, Germany, in June 1999. The general question asked at this meeting was: What can one, with the help of historically informed social-scientific models, know about the "historical" Jesus from the New Testament that cannot be known by other approaches? Most contributors to this book adhered to this theme. The Tutzing meeting proved to be successful in generating scholarly interaction among Context Group members and their German New Testament colleagues. Yet one of the founding members of the Context Group could not attend, and we would like to dedicate this volume to him.

Since the inception of the Context Group in 1989 and of its predecessor, the Social Facets Group of the Jesus Seminar, in the early 1980s, John H. Elliott has structured our annual national programs. Like all Context Group members, Jack came to social-scientific biblical interpretation through a distinctive set of circumstances.

A native of New York City, Elliott received his Bachelor of Arts, Bachelor of Divinity, and Master of Divinity degrees from Concordia Seminary, St. Louis, Missouri, and his degree of Doktor der Theologie from the Westfälische Wilhelms-Universität (1963). He was ordained a Lutheran clergyman in 1963. He taught at Concordia Seminary (1963–67) and at the University of San Francisco from 1967 until his retirement in 2001.

Jack Elliott takes pride in his career of liberal activism. In the 1960s, he protested the Vietnam War and marched in Selma, Alabama. Finding that he shared intellectual interests with a number of his fellow protesters — many of them from Berkeley — Elliott met with them off the streets to explore the intersection of politics and theology. They called themselves the Bay Area Seminar for Theology and Related Disciplines—BASTARDs. Searching for new theological perspectives to deal with the political situation, he began reading widely in sociology and political science. He asked many of the same questions as the liberation theologians active at the time, but he found that they were not systematic or rigorous enough in their analysis.

Jack had written his doctoral dissertation about 1 Peter (*The Elect and The Holy: An Exegetical Examination of 1 Peter 2:4–10 and the Phrase "Basileion Hierateuma,"* NovTSup 12 [Leiden: Brill, 1966]). The nature of the times pressed him to get beyond the scholarship that saw 1 Peter through spiritual lenses and to consider the document in terms of the concrete concerns of real people. Using sociology, he recognized many of the church members addressed in 1 Peter as recent migrants to the places in which they resided. They were resident aliens looked down upon by the native inhabitants. First Peter's author gave a positive interpretation to their condition, pointing to their home with God. Jack published his insights as *A Home for the Homeless: A Sociological Exegesis of 1 Peter, Its Situation and Strategy* (Philadelphia: Fortress Press, 1981). Elliott developed a sociological framework for answering such questions, both in contemporary church experience as well as in the experience of early Jesus group members.

In 1978, Jack was the first Lutheran clergyman to teach at the Pontifical Biblical Institute in Rome, where he found himself in the remarkable position of teaching New Testament to future Roman Catholic professors of biblical studies. In the summer of that year, Elliott attended the Catholic Biblical Association annual meeting, where he gave an address on *Home for the Homeless*. After this address, I sought him out and suggested that we work together based on our shared scholarly concerns. Since 1974, I had chaired a study group exploring sociolinguistics and cultural anthropology for new perspectives on biblical studies. Jack and I immediately hit it off, sparking a lifelong friendship. Eventually like-minded scholars formed the nucleus of a group dedicated to the application of social sciences in New Testament study. In 1986 Elliott chaired a first meeting of a group associated with Robert Funk's Jesus Seminar, the Social Facets Group. The first issues of the Jesus Seminar's journal, *Forum*, witnesses to the prolific scholarship of the Social Facets Group. Yet Jack was likewise one of the first to see that the Jesus Seminar was little concerned with our social-science methods and research. Funk's goal-oriented agenda, focused on immediate results, sought consensus on a number of topics that members of the Social Facets Group thought needed fundamental research. Thanks to an ongoing invitation from Richard Rohrbaugh, Elliott and colleagues severed their association with the Jesus Seminar and assembled annually under the banner of a newly formed Context Group at the Franciscan Retreat Center in Portland, Oregon.

A jovial extrovert, Jack is an indefatigable and indomitable networker. At the same time, he has always been a very careful scholar, a very capable and insightful critic. He has consistently been a source of support for people in our group, in whatever direction their research took them.

His list of scholarly accomplishments is long and can be found in the Context Group bibliography (http://www.kchanson.com/elliott.html). This list of publications has recently culminated in his masterly, encyclopedic commentary on 1 Peter in the Anchor Bible: *1 Peter: A New Translation with Introduction and Commentary*, AB 37b (New York: Doubleday, 2001). Among his other works, perhaps his most significant writings have been the aforementioned *Home for the Homeless* (the second edition has the more precise subtitle *A Social-Scientific Criticism of 1 Peter, Its Situation and Strategy* [Minneapolis: Fortress Press, 1990]), in which he experimented with sociological methods. And in his *What Is Social-Scientific Criticism?* GBS (Minneapolis: Fortress Press, 1993), Jack has amassed a thorough bibliography and presented a sociology-based program systematically listing what needs to be known to understand a social system fully. Equally significant have been his sociological pursuit of sect typology, his anthropological research into the evil eye in antiquity, and his relentless underscoring of the anachronism of finding equality in ancient documents, including the New Testament.

Given the plethora of naive statements and dead-end insights often offered under the label of "new paradigm," or "paradigm shift," or of some "socio-" hyphenated adjective, as well as the frequent confusion of the "social" with sociology, and of sociology with cultural (U.S.) or social (British) anthropology, it is often difficult not to be suspicious of this hermeneutic of the immediately relevant, ecclesiologically oriented, ethnocentric anachronism. In the name of a hermeneutics of relevance, people continue to find a Jesus or Paul who supports their twenty-first-century agenda, ranging from the feminist to the patriarchal. Elliott has always been patient with the naive and diplomatic with the ignorant in the guild. Ever attuned to anachronism and ethnocentrism, Elliott the social activist has always refused to rewrite history and to pretend that Jesus and his followers were social reformers with twenty-first-century sensibilities.

Yet all of his essays, presentations, and books have one thing in common. They are fresh and insightful, and no one can leave them without having learning something new and useful. *Ad multos faustissimosque annos* to a capable colleague, dear friend, and devoted New Testament scholar.

Bruce J. Malina
Creighton University
July 4, 2001

Abbreviations

1QM	War Scroll (*Milḥamah*)
1QpHab	Habakkuk Pesher
1QS	Rule of the Congregation
1QSa	Rule of the Congregation (Appendix A to 1QS) 1Q28a
4Q274	4Q Purification Rules A (*Tohoroth A*)
4Q560	Against Demons (Exorcism 2r)
4QDᵈ	Damascus Document (4Q269)
4QMMT	*Miqṣat Ma'asê ha-Torah* (4Q394)
11QTemple	Temple Scroll (11Q19)
AB	Anchor Bible
ABD	*Anchor Bible Dictionary*
ABRL	Anchor Bible Reference Library
AGAJU	Arbeiten zur Geschichte des antiken Judentums und des Urchristentums
AJS	*American Journal of Sociology*
ANRW	*Aufstieg und Niedergang der römischen Welt*
Ant.	Josephus, *Antiquities of the Judeans*
Ap.	Josephus, *Against Apion*
Aphor.	The Hippocratics, *Aphorisms*
ARA	*Annual Review of Anthropology*
b.	Babylonian Talmud
BA	*Biblical Archaeologist*
BAR	*Biblical Archaeology Review*
BASOR	*Bulletin of the American Schools of Oriental Research*
BETL	Bibliotheca ephemeridum theologicarum lovaniensium

BETTA	Beiträge zur evangelischen Theologie, theologische Abhandlungen
BibInt	*Biblical Interpretation*
BibIntSer	Biblical Interpretation Series
BJSP	*British Journal of Social Psychology*
BNTC	Black's New Testament Commentary
B. *Qam.*	*Baba Qamma*
BR	*Biblical Research*
BRev	*Bible Review*
BTB	*Biblical Theology Bulletin*
BZ	*Biblische Zeitschrift*
BZNW	Beihefte zur ZNW
CBQ	*Catholic Biblical Quarterly*
CC	Continental Commentaries
Crass.	Plutarch, *Crassus*
CRINT	Compendia rerum iudaicarum ad Novum Testamentum
CSSA	*Cambridge Studies in Social Anthropology*
CSSH	*Comparative Studies in Society and History*
CurTM	*Currents in Theology and Mission*
Did.	*Didache*
EKKNT	Evangelisch-katholischer Kommentar zum Neuen Testament
Ep. Apos.	*Epistle to the Apostles*
EvQ	*Evangelical Quarterly*
EvTh	*Evangelische Theologie*
ExpTim	*Expository Times*
FBESG	Forschungen und Berichte der evangelischer Studiengemeinschaft
FGH	*Die Fragmente der griechischen Historiker.* Edited by F. Jacoby
FRLANT	Forschungen zur Religion und Literatur des Alten und Neuen Testaments
FTod	*Folklore Today*
FTS	Frankfurter theologische Studien
GBS	Guides to Biblical Scholarship
Gos. Eb.	*Gospel of the Ebionites*
Gos. Thom.	*Gospel of Thomas*
Gos. Naz.	*Gospel of the Nazarenes*
Gyn.	Soranus, *Gynaeciorum*

Ḥag.	*Ḥagigah*
HeyJ	*Heythrop Journal*
Hist. eccl.	Eusebius, *Histoia ecclesiastica*
Hor.	*Horayot*
HR	*History of Religions*
HTR	*Harvard Theological Review*
HTS	*Hervormde Teologiese Studies*
HUCA	*Hebrew Union College Annual*
IDB	*Interpreter's Dictionary of the Bible*
IEJ	*Israel Exploration Journal*
Int	*Interpretation*
ITQ	*Irish Theological Quarterly*
JAAR	*Journal of the American Academy of Religion*
JBL	*Journal of Biblical Literature*
JBTh	*Journal of Biblical Theology*
JCCP	*Journal of Cross-Cultural Psychology*
JECS	*Journal of Early Christian Studies*
JETS	*Journal of the Evangelical Theological Society*
JJS	*Journal of Jewish Studies*
JPS	*Journal of Peasant Studies*
JRASup	Journal of Roman Archaeology Supplements
JRH	*Journal of Religious History*
JRS	*Journal of Roman Studies*
JSI	*Journal of Social Issues*
JSJ	*Journal for the Study of Judaism in the Persian, Hellenistic, and Roman Periods*
JSNT	*Journal for the Study of the New Testament*
JSNTSup	JSNT Supplement Series
JSocSci	*Journal of Social Sciences*
JSOTSup	Journal for the Study of the Old Testament Supplement Series
JSPSup	Journal for the Study of the Pseudepigrapha Supplement Series
JTS	*Journal of Theological Studies*
Ketub.	*Ketubot*
KJV	King James Version (Authorized Version)
KTA	Kroners Taschenausgabe
LCL	Loeb Classical Library
LEC	Library of Early Christianity

LSEMSA	London School of Economics Monographs on Social Anthropology
LSJ	H. G. Liddell, R. Scott, H. S. Jones, *A Greek-English Lexicon*. 9th ed. with revised supplement
LUÅ	Lunds Universitets Årsskrift
LXX	Septuagint
m.	Mishnah
Meg.	*Megillah*
MM	J. H. Moulton and G. Milligan, *The Vocabulary of the Greek Testament*
MT	Masoretic Text
NAB	New American Bible
Nat. hist.	Pliny, *Natural History*
NEB	New English Bible
NIBC	New International Bible Commentary
NICNT	New International Commentary on the New Testament
NIV	New International Version
NJB	New Jerusalem Bible
NovT	*Novum Testamentum*
NovTSup	NovT Supplements
NRSV	New Revised Standard Version
NSK.AT	Neue Stuttgarter Kommentar: Altes Testament
NTL	New Testament Library
NTOA	Novum Testamentum et Orbis Antiquus
NTR	New Testament Readings
NTS	*New Testament Studies*
NTTS	New Testament Tools and Studies
OBT	Overtures to Biblical Theology
OEANE	*Oxford Encyclopedia of Archaeology in the Near East.* Edited by E. M. Meyers
Or.	Dio Chrysostom, *Orations*
ÖTNT	Ökumenischer Taschenbuchkommentar zum Neuen Testament
PACE	*Professional Approaches for Christian Educators*
par.	parallel(s)
P.Fiorentini	Fiorentini Papyri
Pesaḥ.	*Pesaḥim*
PGM	*Papyri graecae magicae: Die griechischen Zauberpapyri.* Edited by K. Preisendanz

P.Oxy.	*Oxyrhynchus Papyri*
Q	The Sayings Source Q
Qidd.	*Qiddušin*
REB	Revised English Bible
RevExp	*Review and Expositor*
RGG⁴	*Religion in Geschichte und Gegenwart: Handwörterbuch für Theologie und Religionswissenschaft.* Edited by H. D. Betz et al. 4th ed.
RivB	*Rivista biblica italiana*
Roš. Haš.	*Roš Haššanah*
RSR	*Recherches de science religieuse*
RSV	Revised Standard Version
SBEC	Studies in the Bible and Early Christianity
SBL	Society of Biblical Literature
SBLDS	SBL Dissertation Series
SBLSP	*SBL Seminar Papers*
SBLSymS	SBL Symposium Series
SBT	Studies in Biblical Theology
Šeb.	*Šebiʿit*
Šeqal.	*Šeqalim*
Šabb.	*Šabbat*
SHJ	Studying the Historical Jesus
SJLA	Studies in Judaism in Late Antiquity
SJT	*Scottish Journal of Theology*
SNTSMS	Society for New Testament Studies Monograph Series
SNTSU	Studien zum Neuen Testament und seiner Umwelt
SocProb	*Social Problems*
SocQ	*Sociological Quarterly*
Spec. Leg.	Philo, *Special Laws*
SUNT	Studien zur Umwelt des Neuen Testaments
SV	Scholars Version
t.	Tosephta
T.Gad	*Testament of Gad*
Ta'an.	*Ta'anith*
TBT	*The Bible Today*
TDNT	*Theological Dictionary of the New Testament.* Edited by G. Kittel and G. Friedrich
TEV	Today's English Version
Top.	Aristotle, *Topics*

T.Sol.	*Testament of Solomon*
TRE	*Theologische Realenzyklopädie*
UJT	Understanding Jesus Today
WUNT	Wissenschaftliche Untersuchungen zum Neuen Testament
y.	Jerusalem Talmud (Yerusalmi)
ZNW	*Zeitschrift für die neutestamentlichen Wissenschaft*
ZTK	*Zeitschrift für Theologie und Kirche*

Introductory Perspectives

1

Social-Scientific Methods in Historical Jesus Research

Bruce J. Malina

Social-scientific interpretation of New Testament documents involves reading some New Testament writing by first selecting a suitable model accepted in the social-scientific community,[1] and using the model to form adequate scenarios for reading the document in question (see Malina 1991b, reprinted in 1996d). Forming adequate scenarios involves retrojecting an appropriate model to the first-century eastern Mediterranean culture area by a process of abduction, while making it applicable by using proper filters to keep out anachronism and ethnocentrism (Malina 1991a; 1996c). When I speak of social-scientific interpretation and the historical Jesus, I refer to a process like the one just described (see Malina 1981; 1982; 1983; 1997c; Elliott 1993; Pilch 1994a; May 1997).[2] The purpose of this presentation is to highlight what social-scientific research in New Testament studies offers the various quests for the historical Jesus (see Moxnes 1997, "Theological Importance"; Theissen and Merz 1998:1–15).

It is perhaps important to note that North American Context Group scholars who employ the social sciences in biblical research teach, for the most part, at the undergraduate level (the German upper Gymnasium level). The quest for the historical Jesus that the Context Group members might take up is triggered largely, if not exclusively, by the fact that group members teach undergraduates who want to know about Jesus in the same way they know about other persons and things. In other words, the work of these scholars is not ecclesiastically driven. While it is true that they are aware of what the guild is seeking, their concerns are to answer their students' questions within the students' undergraduate training and context (many, if not most, know about the social sciences and many know the natural sciences).[3] What these scholars "prove" has to make sense to these students and to the invisible audience of their Context Group peers. Furthermore, they teach in institutions that do not have hermetically sealed departments. This means that they do in fact interact with faculty members and students from a range of departments. Finally, as U.S.-enculturated persons, they are rationalistic pragmatists. As pragmatists, they believe that reality exists all around; as socially enculturated rationalists, they believe that this reality has been and is socially interpreted (not socially constructed).[4]

For the most part, social-scientific research in New Testament studies has been concerned with interpreting written documents, not with the general storytelling of historians. In other words, its concerns have been exegetical, not historiographical (see Malina 1991a; 1991c). This is perhaps why, so far, there has been no "life" of the historical Jesus based on social-scientific interpretations (but see Herzog 2000; Moxnes 1999; Stegemann and Stegemann 1999). Nonetheless, what has been done with the social sciences is significant, much of it important enough to be plagiarized by John Dominic Crossan.

Mid-Twentieth-Century Presuppositions about Socialization and Enculturation

The presuppositions for the social-scientific perspectives developed here are the following truisms, largely of the mid–twentieth century.

First, human beings are socialized and enculturated in a specific social system, at a given time and place. So, too, Jesus.

Second, because of their socialization and enculturation, human beings share meanings with others in their social group, and these meanings are expressed in language, gesture, artifacts, and the like. The meanings expressed in language, gesture, and artifacts derive from and express the social system at a given time and place, into which the persons communicating have been enculturated. So, too, Jesus.

Third, whatever persons perceive, they perceive according to the social presuppositions they bring to the events they perceive. So, too, Jesus. (These three presuppositions are truisms common to the social sciences, as any textbook in the field will demonstrate).

Fourth, it is certain that Jesus was socialized and enculturated in an eastern Mediterranean society uninfluenced by globalism, universalism, scientism, the modern city, the industrial revolution, nation-state, the Enlightenment, international law, the Renaissance, Arab-European scholasticism, Justinian's Code, Constantine's Christendom, the talmudic Jewish religion, and the like. It is certain that he was socialized and enculturated in hellenized Israelite peasant society, hence influenced by what we today call Hellenism as it was assimilated in Israelite peasant village life in that section of the Roman province of Syria called Galilee.

And fifth, it is equally certain that Jesus was socialized and enculturated into a high-context society. High-context societies produce sketchy and impressionistic documents, leaving much to the reader's or hearer's imagination and common knowledge. Since people in such societies believe that few things have to be spelled out, few things are in fact spelled out. This is so because people have been socialized into widely shared ways of perceiving and acting (Malina 1991b). Hence, much can be accurately assumed.

The fourth and fifth presuppositions, as abstract as they may seem, derive from the Enlightenment passion for accurate chronology typical of historians, who as a rule work from a perspective of "immaculate perception."[5] They believe that the facts, the evidence, are there for the picking—"just read the sources!" While I do not for a moment believe in "immaculate perception," I share the historians' chronological data set and come to the following conclusions.

A Basic Certainty and Its Corollaries

The basic certainty underlying this approach is that Jesus of Nazareth was socialized in a specific first-century, eastern Mediterranean set of social institutions, that he was enculturated in a set of value orientations and values specific to the social system in question, and that he behaved according to the general norms of modal personality operative in that social system. Social systems consist of social institutions, value configurations, and modal personalities. Social institutions are fixed forms of social life. Since the separation of church and state, and of market/bank and state, occurred in the eighteenth century, we can safely say that in the world of Jesus there were only two focal social institutions, kinship and politics. Economics and religion were embedded; hence, the roles, statuses, and values of kinship and politics were used to express and understand economics and religion (Malina 1986g; 1994e; 2001).

A number of other certainties are relevant to the story of Jesus (for data from historians, see the useful sources compiled in Hanson 1996). First, we know that persons in antiquity were enculturated in collectivistic societies; hence, they were collectivistic personalities. They were not individualistic (Malina 1978c; 1979; 1989b; 1990b; 1992; 1993b; 1993c; 1994d; 1995b; 1996e; Malina and Neyrey 1991b; 1996; Pilch 1997b). Their concerns had to do with group integrity—the integrity of their families, forced to be nucleated in Galilee (Guijarro 1997; 1998). They were likewise concerned with the integrity of their fellow villagers, of the people of Galilee whose dialect they shared, and of Israelites in general, all chosen by the God of Abraham, Isaac, and Jacob.

Furthermore, we are sure of the value orientations and the values that influenced Jesus' contemporaries in their interaction with others. If we consider the standard value objects found in all societies (self, others, nature, time, space, and the All; see Pilch and Malina 1993; 1998), we can safely say that Jesus and those he recruited defined self in terms of gender, genealogy, and geography (Malina and Neyrey 1996). In terms of gender, their society was patriarchal, with females embedded in related males, and lower-status bonded males likewise embedded in higher-status males; a higher-status female was of greater value than any male of lesser rank. The patriline (male and female offspring) had entitlements, but not the matriline. Interactions followed the pathways of honor and shame with challenge and riposte, which were duly engendered (Malina 1981; 1993b; Malina and Neyrey 1991c; Neyrey 1998).

As far as others were concerned, people and groups were assessed in terms of in-group and out-group boundaries, drawn in terms of general group patterns (e.g., family, village, region, and ethnic group are always in-group versus other families, villages, regions, and ethnic groups). This in-group/out-group perception replicated thinking in terms of either/or (both/and does not emerge until the seventeenth century). All groups were ethnocentric, using their in-group as the norm for what is human. This ethnocentrism included the authors of the Gospels and the authors' communities. In fact, all New Testament documents were ethnocentric, and the "ethnos" or in-group was Israel. To find "anti-Semitism" (nineteenth-century coinage) in the New Testament is certainly and totally anachronistic (Malina 2000b).

People lived subject to nature, with great concern to understand entities that impinged on their lives, whether visible entities like stars and planets or invisible ones like spirits, angels, and demons. Human nature—hence, human character—never changed (Malina and Neyrey 1996). Stories of the past were very useful since they offered direction for behavior in the present. What people knew for certain was that they were not in control of their existence and, for the most part, were not responsible for what was happening to them (Malina 1992). Everyone, from king to beggar, knew that all goods in life were limited. As with land, there was no way to increase the amount of the good things in life without impinging on another (Malina 1978b; 1993b:90–116). Perceptions of limited good inevitably entailed awareness of envy, which, in its Mediterranean configuration, was usually characterized by the evil eye (see Elliott 1988; 1990; 1992; 1994; Neyrey 1988).

Notions of time focused on a broad present that included the immediate past (to which Jesus' contemporaries were living witnesses) and the forthcoming (deriving from present behavior). Knowledge of the distant past or the distant future was unavailable to human beings. Only God knew the past and the future—and God might reveal that information, if necessary, to God's prophets, like Moses, who describes creation, and Samuel, who wrote of his own period and of Israel's kings.

This was the peasant worldview. Its temporal orientation was to the broad present in a way that was pre-clock, pre-monastic, pre-Newtonian, pre-Enlightenment, pre–Industrial Revolution, and pre-Einstein (Malina 1989a). In the first-century Mediterranean, everyone knew that nature was running down, in a process of devolution as we would say (an analogy deriving from animate beings) (Malina 1997b; 1998).

Space was interpreted in terms of territoriality—that is, marked off and controlled by persons with force to back up their claims. Society was ruralized, with central places (Heb. 'ir; Gk. polis) serving as part-time residences for elite farmers and ranchers, to produce power to control the surround and beyond. There was little clear division between town and country, since elites had their primary residence in the country (see Greene 1986:140; Malina 2000a). Just as there was geographical territoriality, there was also celestial territoriality, with celestial entities having significant impact on the lands below (Malina 1993a).

Even with this limited general overview, one can see the types of collectivistic persons that made up the core members of the Jesus group, who were intent on proclaiming theocracy to Israel. They were to perform this task in a ruralized society characterized by force, cruelty, and extortion from elites toward nonelites (Hobbs 1995; Malina 1994b; 2000b; Seland 1995). To avoid the full impact of such elite power, persons had to find duly placed patrons (Elliott 1996; Malina 1978a; 1988b; Moxnes 1991).

Historical Certainties

Jesus Proclaimed Theocracy

All critics agree that if Jesus did anything, he proclaimed the kingdom of heaven, a politically correct Israelite way of saying "kingdom of God" (Malina 2001). This expression fell under the category of politics, specifically political religion. In more abstract language, the kingdom of heaven was a form of theocracy. The repentance required for participation in the forthcoming kingdom consisted in persons getting their lives in order for living in the new political order.

If one were to apply the prevailing criteria of authenticity,[6] then, to Jesus' proclamation of a forthcoming kingdom of God (or of heaven or of the sky;

Matt 4:17; Mark 1:15; Luke 4:42), criteria involved would be embarrassment
(no such theocracy emerged); incongruity (behavior urged in Matthew and
Luke is for fictive kin groups, not theocracy); multiple attestation (all Synoptics, notably lacking in Paul); and coherence (Jesus was crucified for causing
political unrest).

Jesus Formed a Political Faction

All sources agree that, after Jesus' career was over, a group existed that previously
had been closely connected to Jesus (Malina 1988b). If such a group did exist, it
must have been formed within the framework of Jesus' concern. If Jesus' concern
was with theocracy, then this group was related to theocracy, a set of persons who
witnessed to Jesus' program. Within a political institution, a group formed to
support someone's program is called a faction. Hence I believe it is certain that
Jesus formed a faction. Factions by definition are coalitions, that is, groups
formed by a central person for a specific purpose and a specific time.

Again, using the usual criteria, Jesus recruited a group of persons to assist
him in proclaiming the forthcoming theocracy (Matt 4:18–22; Mark 1:16–20;
Luke 5:1–11). Criteria involved include embarrassment (the proclamation
proved vacuous); incongruity (in the Synoptics, these recruits act like a faction
of a political religion rather than fictive kin-group founders); multiple attestation (all Synoptics mention this recruitment and an initial attempt at proclamation); and coherence (all Synoptics report that group members accompany
Jesus on his final trip to Jerusalem; they flee).

Jesus Was Concerned with Israel Alone

Jesus' proclamation of a forthcoming theocracy looked to Israel alone (Malina
2000b). The theocracy has nothing to do with non-Israelites. Only Israel and Israelite tradition have a social role of Messiah, and only Israel's tradition has a
cosmic figure known as the "son of man" connected with Israelite theocracy.

The theocracy proclaimed by Jesus and his group was an exclusively Israelite theocracy (Matt 10:5, explicitly; Mark 6:7; Luke 9:2, contextually). Criteria include embarrassment (in Matthew, no Samaritans, while Luke includes
them; in Acts and Paul problems with admitting non-Israelites to Jesus messianist groups; no word of Jesus on this score); incongruity (none in Matthew,
Mark, or John, which are solidly against non-Israelites; for John, Samaritans are
Israelites but not Judeans; the incongruity surfaces in Acts and in Paul's Galatians); multiple attestation (all Synoptics report Jesus having no theocratic out-
reach to non-Israelites; at most there are healings, which are not distinctive to
Jesus); and coherence (all Synoptics report that Jesus' career is oriented to Israel, to Jerusalem, to obeying the God of Israel).

As for the son of man again:

> The harbinger of this kingdom, Jesus said, would be a celestial or astral entity
> called "the Son of Man" (Matt 24:30; Mark 13:26; Luke 21:27; see also Matt
> 16:27; Mark 8:38; Luke 9:26): criteria involved would be embarrassment (no
> such celestial entity appeared); incongruity (Jesus is identified with this celestial
> entity); multiple attestation (all the Gospels mention this, notably lacking in
> Paul); coherence (Jesus often spoke of celestial or astral phenomena; final dis-
> course is in astrological forecast terms). (Malina 1997b)

Perhaps at this point it is useful to mention that the categories Jew/Jewish,
Christian, and pagan are anachronistic in historical Jesus research (see Malina and Rohrbaugh 1992:32–34; 1998:44–46; Pilch 1993b; 1996b; 1997a;
1998b). In modern usage, these words point to groups and values that post-
date Constantine. All Jews on the planet today trace back to the Talmud (with
Ashkenazi Jews being eighth-century C.E. central Russian Khazar converts).
Christians trace back to Christendom, the political religion of Constantine
and its subsequent councils. And the word "pagan" was coined after Constantine by Christian elites to label non-Christians (O'Donnell 1979). For more
appropriate designations, I suggest Judean/Israelite, Messianist, and Gentiles
or non-Israelites.

Jesus Spoke Only of the God of Israel

There is no evidence of universalism of any sort in antiquity (Malina 1992).
The deities of various ethnic groups were the groups' traditional gods, even if
Hellenistic theology began to see equivalence among the many gods of the
Roman *oikoumene.* But this would be apparent only to persons living among
outsiders. This was not Jesus' experience, to the best of our knowledge. Just as
stars had impact only on the lands over which they were to be found (Malina
1993c; 1994a), so, too, the deities in the sky (and often visiting the temples on
land below). In his concern for theocracy in Israel, Jesus proclaimed this theocracy in the name of the God of Israel, the God confessed in the Shema.

The "God" to whom Jesus refers and relates is always "the God of Israel"
(Matt 15:31; Mark 12:29; Luke 1:68; ancestral God, Matt 22:32; Mark 12:26;
Luke 20:37; Acts 3:13; 7:32; Matt 8:11, and compare Luke 13:29). The criteria
involved again include embarrassment (in Paul and Revelation, there is but
one God, no specific "God of Israel"); incongruity (none in the Synoptics,
hints of incongruity in Acts, e.g., in Peter's vision of one God of all people, and
in Paul and Revelation); multiple attestation (all Synoptics report Jesus relating
to the traditional God of Israel, referring to the Shema which refers explicitly to

Israel's God); and coherence (all Synoptics report that the theocracy Jesus proclaimed refers to the rule of Israel's God over Israel).

Jesus Necessarily Spoke of Political Religion and Political Economy

If Jesus proclaimed theocracy, which is certain, his proclamation must have included religious (Hanson and Oakman 1998; Malina 1986g; 1994e; 2001) and economic dimensions (Oakman 1986; 1999; Moxnes 1988), since, during that period, religion and economics were embedded in politics and necessarily included in it. Since the forthcoming theocracy would revitalize Israel, it would entail "proper" approaches to God as well as "proper" provisioning of Israelite society, whatever these aspects may have been in detail.

The Life of Jesus: A Collectivistic Life, from Group Formation to Adjourning

One can readily produce a general description of the life of Jesus from the fact that Jesus recruited a faction (a certainty). This life of Jesus consists of a chronology of Jesus' activity, of his social movement. This outline does not require any of the time sequences in the Synoptics or John, but it does help frame Jesus' career. Data in the Gospels might then be attached to this outline and flesh out a highly probable life of Jesus.

The reason for this assertion is that group formation and group development are rigidly structured at a high level of abstraction (as rigidly structured as the human skeleton). The structures have been verified in a wide range of cross-cultural situations so as to be self-evident. To say that the structures are so abstract as to be historically worthless denies what historians do: begin with an abstract pattern of structures, gather data to fit those patterns, then tell a story that unfolds the patterns in terms of the data. There is no "immaculate perception." At least with these structures, which human beings inevitably follow, we have skeletal certitude (the same certitude European scholars used to identify the "Ice Man" as human!).

I begin with the usual pattern of group development. There are, generally speaking, two types of groups: task groups and support groups. If Jesus' faction intended to proclaim the forthcoming theocracy to Israel, it was a task group. Task groups have five phases: forming, storming, norming, performing, and adjourning. These five phases form a chronological sequence in Jesus' public career. (Since he had a public career, he must have been born and developed before launching that career. And since, in antiquity, all infancy descriptions originate after a person's career is complete, such accounts might readily be attached to a life of Jesus—with the same verisimilitude as other ancient, unwitnessed infancy stories.)

Why Jesus Formed a Group: Stages in Small-Group Formation

The story of Jesus' career begins with the formation of a small group, Jesus' faction (see Malina 1995a). Such small-group formation implies that the founder has a project, so as to recruit a group to assist. Group formation is always rooted in the solution to some problem. It is a truism in small-group research that small groups emerge because some person becomes aware of a need for change. That person shares this awareness with others, who nurture hope of success in implementing the change in a societal context in which group formation is expected (Zander 1985; Ross and Staines 1972). Since Jesus did proclaim a kingdom and looked on God as father (that is, proclaimed a political, political-religious, and political-economic theocracy to Israel; see Malina 1988b, reprinted in Malina 1996d), he was aware of a solution to Israel's political problems and was in the process of sharing that solution with others. That Jesus offered such a solution likewise indicates that Israel had political problems that some believed required solution. Those who heard Jesus' solution would compare that solution with other available solutions, and if they found it feasible, they would adopt it and tell others about it. At this point, people would be amenable to forming a small group around Jesus. If the solution were rejected, then Jesus' proclamation would be without effect. In brief, the features of small-group formation may be summed up as aware, share, compare, declare (Malina 1995a). Here Jesus is prophet as problem solver.

The Life of Jesus as Reflected in Small-Group Development

Group development concerns changes in the group over time as well as changes in the relationship between the group and each of its members. The development of the Jesus group likewise marks the unfolding of Jesus' activity over time—a life of Jesus. Hence the value of knowing how the Jesus group developed. Cross-cultural study of small groups has produced the following model of their stages, with verifiably predictable behavior at each stage. The stages are forming, storming, norming, performing, and adjourning (based on the work of Tuckman 1965; Tuckman and Jansen 1977; and further corroborated by Moreland and Levine 1988).

Forming. The forming stage occurs when the group is put together. Groups are formed either to accomplish some extragroup task or for intragroup social support. The faction recruited by Jesus was a group with an extragroup task to perform. The activity of this group is articulated variously in the Synoptic tradition. At first it is vague, expressed as "fishers of men" (Mark 1:17; Matt 4:19; see Hanson 1997; Q 10:2 remembers a reference to "harvest," as does John 4:35; Rom 1:13). In the so-called mission charge, the vague project is expanded: to proclaim that God soon will take over the country, to urge Israelites to get their affairs in order, and to heal those in need of healing. Mark implies that group members were chosen with healing ability in tow (Mark 3:15 and 6:7 mention only that Jesus gave the Twelve authority over unclean spirits; yet, when they return, "they anointed with oil many that were sick and healed them," 6:13). Matthew 10:6 and Luke 9:1 (10:9 is unclear on this score), on the other hand, state that Jesus bestowed this healing ability on his recruits (see Pilch 1992; 1993a; 1995b; 2000). During the forming stage, group members discuss the nature of their task and how it might be performed. The behavior of group members toward each other is tentative; commitment to the group is low.

Storming. At the storming stage, persons invited to join the group jockey for position and ease into interpersonal stances. Members of task groups such as the Jesus faction resist the need to work closely with one another. Conflict among members emerges, with emotions getting free expression. Group members at this stage become more assertive, and each tries to change the group's purposes to satisfy personal needs. Members' commitment to the group is higher than it was before (on conflict, see Malina 1988a; Malina and Neyrey 1991a).

In the Synoptics, we have many remembrances of this phase: the dispute about who is greatest (Mark 9:33–37; Mark 18:1–5; Luke 9:46–48); a general argument about precedence (Mark 10:41–44; Matt 20:24–27; Luke 22:24–27); concern for sitting next to Jesus in the kingdom (Matt 20:20–23; Mark 10:35–40; not in Luke); and the general concern about rewards (Mark 10:28–31; Matt 19:27–30; Luke 18:28–30). Peter's rebuke to Jesus after talk about suffering and death is an attempt to persuade Jesus to change goals to fit the group concern (Mark 8:32–33; Matt 16:22–23; not in Luke).

Norming. The norming stage is marked by interpersonal conflict resolution in favor of mutually agreed-upon patterns of behavior. This phase is one of exchange in task groups such as the Jesus faction. Everyone in the group shares ideas about how to improve the group's performance. Norming involves group members in the attempt to resolve earlier conflicts, often by negotiating clearer guidelines for group behavior.

The task norms for Jesus' core group are listed in the so-called mission discourse (Matt 10:5–16 and expanded with vv. 17–25; Mark 6:7–11; see 3:13–15; Luke 9:1–5).

Performing. With the performing stage, group participants carry out the program for which the group was assembled. Performing marks the problem-solving stage of task groups. Members solve their performance problems and work together productively. From the evidence provided in the New Testament documents, it is clear that the Jesus faction moved into a performing stage (return from successful task performance: Mark 6:12–13; Luke 9:6; no report in Matthew). The sending of the seventy(-two) and their success (Luke 10:1–20) points to enlarged activity. This implies further recruitment or forming, with subsequent storming and norming, leading to greater performing.

What the performing consisted of, by all accounts, was proclamation and healing. Healing took place in a context of political religion and, hence, readily threatened those in authority (see Hollenbach 1982). The purpose of healing was to restore the ill person to his/her station in society (Pilch 1992; 1993a). Jesus himself had healing abilities, as did his core group members (Pilch 1995b; 2000). They likewise knew how to enter altered states of consciousness (Pilch 1993c; 1995c; 1996a; 1998a). Jesus' own altered state of consciousness experiences made it easy for his core group and his fellow Galileans to consider him a holy man (shaman) (Malina 1999a; Pilch 1998c; Craffert 1998) and prophet (Pilch 1998a; Malina 1997b).

It was his healing behavior that called Jesus to the attention of Jerusalem authorities ("by what authority do you *do* these things"; see Hollenbach 1982). This led to the group's adjourning.

Adjourning. With adjourning, group members gradually disengage from activities in a way that reflects their efforts to cope with the group's approaching end. Of course, the event that precipitated the adjourning of the Jesus group was Jesus' crucifixion. Crucifixion, like any public execution, was a status-degradation ritual (Malina and Neyrey 1988). All typical features of the status-degradation ritual appear in all the Gospel accounts. The specific features can easily be described (Neyrey 1994; Pilch 1995a). The motive for Jesus' death was reported as envy—a motive that perfectly fits the general Mediterranean culture area, the perception of limited good, and concern for honor (Hagedorn and Neyrey 1998). Envy certainly seems to be the motive of the collectivistic persons who had Jesus put to death.

The Aftermath of the Jesus Group

Forming again. In the Gospel story, the performing phase comes to a rather abrupt end, marked by the crucifixion of Jesus. With regard to Jesus' core group, the postcrucifixion stories attest liberally to preparations for adjourning, quashed by the appearance of the risen Jesus, an altered state of consciousness experience (Pilch 1998a; see also Malina and Rohrbaugh 1998). With this experience, a feedback loop enters the process with new storming, norming, and subsequent performing, as described telescopically in the final sections of Matthew and Luke, but at length in opening of Acts (for Matthew's community, see, notably, Duling 1995a; 1995b; 1997; 1999). The trigger event for this loop was the core group's experience of Jesus after his death, an experience understood as the work of God, now perceived as "He who raised Jesus from the dead" (Acts 3:15; Rom 8:11). God thus indicated that Jesus is Israel's forthcoming Messiah. The new storming among the remaining Jesus-group members led to what I call a Jesus Messiah group.

Telescoped storming and norming in Matthew and Luke. For the Jesus Messiah group, political concerns were still at the forefront, notably in Acts. Jesus is Israel's Messiah, to come soon. This message would make sense to Israelites. But Paul (and the story of Cornelius in Acts) gives evidence of non-Israelites coming to join Jesus Messiah groups (God calls—this is not the outcome of recruiting). The New Testament documents point to two solutions to the problem of non-Israelite presence. One held that they were like resident aliens in Israel (Acts 15, using Leviticus 17–18). This view would only make sense in locations where Israelites were in the ascendancy: in Judea, Galilee, Perea, Israelite quarters of Alexandria, Antioch, Damascus, and the like. Note that these are places where Paul did not found churches; these regions are called "the circumcision" in Galatians. I call these groups in Israelite territories "Messianic Jesus groups" (in Acts, Jesus followers were called "messianists"). On the other hand, in regions where Israelites were not ascendant, where, in fact, they were resident aliens, it made little sense to treat non-Israelites as resident aliens. In such places, Paul and his colleagues founded churches. I call these churches "Resurrected Jesus groups." But this takes us far beyond the life of Jesus. Yet these groups are no longer political religious groups, but fictive-kin religious groups, a form patterned on domestic religion, with "brothers and sisters." People who joined these groups were interested in a way of life; being a disciple of Jesus was, for them, to follow a way of life, not to await the kingdom of heaven in Israel. This development needs to be mentioned since the Gospel documents as we have them evidence fictive-kin groups that do not trace back to Jesus.

The development, running from the political religion of the Jesus Messiah group to the kinship religion of Messianic Jesus groups and Resurrected Jesus groups, permeates the Gospels. Experiences of these fictive-kin groups evoke words of Jesus, given their newly discovered way of life "in Christ."

In sum, we know with certainty that Jesus proclaimed theocracy, formed a political faction, was concerned with Israel alone, and spoke only of the God of Israel in typical ethnocentric fashion, and thus necessarily dealt with political religion and political economy in Israel. We can with certainty sketch his career in terms of the stages of small-group development, from formation to adjournment. We can likewise use social psychology to sketch the collectivistic modal personality of the time and place. All this information is useful for assessing the traditions about Jesus presented in the Gospels, canonical and otherwise. While the information may be too abstract to form an adequate biography of Jesus, it surely provides boundaries that will warn us when a historian's biography is erroneous.

Notes

1. I have disallowed the use of Festinger's model of what happens "when prophecy fails" (Malina 1982) as well as Weber's model of the charismatic (Malina 1984) because social scientists in the United States claim that these models cannot be verified in human behavior. Biblical scholars wishing to admit these models in their research by criticizing my position would do better to take up the issue with the social scientists, not with me. I still stand behind the principle that if a social-scientific model is called into question or rejected by reputable social scientists, we would do well not to apply it in social-scientific interpretation.

2. As a rule, social-scientific interpretation of the Bible is confused with social history. In 1982, I warned about the lack of precision developing in the terminology in social history and in some social-scientific approaches to biblical interpretation. In French and German, there is little if any difference between "social" and "sociological," while in English the difference is notable. "Social description" and "social history" are no more "sociology" than "policy" and "politics" are identical, although the word "sociology" in French and German refers to both disciplines. For most nonpractitioners, there is little difference between sociology and anthropology (although British social scientists are given to fuse the two). It is unfortunate if these imprecisions in terminology have been imported into the lexicon of biblical scholarship (see, for example, the works of Barton, Holmberg, Kee, Malherbe, Meeks, and Peterson, to name a few; and, most recently, see Horrell 1999). Use of the social sciences in biblical interpretation should at least be acceptable to and recognizable by social scientists and by undergraduate students who take courses in the social sciences. While social historians

use concepts and hypotheses as a basis for selection and interpretation, and cannot proceed otherwise (although "immaculate perceptionists" believe they do), there are in fact two main differences between social historians and social scientists. The first is that the social historian's conceptualizations are invariably implicit, arbitrary, and unsystematic, while the social-scientific interpreter's are explicit and systematic. The second is the social historian's tendency to evade, as far as possible, the theoretical issues that underpin historiography, because what historians consider to be sources usually provide them a loose narrative pattern to which the facts can be related. In other words, social historians prefer not to deal with the underlying structures and cultural value orientations; rather, their concern is with so-called events and personalities, which are usually more sharply delineated in historical records (narratives) than in the materials social-scientific interpretation uses (see especially Barraclough 1978:45–64).

3. It is important for non-Americans to realize that all Americans are enculturated to believe that they are totally competent in making decisions relative to politics, religion, and sex. Relative to religion, Zöller writes: "The religious culture of America provides an example of this separate American development, which counters expectations that advancing modernization, with its loosening of social ties, would lead to the disappearance of religion. Initially, the development of religion in America appeared to be merely a variation on English patterns. But as early as the late eighteenth century there arose specifically American forms of religion that, despite their diversity, shared the conviction that individuals not only had the *right* to choose their religious affiliation but were also *competent* to evaluate their religious choices" (1998:10). For the most part, persons who take our courses in the life of Jesus come believing that they know all there really is to know about Jesus and that the course will simply reinforce it.

4. The perception of the "social construction of reality" is quite idealistic (see Malina 1999a:355). It derives from that Kantian spin-off known as the "sociology of knowledge" (often confused in religious studies with the academic discipline of sociology). It is a Romantic view that normally conflicts with U.S. pragmatism, which insists that reality is not socially constructed, but the social conceptions by which we produce our culturally rooted perceptions. The metaphor "social construction of reality" is inadequate and clearly misleading, unless it means "social construction of socially constructed reality." In the latter case it is just silly, since it presumes two types of reality: socially constructed and non–socially constructed. This leads some to believe that non–socially constructed reality cannot be known. Again, this is silly, since anything human beings know intuitively and directly is known intuitively and directly by all members of the species, even though such experiences lack a social component, for example, pain, joy, fatigue, exhilaration, and the like. Such pragmatic experiences indicate that reality is socially interpreted, not socially constructed. While these social interpretations are based largely on direct experience, these social interpretations of reality leave reality intact. This is why there are many different cultures—each a social

interpretation of reality. This is also why there are many difficulties with translation or hermeneutics—moving from the social systems that gave meaning to biblical documents, to social systems in which those documents can make sense only with contortions called appropriation (see Prickett 1996).

Hermeneutics, as a rule, is conceived as the task of translating the essence of a text into contemporary terms. New Testament mythology (i.e., culturally irrelevant stories) is translated into existential categories compatible with and understandable to "the modern mind" (i.e., a different social system). Social-scientific interpretation, on the other hand, conceives its task as translating (transferring) a contemporary person into the social system of persons who authored and populate the pages of the New Testament. With social-scientific interpretation, contemporary persons with their "modern minds" are made compatible with and sensitive to the categories of New Testament mythology within the social systems in which that mythology produced and sustained meaning.

5. Like Edwin A. Judge earlier (1980), Richard A. Horsley represents this approach: "To establish an adequate historical sociology or anthropology, we must move beyond illustrating models (such as those of structural-functional sociology or pan-Mediterranean cultural anthropology) to a more dialectical movement between textual and other evidence for ancient social structures, conflicts and meanings analyzed with the help of modern Western sociological methods, on the one hand, and [between] models and methods which we critically adapt and revise on the basis of our historical analysis of texts and cultural artifacts, on the other" (1994:12). "Such studies illustrating social science models from NT texts involve a questionable presumption of continuity (in effect) from findings of modern anthropologists to the realities of ancient Hellenistic Roman life. . . . If in the absence of literary or other evidence, we are to give credence to presumptions of historical continuity, then for the Palestinian peasantry among whom the Synoptic Gospel traditions originated it would make far more sense to imagine continuity with the lore and values we know through biblical literature and history in the preceding centuries. Such continuity, moreover, would appear to be confirmed by the values manifested in ancient popular movements more contemporary with Jesus known through Josephus and other ancient writers" (14 n. 22). The attitude of "immaculate perception" continues; most recently, in an unrelated book review, Blake Leyerle of Notre Dame writes: "Models, especially those developed by B. Malina and other members of the Context group, are too often presented as reality rather than as hermeneutical tools" (1999:170). How does one present reality except in terms of models (i.e., hermeneutical tools)?

6. "The rather abstract, general principles used to evaluate the authenticity of statements attributed to Jesus include the following: criteria of discontinuity, embarrassment, incongruity, multiple attestation, explanation and coherence" (Barr 1995:467–73; Duling and Perrin 1994:520–23). There is general consensus that statements ascribed to

Jesus militating against Second Temple Israelite behavior, as well as against behavior espoused by later Jesus Messiah groups (discontinuity), trace back to Jesus with high probability. Similarly, Jesus' statements that express sentiments and values awkward for Jesus Messiah groups (embarrassment) have a very high probability of tracing back to Jesus himself. Further, there is likewise general consensus that a statement attributed to Jesus in tension with other ideas in the same text (incongruity), as well as a statement found in a number of early sources (multiple attestation), has a high probability of tracing back to Jesus himself. Statements attributed to Jesus that account for his rejection and crucifixion (explanation) along with those that produce a cogent portrait of a "believable" person (coherence) are generally viewed as "possible to probable in value" (Malina 1999b:27–28). Theissen (1996) seeks to refine these criteria in face of "Lessing's Yawning Gulf." The way I read Lessing, the problem is one of true and false criteria emerging from Piaget-like formal operational thinking, in the face of judgments of validity and nonvalidity emerging in post-formal operational thinking characterized by commitment (see the data and model provided by Perry 1970). Lessing's "cogent truths of reason" are abstract, true or false propositional judgments, while his "contingent truths of history" are abstract statements of validity or nonvalidity based on a person's cognitive development and social situation (who, with whom, when, where, why). As Lessing states: "Contingent truths of history can never serve to prove cogent truths of reason" (cited in Theissen 1996:148). People who think in terms of true/false can never make commitments unless they pass through a heavy dose of multiplicity (experiential awareness of both/and) and relativity (experiential awareness that everything is related to something or someone else, and nothing or no one really stands alone, i.e., is absolute; see Perry 1970).

Works Cited

Barr, David L. 1995. *New Testament Story: An Introduction.* 2d ed. Belmont, Calif.: Wadsworth.

Barraclough, Geoffrey. 1978. *Main Trends in History.* Main Trends in the Social and Human Sciences 2. New York: Holmes & Meier.

Craffert, Pieter. 1998. "Jesus and the Shamanic Complex: Social Type and Historical Figure." Paper delivered at the Annual Meeting of the Society of Biblical Literature, Orlando, Florida.

Duling, Dennis C. 1990. "Binding and Loosing (Matt 16:19; 18:18; John 20:23)." *Forum* 3, no. 4:3–31.

———. 1995a. "The Matthean Brotherhood and Marginal Scribal Leadership." In Esler 1995:159–82.

———. 1995b. "Matthew and Marginality." *HTS* 51:1–30.

———. 1995c. "Small Groups: Social Science Research Applied to Second Testament Study." *BTB* 25:179–93.

———. 1997. "Egalitarian Ideology, Leadership, and Factional Conflict in the Gospel of Matthew." *BTB* 27:124–37.

———. 1999. "Matthew 18:15–17: Conflict, Confrontation, and Conflict Resolution in a 'Fictive Kin' Association." *BTB* 29:4–22.

Duling, Dennis C., and Norman Perrin. 1994. *The New Testament: Proclamation and Parenesis, Myth and History.* 3d ed. Fort Worth, Tex.: Harcourt, Brace.

Elliott, John H. 1988. "The Fear of the Leer: The Evil Eye from the Bible to Li'l Abner." *Forum* 4, no. 4:42–71.

———. 1990. "Paul, Galatians, and the Evil Eye." *CurTM* 17:262–73.

———. 1992. "Matthew 20:1–15: A Parable of Invidious Comparison and Evil Eye Accusation." *BTB* 22:52–65.

———. 1993. *What Is Social-Scientific Criticism?* GBS. Minneapolis: Fortress Press.

———. 1994. "The Evil Eye and the Sermon on the Mount: Contours of a Pervasive Belief in Social-Scientific Perspective." *BibInt* 2:51–84.

———. 1996. "Patronage and Clientage." In Rohrbaugh 1996:144–56.

Esler, Philip F., ed. 1995. *Modelling Early Christianity: Social-Scientific Studies of the New Testament in Its Context.* New York and London: Routledge.

Greene, Kevin. 1986. *The Archaeology of the Roman Economy.* Berkeley: University of California Press.

Guijarro, Santiago. 1997. "The Family in First-Century Galilee." In Moxnes, ed., 1997:42–65.

———. 1998. *Fidelidades en conflicto: La ruptura con la familia pro causa del discipulado y de la misión sinóptica.* Plenitudo Temporis 5. Salamanca, Spain: Universidad Pontificia de Salamanca.

Hagedorn, Anselm C., and Jerome H. Neyrey. 1998. "'It Was Out of Envy That They Handed Jesus Over' (Mark 15.10): The Anatomy of Envy and the Gospel of Mark." *JSNT* 69:15–56.

Hanson, K. C. 1996. "Greco-Roman Studies and the Social-Scientific Study of the Bible: A Classified Periodical Bibliography (1970–1994)." *Forum* 9, nos. 1–2:63–119. <http://www.kchanson.com/CLASSIFIEDBIB/grstud.html>

———. 1997. "The Galilean Fishing Economy and the Jesus Tradition." *BTB* 27:99–111. <http://www.kchanson.com/ARTICLES/fishing.html>

Hanson, K. C., and Douglas E. Oakman. 1998. *Palestine in the Time of Jesus: Social Structures, Social Conflicts.* Minneapolis: Fortress Press.

Herzog, William, II. 2000. *Jesus, Justice, and the Reign of God: A Ministry of Liberation.* Louisville: Westminster John Knox.

Hobbs, Raymond. 1995. "The Language of Warfare in the New Testament." In Esler 1995:259–73.

Hollenbach, Paul W. 1981. "Jesus, Demoniacs, and Public Authorities: A Socio-Historical Study." *JAAR* 49:567–88.

Horrell, David G., ed. 1999. *Social-Scientific Approaches to New Testament Interpretation*. Edinburgh: T. & T. Clark.

Horsley, Richard A. 1994. *Sociology and the Jesus Movement*. 2d ed. New York: Crossroad.

Judge, Edwin A. 1980. "The Social Identity of the First Christians: A Question of Method in Religious History." *JRH* 11:201–17.

Leyerle, Blake. 1999. "Review of *Constructing Early Christian Families*, ed. H. Moxnes." *JECS* 7:169–70.

Malina, Bruce J. 1978a. "Freedom: The Theological Dimensions of a Symbol." *BTB* 8:62–76.

———. 1978b. "Limited Good and the Social World of Early Christianity." *BTB* 8:162–76.

———. 1978c. "The Social World Implied in the Letters of the Christian Bishop-Martyr (Named Ignatius of Antioch)." In *SBLSP 1978*. 2:71–119. Missoula, Mont.: Scholars.

———. 1979. "The Individual and the Community: Personality in the Social World of Early Christianity." *BTB* 9:126–38.

———. 1980. "What Is Prayer?" *TBT* 18:214–20.

———. 1981. *The New Testament World: Insights from Cultural Anthropology*. Atlanta: John Knox.

———. 1982. "The Social Sciences and Biblical Interpretation." *Int* 37:229–42.

———. 1983. "Why Interpret the Bible with the Social Sciences." *American Baptist Quarterly* 2:119–33.

———. 1984. "Jesus as Charismatic Leader?" *BTB* 14:55–62.

———. 1985a. "Banquet," "Cup," "Hospitality," "Humility," "Laying on of Hands," "Pity," "Service." In *Harper's Bible Dictionary*, edited by P. J. Achtemeier. San Francisco: Harper and Row.

———. 1985b. *The Gospel of John in Sociolinguistic Perspective*. Forty-eighth Colloquy of the Center for Hermeneutical Studies. Edited by H. Waetjen. Berkeley, Calif.: Center for Hermeneutical Studies.

———. 1986a. *Christian Origins and Cultural Anthropology: Practical Models for Biblical Interpretation*. Atlanta: John Knox.

———. 1986b. "Interpreting the Bible with Anthropology: The Question of Poor and Rich." *Listening: Journal of Religion and Culture* 21:148–59.

———. 1986c. "Miracles or Magic II." *RSR* 12:35–39.

———. 1986d. "Normative Dissonance and Christian Origins." *Semeia* 35:35–59.

———. 1986e. "Reader Response Theory: Discovery or Redundancy." *Creighton University Faculty Journal* 5:55–66.

———. 1986f. "The Received View and What It Cannot Do: III John and Hospitality." *Semeia* 35:171–94.

———. 1986g. "Religion in the World of Paul: A Preliminary Sketch." *BTB* 16:92–101.

———. 1987. "Wealth and Poverty in the New Testament and Its World." *Int* 41:354–67.

———. 1988a. "Mark 7: A Conflict Approach." *Forum* 4, no. 3:3–30.

———. 1988b. "Patron and Client: The Analogy behind Synoptic Theology." *Forum* 4, no. 1: 2–32.

———. 1989a. "Christ and Time: Swiss or Mediterranean?" *CBQ* 51:1–31.

———. 1989b. "Dealing with Biblical (Mediterranean) Characters: A Guide for U.S. Consumers." *BTB* 19:127–41.

———. 1990a. "From Isis to Medjugorje: Why Apparitions?" *BTB* 20:76–84.

———. 1990b. "Mary—Woman of the Mediterranean: Mother and Son." *BTB* 20:54–64.

———. 1991a. "Interpretation: Reading, Abduction, Metaphor." In *The Bible and the Politics of Exegesis: Essays in Honor of Norman K. Gottwald on His Sixty-fifth Birthday*, edited by D. Jobling et al., 253–66. Cleveland: Pilgrim.

———. 1991b. "Reading Theory Perspective: Reading Luke-Acts." In Neyrey 1991:3–23.

———. 1991c. "Scienze sociali e interpretazione storia: La questione della retrodizione." *RivB* 39:305–23.

———. 1992. "Is There a Circum-Mediterranean Person? Looking for Stereotypes." *BTB* 22:66–87.

———. 1993a. "Apocalyptic and Territoriality." In *Early Christianity in Context: Monuments and Documents. Essays in Honour of Emmanuel Testa*, edited by F. Manns and E. Alliata, 369–80. Jerusalem: Franciscan Printing Press.

———. 1993b. *The New Testament World: Insights from Cultural Anthropology*. 2d ed. Louisville: Westminster John Knox.

———. 1993c. *Windows on the World of Jesus: Scenarios for New Testament Interpretation*. Louisville: Westminster John Knox.

———. 1994a. "The Book of Revelation and Religion: How Did the Book of Revelation Persuade." *Scriptura* 51:27–50.

———. 1994b. "Establishment Violence in the New Testament World." *Scriptura* 51:51–78.

———. 1994c. "John's: The Maverick Christian Group—The Evidence of Sociolinguistics." *BTB* 24:167–82.

———. 1994d. "'Let Him Deny Himself' (Mark 8:34//): A Social Psychological Model of Self-Denial." *BTB* 24:106–19.

———. 1994e. "Religion in the Imagined New Testament World: More Social Science Lenses." *Scriptura* 51:1–26.

————. 1995a. "Early Christian Groups: Using Small-Group Formation Theory to Explain Christian Organizations." In Esler 1995:96–113.

————. 1995b. "Maria, Doncella y Madre Mediterranea: Mundo mediterráneo: trasfondo mítico de los siglos I–IV." *Ephemerides Mariologicae* 45:69–91.

————. 1995c. "Power, Pain, and Personhood: Asceticism in the Ancient Mediterranean World." In *Asceticism*, edited by V. L. Wimbush and R. Valantasis, 162–77. New York: Oxford University Press.

————. 1996a. "Mediterranean Sacrifice: Dimensions of Domestic and Political Religion." *BTB* 26:26–44.

————. 1996b. "Review Essay: The Bible—Witness or Warrant? Reflections on Daniel Patte's *Ethics of Biblical Interpretation*." *BTB* 26:82–87.

————. 1996c. "Social-Scientific Criticism and Rhetorical Criticism: Why Won't Romanticism Leave Us Alone?" In *Rhetoric, Scripture, and Theology: Essays from the 1994 Pretoria Conference*, edited by S. E. Porter and T. H. Olbricht, 71–101. JSNTSup 131. Sheffield: Sheffield Academic.

————. 1996d. *The Social World of Jesus and the Gospels*. London: Routledge.

————. 1996e. "Understanding New Testament Persons: A Reader's Guide." In Rohrbaugh 1996:41–61.

————. 1996f. "Wealth and Poverty in the New Testament World." In *On Moral Business: Classical and Contemporary Resources for Ethics in Economic Life*, edited by M. L. Stackhouse et al., 88–93. Grand Rapids: Eerdmans, 1995.

————. 1997a. "Embedded Economics: The Irrelevance Of Christian Fictive Domestic Economy." *Forum for Social Economics* 26, no. 2:1–20.

————. 1997b. "Jesus as Astral Prophet." *BTB* 27:83–98.

————. 1997c. "Mediterranean Cultural Anthropology and the New Testament." In *La Bíblia i el Mediterrani—La Biblia y el Mediterráneo—La Bible et la Méditerranée—La Bibbia e il Mediterraneo: Actes del Congrés de Barcelona 18–22 de setembre de 1995*, edited by A. Borrell et al. Vol. 1:151–78. Abadia de Montserrat, Spain: Associació Bíblica de Catalunya, 1997.

————. 1998. "How a Cosmic Lamb Marries: The Image of the Wedding of the Lamb (Rev 19:7 ff.)." *BTB* 28:75–83

————. 1999a. "Assessing the Historicity of Jesus' Walking on the Sea: Insights from Cross-Cultural Social Psychology." In *Authenticating the Activities of Jesus*, edited by C. A. Evans and B. Chilton, 351–71. NTTS 28/2. Leiden: Brill.

————. 1999b. "Criteria for Assessing the Authentic Words of Jesus: Some Specifications." In *Authenticating the Words of Jesus*, edited by C. A. Evans and B. Chilton, 27–45. NTTS 28/1. Leiden: Brill.

————. 2000a. *The New Jerusalem in the Revelation of John: The City as Symbol of Life with God*. Zacchaeus Studies. Collegeville, Minn.: Liturgical.

————. 2000b. "Three Theses for a More Adequate Reading of the New Testament." In *Practical Theology: Perspectives from the Plains*, edited by Michael G. Lawler and Gail S. Ritsch. Omaha, Neb.: Creighton University Press.

————. 2001. *The Social Gospel of Jesus.* Minneapolis: Fortress Press.

Malina, Bruce J., and Jerome H. Neyrey. 1988. *Calling Jesus Names: The Social Value of Labels in Matthew.* Sonoma, Calif.: Polebridge.

————. 1991a. "Conflict in Luke-Acts: A Labelling and Deviance Theory." In Neyrey, ed., 1991:97–122.

————. 1991b. "First-Century Personality: Dyadic, Not Individual." In Neyrey, ed., 1991:67–96.

————. 1991c. "Honor and Shame in Luke-Acts: Pivotal Values of the Mediterranean World." In Neyrey, ed. 1991:25–65.

————. 1996. *Portraits of Paul: An Archaeology of Ancient Personality.* Louisville: Westminster John Knox.

Malina, Bruce J., and John J. Pilch. 2000. *Social-Science Commentary on the Book of Revelation.* Minneapolis: Fortress Press.

Malina, Bruce J., and Richard L. Rohrbaugh. 1992. *Social-Science Commentary on the Synoptic Gospels.* Minneapolis: Fortress Press.

————. 1998. *Social-Science Commentary on the Gospel of John.* Minneapolis: Fortress Press.

May, David M. 1997. "'Drawn from Nature or Common Life': Social and Cultural Reading Strategies for the Parables." *RevExp* 94:199–214.

Moreland, Richard L., and John M. Levine. 1988. "Group Dynamics over Time: Development and Socialization in Small Groups." In *The Social Psychology of Time: New Perspectives*, edited by J. E. McGrath, 151–81. Newbury Park, Calif.: Sage.

Moxnes, Halvor. 1988. *The Economy of the Kingdom: Social Conflict and Economic Interaction in Luke's Gospel.* OBT. Philadelphia: Fortress Press.

————. 1991. "Patron-Client Relations and the New Community in Luke-Acts." In Neyrey, ed., 1991:241–68.

————. 1997. "The Theological Importance of the 'Third Quest' for the Historical Jesus." In *Whose Historical Jesus?* edited by W. E. Arnal and M. Desjardins, 132–42. Studies in Christianity and Judaism 7. Waterloo, Ontario: Wilfrid Laurier University Press.

————. 1999. "The Historical Jesus: From Master Narrative to Cultural Context." *BTB* 29:135–49.

————, ed. 1997. *Constructing Early Christian Families: Family as Social Reality and Metaphor.* New York: Routledge.

Neufeld, Dietmar. 1996. "Eating, Ecstasy, and Exorcism (Mark 3:21)." *BTB* 26:152–62.

Neyrey, Jerome H. 1988. "Bewitched in Galatia: Gaul and Cultural Anthropology."
    CBQ 50:72–100.

———. 1991a. "Ceremonies in Luke-Acts: The Case of Meals and Table Fellowship."
    In Neyrey, ed., 1991:361–87.

———. 1991b. "The Symbolic Universe of Luke-Acts: 'They Turn the World Upside
    Down.'" In Neyrey, ed., 1991:271–304.

———. 1994. "Despising the Shame of the Cross: Honor and Shame in the Johan-
    nine Passion Narrative." *Semeia* 68:113–37.

———. 1995. "Loss of Wealth, Loss of Family, and Loss of Honour: The Cultural
    Context of the Original Makarisms in Q." In Esler 1995:139–58.

———. 1996a. "Clean/Unclean, Pure/Polluted, and Holy/Profane: The Idea and Sys-
    tem of Purity." In Rohrbaugh 1996:80–104.

———. 1996b. "Meals, Food, and Table Fellowship." In Rohrbaugh 1996:159–82.

———. 1998. *Honor and Shame in the Gospel of Matthew.* Louisville: Westminster
    John Knox.

———, ed. 1991. *The Social World of Luke-Acts: Models for Interpretation.* Peabody,
    Mass.: Hendrickson.

Oakman, Douglas E. 1986. *Jesus and the Economic Questions of His Day.* SBEC 8.
    Lewiston, N.Y.: Mellen.

———. 1994. "The Archaeology of First-Century Galilee and the Social Interpreta-
    tion of the Historical Jesus." In *SBLSP 1994,* 220–51. Atlanta: Scholars.

———. 1999. "The Lord's Prayer in Social Perspective." In *Authenticating the Words
    of Jesus,* edited by C. A. Evans and B. Chilton, 137–86. NTTS 28/1. Leiden: Brill.

O'Donnell, James J. 1979. "The Demise of Paganism." *Traditio* 35:45–88.

Perry, William G., Jr. 1970. *Forms of Intellectual and Ethical Development in the Col-
    lege Years: A Scheme.* New York: Holt, Rinehart & Winston.

Pilch, John J. 1992. "BTB Readers Guide: Understanding Healing in the Social World
    of Early Christianity." *BTB* 22:26–33.

———. 1993a. "Insights and Models for Understanding the Healing Activity of the
    Historical Jesus." In *SBLSP 1993,* 154–77. Atlanta: Scholars.

———. 1993b. "Jews or Judeans: A Translation Challenge." *Modern Liturgy* 20, no. 3:19.

———. 1993c. "Visions in Revelation and Alternate Consciousness: A Perspective
    from Cultural Anthropology." *Listening* 28:231–44.

———. 1994a. "Illuminating the World of Jesus with Cultural Anthropology." *The
    Living Light* 31:20–31.

———. 1994b. "Secrecy in the Mediterranean World: An Anthropological Perspec-
    tive." *BTB* 24:151–57.

———. 1995a. "Death with Honor: The Mediterranean Style Death of Jesus in
    Mark." *BTB* 25:65–70.

———. 1995b. "Insights and Models from Medical Anthropology for Understanding the Healing Activity of the Historical Jesus." *HTS* 21:314–37.

———. 1995c. "The Transfiguration of Jesus: An Experience of Alternate Reality." In Esler 1995:47–64.

———. 1996a. "Altered States of Consciousness: A 'Kitbashed' Model." *BTB* 26:133–38

———. 1996b. "Jews and Christians: Anachronisms in Bible Translations." *PACE* 25 (April): 18–25.

———. 1997a. "Are There Jews and Christians in the Bible?" *HTS* 53:1–7.

———. 1997b. "BTB Readers Guide: Psychological and Psychoanalytical Approaches to Interpreting the Bible in Social-Scientific Context." *BTB* 27:112–16.

———. 1998a. "Appearances of the Risen Jesus in Cultural Context: Experiences of Alternate Reality." *BTB* 28:52–60.

———. 1998b. "No Jews or Christians in the Bible." *Explorations (Rethinking Relationships among Protestants, Catholics, and Jews)* 12, no. 2:3.

———. 1998c. "A Window into the Biblical World: Walking on the Sea." *TBT* 36: 117–23.

———. 2000. *Healing in the New Testament: Insights from Medical and Mediterranean Anthropology.* Minneapolis: Fortress Press.

Pilch, John J., and Bruce J. Malina, eds. 1993. *Biblical Social Values and Their Meanings: A Handbook.* Peabody, Mass.: Hendrickson.

———. 1998. *Handbook of Biblical Social Values.* Rev. ed. Peabody, Mass.: Hendrickson.

Prickett, Stephen. 1996. *Origins of Narrative: The Romantic Appropriation of the Bible.* Cambridge: Cambridge University Press.

Rohrbaugh, Richard L., ed. 1996. *The Social Sciences and New Testament Interpretation.* Peabody, Mass.: Hendrickson.

Ross, Robert, and Graham L. Staines. 1972. "The Politics of Analyzing Social Problems." *SocProb* 20:18–40.

Seland, Torrey. 1995. *Establishment Violence in Philo and Luke: A Study of Non-conformity to the Torah and Jewish Vigilante Reactions.* BibIntSer 15. Leiden: Brill.

Stegemann, Ekkehard W., and Wolfgang Stegemann. 1999. *The Jesus Movement: A Social History of the First Century.* Translated by O. C. Dean Jr. Minneapolis: Fortress Press.

Theissen, Gerd. 1996. "Historical Scepticism and the Criteria of Jesus Research or My Attempt to Leap across Lessing's Yawning Gulf." *SJT* 49:147–76.

———. 1998. "Jésus et la crise sociale de son temps: Aspects socio-historique de la recherche du Jesus historique." In *Jesus de Nazareth: Nouvelles approches d'une énigme,* edited by C. A. Evans and B. Chilton, 137–86. Le Monde de la bible 38. Geneva: Labor et Fides.

Theissen, Gerd, and Annette Merz. 1998. *The Historical Jesus: A Comprehensive Guide*. Translated by J. Bowden. Minneapolis: Fortress Press.

Tuckman, Bruce W. 1965. "Developmental Sequence in Small Groups." *Psychological Bulletin* 63:384–99.

Tuckman, Bruce W., and M. A. C. Jansen. 1977. "Stages of Small-Group Development Revisited." *Group and Organization Studies* 2:419–27.

Zander, Alvin. 1985. *The Purposes of Groups and Organizations*. San Francisco: Jossey-Bass.

Zöller, Michael. 1998. *Bringing Religion Back In: Elements of a Cultural Explanation of American Democracy*. Occasional Paper 21. Washington, D.C.: German Historical Institute.

2

Ethnocentrism and Historical Questions about Jesus

Richard L. Rohrbaugh

It is a commonplace in New Testament scholarship to say that the answers we get are determined by the questions we ask. Yet it does not appear to have dawned on many historical Jesus researchers that ethnocentric results are frequently the result of questions that are themselves rooted in ethnocentric bias. In order to explore this possibility, I examine one of the central questions in historical Jesus research: the question of the so-called messianic self-consciousness of Jesus. Few questions in historical Jesus research have generated more print, or more disagreement, than this one.

To tread on this ground might at first seem dangerous. After all, Western scholars have debated it intensively for a century and a half and yet remain deeply divided. My purpose, however, is neither to review nor to analyze the enormous literature on this subject.[1] Rather, I examine the question about Jesus' self-understanding to determine (1) whether the question itself is inappropriate and (2) whether the question predetermines a range of answers that are peculiarly Western in character and, therefore, inevitably ethnocentric. Should this turn out to be true, it seems likely to call into question a considerable portion of the Western scholarly effort to understand who Jesus was.

The Nature of the Question

First, let us explore the nature of the question being asked. The question appears in the titles of books and articles throughout the twentieth century.[2] In its most basic form, the question inquires into the *self*-understanding of Jesus. Exactly who did he think he was? Was he acting out an identity of his own choosing? Did he have a conscious agenda of his own? Did his *self*-understanding define his mission? That is the heart of the matter.

Many researchers have asked these questions in rather naive fashion, as if we somehow could do a psychological inquiry into Jesus' sense of self. Ragnar Leivestad, for example, claims that "if there is no possibility of attaining any psychological understanding and insight," then the person of Jesus will inevitably be an "unapproachable enigma and his proclamation abstract and distant" (1987:12).[3] Others, however, have grasped that this understanding is not possible. Thus, Joachim Gnilka readily acknowledges that the Gospels do not contain psychological texts with which to work (1997:248).

What virtually all of the many inquiries into this question have in common has recently (and forcefully) been asserted in an article by Ben F. Meyer: "We take it, for our part, that Jesus was a man with a definite view of himself" (1994:341).[4] That Jesus had a definite view of himself is taken for granted by virtually all Western scholars addressing the issue. Yet this underlying assumption has remained almost completely unexamined in the historical Jesus literature to date. That is true, I believe, because *self*-understanding is so fundamental to the Western perception of what it is to be human that it is nearly impossible for us to conceive of a human being without it.

The Self as Cultural Construct

Missing in the discussion is recognition that the concept of the "self" is a cultural construct that differs markedly from one society to the next. As hard as it is for Westerners to conceive, social scientists have demonstrated that not everyone shares our understanding of what it is to be a human self. Moreover, as Edward Stewart and Milton Bennett have argued, few cultural realities contain the potential for more misunderstanding than this one (1991:129–47).

According to social scientists, societies may be placed along a continuum in regard to views of the self. On the one hand, some societies understand persons individualistically. In these societies, the individual is seen as a bounded and unique center of consciousness, a more or less integrated cognitive and motivational universe. The key to understanding persons in such societies is the psychological makeup of the individual. On the other hand, some societies view the self as fundamentally collective. Persons are so embedded in groups that the group and the individual are in large measure coextensive, both psychologically and in every other way.

Americans and, to varying degrees, most other Westerners, stand at the individualist end of this spectrum. Mediterranean persons, however, including those of the biblical period, must be located primarily at the collectivist end. The difference between Westerners and Mediterranean persons is thus rather substantial. Moreover, it is a difference that New Testament scholars cannot afford to overlook. As F. Sushila Niles has recently argued, a near consensus among social scientists is that such individualist-collectivist differences may be the most important factor in determining social behavior (1998:315–16).

Individualist Cultures

In all the individualistic cultures of the West, then, and especially in the United States, individualism rests on the fundamental notion that "each person is not only a biological entity, but also a unique psychological being" (Stewart and Bennett 1991:129). The self is fundamentally subjective; hence, individuals are endowed with unique perception, unique personal opinions, their own creativity, and personal preferences (130). Being subjective, this Western self can best be examined via its own subjectivity. As a result, the Western individualistic self is highly introspective and, in the last analysis, can finally and completely be known only to itself. For Westerners, therefore, *self*-understanding is always the heart of the matter.

Variations among individualist cultures exist, of course, and I say more about these below. But the differences notwithstanding, most individualists share certain key characteristics. First, they base identity on personal experiences, personal achievements, possessions, abilities, and personal preferences (Triandis 1995:71). They tend to attribute actions to internal causes and to personal choices in ways that collectivists do not.[5] They focus on personal rights, needs, and abilities. They are relentless in seeking cognitive consistency. Individualists attribute motives to internal needs and aspirations. They give greater priority to attitudes than to norms and treat values as matters of individual choice. They value privacy and private property. Career, life work or mission, purpose, and even religion are matters to be worked out by individual choice. Above all, individualists assume that ability, effort, and responsibility are the basis for personal success.

This sort of individualism, however, has been rare in world culture. It is nearly absent in the Middle East today and almost certainly was in antiquity as well. Most important, there is virtually nothing in the New Testament or in the Jesus tradition that suggests an individualistic culture (Malina 1993:67). The Western type of individualism simply did not exist. To my knowledge, however, recognition of this fact has been virtually absent from historical Jesus research to date — even though applying these concepts to the historical Jesus is certainly an ethnocentric mistake. That will be clearer if we take a moment to contrast individualist cultures with the collectivist cultures of the biblical period.

Collectivist Cultures

It is first necessary to clarify what we mean by a collectivist culture. It may be defined as a culture in which persons understand themselves as parts of groups or collectives such as family, tribe, or nation (Triandis 1995:2). Persons are defined by the groups to which they belong and do not understand themselves as having a separate identity. They are motivated by group norms rather than individual needs or aspirations, and strenuously avoid articulating personal goals or giving them priority over the goals of the group. For most collectivists, the primary identity group is the family, although belonging to additional in-groups is common. Since personal identity and group identity are completely inseparable, however, separation from a group in these societies always involves a loss of self (Malina 1993).

It is important to recognize that collectivism is both a historical development and one involving considerable variation. Geography, ecology, language, mode of production, family size, age structures, affluence, urbanism, and the presence or absence of personal choice all shape human patterns of self-perception. Thus anthropologists see evidence that hunter-gatherers were primarily individualists. By contrast, agrarian societies, and especially agrarian societies in which peasant farming provides a marginal living for the vast majority, have been almost exclusively collectivist. Both agricultural practices and marginal resources require extensive cooperation for simple survival (Triandis 1995:82–83). Thus Triandis argues that 70 percent of the world's population is currently collectivist rather than individualist (1995:13). Others put the figure as high as 80 percent (Pilch 1997:113). Most important, since nearly all agrarian cultures are and have been collectivist, it is likely that ancient Mediterranean society was no exception.

If all these observations are true, we cannot assume a definition of the self when we inquire about the self-understanding of Jesus. We certainly cannot assume a Western definition. Indeed, we have to ask whether questions Westerners have been using since the time of Reimarus are appropriate. As Harry Triandis, the foremost researcher in this field, has pointed out, the individualism-versus-collectivism distinction is a fundamental challenge to the universal applicability of Western psychological understandings (1995).[6]

Horizontal and Vertical Cultures

Not all individualist or collectivist cultures are individualist or collectivist to the same degree, or for the same reasons, or in the same fashion. Thus we can make an additional set of distinctions that will aid in locating contemporary

Western cultures in relation to ancient Palestine. Triandis distinguishes between what he calls "horizontal" and "vertical" cultures, each of which produces individualism and collectivism of a different type (1995:44ff.).

Cultures that tolerate relatively small differences in status, power, and privilege Triandis calls horizontal. The range of social stratification in these societies is thus rather small. By contrast, societies in which differences in status, power, and affluence are much greater, Triandis calls vertical. In vertical societies, social stratification is both marked and rigid. Thus, if we examine this cultural characteristic in relation to individualism and collectivism, we obtain the results in figure 2.1.

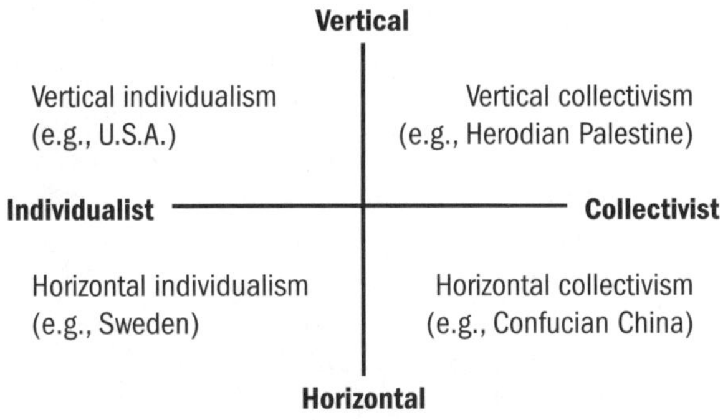

Vertical

Vertical individualism
(e.g., U.S.A.)

Vertical collectivism
(e.g., Herodian Palestine)

Individualist ———————————————————— **Collectivist**

Horizontal individualism
(e.g., Sweden)

Horizontal collectivism
(e.g., Confucian China)

Horizontal

Figure 2.1: Types of individualist and collectivist societies

First, as the diagram indicates, cultures in which persons maintain a high degree of independence, and yet which tolerate only small differences in power, status, and affluence, produce a horizontal individualism. Triandis cites Sweden as an example. Second, cultures that likewise tolerate relatively small differences in status and power, and yet hold a collectivist view of the self, can be termed horizontal collectivist. Confucian China is perhaps an example. Third, cultures that tolerate significant differences of status, hence that are vertical, but that, at the same time, are also individualist, produce achievement-oriented, hedonistic, acquisitive, and competitive social behavior. A prime example is obviously the United States. Finally, cultures that tolerate wide differences of status and power, yet that are predominantly collectivist in outlook, produce the kind of vertical collectivism that characterized the Mediterranean societies of antiquity.

Individualism in Vertical Collectivist Societies

It is important to recognize that no society is one way or the other, either completely individualist or collectivist. For example, although certain kinds of individualists exist in predominantly (vertical) collectivist societies, we cannot assume that all persons in all collectivist societies are to be characterized in the same way. Individualistic behavior did exist in the vertical, collectivist societies of the ancient Mediterranean world.

That said, however, we must point out that these "individualistic" persons in collectivist societies are not the equivalent of the introspective, psychologically minded, self-reliant individualists familiar to modern Americans. Rather, they are either (1) elite, idiocentric (Malina 1993:113), acquisition-oriented, self-indulgent, and competitive persons or (2) rootless, disconnected, marginalized persons whose outlook, in both cases, derives from the special positions they occupy in the social system. Since they share some, but not all, of the characteristics of individualists with whom we are familiar, perhaps we should call these persons quasi-individualist, in order to distinguish them from the American model. Figure 2.2 further identifies who such persons are.

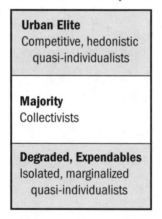

Urban Elite
Competitive, hedonistic
quasi-individualists

Majority
Collectivists

Degraded, Expendables
Isolated, marginalized
quasi-individualists

Figure 2.2: Quasi-individualism in predominantly vertical, collectivist societies

Especially important for anyone studying the New Testament is that strongly vertical collectivist societies, hence that contain wide variations in status and rigid social stratification, tend to produce pockets of individualistic behavior in otherwise collectivist situations. Status and affluence obviously bring independence and choice. Thus, the elite members of otherwise collectivist societies quickly become quasi-individualists. They are often motivated by pleasure, personal needs, or aspirations to achieve. Triandis cites Latin America as a contemporary example (1995:82), in which the elite indulge in conspicuous consumption such as carnivals, trade, luxury goods, and so on. The picture is not unlike that in ancient Rome. In Rome, a similar quasi-individualism emerged among the urban elite, who differed markedly from the collectivists that predominated elsewhere.

Equally important for Jesus scholars is another factor that creates pockets of individualistic behavior in otherwise collectivist societies. At extreme levels of poverty, what Triandis calls "anomic individualism" appears (1995:82). The term refers to a society's most marginalized individuals, who are cut off from the in-groups that guarantee survival in collectivist cultures. Beggars, prostitutes, disinherited sons, orphans, or children that families cannot support—abandoned to the streets to fend for themselves—are all obvious examples.

One caution, however, in adopting Triandis's terminology is relevant to consideration of Roman Palestine. Beggars, orphans, prostitutes, and the like may not have conformed to the mainstream, but no one in Roman Palestinian society, not even beggars and prostitutes, lived outside the social norms prescribed for those in their positions. Their behavior fit recognizable patterns. Thus, the term "anomic" is not quite appropriate. The key fact about such persons is that they are isolated from groups and left to fend for themselves.

It is important to recognize, therefore, that the individualistic behavior of these people does not result from personal choice. It is forced on them by their circumstances. The result is that their individualism does not produce a modern individual with a "definite view of himself." Instead, it produces a horizontal, marginalized sense of isolation.

In sum, although the Mediterranean societies of antiquity were predominantly collectivist in outlook, two types of individualistic behavior also existed. First was the vertical, narcissistic, and hedonistic behavior of the urban elite, and second was the horizontal, solitary behavior of the marginalized and degraded. The first outlook derived from privilege and choice, the second from isolation and despair. It is important to recognize that both types of individualistic behavior are present in the Jesus traditions.

Facets of the Self

One additional aspect of the self will aid our discussion. Greenwald and Pratkanis have identified several facets that play distinct roles in determining our identity (1984:158). First is what they call the *private* self, which emerges when one's inner audience evaluates its own opinions, attitudes, and actions. This is the foundational self in most individualistic cultures in the West and is, in fact, the classic subjective self assiduously sought in Western psychoanalysis. In many respects, the vast majority of historical Jesus researchers seek this private self when they inquire about the *self*-understanding of Jesus.[7]

Second is the *public* self that is the result of a general evaluation by others. It consists of both expectations and reports that the individual internalizes. The intense interest of collectivist societies in gossip as a means of evaluating others is ready testimony to the importance, to them, of the public self. Moreover, as my study on that topos indicates, gossip played a critical role in the public evaluation of Jesus (Rohrbaugh 2001).

Third, Greenwald and Pratkanis describe the *collective* self, or what Malina has called the "in-group" self (Malina 1994:113). This self emerges as one internalizes the values, expectations, and descriptions of an in-group in which one is embedded. For most ancient Mediterranean persons, of course, this would have been the biological family. For Jesus, this in-group early on may have been his biological family, but, at least according to the Gospels, it eventually became the followers with whom he was most closely associated.

We recognize now that the relationship among these three selves—the private, the public, and the in-group—works out differently in individualist and collectivist societies.

As figure 2.3 indicates, the private and public selves are expected to match in individualist societies. Failure in this regard is considered hypocrisy. The result is that individualistic persons are extremely sensitive to the nuances involved in relating private to public self. By contrast, in collectivist societies persons are socialized to monitor the relation between public self and in-group

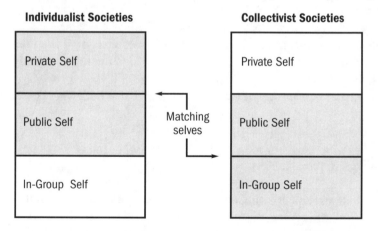

Figure 2.3: Diagram illustrating "matching" selves (adapted from Malina and Rohrbaugh 1998:143–45)

self. These two selves must match for collectivists, because meeting the expectations of others is the standard by which all collectivist persons are judged.

Of special importance for our inquiry is that, in collectivist cultures, the private self is never revealed in public. It is hidden behind an intensely maintained mantle of secrecy. In fact, as John Pilch has shown, lying in order to keep the private self concealed is considered honorable behavior in collectivist societies (1994). Public declaration of one's uniqueness, that is, the ways one is different from others, demonstrates lack of loyalty to the in-group, which is the highest value that collectivist societies acknowledge. Thus, collectivist people present themselves publicly in terms of what their neighbors want to hear; to do anything less is shameless behavior.

Collectivism and Quasi-individualism in First-Century Palestine

By clarifying these aspects of the cultural construction of the self, one can begin locating the historical Jesus in the ancient Mediterranean society from which he emerged. That society was predominantly vertical and collectivist. Among the urban elite, however, narcissistic and hedonistic individualistic behavior resulted from status and wealth. At the same time, substantial isolation existed among those left to fend for themselves.

A broad-brush collectivist/quasi-individualist profile of Herodian Palestine results if we compare our results with Dennis Duling's macrosociological profile of typical agrarian societies.

As figure 2.4 suggests, the elite accounted for 1 to 2 percent of the population. In highly stratified collectivist societies, as noted above, such persons were likely to be self-indulgent, idiocentric, acquisition-oriented quasi-individualists. Their survival was not at stake, and thus they could afford to act as a law unto themselves, beholden to no one. Their honor was displayed in their achievements and possessions, not in their conformity or loyalty to a group. Those features are what we find among the urban elite of Palestine in the Roman period.

At the other end of the social spectrum were the unclean, degraded, and expendables. Such persons accounted for about 10 percent of the population in the Herodian period; the Triandis model would predict isolated quasi-individualism among such persons. A clear example in the Jesus tradition is the beggar in John 5 who had no friend to put him in the pool. Beggars, prostitutes, tanners, sailors, the poorest day laborers, bandits, ass drivers, usurers, dung collectors, shepherds, and the like fell into this category. Their individualistic behavior came not from the affluence or status that brought choice, but from their isolation from any group on which to draw a sense of identity. They had loyalty to no one and none had loyalty to them.

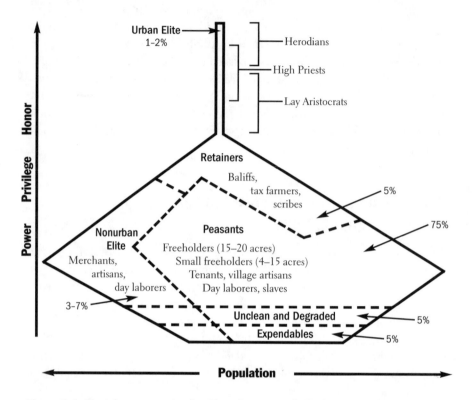

Figure 2.4: Social structure in the Herodian period (Duling 1994:56)

The Identity of Jesus

We are now in a position to inquire more directly about the identity of Jesus. Was he a typical agrarian collectivist? Or might he have been one of the two kinds of quasi-individualists we have identified in a typical agrarian, vertical, collectivist society?

One possibility is that Jesus was an individualistic exception of the hedonistic, narcissistic, indulgent, competitive, achievement-oriented sort that emerged among the urban elite. Yet nothing in the texts gives us reason to locate Jesus here. He was a village artisan from Nazareth, a tiny village in a rural area. Moreover, as figure 2.4 indicates, village artisans were among the lowest-status persons in agrarian societies. Hence, on the basis of his origins, Jesus cannot plausibly be placed among the urban elite. The teachings of Jesus do not suggest he shared these elitist values.

The other possibility is that Jesus lived among the marginalized, whose position resulted from extreme poverty and isolation. Should we place Jesus here? I argue that there is no New Testament data that would lead us to do so.

It is true that Jesus appears to have broken with his biological roots, which would mean a loss of group-centered identity. But two things argue against using this as data for quasi-individualism. One is that the break appears to have been voluntary. We learn of nothing in Jesus' life suggesting that he was forced onto the streets to fend for himself. Moreover, the teachings of Jesus suggest the opposite of this type of individualism. His teachings offer a home to the homeless rather than an expression of isolation or despair.

Another argument against seeing Jesus as a marginalized quasi-individualist is that, while he broke with one group, his family, he appears to have quickly reestablished new in-group relationships, probably first with the Baptist's movement, but then later with followers of his own. My conclusion, therefore, is that we cannot locate Jesus among either of the individualistic groups present in Herodian Palestine. Rather, we must assume that he shared the collectivist outlook that predominated in the ancient world.

Equally important is to recognize that, like other collectivist persons, what would have concerned Jesus was his public and his in-group self, not his private self. The private self is an issue only for Westerners. That is the self that we see as essential for all human persons. We see it as the seat of motives and the explanation for personal actions. To explain what Jesus did and why he did it, therefore, Westerners require an account of Jesus' private self. We know nowhere else to locate his motives or sense of mission. Yet it is this very private self that Middle Easterners do not consider central, do not reveal, indeed, do not even admit to having in public. In the Gospel traditions we should expect to find material describing the public and the in-group selves of Jesus, not his private self. As it turns out, this is exactly the case.

Evidence in the Gospels

Space does not permit examination of all relevant New Testament texts, but at least one cannot be overlooked. The *locus classicus* of this issue is Mark 8:27–30, which has played a key role in the debate since the time of Reimarus. The overwhelming majority of scholars consider this anecdote to be a later creation of the church, and in its present form it almost certainly is. Erich Dinkler was among the first to argue—persuasively, in my view—that a much older tradition lies behind this Markan narrative (1971:192).

The nearly universal Western interpretation of this passage is that Jesus himself knows who he is, and that he is quizzing his followers to see whether they do (Schweizer 1975; Hooker 1991; Williamson 1983; Myers 1988; Hurtado 1989; and others). Up to this point, Jesus' followers have not identified him correctly, so his questions are a kind of test. Peter's half-understood exclamation that Jesus is the Messiah is thus understood to represent a climactic confessional moment in the Gospel narrative.

Yet if it is correct that Jesus is a collectivist person, we can make no assumption that Jesus possesses self-knowledge. Nor can we assume that he either is trying to determine whether the disciples have understood him correctly or that he is trying to provoke their recognition. That seems to me an entirely Western approach, based on the assumption of private self-knowledge. Rather, we have to assume that Jesus *does not know who he is* and that, if he wishes to know, he will have to ask the significant others in whom he is embedded.

Note carefully the questions Jesus puts to the disciples in Mark 8:27–29. He asks first, "Who do the people say I am?" That is an inquiry about his *public* self. And the answers appropriately come *from the public*. Then Jesus asks, "Who do you say that I am?" That is an inquiry about his *in-group* self. That is of critical importance in collectivist societies, because the in-group *determines* who a person is. In Jesus' culture, the answer must come *from the in-group*, not from Jesus. Moreover, note that, in each case, the answers provided suggest stereotypical roles, *not personal qualities or individual choices*.

In other words, the anecdote narrates Jesus asking an in-group to identify both his public self and his in-group self. Conspicuous by its absence, however, is talk about Jesus' private self, either from the disciples or from Jesus. Such talk simply is not there, and it can be put there only by importing Western assumptions into the text. This story has in view only the public and in-group selves of Jesus.

More precisely, in this story Jesus is inquiring about the *match* between his newly emerging public and in-group identities. Who do people (public) say that I am? Who do you (in-group) say that I am? This is precisely the match that is central in collectivist societies. There are thus significant social grounds for assuming, as Dinkler does on form-critical grounds, that a historical tradition may lie behind the Markan version of events at Caesarea Philippi.

When one thinks about it, it is not surprising that confusion developed over the identity of Jesus, not only in the mind of his followers but in Jesus' mind as well. In addition to Mark 8:27–30, there is widespread speculation in the Gospels about Jesus' identity.[8] The scope of speculation suggests that something historical lies behind it. While space unfortunately does not permit an analysis of all the texts, the point would not be to answer the question about who Jesus thought he was. That question is inappropriate, even if it could be answered. The point is that speculation about Jesus' identity was going on *in public*, exactly where it should occur in a collectivist society.

Conclusion

At the beginning of his article on the historical Jesus, quoted above, Ben F. Meyer makes the following claim (here now in its entirety): "We take it, for our part, that Jesus was a man with a definite view of himself and his time, a man with a mission, equipped with great resources for accomplishing it and confronted with not easily manageable obstacles in the way of its accomplishment" (1994:341). It would be hard to imagine a more ethnocentric and anachronistic understanding of Jesus. It is a virtual projection of the Western, individualistic, private self onto the Jesus of history. Its plausibility in the collectivist society of antiquity is near zero. Western assumptions about the nature of the self have determined the outcome before the inquiry starts.

Did Jesus think of himself as the Messiah? I do not know. But I suggest that, if he did, and if he was at all typical of collectivist personalities, he would have been extremely careful about asserting it either in public or in his in-group. To assert a private self would have been shameful behavior. If Jesus did have a private self, neither his followers, in-group, the public, nor you and I would have heard of it during his lifetime.

In the end, however, it seems that the question about Jesus' private self is inappropriate, not just because it is unanswerable, but because it is culturally ethnocentric. It is a question only a Westerner would ask. All of the legitimate questions about Jesus have to do with groups. In what group was Jesus embedded? What was their opinion of him? In what way did he embody and defend their goals? If he detached himself from his biological family, by what means did he reestablish a collectivist identity? All such questions presume the collectivist understanding of human beings that is the only one appropriate for understanding the historical Jesus.

As I said at the outset, the questions one asks determine the answers one gets. It is important to recognize that, in seeking the person of Jesus, we have been asking questions of the wrong kind.

Notes ━━

1. That has conveniently been done by a number of scholars over the years, though perhaps most clearly and systematically in the recent work of Gerd Theissen and Annette Merz (1998).

2. Articles by Western scholars addressing the "self-consciousness" of Jesus are far too numerous to list in this short article. The bibliography offers a representative sample from recent decades.

3. Theology, it seems, also requires an answer. Wolfhart Pannenberg asserts that "Christology cannot avoid the question of Jesus' self-consciousness, however difficult it may be exegetically and historically" (1968:326).

4. Or as Gwilym Beckerlegge puts it, "Any approach to Jesus which accepts both his humanity and his rationality is based on the presupposition that Jesus had a self-consciousness" (1978:370).

5. Thus they produce countless introspective sermons on the meaning of *metanoia*.

6. For excellent discussions of collectivist views in relation to New Testament study, see Malina 1989; 1992; Malina and Neyrey 1991.

7. It is the psychological self of Jesus sought, for example, by Ragnar Leivestad in his psychologically oriented book (1987).

8. In Mark 6:1–6, the crowd asks, "Where did this man get all this?" "Is not this the carpenter, the son of Mary and brother of James and Joses and Judas and Simon, and are not his sisters here with us?" In Luke 4:22, the synagogue goers ask, "Is not this Joseph's son?" In John 7:15, people are puzzled. "How does this man have such learning when he has never been taught?" Later they add, "Can it be that the authorities really know that this is the Messiah?" They are confused because they "know where this man [Jesus] is from" (7:27). Finally, division breaks out among the people, who cannot decide whether Jesus is a prophet, the Messiah, or a fraud. Some cannot believe a Messiah could come from Galilee (7:40–43). The similarity between John's story and Mark 8:27–30 is striking.

Elsewhere in the Synoptics, Jesus' disciples ask, "What sort of man is this?" (Matt 8:27). The authorities ask him, "Tell us by what authority you do these things" (Luke 20:2). They are really asking Jesus who he thinks he is, but he refuses to answer. Elsewhere, crowds wonder at him (Mark 1:27; 2:12; 5:20; 5:42; 12:17; Matt 9:33; 12:23; 15:31; 22:22; 27:14; Luke 4:36; 5:26; 9:43; 11:14; 20:26), as do the disciples (Mark 4:41; 6:52; 10:32). Even Jesus' parents wonder who he is (Luke 2:33, 47–48). Demons seem to know who he is (Mark 1:24, 34; 3:12; 5:7), but everyone else wonders and speculates.

Works Cited

Aune, David E. 1973. "A Note on Jesus' Messianic Consciousness and 11QMelchiz-
idek." *EvQ* 45:161–65.
Beckerlegge, Gwilym. 1978. "Jesus' Authority and the Problem of His Self-Consciousness." *HeyJ* 19:365–82.
Betz, Otto. 1963. "Die Frage nach dem messianischen Bewusstsein Jesu." *NovT* 6:20–48.
Brown, Raymond E. 1967. "How Much Did Jesus Know? A Survey of the Biblical Evidence." *CBQ* 29:315–45.
———. 1985. "Did Jesus Know He Was God?" *BTB* 15:74–79.
Bultmann, Rudolf. 1919. "Die Frage nach dem messianischen Bewusstsein Jesu und
das Petrusbekenntnis." *ZNW* 19:165–75.
———. 1951–55. *Theology of the New Testament.* Translated by K. Grobel. 2 vols.
New York: Scribner.
———. 1958. *Jesus and the Word.* Translated by L. Smith and E. Lantero. New York:
Scribner.
Chilton, Bruce D. 1982. "Jesus ben David: Relections on the Davidssohnfrage." *JSNT*
14:88–112.
Dinkler, Erich. 1971. "Peter's Confession and the 'Satan' Saying: The Problem of
Jesus' Messiahship." In *The Future of Our Religious Past: Essays in Honour of
Rudolf Bultmann,* edited by J. M. Robinson, translated by C. E. Carlston and R. P.
Scharlemann, 169–202. New York: Harper & Row.
Duling, Dennis C. (and Norman Perrin). 1994. *The New Testament: Proclamation and
Parenesis, Myth and History.* 3d ed. New York: Harcourt Brace.
Fiensy, David A. 1991. *The Social History of Palestine in the Herodian Period: The
Land Is Mine.* SBEC 20. Lewiston, N.Y.: Mellen.
Gnilka, Joachim. 1997. *Jesus of Nazareth: Message and History.* Translated by S. S.
Schatzmann. Peabody, Mass.: Hendrickson.
Greenwald, Anthony G., and Anthony R. Pratkanis. 1984. "The Self." In *Handbook of
Social Cognition,* edited by R. S. Wyler and T. K. SrullWyler. Vol. 3, 129–78. Hills-
dale, N.J.: Erlbaum.
Hooker, Morna D. 1991. *The Gospel according to Saint Mark.* BNTC. Peabody,
Mass.: Hendrickson.
Hui, Harry C., and Harry C. Triandis. 1989. "Individualism-Collectivism: A Study of
Cross-Cultural Researchers." *JCCP* 17:225–48.
Hurtado, Larry W. 1989. *Mark.* NIBC 2. Peabody, Mass.: Hendrickson.
Leivestad, Ragnar. 1987. *Jesus in His Own Perspective: An Examination of His Sayings,
Actions, and Eschatological Titles.* Translated by D. E. Aune. Minneapolis: Augsburg.
Lenski, Gerhard, and Jean Lenski. 1987. *Human Societies: An Introduction to
Macrosociology.* 5th ed. New York: McGraw-Hill.

Longenecker, Richard N. 1969. "'Son of Man' as a Self-Designation of Jesus." *JETS* 12:151–58.

Malina, Bruce J. 1989. "Dealing with Biblical (Mediterranean) Characters: A Guide for U.S. Consumers." *BTB* 19:127–41.

———. 1992. "Is There a Circum-Mediterranean Person? Looking for Stereotypes." *BTB* 22:66–87.

———. 1993. *The New Testament World: Insights from Cultural Anthropology.* 2nd ed. Louisville: Westminster/John Knox.

———. 1994. "'Let Him Deny Himself' (Mark 8:34 & Par): A Social-Psychological Model of Self-Denial." *BTB* 24:106–19.

Malina, Bruce J., and Jerome H. Neyrey. 1991. "First-Century Personality: Dyadic, Not Individualistic." In *The Social World of Luke-Acts: Models for Biblical Interpretation*, edited by J. H. Neyrey, 67–96. Peabody, Mass.: Hendrickson.

Malina, Bruce J., and Richard L. Rohrbach. 1998. *Social-Science Commentary on the Gospel of John.* Minneapolis: Fortress Press.

Meyer, Ben F. 1994. "Jesus' Ministry and Self-Understanding." In *Studying the Historical Jesus: Evaluations of Current Research*, edited by B. Chilton and C. A. Evans, 337–52. New York: Brill.

Meyer, Paul W. 1960. "The Problem of the Messianic Self-Consciousness of Jesus." *NovT* 4:122–38.

Myers, Ched. 1988. *Binding the Strong Man: A Political Reading of Mark's Story of Jesus.* Maryknoll, N.Y.: Orbis.

Niles, F. S. 1998. "Individualism-Collectivism Revisited." *Journal of Cross-Cultural Research* 32:315–41.

Pannenberg, Wolfhart. 1968. *Jesus—God and Man.* Translated by L. L. Wilkins and D. A. Priebe. Philadelphia: Westminster.

Pilch, John J. 1994. "Secrecy in the Mediterranean World: An Anthropological Perspective." *BTB* 24:151–57.

———. 1997. "Psychological and Psychoanalytical Approaches to Interpreting the Bible in Social-Scientific Context." *BTB* 27:112–16.

Rohrbaugh, Richard L. 1991. "Legitimating Sonship—a Test of Honour: A Social-Scientific Study of Luke 4:1–30." In *Modelling Early Christianity*, edited by P. F. Esler, 183–97. New York and London: Routledge.

———. 1993. "The Social Location of the Markan Audience." *BTB* 23:114–27.

———. 2001. "Gossip in the New Testament." In *Social-Scientific Models for Interpreting the Bible: Essays by the Context Group in Honor of Bruce J. Malina*, edited by J. J. Pilch. 239–59. BibIntSer 53. Leiden: Brill.

Sabourin, Leopold. 1983. "About Jesus' Self-Understanding." *Religious Studies Bulletin* 3:129–34.

Schweder, Richard A., and E. J. Bourne. 1982. "Does the Concept of Person Vary Cross-Culturally?" In *Cultural Conceptions of Mental Health and Therapy*, edited by A. Marsella and G. White, 97–137. Boston: Reidel.

Schweizer, Eduard. 1975. *The Good News according to Mark*. Translated by D. H. Madvig. Richmond: John Knox.

Stewart, Edward C., and Milton Bennett. 1991. *American Cultural Patterns: A Cross-Cultural Perspective*. Yarmouth, Maine: Intercultural.

Theissen, Gerd. 1992. "Gruppenmessianismus: Überlegungen zum Ursprung der Kirche im Jüngerkreis Jesu." *Jahrbuch für biblische Theologie* 7:101–23.

Theissen, Gerd, and Annette Merz. 1998. *The Historical Jesus: A Comprehensive Guide*. Translated by J. Bowden. Minneapolis: Fortress Press.

Triandis, Harry C. 1987. "Cross-Cultural Studies in Individualism and Collectivism." In *Nebraska Symposium on Motivation 1989*, edited by R. Dienstbier, 41–133. Lincoln: University of Nebraska Press.

———. 1995. *Individualism and Collectivism*. New Directions in Social Psychology. San Francisco: Westview.

Triandis, Harry C., et al. 1992. "An Etic-Emic Analysis of Individualism and Collectivism." *JCCP* 24:366–83.

Williamson, Lamar. 1983. *Mark*. Interpretation. Atlanta: John Knox.

Witherington, Ben, III. 1990. *The Christology of Jesus*. Minneapolis: Fortress Press.

Wright, N. T. 1996. "How Jesus Saw Himself." *BRev* 12:22–29.

3

The Contextual Ethics of Jesus

Wolfgang Stegemann

Jesus' ethics are an integral part of the symbolic moral system of his society. Hence, his ethics cannot be understood without knowledge of this moral system. What this mainly means is that the ethics of Jesus must be interpreted within the symbolic moral system of his society, not in contrast with it. More to the point, Jesus did not step out of the moral world of his society and design his own, new, symbolic moral system. Rather, he developed and articulated his own perspective within this symbolic system and put specific emphases on some dimensions of it.

Four Critical Observations on the Traditional Understanding of the "Ethics" of Jesus

A Conceptual Theory of Ethics

When broaching the theme of Jesus' ethics, scholars generally understand the subject as part of the "ethics" of early Christianity or the "ethics" of the New Testament. Although the term "ethics" has become established in exegesis, it seems in need of revision. The term "ethics" describes, "since Aristotle, an exercise in theory" that, among other things, has as its object "criteria of right behavior" (Herms 2000:1598). Hence one may say that ethics is a conceptual theory that establishes or formulates moral rules and norms of human behavior. The *Oxford English Dictionary* defines "ethics" as "the science of morality." Meeks prefers to speak of "morality" when dealing with early Christianity; he understands the term "ethics" to refer to "a reflective, second-order activity" (1993:4).

However we define the term, it is clear in any event that Jesus did not formulate an ethics in the sense of a theoretical construct. Jesus did not design a theory of proper behavior, nor did he develop criteria for a moral way of life. Rather, he had himself acted within the framework of the values, norms, and conventions of his society. And he did criticize individual norms and values or customs of his society. Yet if we insist on taking the term "ethics" in its technical sense and apply it to Jesus in a broad sense, that is, not necessarily in the reflexive sense of a theory of morality, the difficulty is that the term always suggests that Jesus did in fact have or formulate his own concept of ethics. Did he really? For some time now scholars have attempted to articulate this concept, to spell out its explicit and hidden fundamental motives or principles.

The Search for a Fundamental Principle behind the Moral Statements of Jesus

It would seem worthwhile to inquire again into whether Jesus' ethics was controlled by some fundamental motive or guiding hermeneutical principle (see below) or any type of central theme in his moral teaching. One widespread opinion is that the "ethics" of Jesus is determined by his eschatological proclamation, for example, Schrage in his standard work, *The Ethics of the New Testament.* There is a chapter in the work entitled "Jesus' Eschatological Ethics." For Schrage, Jesus' statement in Mark 1:15 is programmatic: "Repent, *for* the kingdom of God is at hand" (1989:33). Schrage understands the "ethics" of Jesus to be a consequence of his proclamation of the proximate arrival of the kingdom of God. It is commonly known that, since Johannes Weiss and Albert Schweitzer, "Jesus' eschatological message is the critical basis and guideline for his ethics." (Schrage 1989:30). This led Schweitzer to his thesis of "interim ethics." Rudolf Bultmann, on the other hand, saw the organizing principle of Jesus' morality in Jesus' understanding of existence, the deeper meaning of which was that humans are being directed into their "Now as hour of decision for God" (1961:21). Others again hold Jesus' concept of God as the "center" of his statements, since Jesus always was concerned "radically about God" in his moral demands. These examples can be multiplied readily. What they have in common is that they look for a fundamental motif or central point that gives specific shape to Jesus' moral statements. Here I briefly go into the oft-advocated emphasis on rooting Jesus' ethics in his proclamation of the kingdom of God.

I do not doubt that a particular worldview—here the expectation of the proximate realization of the rule of God in Israel, as it already functioned in the sky—determines moral convictions and can lead to lasting moral consequences. In the case of Jesus, one might argue that his expectation of God's kingdom (*basileia tou theou*) focused on and favored in a special way socially marginal groups in Israel (the poor, prostitutes, tax collectors, children). On the other hand, he set forth an unfavorable eschatological prognosis for the authorities behind the groups, whom he designated "the rich." "Blessed are you poor, for the kingdom of God is yours" (Luke 6:20), or "It is easier for a camel to pass through the eye of a needle than for a rich person to enter the kingdom of God" (Mark 10:25). But these are not exactly moral consequences drawn by Jesus from his expectation of the proximate realization of the kingdom of God. A moral consequence of this expectation would be, for example, if Jesus had required (voluntary) poverty as a way of life and then demanded this as requirement for entrance into the kingdom of God. Jesus did do this in a certain sense — but only with the "rich" (for example, Mark 10:21); but he did not need to require this poverty from his "clients," since one need not require what already exists.

These passages — along with other references I do not discuss here — indicate that (voluntary or involuntary) poverty was not for Jesus a moral ideal that followed from the proximity of the kingdom of God. Rather, what followed from the nearness of the kingdom for Jesus was a positive future for those now poor and a negative one for those now rich, a reversal of present (unjust) social relations. Jesus had blessed the poor, not poverty (as a way of life)! He required no "asceticism in the world" (Max Weber), but expected God to intervene soon in favor of the poor. Those who now hunger will be filled; those who now mourn will laugh (Luke 6:21). A rich person who sought to escape what Jesus described as a negative fate could enter the company of the saved by selling his riches. In fact, the rich person need not practice a morally significant way of life. All he had to do was join the poor by renouncing his riches. In other words, renunciation of wealth was a condition of belonging to the saved. It was not an ascetic ideal characterizing a way of life. To sum up, it is doubtful that Jesus deduced some ideal of poverty (or some ideal of chastity) from his belief in the proximate realization of the kingdom of God.

On the contrary, there is little doubt that, for the poor, the promise of the kingdom of God had significance, that it led them to a change of thinking, in self-awareness, and, thus, had an impact on their behavior. That is one thing. But the other is the question whether Jesus himself preached a set of moral principles influenced or motivated by his eschatological expectation. Can the moral values he championed be traced to this proclamation of the kingdom? While it may be true that one or another of Jesus' value statements may have been marked by his apocalyptic hope in the kingdom of heaven, I do not see that this expectation was the characteristic motive behind his moral positions. Quite the contrary. Many of Jesus' moral demands or assertions in the Gospels trace neither directly nor indirectly to his kingdom expectation. Consider Jesus' prohibition of divorce or his interpretation of the Sabbath command, or his position on purity or his requirement to love one's enemy. These as well as other moral declarations of Jesus were grounded in different motives, for example, in the motive of reward and punishment or judgment or the Golden Rule or the order of creation, or simply by a reference to the Torah.

The Quest for Fundamental Hermeneutical Principles of Jesus' "Ethics"

In exegetical discussions, Jesus' interpretation of Torah prescriptions is usually traced to fundamental hermeneutical principles. For instance, some hold that the center of Jesus' perspective is the principle of love. This alleged core is then made to serve as the guideline for Jesus' reading of other Torah prescriptions. In this context, some even maintain that Jesus transgressed Torah commands out of love. Other attempts to discover comprehensive hermeneutical categories for Jesus' moral posture go so far as to stamp Jesus' relation to the Torah as radical (or, more concretely, as "mitigating" the Torah or "intensifying" the Torah) (see Theissen and Merz 1998). Such positions are less descriptions than evaluations.

Thus, for example, Jesus' interpretation of the prohibition of divorce (Exod 20:14) in the second antithesis of the Sermon on the Mount (Matt 5:27–30) is interpreted as "intensification of the Torah." For the passage states: "But I say to you: whoever looks upon a woman to desire her has already committed adultery in his heart" (Matt 5:28). The word "intensification" presupposes that the Torah prescription itself is more open, "weaker," or "more broad-minded." But one might ask whether this assessment is correct. For who can say what the Torah prescription ("You shall not commit adultery") "originally" meant, whether it originally was open to "weak" or "broad" interpretation? One might also ask if Jesus' Sabbath halakah is Torah-mitigating. Or, conversely, is his application of the command to love one's neighbor to enemies an intensification of the Torah? From where does one derive a criterion for such judgment? Let us stick to the subject of divorce. Jesus' contemporaries—to the extent that he spoke in the way the second antithesis of the Sermon on the Mount suggests—would hardly find his statement as an intensification of the Torah, nor even especially original (see Luz 1989:295). Montefiore has noted: "No simple rabbinic Jew . . . would find in it [in the second antithesis] anything startling except the implication that there was any opposition between the old Law and the new" (quoted in Luz 1989:295). This should make one proceed carefully in applying evaluative terms to the few known examples of Jesus' Torah interpretation.

The Impulse to One-Upmanship

"The world before Christ came was a world without love." That is how Gerhard Uhlhorn formulated the situation at the beginning of his learned work on Christian love activity (1895:7). Uhlhorn in fact understood the love command in the mouth of Jesus as a new commandment (with reference to John 13:34). It was new both for the gentile world as well as for Israelites. Although Uhlhorn later limited his judgment to the gentile world, he persisted in holding that "paganism did not produce any actual activity of love aside from occasional expressions of sympathy" (29). And the learned Uhlhorn was not bothered by the fact that the command to love one's neighbor is in the Torah (Lev 19:17). The Old Testament command to love is for him only a "bud of a developing life of love that comes to full bloom in the New Testament"—a bud, to be sure, but only a bud (31). Between Jesus and the Old Testament, Uhlhorn perceives "post-exilic Judaism" at work. Postexilic Judaism stunted the growth of the "seeds of a free and universal exercise of love" present in the Old Testament. The fault lies with—we might have guessed it from what we know of the Christian stereotype of Judaism—the "works of the law" and the "national pride" of the Jews (33). Uhlhorn would not deny that a widespread practice of almsgiving existed in Judaism at the time of Jesus. "But if alms sufficed, love was hardly present." Alms were given only out of "legal obligation" and for the sake of merit, and finally only to "fellow Jews" (33–34). Uhlhorn thus criticizes Judaism for giving alms without the right intention (love) and not to all people. It was this deficiency, according to Uhlhorn, that Jesus sought to rectify.

I have quoted Uhlhorn because he vividly represents a dominant tendency in the way Christians deal with the "ethics" of Jesus. This is the tendency to one-upmanship. As far as Jesus is concerned, everything is fundamentally one up: nicer, better, greater, or even newer in relationship to the gentile or Israelite world. While true that no one today would say that the world before Jesus was a world without love, now, as previously, the "ethics" of Jesus is understood as outdoing the moral viewpoints of the Judaism of his day. In this context, the command of love of neighbor is given a central role.

In his article on the ethics of Jesus, Hurst concedes that Jesus, too, connected his moral demands with the ideas of reward and punishment. Among other passages, Hurst cites Matt 6:4, 6, 18; 16:27 (reward), and Matt 5:22, 29–30; 7:19; 10:28 (punishment). While reward and punishment are ethically inferior concepts for Hurst, they are fine for Jesus, but to be criticized when advocated by the Pharisees. In Jesus' favor, he states that the motive is an element of his ethics' pragmatism, while, for (most) Pharisees, what is commanded is to be done out of "naked obedience," "simply because it was commanded." Above all, for Jesus the "character" of a human being has priority over the Pharisees' external motives for behavior (Hurst 1992:214).

The tendency to one-upmanship exists today even in relationship to gentile culture. Thus Crossan, among others, champions the thesis that the Jesus movement sought to displace prevailing Mediterranean values such as honor and shame through its egalitarian and open table fellowship: "For Jesus . . . commensality was, rather, a strategy of building or rebuilding peasant community on radically different principles from those of honor and shame, patronage and clientage" (Crossan 1991:344).

According to Crossan, the same would hold comparably for so-called Mediterranean patriarchalism as well (I turn to this below). In brief, Jesus remains the humane critic and moral one-upman in relation to the central values of Mediterranean culture.

There seems to be a type of (Christian) impulse to interpret the moral statements of Jesus mainly as articulating something new, distinctive, and incomparable, in contrast to all other moral positions of his day. But this involves a petitio principii, as the formulation of Meeks indicates. Meeks assesses the Christian movement as follows: "[W]e cannot . . . escape the tectonic shift of cultural values that was set in motion by those small and obscure beginnings. . . . What had changed was morality" (1993:1–2). He does not, however, tell us what the new features, the new moral praxis, the new values were that came into the world with the Christian movement.

> To be sure, it is curiously difficult to say exactly what was new about Christian morality, or to draw firm boundaries around it. The language of virtue that Christians spoke was adapted from older traditions of moral discourse. . . . The daily practice of most church members was doubtless indistinguishable in most respects from that their unconverted neighbors (1993:2).

What then is new about early Christian morality? Perhaps, because the presumptions behind this position are inaccurate, it is not easy to say. Perhaps that means that neither Jesus' ethics nor the ethics of early Christianity were in fact a "tectonic shift" in the symbolic moral world and practice of Mediterranean culture. I find it noteworthy that Meeks fails to name anything new. I do not maintain that one must not expect anything new from Jesus. What I mean is that we ought to free ourselves from the impulsive interest always to interpret the ethics of Jesus as new, distinctive, incomparable in comparison with other moral positions. It is not necessary that great and grave differences characterize his morality. It seems to me that it is a question of "fine distinctions," to use a phrase of Bourdieu (1984).

Summary

The term "ethics" is inappropriate to describe Jesus' position toward the morally relevant problems of his society. On the one hand, this term is used for theoretical moral discourse, and, on the other, it suggests that Jesus possessed something like a reflexive theory of moral behavior. It likewise seems inappropriate to me to assume that fundamental motives or foundational hermeneutical principles undergird the so-called ethics of Jesus. Thus, for example, the thesis that the total moral posture of Jesus is embedded in his message of the proximity of the kingdom of God does not stand up to scrutiny. I also find it a problem that, in relation to Israelite morality, Jesus' ethics is categorically overrated (e.g., as the "radicalization" of the Torah). With this label, the ethics of Jesus is ascribed a special or even an exceptional place within the symbolic world of Judaism. This interest in underscoring the distinctive quality of the moral statements of Jesus is further reinforced by what I have called the impulse to one-upmanship: ascribing, a priori, a superior moral quality to the ethics of Jesus so that it outranks all other moral systems.

The Contingency and Contextuality of Jesus' Moral Position

In contrast to the problematic points cited above, I now demonstrate in two sections that Jesus' moral position was fairly ad hoc. It derived in part from his need to defend his behavior from accusations of deviance or to respond to questions. In contrast to the tendency to radicalization and one-upmanship, I point to how the ethics of Jesus was an integral part of the symbolic moral system of his culture. This does not preclude that Jesus may have emphasized certain features within his society's moral world.

The Contingent Character of Jesus' Morally Relevant Position

One does not find a theoretical system of moral behavior in the Gospels. On the one hand, what we find are moral statements of Jesus. By that I mean that Jesus states his position on certain norms, rules, and conventions of his society. On the other hand, certain behavior from Jesus and his followers is morally relevant. I offer a few examples, for brevity's sake. Jesus did express himself on Torah prescriptions. On the Sabbath prohibition, for example, Jesus explains why one can pluck ears of grain (hence carrying out a type of harvest labor), although the recognized Israelite norm proscribes it (Mark 2:23–28 par.). Jesus also, in answer to a question whether and under what conditions it is possible to dissolve a marriage, expresses his views on the prohibition of divorce (Mark 10:2–11 par.).

In these cases, Jesus took an explicit position on norms or rules of Israelite society that were fixed in writing and further developed through oral discourse.

An implicit moral position can be discerned in the practice of Jesus insofar as he (or his followers) behaved in a certain way related to specific moral norms. Jesus was considered, for example, a "friend" of tax collectors and sinners; that is, he had interacted socially with them by participating in common meals with these despised social groups (Mark 2:15–17). This behavior involves a breach of conventions (in this case, commensality) through which the cultural value system of Israelite society, as generally in Mediterranean societies, was ordered. Jesus thus directly or indirectly expressed himself on the moral values of his society, indicated by his opponents' questioning of his deviant praxis. His answers are formulated ad hoc, rather than arising from some preexisting, reflexive, general moral system of his own. Jesus did, indeed, presuppose a general moral system, namely the ethos (that is, guiding beliefs) of his society. It was within this social system that he formulated his moral emphases. Hence we perhaps should talk of Jesus' ethos rather than his ethics.

The Ethos of Jesus as an Integral Part of the Ethos of His Culture and Society

The ethos of Jesus arose in a real-life context. This context is generally determined by the social system and cultural value orientations of his society. For heuristic reasons I distinguish three contexts.

The cultural meaning system of Jesus' society is marked in a special way by the Israelite tradition, both by the Torah and its interpretation as well as by other Israelite traditions. Jesus' ethos is thus Israel's ethos; the Israelite traditions of his day form the first observable context of the moral praxis of the Jesus movement and of the moral statements of Jesus.

To be sure, the moral world of Israel, with all its peculiarities, was part of the value system of the Mediterranean world in general. To understand the Israelite ethos of Jesus, it is necessary to consider a second context, that of the cultural values and conventions of the ancient societies of the Mediterranean.

Finally, since moral value orientations are realized in specific social institutions, the political and domestic structuring of Israelite society must be considered as a third context.

I cannot go into each context here. But I make several observations about value orientations and social institutions. To this end, I refer to the introduction to *Handbook of Biblical Social Values*, edited by Pilch and Malina: "The word 'value' describes some general quality and direction of life that human beings are expected to embody in their behavior. A value is a general, normative orientation of action in a social system" (1993:xiii).

A general value takes on concrete significance through its realization in a social institution, for example, in the social institution of family, which in Mediterranean society was the focal social institution (Pilch and Malina 1993:xviii).

Parenthetic Remarks

To begin, I once more insist that Jesus' ethos was a constituent part of the symbolic moral world of his society. We cannot—and Jesus could not—remove our society's or group's symbolic moral world like a garment. It is like one's skin, out of which human beings cannot come. In this regard, Meeks writes: "Morality is an integral part of a community's culture" (1993:10). From this, the improbability of Jesus stepping out of his society's moral world follows. In general, it is a false presumption to think that Jesus had a reflexive or distanced relationship to the symbolic moral world of his people, similar to the one we can adopt as historical observers. People normally orient themselves unconsciously in their social behavior, guided by traditional meaning systems, by the values of their society or group. Only when one's own social praxis deviates from the expectations of others does a conscious discussion about the symbolic moral world take place. But even in conflict it is clear that we make our moral decisions, not in the free choice of theoretical or speculative possibilities, but within the symbolic moral world of our society or group. I illustrate with an example, the Sabbath conflict in Mark 2:23–27.

We find Jesus' explanation of the Sabbath command in a conflict story in which Jesus' disciples pluck grain on the Sabbath. But his explanation does not provide a new moral principle, as is frequently maintained. What is implied is that a human being has precedence over cultic law. The fact is that, contrary to the general view, Jesus does not maintain that work on the Sabbath is allowed. Jesus goes back to the Sabbath halakah of the traditional symbolic world of Israelite society. He grounds his followers' behavior within what was possible in this halakah. Traditional Sabbath halakah allows the suppression of Sabbath prohibitions in favor of other norms, for example, to avoid danger to life. This case in Mark 2 can be summed up as follows: poverty suppresses the Sabbath.

As this example shows, Jesus made specific moral emphases. But in no way did these emphases result from a single motive, for example, from the proximate establishment of the kingdom of God. The expectation of the kingdom of God does not play any role in the reasons Jesus adduces for the previously cited Sabbath-breaking. As already indicated, many and varying reasons have influenced Jesus' specific moral emphases. Neither Jesus' specific interpretation of the Sabbath command nor his restrictive opinion relative to the possibility of divorce traces back in any knowable relation to the urgent expectation of the kingdom of God. This is more noteworthy since the proximate in-breaking of God's kingdom would have been relevant to the question of divorce (as Paul in 1 Corinthians 7 shows in his own way). In fact, Jesus cites the biblical creation story in favor of his position that divorce is not allowed.

"From the beginning of creation God made them male and female . . . therefore a man will leave his father and mother and the two will become one flesh" (Gen 1:27; 2:24; see Mark 10:6). Jesus adduces Israelite Scripture to ground his prohibition of divorce. From these sources, he concludes that the meaning of the creation of two sexes lies in the marital union of man and woman. It means separation from the family of origin with a view to forming the nucleus of a new group of relatives. Such reasons also appear in other Israelite documents and, hence, seem to connect with a corresponding value concept.

Another example comes in Jesus' reasons for fellowship with tax collectors and sinners: "I have not come to call the just, but sinners" (Mark 2:17). The reason adduced is Jesus' own consciousness of mission, but it implicitly discloses his social perspective.

To summarize, Jesus' moral positions are contingent and contextual. They do not allow for tracing them back to a single or central principle, motive, or even abstract concept. Rather, Jesus' ethos entails a range of reasons that, in general, were present in the symbolic moral world of his culture. In place of the dominant petitio principii that dissociates Jesus' morality from his culture and society, I argue for an integrating interpretive approach. Jesus' ethos is part of the comprehensive cultural and social system that I have designated, all too simply, as Israelite tradition, Mediterranean culture in general, and the social institutions of Israel.

Two Examples

I offer two examples to illustrate the suggested approach. On the one hand, some interpret the following of Jesus as an expression of a radical ethos. It was not the ethos that was radical, however, but the social rupture that members of the Jesus movement experienced. The correlative question concerns the effects that his followers' departure from family had on their estimation of family values. Did Jesus thereby criticize or wish to criticize his culture and society? The second example deals with Jesus' transformation of love of neighbor to love of enemies. I describe the prevailing understanding of love that, for the most part, proceeds from modern conceptions and compare this understanding with an approach more appropriate to the culture and social experience of the New Testament world.

Leaving the Family and a Break with Convention

Was following Jesus an ethical act, a renunciation of possessions, homeland, marriage, and family? Are exile, celibacy, and poverty in the following of Jesus, therefore, an expression of a radical ethos? Are they virtuous behaviors on the part of those who have decided to follow Jesus? In other words, was the lifestyle of Jesus' disciples exemplary, a model for a morally virtuous life (or, in any event, what Jesus had imagined to be a morally virtuous life)? Jesus research has been occupied with these questions for some time already. For example, Theissen interprets Jesus' charge to follow him as a demand to renounce property, marriage, and home region. This act of renunciation was understood as the expression of a radical ethos, an a-family ethos, an ethos of exile, and so on. Theissen moved Jesus and his followers into the ideological neighborhood of Cynic wandering philosophy (Theissen 1978). Comparisons between the Jesus movement and Cynics have recently been expanded and intensified. As an example, I cite Mack, who, looking to explain the morally relevant statements (imperatives or rules) of the so-called logia (sayings) source, maintains: "The lifestyle of the Jesus people bears remarkable resemblance to the Greek tradition of popular philosophy characteristic of the Cynics. Cynics also promoted an outrageous lifestyle as a way of criticizing conventional mores and the themes of the two groups, the Cynics and the Jesus people, are largely overlapping" (1995:50).

Mack therefore sees great similarities between the lifestyle and agenda of the Cynics and the lifestyle or motives of Jesus people. For Crossan, Jesus is "a peasant Jewish Cynic" (1991:421). His "radical social egalitarianism" puts the patriarchal family of the Mediterranean world in question (299). By amassing various passages—he clusters, among other things, the leaving of family in the course of following Jesus—Crossan maintains that Jesus had criticized the patriarchalism of Mediterranean culture: "Jesus will tear the hierarchical or patriarchal family in two along the axis of domination and subordination" (300).

The attempt to interpret the Jesus movement by comparison with Cynic wandering philosophy is, in my estimation, rather old. The author of the Gospel of Luke had already depicted the Jesus movement with typical features of Cynic wandering philosophy (renunciation of property, renunciation of family and marriage) (Stegemann 1984; see also Draper 1999). Yet we might ask whether the cynicizing of Jesus' followers is an appropriate model for the historical phenomenon of the Jesus movement. Did membership in the Jesus movement constitute membership in a moral organization? Was following Jesus a virtue, a model of right living, and, at the same time, a criticism of false living? For some Cynics, one can in fact hold that their style of living, their partially demonstrative and provoking lifestyle, was an expression of virtues (for example, of freedom from needs, self-sufficiency, of the natural and simple life) as well as criticism of present societal praxis (of riches, luxury, etc.). Did members of the Jesus movement freely become poor, did they freely renounce possessions in order to criticize wealth and luxury? Did they live in poverty, in order to practice and demonstrate radical self-sufficiency (autarchy) and the ideal of a simple life? Did they leave their families and spouses in order to renounce the obligations of family, which would stand in the way of their striving for independence and self-sufficiency? Did their departure from family intend to expose the traditional hierarchy of Mediterranean families, which we call patriarchal? No, I do not believe so. I am convinced that Cynic interpretations and, with them, the moralizing interpretations of the historical Jesus movement are mistaken. This must be demonstrated in detail, yet this is a broad field. Here I treat only the problem of leaving the family.

Jesus and his followers took a significant social step when they left their families (and jobs). Family, or kinship, was the most important social institution of Mediterranean society. Leaving the family in the course of following Jesus would have been ascribed preponderant significance. The family that a disciple left would experience an important disruption in self-provision, among other things. The disciples who left would neglect family obligations and loyalty to the family. Given the high significance of family ties, it is no accident that the Gospels speak several times of breaks with family initiated by Jesus' followers.

Matthew 8:18–22 (cf. Luke 9:57–62) reflects this problem clearly. The most acute statement in this regard is perhaps Matt 8:22, in which Jesus forbids a would-be follower from burying his father. Can this verse be properly understood other than hyperbolically? Other passages are Mark 3:20–21; 10:28–30; Luke 12:49–53 (see also Matt 10:34–36; Luke 14:26).

I have already mentioned that Crossan in this context defends the thesis that Jesus criticized the hierarchical order of the patriarchal Mediterranean family. In my opinion, the frequent mention of leaving family in the Gospel accounts indicates just the opposite. The stories indicate that persons were aware of the outrageous rupture with the conventions that concerned appropriate behavior in the family. But if the leaving of family is noted so frequently and, especially, justified with a special commission by Jesus, then the deviant behavior in question is knowingly understood as an exception. As the proverb has it, exceptions prove the rule! In sum, I do not see evidence for an attack by Jesus on Mediterranean patriarchalism in any of the passages that Crossan cites.

Love of Neighbor and Love of Enemies

Many interpretations of love of neighbor or love of enemies proceed from the position that the term "to love" (*agapan*) means an affectionate, emotional inclination toward some person. With this presupposition in mind, Sigmund Freud, for example, describes the command to love one's neighbor as an "ideal demand of civilized society" (1961:109). Freud criticizes this command by observing that it ultimately requires something unjust of human beings. For love of neighbor would require one to love and to show affection to strangers; but human beings ought to have such affection only for their own—their family, relatives, and friends. Later, Freud focuses criticism on Jesus' command to love one's enemies. When considered closely, this command, according to Freud, adds nothing new to love of neighbor. What was offensive to Freud (and to others as well) is that the command to love neighbor or enemy required feelings or behaviors that, generally speaking, were expected in the social institution of partnership (marriage), in the family or kinship, or in friendship (Freud 1969: 109–12). But this interpretation bespeaks misunderstanding of the words *agapan/philein* in the ancient Mediterranean and in the Bible. While these verbs can in fact refer to emotional ties, their main meaning is social, that is, in referring to a social relationship between individuals and groups. Malina contrasts the biblical concept of "love" with the modern, Western understanding of the term: "In Western culture generally speaking, love is an affect of the heart which is usually experienced individualistically toward another or other individuals. It does not necessarily involve attachment" (Pilch and Malina 1993:113). In Mediterranean values, love "is the value of group attachment and group bonding. It may or may not be coupled with feelings of affection. Such group attachment and group bonding are one type of social glue that keeps groups together. . . . Thus, to love someone is to be attached and bonded to the person" (110).

A husband who "loves" his wife, for example, gives up his attachment to his parents, that is, to his family of origin, and forms a new attachment with his spouse, with whom he becomes one flesh (i.e., forming the nucleus of a new kin group). On the contrary, the word "hate" (*misein*) can mean the dissolution of family ties. Thus, in Luke 14:26: "Whoever comes to me and does not hate his father and mother and wife and children, brothers and sisters, even his own life, cannot be my disciple."

Attachment to Jesus is here characterized as the dissolution of attachment to one's family. The family in the Mediterranean world is undoubtedly an important social institution for realizing the general value of "love." But it is not the only one. Love of neighbor is practiced in relations with friends and neighbors as well. Ancient love of neighbor or love of enemies related to social practices that we today would sooner place in the economy. More specifically, such practices concern the most elementary exchange of goods and services, or reciprocity.

Reciprocity entails a network of mutual services among persons and social groups with comparable social status. Reciprocity ultimately rests quid pro quo on mutuality and is not oriented toward profit (uneven or negative reciprocity). In principle, reciprocity presupposes symmetry or balance of exchange and is normally associated with careful reckoning of mutual services.

A typical example is Luke 11:5–8. A traveler comes at night to his friend's house; the latter takes him in as a guest. Since the host has nothing more to eat in his house, he goes to his neighbor, knocks on his door, and borrows some bread.

This brief description of ancient reciprocity must suffice for now (extensive examples appear in Stegemann and Stegemann 1999:34–36). I cite Luke 6:27ff. for the interpretation of Jesus' requirement of love of enemy (I take this passage as more original than the version in the Sermon on the Mount). To state it up front, I believe that Luke 6:27ff., which we generally title "love of enemies," concerns the ancient practice of reciprocity. In this I agree with Malina and Rohrbaugh (1992:56–57, 325). The passage teaches us about the everyday practice of reciprocity:

> If you love those who love you, what credit is that to you? For even sinners love those who love them. And if you do good to those who do good to you, what credit is that to you? For even sinners do the same. And if you lend to those from whom you hope to receive, what credit is that to you? Even sinners lend to sinners, to receive as much again. (Luke 6:32–34)

From this common practice, love of enemies is derived: "But love your enemies, and do good, and lend, expecting nothing in return; and your reward will be great, and you will be sons of the Most High; for he is kind to the ungrateful and the selfish" (Luke 6:35). Even earlier, Jesus had said, "But I say to you that hear, Love your enemies, do good to those who hate you, bless those who curse you, pray for those who abuse you" (Luke 6:27–28).

In my opinion, Jesus' requirement to love one's enemies is to be understood as follows: The term "love" refers to a social praxis—group attachment—and this in the context of reciprocal relations among neighbors. In contrast with the way reciprocity was normally practiced among equals, the love of enemies requires two changes in behavior.

On the one hand, it extends reciprocal relations to social enemies, a feature that stands in the foreground of the discussion. The communicative significance of this requirement is to restore communal relationships; one might say it concerns the reattachment of social enemies to the group.

On the other hand, love of enemies requires giving without the hope of getting anything in return. Here it might involve giving to the economically weaker partner. Further, Luke 6:35 ("he [God] is kind to the ungrateful and the selfish") suggests that one ought to extend relations of reciprocity even to ungrateful (*acharistos*) neighbors, hence to those who receive goods and services but who do not reciprocate.

To express this idea in modern terms, love of enemies is a type of business ethics. It relates to elementary gift exchange in an agrarian society. Jesus' demand seeks to bring social enemies and the ungrateful (those who do not reciprocate gifts received) back into a relationship of solidarity.

Yet, even with these emphases, Jesus' interpretation of love of neighbor as love of enemies remains within the framework of ancient reciprocity. This follows from the context of the passage, concerning love of enemies. The passage in Luke offers two important reasons for the required behavior. The first cites the Golden Rule: "And as you wish that people do to you, do so to them" (Luke 6:31). In this context, the statement cannot mean that one should repay like with like; rather, one should presuppose that one's own needs and expectations are those of others as well. The second reason promises a reward for the required behavior: ". . . and your reward will be great and you will be sons of the Most High" (Luke 6:35). God repays the gift when the human recipient does not. The compensation consists in a status elevation or, as one could say, in an enormous gain in honor. It would be possible to compare Jesus' emphasis on reciprocity, which we call love of enemy, with Israelite and gentile morality. Again the outcome would be that Jesus' position in no way falls outside the framework of the Israelite or Mediterranean symbolic moral world.

Conclusion

I conclude with four theses:

1. Jesus' ethos is a contextual ethos. In other words, it was formulated within the Israelite or general Mediterranean symbolic moral world and in the context of the social institutions of his society.
2. The insights gained through New Testament social history or cultural anthropology, and through modern research into Judaism at the time of Jesus, demonstrate the dominant tendency to one-upmanship in the

interpretation of Jesus' ethos as a petitio principii. Such interpretation corresponds to the misguided "criterion of dissimilarity." Instead of this criterion, we ought to consider the possibility of comparisons between the symbolic moral world of Jesus and Israelite or gentile society.

3. What recommends itself, therefore, is an integrating approach to the New Testament passages, one highlighting Jesus' ethos. The search for a motivating center of Jesus' "ethics" is doomed to failure if only because the Gospels themselves adduce differing reasons for the moral positions that Jesus adopts.

4. As I see it, social-scientific Jesus research requires a fundamentally new assessment and presentation of what has hitherto been labeled the "ethics" of Jesus.

Works Cited

Bourdieu, Pierre. 1984. *Distinction: A Social Critique of the Judgment of Taste*. Translated by R. Nice. Cambridge: Harvard University Press.

Bultmann, Rudolf. 1961. *Theologie des Neuen Testaments*. 4th ed. Tübingen: Mohr/Siebeck. Translated by K. Grobel under the title *Theology of the New Testament*. 2 vols. New York: Scribner, 1951–55.

Crossan, John Dominic. 1991. *The Historical Jesus: The Life of a Mediterranean Jewish Peasant*. San Francisco: HarperSanFrancisco.

Draper, Jonathan A. 1999. "Wandering Charismatics and Scholarly Circularities." In *Whoever Hears You Hears Me: Prophets, Performance, and Tradition in Q*, edited by R. A. Horsley and J. A. Draper, 29–45. Harrisburg, Pa.: Trinity Press International.

Freud, Sigmund. 1961. *Civilization and Its Descendants*. In The *Standard Edition of the Complete Psychological Works of Sigmund Freud*. Vol. 21. Trans. and ed. James Strachey. London: Hogarth (reprint 1930).

Herms, Eilert. 2000. "Ethik." In *RGG*⁴ 2:1598ff. Tübingen: Mohr/Siebeck.

Hurst, L. D. 1992. "Ethics of Jesus." In *Dictionary of Jesus and the Gospels*, edited by J. Green and S. McKnight, 210ff. Downers Grove, Ill.: InterVarsity.

Luz, Ulrich. 1989. *Matthew 1–7*. Translated by W. C. Linss. CC. Minneapolis: Augsburg.

Mack, Burton L. 1995. *Who Wrote the New Testament? The Making of the Christian Myth*. San Francisco: HarperSanFrancisco.

Malina, Bruce J., and Richard L. Rohrbaugh. 1993. *Social-Science Commentary on the Synoptic Gospels*. Minneapolis: Fortress Press.

Meeks, Wayne A. 1993. *The Origins of Christian Morality: The First Two Centuries*. New Haven: Yale University Press.

Pilch, John J., and Bruce J. Malina, eds. 1993. *Handbook of Biblical Social Values*. Peabody, Mass.: Hendrickson.

Schrage, Wolfgang. 1989. *Ethik des Neuen Testaments.* Göttingen: Vandenhoeck & Ruprecht. Translated by D. E. Green under the title *The Ethics of the New Testament.* Philadelphia: Fortress Press, 1988.

Stegemann, Ekkehard W., and Wolfgang Stegemann. 1999. *The Jesus Movement: A Social History of Its First Century.* Translated by O. C. Dean Jr. Minneapolis: Fortress Press.

Stegemann, Wolfgang. 1984. "Vagabond Radicalism in Early Christianity? A Historical and Theological Discussion of a Thesis Proposed by Gerd Theissen." In *God of the Lowly: Socio-Historical Interpretations of the Bible,* edited by W. Schottroff and W. Stegemann, 148–68. Maryknoll, N.Y.: Orbis.

Theissen, Gerd. 1978. *Sociology of Early Palestinian Christianity.* Translated by J. Bowden. Minneapolis: Fortress Press.

Theissen, Gerd, and Annette Merz. 1998. *The Historical Jesus: A Comprehensive Guide.* Translated by J. Bowden. Minneapolis: Fortress Press.

Uhlhorn, Gerhard. 1895. *Die christliche Liebesthätigkeit.* 2d ed. Stuttgart: Gundert. Translated under the title *Christian Charity in the Ancient Church.* New York: Scribners, 1883.

Social-Psychological Perspectives

4

Jesus as Fatherless Child

Andries van Aarde

Psychohistory—the Problem

The discomfort of many European exegetes with psychohistorical portrayals of Jesus can be attributed to Albert Schweitzer's sharp criticism of psychopathologists' attempts to analyze Jesus ([1913] 2001:292–95; 1948:33, 46–53). Some of these psychological studies were triggered by Schweitzer's own work. He had emphasized Jesus as an apocalyptic figure. This, and the reference in Mark 3:21 that Jesus' own family thought him to be insane, led to psychologists questioning Jesus sanity. It caused Schweitzer to write his second dissertation on a psychopathological analysis of Jesus (1948). Schweitzer was not only interested, however, in therapeutic matters (see Joy 1948:23). He also had a problem with the psychopathologists' unsophisticated use of historical and textual evidence.

In the same vein, Martin Kähler pointed out that a *biography* of Jesus would be impossible since sources did not mention Jesus' "psychological disposition" ([1896] 1969:14). Rudolf Bultmann conceded that, "psychologically speaking," we know virtually nothing of the "life" and "personality" of Jesus ([1926] 1988:8–19; see Käsemann 1960). But, according to Walter Schmithals, in the afterword to Bultmann's Jesus book, a gross misunderstanding could arise here (1988). It is misleading to believe that Bultmann (or Schweitzer, for that matter) considered it impossible to carry out a historical investigation of Jesus. Bultmann also said that we know enough of Jesus' message to be able to draw a coherent picture of him ([1926] 1988:13). The question remains, however, whether it is in any way possible to study Jesus from the viewpoint of social psychology without being guilty of a "psychological fallacy" (see, for example, Miller 1997).

It has been especially John J. Pilch who has pointed to the shortcomings of modern psychiatry and psychology in describing the behavior of the people of whom we read in the New Testament (1996; 1997a; 1997b). Modern psychiatry and psychology function within modern Western categories. Pilch has demonstrated why individualism (as a modern Western category) cannot serve as an explanation for the collectivistic personalities of first-century Mediterranean people.

In his 1980 work, David Stannard pointed out four problems in the works of historians who make use of psychoanalytical investigations within the Freudian paradigm: therapy, logic, theory, and culture. In this essay I illustrate some aspects of his thesis. Yet I also show a viable possibility of seeing Jesus from the viewpoint of social psychology, in cross-cultural perspective.

My presupposition is that Jesus probably grew up without a father playing a role in his life. My understanding of Jesus' baptism is that it was a ritual event through which "sinful sickness" was addressed and healed. Why would Jesus want to be baptized? The unfortunate relationship with his family and his critique of the patriarchal family as such provide probable clues. Moreover, what does Jesus' birth record tell us about his relationship with his family and his townsfolk in Nazareth? What does his birth record reveal about his vision, notably of children and of other "nobodies" in his society?

The answers to these questions rest on a construct, an ideal type, of someone in first-century Herodian Palestine who was "healed" from the stigma of being a fatherless son and who started a career healing "sinners." Jesus died because of the subversiveness of this ethos. It all happened against the background of the ideology of the Second Temple and Roman imperialism.

The Ideal-Type Model

Stannard's "problem of logic" pertains to conclusions reached about someone's behavior on the basis of psychoanalysis that completely lacks empirical observation (1980:53–82). This does not mean, however, that the historian is unable to construct a coherent mosaic of probabilities from scattered, isolated evidence. In this regard, Max Weber's notion of "ideal type" can be helpful. In constructing an ideal type, however, one does not attempt to provide a record of concrete historical situations based on empirical data. According to Max Weber, an ideal type is a theoretical construct in which possible occurrences are brought into a meaningful relationship with one another, so that a *coherent image* may be formed from data of the past (1949:89–112). In other words, as a theoretical construct, an ideal type is a conceptualization that will not necessarily correspond with empirical reality. Yet as a construct displaying a coherent image, the ideal type influences the conditions of investigations into what could have happened historically. The purpose of establishing an ideal type is to develop an intelligible account of interrelationships between discrete historical events. Such a coherent construct is not formed by or based on a selection from what is regarded as universally valid. Rather, it consists of a culturally circumscribed sampling of what is common to all relevant cases—to similar concrete situations that could, in reality, happen. It is, therefore, no logical-positivist choice based on either inductive or deductive reasoning.

I wish to develop, and to contribute to historical Jesus research, a construct of Jesus as a fatherless figure who called God his Father. In using the epistemological construct of an ideal type as the point of departure, I am not claiming that my historical Jesus construct is based on what is common to all fatherless people in first-century Galilee. That would amount to inductive historical reasoning. Nor is it based on what is common to most cases of fatherless people in Galilee. That, again, would amount to deductive historical reasoning.

The ideal-type construct enables one to concentrate on the most favorable cases. I focus on the data that can lead to a better understanding and explanation of some of Jesus' sayings and deeds. I am particularly interested in why the historical Jesus linked up with John the Baptist and submitted to the baptism for the remission of sins. I am also interested in why Jesus, once his road deviated from the Baptist, became involved, so unconventionally for his time, with the fate of fatherless people, especially women without "patriarchs" in their life and children without fathers. The aim of my construct is to provide an explanation of the historical figure of Jesus, trusting God as his Father, destroying conventional patriarchal values and, at the same time, caring for the fatherless within the macrosociological framework of family disintegration and divine alienation in the time of Herodian Palestine. The ideal type should be historically intelligible and socially explanatory.

Jesus as Fatherless Child

Apart from the reference to Joseph in the genealogy of Jesus, Joseph is called an artisan in the Gospel of Matthew, when Jesus is mentioned as his son. Mark only mentions that Jesus is an artisan. Luke does not make any reference in this regard. Luke does, however, indicate that Jesus is Joseph's son. There are no other references to Joseph in any document originating before 70 c.e. In the New Testament documents originating after 70 c.e., reference is made to Joseph's righteousness, his Davidic ancestry, his dream and the angel's conversation with him, his "holy marriage" to the "impure" Mary, his trip to Egypt with his family, and his trip to the temple with Mary and Jesus.

In documents originating from the second century onward, we find an elaboration on the fact that Joseph was a woodworker, further mentioning that he was righteous, that he was very old (89) when he took Mary as his wife, that he never had sex with her, that his youngest son, James, was still a child when this happened, that he also had other children, and that he died at the age of 111 (see Schaberg 1994a). From a historical viewpoint, it becomes highly questionable to refer to Joseph as the father of Jesus. References to Joseph do not occur in writings antedating the separation of the Pharisaic synagogue and Jesus groups after the destruction of Jerusalem in 70 C.E., and the termination of the earliest Jesus groups in Jerusalem. No known father played a role in the life of the historical Jesus.

With this backdrop, an altogether different portrait of Jesus' initial activity emerges. It is a picture of a "sinner," away from his home village, trapped in a strained relationship with relatives, but experiencing a fantasy homecoming in God's kingdom. Through the "altered state of consciousness" experienced at his baptism, Jesus probably encountered an "imaginary reality," created by the Spirit of God, which developed his perception of the care of a heavenly Father. He both attested to and lived this reality. Through the stories and letters of associates, Jesus became the icon of God's forgiveness of sin and providential care.

My thesis is that the "ethical example" that the figure of Joseph in the Old Testament provided in Hellenistic-Semitic literature served as a model for the transmitters of the early Jesus tradition. The authors of the Gospels of Matthew, Luke, and John knew the Joseph tradition. They found themselves (likes others from 70 to 135 C.E.) in controversies with fellow Israelites about, among others, Jesus' "illegitimacy." They counteracted by positioning Jesus as the "son of Joseph, the son of Jacob."

The patriarch Joseph sired children by his gentile Egyptian spouse Asenath. Asenath's virginity is not mentioned in the Genesis account. However, both the nature of Joseph's marriage to Asenath and her virginity were already widespread literary topics in the first century C.E. For example, when dealing with Joseph and Asenath, Josephus (*Ant.* 2.9) referred to their "most distinguished marriage" and Asenath's virginity (see Niehoff 1992:106). It is, furthermore, remarkable to notice that "rabbinic Midrash is . . . concerned with Asenath's alien origin and [that] this disturbing fact is accounted for in numerous ways" (Aptovitzer 1924; see also Niehoff 1992:107).

The children of Joseph and Asenath, the Makarites, became the forefathers of the Israelites who settled in the northern parts of Israel (see Michaud 1976:77–135). The Judeans labeled them "Samaritans" (Montgomery [1907]

1968:180–81; Egger 1986; Coggins 1975:53). Joseph and Judah became the symbols of *challenge and riposte* (see Malina 2001:27–57) with regard to impurity and purity in cultic life. In John's Gospel, after implying that Jesus was of illegitimate birth (8:41), the Judeans labeled Jesus a "Samaritan" and "demon possessed" (8:48).

In Hellenistic-Semitic literature, such as *The Testaments of the Twelve Patriarchs* (see Hollander 1981; Sklar 1996; Zerbe 1993; Argyle 1951–52) and *Joseph and Asenath*, the "righteous" Joseph, despite defamation, became the ancestor of children whose sins were forgiven, who were given their daily bread, and who were instructed to forgive others their trespasses, to give them their share of God's daily bread, and to ask God that they not be tempted to disobey their father's will. The compassion and forgiveness of sin by Joseph the patriarch is also the most outstanding theme in *The Testaments of the Twelve Patriarchs*.

> It is the patriarch Joseph above all who plays a pre-eminent role in the ethics of the Testaments. Not only in his farewell discourse is Joseph put forward as a good example for his sons, but his brothers too refer to him on their deathbeds, exhorting their sons to be like Joseph. He was one who kept himself free from adultery, who never stopped loving his brothers, who was full of mercy, compassion and forgivingness, who humiliated himself. He was a righteous man tried by God and rewarded and exalted afterwards. (Hollander 1981:65)

The Gospel tradition shared this emphasis and made use of it in striking ways in its depiction of Jesus. In the *Testament of Benjamin* (4:2), one reads: "The good person has not a dark eye. For [s]he shows mercy to all people, even though they are sinners" (Hollander 1981:69–70). *Testament of Benjamin* 4:4d reads: ". . . on the poor person [s]he has mercy; with the weak [s]he feels sympathy." In the *Testament of Zebulon* (6:5; 7:3), the same attitude toward the poor and *sympathy* toward the weak are described as virtues of the patriarch Zebulon, imitating the attitude and feeling of Joseph. In the *Testament of Gad* (4:1–2), in a passage in which Gad instructs his children, a remarkable phrase appears that the Gospel tradition attributed to Jesus: Gad revealed that lawlessness against the Lord amounts to disobedience to the words of God's "commandments concerning the love of one's neighbor, and it [hatred] sins against God" (cf. Sklar 1996:51). These instructions clearly go with the confession of one's own sin and an ongoing forgiveness of the sin of others (see *T. Gad* 6:3–4, 7). Here we have a clear resemblance to Jesus' words in Matthew's Lord's Prayer (6:12) and in Matthew's record of Jesus' summary of the Ten Commandments (22:37–40). These words in the *Testament of Gad* refer to Gad's memory that Joseph had wronged him several times. Gad reminded himself of his bitter hatred toward Joseph, such that he "very often . . . wanted to kill him" (*T. Gad* 2:1), and of his (and Judah's) own covetousness by selling Joseph for "thirty pieces of gold" (see *T. Gad* 2:3–4).

The parallels between the patriarch Joseph and Jesus should not surprise us. In *The Testaments of the Twelve Patriarchs*, later generations were instructed to imitate "our father Joseph." In this regard, it is noteworthy to observe, relative to the Israelite priest and author Flavius Josephus, that the "biblical Joseph's relationship with his brothers emerges as that part of the story which is most similar to Josephus' own life" (compare Josephus, *Ant.* 2.16, with *Life* 306, 314, 333, 389, 353; see Niehoff 1992:101). In her work on *The Figure of Joseph in Post-Biblical Jewish Literature*, Maren Niehoff found: "For one reason or another, Joseph seems to represent for each narrator a certain *Idealtyp*" (1992:52). The same is true with regard to Matthew's Joseph and the Joseph depicted in the romance *Joseph and Asenath* (ca. 100 B.C.E. to 115 C.E.; see Chesnutt 1996:286). This Hellenistic-Semitic romance focuses on God's intervention in the life of Joseph the patriarch (parallel to the Joseph in the Gospel tradition) to take Asenath, a virgin though an "impure" woman, into his house. It is a story of a "holy marriage." Against this background, Greek-speaking Israelites, who became followers of Jesus, retold a segment of the life of Jesus. For some of them, despite the slander, Jesus became the embodiment of God's forgiveness of sin and providential care, thanks to the God of his father (cf. Gen 49:25), Joseph, son of Israel.

We have seen that no writing traceable to 30–70 C.E. mentions Joseph's connection with Jesus. Such a conclusion has far-reaching consequences for historical Jesus research. It seems that Joseph did not die early in Jesus' life. Joseph entered the scene belatedly, after Jesus was crucified. For Greek-speaking Israelites, Joseph was an ethical paradigm. For Pharisees, he was the symbolic adversary of Judah, the forefather of people who either came from the pagan world or who mixed with them. In other words, the Judeans regarded the "Joseph people" as bastard Israelites, because they were a mixture of God's people and Gentiles. Therefore, "Joseph people" were to be regarded as if they had no parentage at all (see van Aarde 1998).

Who was first to claim that the fatherless Jesus was the son of Joseph? Was it the Pharisees, who believed that being fatherless denoted illegitimacy? Or was it Greek-speaking members of the house of Israel, who belonged to a Jesus group and who regarded such a claim to indicate the intervention of God, who turns slander into exaltation? I do not know. The important point is that these two perspectives relate to the way in which one views Jesus.

An Inflation of Historical Probabilities?

From the assumption that Jesus grew up fatherless, I believe that a historical construct of Jesus' life within first-century Herodian Palestine can be built according to an imaginative ideal type. It is not an inflation of historical probabilities to say that the following features go together:

- a record of having been born out of wedlock;
- the absence of a father figure;
- having been an unmarried bachelor;
- a tense relationship with mother and other siblings;
- the shift, probably forced, from farming to woodworking;
- sinfulness that led to an association with a "revolutionary" baptizer;
- an altered-state-of-consciousness experience in which God was present and acted like a father;
- abandoning the craft of woodworking;
- "homelessness" that led to an itinerant lifestyle along the lakeside;
- a journey that never seemed to take him inside the cities Sepphoris and Tiberias, but that was restricted to the plains, valleys, and hills of Galilee;
- assembling a core of close companions;
- defending fatherless children, "patriarch-less" women, and other social misfits;
- calling these "misfits" a family by resocializing them into God's household, through empowering healing and by acting as an agent of the Spirit of God;
- offending village elders by subversive teaching and actions;
- outraging Pharisees, Herodians, chief priests, and elders in Jerusalem by criticizing the manipulative ploys and misuse of hierarchical power by the temple authorities;
- crucifixion by the Romans after an outburst of emotion at the outer temple square;
- death without interment in a family tomb;
- believed to be taken up to the bosom of father Abraham to be among the "living dead," as Scriptures foretold;
- more than that, believed to be God's beloved child who was already with God before creation, who is now preparing a dwelling for those who still live by his cause.

I cannot prove that my image of Jesus is the "real" Jesus. This ideal type, however, can be supported when interpreted in terms of a chronological stratification of relevant documents (see Funk, Hoover, and the Jesus Seminar 1997; Funk and the Jesus Seminar 1998; Crossan 1991:427–50) and when seen as congruent with the social stratification of first-century Herodian Palestine (compare Lenski, Nolan, and Lenski 1995:175–222; Fiensy 1991:158; Stegemann and Stegemann 1998:72).

Status Envy and Social Identity

In the peasant society of Jesus' world, the family revolved around the father. The father and the mother were the source of the family, not only in the biological sense, but because their interaction with their children created the structures of society. The socialization process in such communities fostered the child's dependence.

In the 1960s, Harvard University social psychologists conducted a cross-cultural study of the father's position in the family as it relates to the identification of children (see Burton and Whiting 1961). This research developed a "status-envy hypothesis." The evidence focused on the effect of a father's absence in the household. The outcome of the study differed from some other theories of identification in that, in terms of the hypothesis, a relationship that fully satisfies both parties is not conducive to identification. According to the status-envy hypothesis, for a child to identify fully with adults, such as parents, it is necessary that adults openly consume resources denied to the child. In other words, love alone will not produce identification unless the people a child loves withhold something the child wants. This is particularly true during socialization, which familiarizes the child with the privileges and disabilities fundamental to a particular society.

Everyone in society has a social map, precisely defining one's position in terms of identity, kinship, and expected behavior (Scott 1989:79). As part of every society's cultural rules, a status system gives the privileged access to some resources and denies them to others. A resource is a material or nonmaterial commodity, such as food, water, optimum temperature, and freedom from pain—including punishment—which one person may desire but over which another person may have control. Symbolic resources include love, comfort, power, and success. Were these resources inexhaustible, and equally and completely available, there would be no learning by identification, because there would be no such thing as status envy. This, however, is never the case. No one in a household—in any society—has unlimited access to every resource.

Societal taboos make it practically impossible. It is inevitable that some resources will be withheld and that someone will want them. This situation is particularly true in agrarian societies with limited goods and that are patrilocal in nature. In societies with patrilocal residence, a man spends his life in or near his place of birth. This results in a core of closely linked, blood-related male residents, supplemented by wives drawn from neighboring communities. The women are literally and figuratively outsiders. The men are the locus of power and prestige: the "adult males are the ones to be envied" (Burton and Whiting 1961:89).

This hypothesis about the process of identification and the development of identity may be summarized as follows (see Burton and Whiting 1961:85): identification is achieved by the imitation of a status role that is envied. This happens not overtly, but in fantasy, and the driving force is envy of the person who enjoys the privileged status. In every society, statuses have names or labels. In modern Western society, for example, there are the familiar kinship statuses of father, mother, uncle, aunt, brother, sister; the age-determined statuses of infant, child, adolescent, adult, and aged; the occupational statuses such as doctor, lawyer, clerk, and workman; and the sex-determined statuses of male and female.

As previously noted, the family was at the center of the first-century Mediterranean world, and, in the family, the father was central. Beyond the family lay the village, beyond that the administrative city, and further still the limits of the Roman Empire, encompassing "the world." This understanding of society served as an analogy for the concept "kingdom of God" (Scott 1989:79). The father's role in the family was not only that of God's representative but also that of the guarantor of proper worship of and obedience to God. One had to belong to a family to enjoy God's blessing, and, within the family, the father's status was divinely ordained (see Hamerton-Kelly 1979:27). And so, the divine and the human met at the most intimate level, the familial.

The identity of a person is his or her position or positions in the status system of a particular society. Three kinds of identity can be distinguished: attributed, subjective, and optative (Burton and Whiting 1961:85). *Attributed identity* consists of the statuses assigned to a person by other members of his or her society. *Subjective identity* consists of the statuses a person sees himself or herself occupying. Finally, *optative identity* consists of statuses a person wishes he or she could occupy, but from which he or she is barred. The aim of socialization is to produce an adult whose attributed, subjective, and optative identities are isomorphic: I see myself as others see me, and I am what I want to be. To attain such isomorphism, however, persons have to be barred from certain statuses in favor of others. They thus experience status envy and reach out from their attributed identity to some optative identity.

One's optative identity derives from status envy, and it would help if it were objective and realistic. In households in which the father is absent, the wish to be a father is not as realistic as the wish to have a father. The wish to have a family seems realistic when a person is barred from having a position in a family. According to this theory, fatherless infants who have been nurtured by their mother alone would not identify with her status, but would desire the privileged statuses in the family from which they had been barred. We can presume that if a man has a strong desire for a family, he did not identify with a father who occupied the privileged status within his biological family during infancy. One could continue the same line of reasoning. If someone within the house of Israel is hailed as a son of Abraham and a son of God, these labels could express status envy and optative identity. The first name expresses a position within the extended genealogical tribe of Israel; the last is a symbolic, fantastic expression of assumed fatherhood. In normal conditions, both labels express attributed identity. Having a position in the family is an identification of secondary nature and having a father is a primary identification.

Applied to a different context, but referring to the eastern Mediterranean, Crossan (1991:269) says that "to be a child was to be a nobody, with the possibility of becoming a somebody absolutely dependent on parental discretion and parental standing on community." In other words, arrangements in infancy lead to primary identification whereas those in childhood lead to secondary identification. But there could also be discrepancy between these two identifications because of status debarment on the primary level that needs to be resolved by an initiation ritual.

Cross-Cultural Perspective

Using anthropology in biblical exegesis does not mean simply studying phenomena by means of analogy. It pertains to cross-cultural comparison—identifying similarities and differences. Cross-cultural studies yield significant variables that bear on the hypothesis as postulated. Specifically, I have judged social structures of a sampling of societies for the degree to which the father and adult males in general occupy privileged statuses as perceived by the infant and, later, by the child (see Burton and Whiting 1961:88–89). One measure of privileged status, and therefore of status envy in childhood, is provided by the prevailing sleeping arrangements (see Whiting, Kluckhorn, and Anthony 1958). Another measure of privileged status pertains to marriage arrangements (see Jeremias 1969:271–73).

Sleeping Arrangements

Because it is the place where resources of greatest value to a child are given or withheld, a child's bed is at the center of its world during infancy. Those who share sleeping arrangements with the child become the child's models for primary identification, and the key question is whether or not the father also sleeps with the mother. A baby sleeping on its own in a separate room is unique. In thirty-six of sixty-four societies examined, the parents sleep apart during the nursing period so that the infant can enjoy the mother's exclusive attention. In the remaining twenty-eight societies, the parents sleep together, with the child sleeping in the bed with them or placed in a crib or cradle within reach of the mother.

It follows that, in terms of the hypothesis, the different situations would have a profound effect on the child's primary identification. If the parents sleep together, they both bestow and withhold resources, so that the envied status would fall to either parent. The infant perceives the juxtaposition of privilege to be between himself or herself and an adult. On the other hand, in cases where the parents sleep apart, the mother assumes a vast importance. The juxtaposition of privilege is between the child and mother and, because she sometimes withholds resources, she is the person envied. In societies in which infants enjoy their mother's exclusive attention in sleeping arrangements, therefore, the optative identity of boys may be expected to be cross-sexual. Those reared in societies in which, because of the sleeping arrangements, both adults withhold resources and are therefore envied, the optative identity of boys is more likely to be directed to adulthood.

Residence patterns provide the conditions for secondary optative identity, also when sex-determined statuses are relatively unprivileged because of primary cross-sex optative identity. Patrilocal societies would produce a conflict between primary and secondary optative sex identity when there are exclusive mother-child sleeping arrangements. In societies with maximum conflict in sex identity, for example, in which a boy initially sleeps exclusively with his mother but in which the domestic unit is patrilocal and, hence, controlled by men, initiation rites at puberty resolve this conflict in identity.

In the above-mentioned sample of sixty-four societies, there are thirteen in which "elaborate initiation ceremonies with genital operations" take place (Burton and Whiting 1961:90). All thirteen have the exclusive mother-infant sleeping arrangements, which (according to the hypothesis) cause a primary feminine identification. Furthermore, twelve of these thirteen have patrilocal residence that produces the maximum conflict in identity and, hence, the need for an institution such as an initiation rite to help resolve this conflict. Initiation rites serve the psychological function of replacing the primary feminine identity with a firmly established male identity (see Burton and Whiting 1961:90). This is accomplished by means of hazing, deprivation of sleep, tests of manliness, and painful genital operations, which are rewarded with the high status of manhood, if the initiate endures them unflinchingly. By means of the symbolic death and rebirth through the initiation rites performed at puberty, a male born in these societies leaves behind the woman-child status into which he was born and is reborn into his optative status and identity as a man. The process is also referred to as a "clarification of status" (see Corbett 1983:712).

In Jesus' time, women fulfilled the primary gender-specific role of childbearing. Typical female behavior included taking the last place at the table, serving others, forgiving wrongs, having compassion, and attempting to heal wounds (see Malina 2001:50). The role of the mother of a household, as household manager, however, was not gender-specific (see Matthews and Benjamin 1993:25). She was the "teacher" of the other women and children in the household. For boys, this role was transferred to the father once the boy became a young man and participated in the communal labor of the village.

Studies that focus on the effect of father-absent households in the early life of boys support the postulated hypothesis of status envy. Specifically, some studies in present-day Western society indicate that "war-born" boys from father-absent households not only behaved like girls in fantasy behavior but also showed very little aggression (see Burton and Whiting 1961:93). This behavior derived from the boys' first, or primary, identification. Their secondary identification led to behavior, overtly and in fantasy, that produced fatherlike performance.

Sigmund Freud held that the male child's identification with his father originates in the child's desire to be like the father, but that this is later replaced by the drive to replace the father in the mother's affections. Contrary to Freud's contention that the father is at the center of consciousness, Hubertus Tellenbach believes that the role of the father figure today has vanished from the Western psyche (1976:7–11). According to Tellenbach, the disappearance of the father is the result of a long process. He traces this process back in art and literature. From a macrosociological perspective, roots of the trend might go back to when "simple agrarian societies" in the Middle East developed into "advanced agrarian societies" (Lenski, Nolan, and Lenski 1995:188–222). Although kinship ties remained of great importance for individuals throughout the agrarian era, they were no longer the "chief integrating force" in advanced agrarian societies (Lenski, Nolan, and Lenski 1995:213).

Such profound social changes, especially with regard to Herodian Palestine, had an inevitable effect on kinship patterns and social relationships. The extended family (the *beth-'ab*) was slowly breaking up (Fiensy 1991:132). The

Hellenistic period inaugurated far-reaching change for many Israelites who had previously lived in extended family units, subsisting through communal labor on isolated farms. They now found themselves most commonly in nucle-ated families, living and working on large estates (Fiensy 1991:121). It seems that only two options were open to peasants, whose "agroeconomic" base had been removed, if they needed to adjust to their income when their families dis-integrated because their "agroeconomic" base was removed (Wolf 1966:15). They could either increase their production or reduce their consumption. The former strategy necessitated putting more labor into their land, but in terms of returns, this was hardly worthwhile. So they were impelled to supplement their income from the land. They could hire themselves out as day laborers, doing seasonal agricultural work or working temporarily in the fishing industry, or perhaps as craftsmen (Fiensy 1991:95). Neighbors in the village courtyard, which became the only viable economic unit, started to function as a socially supportive unit. This was true of village life in the ancient Mediterranean world, and, as children seldom left the village on attaining adulthood, neigh-bors increasingly constituted the socioeconomic basis of relationships (Fiensy 1991:135; Harper 1928:106). Villagers were generally related to each other by ties of blood or marriage.

Marriage Arrangements

Marriage arrangements in Israelite society were tightly linked to the organiza-tion of the Jerusalem temple cult. The temple cult also determined both the classification of people and politics. This means that holiness was understood in a highly specific way: "To be holy meant to be separate from everything that would defile holiness" (Borg 1991:86–87). When someone, according to this ethos of holiness, was considered an outsider within the social body—a no-body—such a person would have no identity and would experience a tense re-lationship with villagers, even with close relatives. Status envy would therefore come as no surprise.

Marriage regulations, determined by the Torah, prescribed who could marry whom. The hierarchy of the temple community was clearly visible in postexilic marriage regulations. Three types of marriage strategies can be dis-tinguished in the world of the Bible: "reconciliatory," "aggressive," and "defen-sive" (Malina 2001:143–59). The term "marriage strategy" refers to the way society was organized through kinship relations. The three marriage types were broadly related to three successive periods in the life of Israel: the period of the patriarchs, the period of the kings, and the postexilic Second Temple period. Marriage regulations during the postexilic Second Temple period were deter-mined strongly by cultic purity regulations. Thus, for instance, marriages were only allowed when they took place within the ambit of one's own group of families, the "family of procreation," that is, the "house of Israel" (Malina 1996:50). Marriages were geared toward the continuation of "holy seed," that is, of the physical "children of Abraham" (Malina 2001:152–53). The practice of circumcision and admission to the temple as the place of God's presence were closely related to this goal. The commandment on divorce, in the marriage reform regulations (Nehemiah 9–10; Ezra 9:10), was meant to dissolve undesirable, "mixed marriages" (see Bossman 1979). These marriage arrangements were embedded in the stratification of people from holy to less holy to impure (Jeremias 1969:271–73; Neyrey 1991:279; Funk 1998:202; this hierarchical construct is inferred from *m. Qidd.* 4:1; *m. Hor.* 3:8; *t. Roš. Haš.* 4:1; and *t. Meg.* 2:7):

1. priests
2. Levites
3. full-blooded Israelites
4. illegal children of priests
5. converts (proselytes) from heathendom
6. converts from the ranks of those who had previously been slaves, but who had been set free
7. bastards (born from mixed-marriage unions or through incest)
8. the fatherless (those who grew up without a father or a substitute father and therefore were not embedded within the honor structures)
9. foundlings
10. eunuchs
11. men who had been eunuchs from birth
12. those with sexual deformities
13. hermaphrodites
14. Gentiles

The principle behind this classification was related to the marriage regulations that obtained during the Second Temple period. These regulations determined who could marry whom and who could enter into the temple. The above fourteen groups may be divided into seven categories (see Malina 2001:174). The (1) priests, (2) Levites, and (3) "full-blooded" Israelites formed the first three categories. Illegal (not illegitimate) children of priests were children born of marriages that were inadmissible to priests. A priest was forbidden to marry a woman who already "belonged to a man," like a widow, divorcée, or rape victim. These "illegal children" of priests (4) formed, with both groups of proselytes (5 and 6), the fourth category. Bastards (7), the fatherless (8), foundlings (9), and the castrated (10) formed the fifth category. We have no information of note on the *fatherless* (men whose father was unknown) and *foundlings* They were forbidden marriage with both Israelites of pure descent and with illegitimate children of priests (*m. Qidd.* 4:1), for their fathers, or their parents, were unknown. In fact, they were suspected of being bastards (cf. *m. Ketub.* 1:8–9); on the other hand, the possibility could not be excluded that they might, without being aware of it, contract a forbidden marriage with a relation (*b. Qidd.* 73a).

Those born eunuchs (11), those with deformed genitals (12), and hermaphrodites (13)—in other words, people who could not marry at all—made up the sixth category. People with another ethnic orientation (14), those, in other words, outside "God's people as people of the covenant," formed the seventh category. Any involvement with these people was very strongly discouraged in Israel. Those from the sixth category could make no biological contribution to the continuation of "holy seed," the "children of Abraham."

"True Israel," actually, consisted only of the first three categories. Persons in those categories could, with certain limitations, freely intermarry. People from the fourth category ("illegal children" of priests and proselytes) did belong to Israel and were allowed to marry Levites and "full-blooded" Israelites, but daughters among these "illegal children" and daughters of proselytes were under no circumstances allowed to marry priests. The fifth category was simply deemed "impure." They were people outside the covenant—doomed, as far as the temple in Jerusalem was concerned. They were not to approach closer than the temple square, the court of the Gentiles; they were obliged to live as if God did not exist (see Sanders 1993:229). If a man from this category wanted to get married, he could do so only with an "impure" woman, among whom the Gentiles, too, were categorized. Otherwise, such a person remained unmarried. In a society in which the honor of a man—in fact, his entire social identity—was determined by his status as a member of the family of Abraham and his contribution to the physical continuation of that family, one's unmarried status had, to put it mildly, serious implications.

Does Jesus Fit the Model?

The image of the historical Jesus as the fatherless woodworker, the unmarried son of Mary, living in a strained relationship with his village kin in Nazareth — probably because of the stigma of being fatherless—and, therefore, a sinner, fits the fifth category described above. Although innocent as a child, who was not supposed to know the nature of sin, the historical Jesus was denied the status of being God's child, doomed not to transmit the status of proper covenant membership, and, therefore, not allowed to enter the congregation of the Lord.

Yet Jesus shared the vision of John the Baptist that remission of sin could be granted by God outside the structures of the temple. Both before and after his baptism and breach with John the Baptist, Jesus was noted for association and friendship with "sinners" and his trust in God as his Father. This attitude was certainly subversive toward the hierarchical, patriarchal values that underlined the marriage strategy of the Second Temple period. The historical claim may therefore be made that, in the criteria of the Second Temple period, Jesus, being fatherless, was considered of illegitimate descent.

John Pilch made a valuable contribution with regard to childrearing in the Mediterranean world and its application to the life of Jesus (1993). Although it was not Pilch's intention to distinguish between the historical Jesus and the Jesus of faith, the results of his study remain of special importance for my own research. Pilch showed how ambivalent Mediterranean society was to its value system, since both the feminine quality of nurture and the male quality of assertion were emphasized. In early childhood, the boy learned nurturing values, but these were displaced by the "clarification of status" that marked his passage at puberty from the gentle world of women to the authoritarian world of men. The transformation developed out of a parenting style in the Near East through which the boy learned from his father (or male next-of-kin) that "Abba Isn't Daddy," in the Western sense of the word (Barr 1988). In the aggressive and hierarchical world of men, Jesus learned, according to Pilch, to reject the comfort of childhood and the warmth of feminine values and to embrace instead the rigors of manhood, subjecting himself in unquestioning obedience to the severity of the treatment that his Father and other males might inflict on him.

If a "clarification of status" was lacking because of fatherlessness, one can anticipate a diffused identity. As Donald Capps suggested with regard to Jesus, it is likely that status envy could cause the "child . . . as an endangered self" to desire "to be another man's son" (1992:21). In the words of Jane Schaberg, "paternity is canceled or erased by the theological metaphor of the paternity of God" (1994a:14). The resources withheld in Jesus' case would be the resources that a father was expected to give his son. Since Jesus called God his Father, it seems that the followers of Jesus interpreted his suffering as a filial act of obedient submissiveness to God, his heavenly Father.

Because of the assumption that his primary identification was never "clarified" by a secondary identification, the fatherless Jesus seemingly behaved in a "motherlike" manner as an adult (see Jacobs-Malina 1993:2). It can be seen in his sayings and deeds, in which he advocated taking the last place at the table, serving others, forgiving wrongs, having compassion, and healing wounds. Such a "conflict-laden" performance caused spontaneous, if not intentional, antipatriarchal behavior.

Jesus' *attributed identity*, based on how the members of his society perceived him, seems to have consisted in his fatherless status. This position, assigned to him because of the temple ideology, would lead to his being barred from status as child of Abraham, that is, a child of God; he would have been a nobody, prohibited from marrying a "full-blooded Israelite." Jesus' *subjective identity* seems to consist of the status he saw himself occupying: as the protector and defender of outcasts, like abandoned women and children, and as a person who gave the homeless a fictive home. Finally, Jesus' *optative identity*—the status that he wished he could occupy, but from which he was excluded— seems to be that of child of Abraham, child of God. That could be the reason why the fatherless Jesus called upon God as Father.

Works Cited

Aptovitzer, Victor. 1924. "Asenath, the Wife of Joseph." *HUCA* 1:239–306.

Argyle, A. W. 1951–52. "The Influence of the *Testaments of the Twelve Patriarchs* upon the New Testament." *ExpTim* 63:256–58.

Barr, James. 1988. "Abba Isn't 'Daddy.'" *JTS* 39:28–47.

Borg, Marcus J. 1987. *Jesus: A New Vision—Spirit, Culture, and the Life of Discipleship*. San Francisco: Harper & Row.

Bossman, David M. 1979. "Ezra's Marriage Reform: Israel Redefined." *BTB* 9:32–38.

Bultmann, Rudolf. [1926] 1988. *Jesus*. New ed. Tübingen: Mohr/Siebeck.

Burton, R. V., and J. W. M. Whiting. 1961. "The Absent Father and Cross-Sex Identity." *Merrill-Palmer Quarterly* 7:85–95.

Capps, Donald. 1992. "The Desire to Be Another Man's Son: The Child Jesus as an Endangered Self." In *The Endangered Self*, edited by R. K. Fenn and D. Capps, 21–35. Princeton: Center for Religion, Self, and Society, Princeton Theological Seminary.

Chesnutt, R. D. 1996. "From Text to Context: The Social Matrix of *Joseph and Aseneth*." In *SBLSP 1996*, 285–302. Atlanta: Scholars.

Coggins, R. J. 1975. *Samaritans and Jews: The Origins of Samaritanism Reconsidered*. Growing Points in Theology. Atlanta: John Knox.

Corbett, J. H. 1983. "The Foster Child: A Neglected Theme in Early Christian Life and Thought." In *Traditions in Contact and Change: Selected Proceedings of the XIVth Congress of the International Association for the History of Religions*, edited by P. Slater and D. Wiebe, 710–13. Waterloo, Ontario: Canadian Corporation for Studies in Religion.

Crossan, John Dominic. 1991. *The Historical Jesus: The Life of a Mediterranean Jewish Peasant*. San Francisco: HarperSanFrancisco.

Egger, Rita. 1986. *Josephus Flavius und die Samaritaner: Eine terminologische Untersuchung zur Identitätsklärung der Samaritaner*. NTOA 4. Göttingen: Vandenhoeck & Ruprecht.

Fiensy, David A. 1991. *The Social History of Palestine in the Herodian Period: The Land Is Mine*. SBEC 20. Lewiston, N.Y.: Mellen.

Funk, Robert W., Roy W. Hoover, and the Jesus Seminar. 1997. *The Five Gospels: The Search for the Authentic Words of Jesus*. New York: Macmillan.

Funk, Robert W., and the Jesus Seminar. 1998. *The Acts of Jesus: What Did Jesus Really Do?* San Francisco: HarperSanFrancisco.

Hamerton-Kelly, Robert. 1979. *God the Father: Theology and Patriarchy in the Teaching of Jesus*. OBT. Philadelphia: Fortress Press.

Harper, M. 1928. "Village Administration in the Roman Province of Syria." *Yale Classical Studies* 1:105–68.

Hollander, Harm W. 1981. *Joseph as an Ethical Model in the "Testaments of the Twelve Patriarchs."* Studia in Veteris Testamenti Pseudepigrapha 6. Leiden: Brill.

Jacobs-Malina, Diane. 1993. *Beyond Patriarchy: The Images of Family in Jesus*. New York: Paulist.

Jeremias, Joachim. 1969. *Jerusalem in the Time of Jesus: An Investigation into Economic and Social Conditions during the New Testament Period*. Translated by F. H. Cave and C. H. Cave. Philadelphia: Fortress Press.

Joy, Charles. R. 1948. "Introduction: Schweitzer's Conception of Jesus." In *The Psychiatric Study of Jesus: Exposition and Criticism*, by Albert Schweitzer. Translated by C. R. Joy. Boston: Beacon.

Kähler, Martin. [1896] 1969. *Der sogenannte historische Jesus und der geschichtliche, biblische Christus*. Newly edited by E. Wolf. 4th ed. Munich: Kaiser.

Käsemann, Ernst. 1960. "Das Problem des historischen Jesus." In *Exegetische Versuche und Besinnungen*, 1:187–214. Göttingen: Vandenhoeck & Ruprecht. Originally published in *ZTK* 51 (1954): 125–53.

Lenski, Gerhard, Patrick Nolan, and Jean Lenski. 1995. *Human Societies: An Introduction to Macrosociology*. 7th ed. New York: McGraw-Hill.

Malina, Bruce J. 2001. *The New Testament World: Insights from Cultural Anthropology*. 3d ed. Louisville: Westminster John Knox.

Matthews, Victor H., and Don C. Benjamin. 1993. *Social World of Ancient Israel, 1250–587 BCE*. Peabody, Mass.: Hendrickson.

Meier, John P. 1991. *A Marginal Jew: Rethinking the Historical Jesus*. Vol. 1: *The Roots of the Problem and the Person*. ABRL. New York: Doubleday.

Michaud, Robert. 1976. *L'Histoire de Joseph, le Makirite (Genèse 37–50).* Lire la Bible 45. Paris: Cerf.

Miller, John W. 1997. *Jesus at Thirty: A Psychological and Historical Portrait.* Minneapolis: Fortress Press.

Montgomery, James A. [1907] 1968. *The Samaritans, the Earliest Jewish Sect: Their History, Theology, and Literature.* Reprint, New York: Ktav.

Neyrey, Jerome H. 1991. "The Symbolic Universe of Luke-Acts: 'They Turn the World Upside Down.'" In *The Social World of Luke-Acts: Models for Interpretation,* edited by J. H. Neyrey, 271–304. Peabody, Mass.: Hendrickson.

Niehoff, Maren. 1992. *The Figure of Joseph in Post-biblical Jewish Literature.* AGAJU 16. Leiden: Brill.

Pilch, John J. 1993. "'Beat His Ribs While He Is Young' (Sir 30:12): A Window on the Mediterranean World." *BTB* 23:101–13.

———. 1996. "Altered States of Consciousness: A 'Kitbashed' Model." *BTB* 26:133–38.

———. 1997a. "Psychological and Psychoanalytical Approaches to Interpreting the Bible in Social-Scientific Context." *BTB* 27:112–16.

———. 1997b. "Review of *Jesus the Healer: Possession, Trance, and the Origins of Christianity,* by Stevan L. Davies." *BTB* 27:71–72.

Sanders, E. P. 1993. *The Historical Figure of Jesus.* New York: Penguin.

Schaberg, Jane. 1994a. "The Canceled Father: Historicity and the New Testament Infancy Narratives." Paper presented at the Westar Institute's Jesus Seminar, Santa Rosa, Calif., October 1994.

———. 1994b. "The Infancy of Mary of Nazareth (Proto-James and Pseudo-Matthew)." In *Searching the Scriptures.* Vol. 2: *A Feminist Commentary,* edited by E. Schüssler Fiorenza, 708–27. New York: Crossroad.

Schmithals, Walter. 1988. "Nachwort." In *Jesus,* by R. Bultmann, 149. New ed. Tübingen: Mohr/Siebeck.

Schweitzer, Albert. [1913] 2001. *The Quest of the Historical Jesus.* Edited by J. Bowden. Translated by S. Cupitt. 1st complete ed. Minneapolis: Fortress Press. Originally published as *Geschichte der Leben-Jesu-Forschung: Zweite, neu bearbeitete und vermehrte Auflage des Werkes von Reimarus zu Wrede* (Tübingen: Mohr/Siebeck).

———. 1948. *The Psychiatric Study of Jesus: Exposition and Criticism.* Translated by C. R. Joy. Boston: Beacon.

Scott, Bernard Brandon. 1989. *Hear Then the Parable: A Commentary on the Parables of Jesus.* Minneapolis: Fortress Press.

Sklar, H. W. 1996. "The Fighter of Horizons: The Story of Joseph as a Model for Social and Spiritual Reconciliation." M.A. thesis, Graduate Theological Union, Berkeley, Calif.

Stannard, David E. 1980. *Shrinking History: On Freud and the Failure of Psychohistory.* New York: Oxford University Press.

Stegemann, Ekkehard W., and Wolfgang Stegemann. 1998. *The Jesus Movement: A Social History of Its First Century.* Translated by O. C. Dean Jr. Minneapolis: Fortress Press.

Tellenbach, Hubertus, ed. 1976. *Das Vaterbild im Mythos und Geschichte: Ägypten, Griechenland, Altes Testament, Neues Testament.* Stuttgart: Kohlhammer.

van Aarde, Andries. 1998. "Jesus' Father: The Quest for the Historical Joseph." *HTS* 54:315–33.

Weber, Max. 1949. *Max Weber on the Methodology of the Social Sciences.* Translated and edited by E. A. Shils and H. A. Finch. Glencoe, Ill: Free Press.

Whiting, J. W. M., R. Kluckhorn, and A. Anthony. 1958. "The Function of Male Initiation Ceremonies at Puberty." In *Readings in Social Psychology,* edited by E. E. Maccoby et al., 359–70. New York: Holt.

Wolf, Eric R. 1966. *Peasants.* Foundations of Modern Anthropology Series. Englewood Cliffs, N.J.: Prentice-Hall.

Zerbe, Gordon M. 1993. *Non-Retaliation in Early Jewish and New Testament Texts.* JSPSup 13. Sheffield: Sheffield Academic.

5

Jesus Heals the Hemorrhaging Woman

Stuart L. Love

Introduction

The purpose of this essay is to assess the historicity of the healing story of the hemorrhaging woman in Matt 9:20–22, primarily by means of a cross-cultural anthropological analysis. The story was chosen for two reasons. First, as Meier points out, the occurrence lacks multiple attestation—there is no other incident of its type, that is, of a woman with a private gynecological problem, perhaps a chronic uterine hemorrhage. This was, according to the levitical law, a constant source of ritual impurity (Meier 1994:707, 709). Meier treats the account's historicity as unclear (*non liquet*; 706–7, 710). Second, the account—having passed through at least the initial compilation and the time of Jesus' activity—no doubt describes the evangelist's setting in life. Accordingly, the final form of the narrative is heavily edited (in comparison to Mark) and tends to suppress certain features for theological reasons (Held 1963).

Historical assessment of the healing stories is most difficult. First, as Malina points out, every "person seeking to evaluate the historical authenticity of Jesus' deeds must necessarily assume and apply some theory of reading, of language and of social meaning, whether they are aware of it or not" (1999a:351–52). Second, for many scholars, the healing deeds of Jesus—a major component of the "miracles" of Jesus—are "problem-ridden behaviors," largely "because there is no room for them among the patterns of conduct and perception available in contemporary U.S. and northern European social systems" (Malina 1999a:352). A final difficulty is that, from the Enlightenment, the deeds of Jesus as a healer have been variously interpreted out of conceptions "available from the contemporary social system" to which scholars have been enculturated (Malina 1999a:353). As Pilch states, "The advent of modern science in about the seventeenth century disrupted the bio-psycho-spiritual unity of human consciousness that had existed until then" (1993:233). Required is an assessment of the "constructs of readers and/or hearers of the Gospel documents" (Malina 1999a:351).

To this end, cross-cultural anthropological models are useful, because the social conceptions of reality described therein are more analogous and indigenous to first-century Mediterranean, Palestinian society. A social-scientific systems analysis provides a thick description based on the cognitive maps of how people in Palestine believed their universe worked. A difficulty, but not an insurmountable problem, is that some models can be analogous both to the periods of Jesus and the evangelist. Even so, I demonstrate that a social-scientific reading of Matthew's account of the healing of the hemorrhaging woman favors the position that the story originated in the activity of Jesus. In other words, Matthew's redaction points in two directions: to the *Sitz im Leben* of the evangelist's day and to the historical period of Jesus as an Israelite healer.

Three social-scientific models will be used: (1) a model of healing in non-Western societies characterized especially by spirit involvement and aggression; (2) a model of social domains; and (3) a native taxonomy of illness involving degrees of impurity. The first model, broad in scope, is designed to better understand illness, healing, and healers in a social-cultural perspective different from the biomedical approach largely operative in advanced industrialized societies like the United States and northern Europe. The notion of spirit aggression assumes that illness is a misfortune caused by cosmic forces. The last two models assist more specifically in reading Matthew's story. The model of social domains concentrates on two foundational spheres—politics and kinship. What does it mean, in light of the political domain, for the woman to be healed in open space? What implications does the healing have for the woman's kinship ties or to Jesus as an Israelite healer? The final model, a taxonomy of degrees of impurity, helps illumine how the human body, in which purity issues are manifest, is a microcosm of the social body. The healing story is not isolated in the narrative, but belongs to the greater fabric of social, religious, and political issues related to Matthew's portrayal of Jesus as a healer.

Social–Scientific Models

Model 1: Healing in Non-Western Societies

How is illness experienced and treated in agrarian societies like the Roman Empire? Robert A. Hahn writes, "Anthropological observers in a variety of non-Western settings have noted that, in addition to roughly equivalent generic terms, sickness is connected to two broader phenomena: cosmological or religious forces, and social relationships and interpersonal conflicts" (1995:24). "Illness" denotes a social-cultural perspective in which "many others besides the stricken individual are involved" (Pilch 1986:102). Both patients and healers are "embedded in a cultural system," and it is the "whole system that heals." Attitudes and actions are embedded in the total fabric of life (Blum and Blum 1965:20). As the Blums add, "Health beliefs and practices must be viewed within the context in which they occur, since focusing on them in isolation distorts or detracts from their meaning and function" (20). Jesus as an Israelite healer should not be viewed in isolation, but in association with the cultural system (Pilch 1985:143). A systems-theory approach, accordingly, takes social relations and cultural expectations of societies into account. Sickness and healing belong to the organized patterns of thinking, judging, and behaving shared by members of a society (Hahn 1995:2; Blum and Blum 1965:chap. 2; Allbaugh 1953). This arrangement is different from the biomedical approach largely operative in advanced industrial societies like the United States and northern Europe, in which the focus too often is on a narrow hierarchy of molecules, cells, organs, and human bodies (Hahn 1995:97). Persons in advanced industrial settings do not readily see Jesus' healing activity as essential to his task in a social-political sense.

In societies like ancient Rome, sickness and healing may be classified along the lines of witchcraft, sorcery, and spirit aggression (Murdock 1980:73; Foster 1976). "Without exception," Murdock states, "every society in the sample which depends primarily on animal husbandry for its economic livelihood regards spirit aggression as either the predominant or an important secondary cause of illness" (1980:82; see Pilch 1991:200–209; 1992). Spirit aggression assumes that sickness is a misfortune due to the effect of cosmic forces on human lives (Pilch 1986:102, 104). Sun and moon belong to the array of cosmic forces. The sun's power gives warmth and life; it also causes headaches. Seeds, women, and the moon wax and wane together. Ill people may be moonstruck (Blum and Blum 1965:31–32).

Evidence for spirit aggression abounds in Matthew. For example, the demon possessed son in chapter 17 (vv. 14–20) is "moonstruck" (v. 15); that is, he is under the moon's cosmic influence or power, a term found only in Matthew (4:24; 17:14–18; see Ross 1978). Cosmic forces have made their habitation within him. Jesus rebukes the demon (17:18) as he does the violent, life-threatening power of a storm on the sea (8:26). Other examples include the Gadarene demoniacs (8:28–34); the Canaanite woman's daughter who "is tormented by a demon" (15:22); John the Baptist, whom Jesus' critics accuse of having a demon (12:18); and the identification of mutes and the blind as demon-possessed persons (9:32; 12:22).

Further, the religious and political implications of the Beelzebul controversy (12:22–32) hinge on whether Jesus "casts out demons by the prince of demons" (9:34; 12:24) or by the Spirit of God (12:26, 28). Matthew's language is unequivocal, forceful, uncompromising, and violent (12:22–30). The spiritual realms of God and Satan are like two kingdoms, cities, or houses that, if divided, cannot stand (12:25–26). The strong man first needs to be tied before his house can be plundered (12:29). Blasphemy against the Spirit will not be forgiven (12:30–31). Accordingly, Matthew presents Jesus as a Spirit-led servant-prophet (see 12:18, based on Isa 42:1–4; Matt 12:28; 3:16; 4:1) who struggles with the religious and political powers of Jerusalem (see 21:14).

Magical practices flourish in preindustrial settings among all social groups, but especially among lower-class urbanites and villagers (Sjoberg 1960:275; Blum and Blum 1965:25, 31–35). Sjoberg states, "Restorative magic has prevailed in feudal orders from the most ancient ones in the Near East to those in the Greek and Roman periods, in Central and Eastern Asia, in medieval Europe and pre-Columbian America, down to those that survive today" (1960:277–78). Since evil spirits upset the order of life, causing illness or other social or physical disasters (Sjoberg 1960:277), magical practices ward off evil and correct imbalances in the spiritual order (Blum and Blum 1965:31–32). Magical rituals presume "the sympathy of word, deed, and concept: peasants believe that by naming their wish, what they wish shall be, with the proviso that the energies of the supernaturals will be enlisted toward this end" (Blum and Blum 1965:32). Whether Jesus is a Hellenistic magician has sparked provocative discussion among scholars (Smith 1978; Hull 1974; Meier 1994:535–75; Twelftree 1993:190–207). Even though Matthew appears to avoid "explicit magical-manipulative connotations" (Duling 1992:109; see Mark 7:31–37; 8:22–26), traces of magical influences possibly remain. My interest is not to decide whether Jesus is a magician or charismatic healer (Theissen and Merz 1998:305–8), but how persons like the hemorrhaging woman might perceive Jesus and respond. Therefore, I use the term "magic" nonpejoratively "as the art of influencing the superhuman sphere of the spirits, demons, angels and gods" (Theissen and Merz 1998:305 n. 22).

Finally, it is necessary to describe the social sectors in which illness is experienced. Based on Arthur Kleinman's cross-cultural materials on healing (1986:29–47; 1989), John Pilch (1988:60–66; 1991; 1992:26–33; 1994) has identified three overlapping social sectors. First is the *popular sector* (1991:194–97), a family-centered environment of sickness and care that manages between 70 to 90 percent of sickness (Kleinman 1986:33); within this sector, "the lay, non-professional, non-specialist popular culture" provides treatment (Pilch 1986:103). Since public-welfare services seldom exist (Sjoberg 1960:251), the family (sometimes assisted by guilds) is the primary welfare-security agency. Persons outside this safety net frequently suffer social and religious isolation and ostracism. Second is the *folk sector*, a community context of care and healing. In this sector, villagers with recognized powers interpret for individuals and their families the presence and absence of illness (Pilch 1991:197–200; Sjoberg 1960:315–16). The deviant condition, illness, is "observed, defined and treated" by a "web of relations involving family, social network, village, etc." (Neyrey 1995:4). Finally, the *professional sector* is comprised of "professional, trained and credentialed healers" (Pilch 1991:192–94; Jackson 1988:9–31; Kee 1986:27–66), who serve mainly the urban upper classes (Sjoberg 1960:315–16). Jesus is not a "professional" healer. Rural and urban lower-class populations—peasants, artisans, outcasts, and expendables— experience health care as mediated by the *popular* and *folk* sectors (Sigerist 1961:2:306; Jackson 1988:138–69). Jesus is a healer among those who experience and treat illness in the *popular* and *folk* sectors.

Model 2: Social Domains

In the ancient Mediterranean there were four "foundational social domains," which now are analyzed by social scientists—politics, economics, religion, and kinship (family) (Hanson 1994). These four spheres, Hanson states, "are never discrete entities that operate in isolation from one another" (183). Rather, they are socially embedded to the extent that one sphere's definition, structures, and authority may be dictated by another sphere. Yet two of the domains, politics and kinship, are polar opposites, so that one may speak of political religion and domestic religion, but not simply of religion (Malina 1999b:30). Or one may speak of political economy and domestic economy, but not simply of economy. The domains of religion and economics, accordingly, are embedded either in politics or the family. For example, religious leaders such as Caiaphas, members of the Jerusalem Sanhedrin, and the Pharisees are political personages, and the Jerusalem temple is a political edifice where sacrifices are made for the public good (Malina 1999b:30). Conversely, domestic religion and economy are family-centered and focused on the kin group (Malina 1999b:31).

Jesus' behavior and words, including his healing activity and that of the Twelve, belong primarily to the public and political Israelite social domain. When Jesus proclaims a coming kingdom of heaven (Matt 4:17), he has an Israelite theocracy in mind (Matt 10:5; 15:24; see Malina 1999b:36). When Jesus heals the misfortunate, the crowds praise "the God of Israel" (Matt 15:31; see 8:11; 22:32). When Jesus recruits the Twelve to help in his theocratic task (Matt 4:18-22; 10:2-4), he commissions them as healers (10:1) and charges them not to go among the Gentiles and Samaritans. Their mission is to the "lost sheep of the house of Israel" (10:5, 6; see 15:24)—to "all the towns of Israel" (10:23; see also 7:6; 19:28-29). These particularistic words probably are authentic to the period of Jesus (Malina 1999b:36). As Malina (1999b:33) puts it, Jesus urges "Israelites to get their affairs in order and to heal those in need of healing (Matt 10:1-16)." The model of social domains sets forth the following social-scientific criterion for authenticating the deeds and words of Jesus. If an activity or statement attributed to Jesus in the healing story "makes direct and immediate political sense, then it is authentic" (Malina 1999b:43).

The kinship domain (household/family), however, as a plurisignificant social institution, also can have political significance. Embedded in the household, kinship is the most basic social organization in agrarian societies (Elliott 1991:221–38). In ancient Israel, the household's core social identity flows out of an ethics of tribal solidarity that "shaped a network of understanding and care that moved beyond the immediate compound family to include . . . the totality of the 'children of Israel'" (Perdue 1997:167). Ancient Israel as a household was a "cosmos for human dwelling" (Perdue 1997:178). Israel's head, Yahweh (Jer 3:4), created and established (Deut 32:6; Mal 2:10) his beloved son (Exod 4:22; Isa 63:16; Jer 3:19; 31:9; Hosea 11), or daughter (Lam 2:13). Household imagery warns Solomon's descendants that Israel would be cut off from the land if they failed to obey the Lord (1 Kings 9:7–8; see Jer 12:7; 22:5). Jesus' lament over Jerusalem echoes this ancient theme: "See, your house is left to you, desolate" (Matt 23:38). Matthew labels the ancient Israelite tabernacle as the "house of God" (12:4) and recalls that God's house "shall be called a house of prayer" (21:13; see Isa 56:7; Jer 7:11). Phrases like "house of Israel" and "house of God," therefore, beyond their historical identity, are social metaphors that particularize Israel. Kinship as a plurisignificant social institution is important, especially when viewed in association with the public, political, social domain.

Model 3: Native Taxonomy of Illness—Degrees of Impurity

A native taxonomy of illness based on "degrees of impurity" (Neusner 1973; 1978; Pilch 1981; 1991:207; Malina 2001:161–97; Neyrey 1986; 1991) follows certain insights of Mary Douglas (1966; 1975). For Douglas, purity is defined as normality and wholeness; pollution and taboo refer to matter "out of place"—dirt—and to a cultural system of order and disorder (1966; Isenberg 1975:179–75; Isenberg and Owen 1977). Purity rules are symbolic norms, a cultural language that expresses and reflects larger social concerns that work in concert with other structures of thought to deliver and support a common message. Douglas identifies four kinds of pollution boundaries: (1) danger pressing on external boundaries; (2) danger from transgressing the internal lines of the system; (3) danger in the margins; and (4) danger from internal contradiction (1966:122). Douglas further indicates that when "rituals express anxiety about the body's orifices, the sociological counterpart is a care to protect the political and cultural unity" of a group (1966:124). Accordingly, Pilch locates so-called leprosy with the boundary of the human body, spirit-possession as an invasion against the boundary, and women's illnesses as a concern for domestic boundaries (1986:104). The healing of the hemorrhaging woman, I affirm, relates not only to pollution boundaries related to the human body but also to pollution boundaries of the public, Israelite, social domain.

The human body is a center at which purity issues are manifest—a microcosm of the social body. Order and chaos at all cultural levels (the individual or the community) indicate social attitudes toward ill persons (Neyrey 1996:93). The Blums state, "Failure to observe the rites of purification, the sensitivities of the spirits, a disregard for the taboos that protect against pollution, are all dangerous omissions—omissions that will bring disaster to the offender" (1965:21). In rural Greece, "one must avoid the menstrual woman for fear of the damage her own power can do the god, the crops, the first bread, or the fighting man" (Blum and Blum 1965:33–34). If the hemorrhaging woman is a menstruant, according to Israelite law she is unclean and should not be touched (Lev 15:19–30). Ordinarily, such a woman remains at home. She may prepare meals and perform her household chores, but the family has to avoid lying in her bed, sitting in her chair, or touching her. For the woman's hemorrhage to last twelve years indicates the abnormality of the condition and the seriousness of the social restriction and/or exclusion. That she is located in open space also suggests a danger of pressing against external boundaries.

The external boundary—that is, the opposite pole, the social body—may be identified as Second Temple Israelite political religion located in Jerusalem.

Purity issues are articulated and measured against biblical stipulations in Lev 21:16–20. Priests with body blemishes, even though not technically impure or unclean, are not to draw near to offer the bread of God (21:17). The Leviticus tradition is known and stressed by Philo (*Spec. Leg.* 1.80; see also 1.117), Josephus (*War* 1.269–70; *Ap.* 1.15; see *Ant.* 14.366 and *t. Parah* 3:8), and the Qumran community. References from Qumran (4QD^d; 1QSa 2:5–10; 1QM 7:3–6), are noteworthy, for the lists they supply are not only for priests but also for those who participate in military action and those who would enter the sacred city and temple. Two passages relate physical impairment and social impurity to sacred locations. The first text (4QMMT B.49–54) excludes the blind and the deaf from the community. The second text (11QTemple 45:12–14) excludes any blind man from entering the holy city where the holy temple is located. Strictures like these possibly illumine the conflict over healing between Jesus and the religious authorities in the temple (Matt 21:14).

Accordingly, acts of touching in a number of the healing stories (the microcosmic level) are cultural issues for leaders of political religion (the macrocosmic level). Guardians of the social order label Jesus a social deviant after he touches and is touched by the impure (Neyrey 1996:91–95). Purity issues cut across Second Temple Israelite society—from the social body to the individual body. Cases in public settings have potential political ramifications for Jesus as an Israelite healer, even though a given example might not describe actual controversy with representatives of the Second Temple's power structure. Matthew's story of the hemorrhaging woman seems to fit this categorization. As Neyrey states, there is a "thorough correlation between socio-political strategy and bodily concerns" (1996:93; against Levine 1996:379–92, who apparently fails to recognize implicit meanings concerning purity issues). This correlation may become clearer in figure 5.1 (for the use of maps, see Neyrey 1996:91–95).

Having set forth the three models, I apply them to the case of the hemorrhaging woman. First, though, I establish a social profile of those healed in Matthew and note Matthew's redaction of Mark's account.

Jesus, Healer of the Hemorrhaging Woman in Matthew's Gospel

Social Profile of Healing Accounts in Matthew

Most of Jesus' healing activity occurs among the "poor"—farmers, artisans, outcasts, and expendables (Matt 11:2–6[Q])—and Jesus' fame as a healer draws large crowds, mostly from rural environs throughout and beyond Palestine

	Social-Religious-Political Elite	Jesus
Political Locus—Temple/Jerusalem/Rome	Network of control: from the Jerusalem Temple to Galilee	No network of control; mostly rural villages and peasants of Galilee
God of Israel	Core value: God's holiness	Core value: God's mercy
	Mission: maintain political control	Mission: inaugurate Israel's theocracy
Structural Implications	Strong boundaries	Weaker boundaries
	Exclusivistic strategy	Inclusivistic strategy among Israelites
Legitimation in Scripture	Law, except Genesis	Genesis and prophets
Strong Purity Concerns	Strong bodily control	Weaker bodily control
	Avoid public, bodily contact with sick, demon-possessed, bodily deformed	Public, bodily contact with sick, demon-possessed, bodily deformed

Figure 5.1: Purity/political map

(4:23–25; 9:35; 14:35–36; 15:29–31). Figure 5.2, on next page, identifies locations in which healing activities are reported and the means by which Jesus heals.

The stilling of the storm (8:23–27) presupposes spirit aggression—the casting out of a demon (compare 8:26 with 17:18). It draws together cosmological forces and social relationships. To classify the story as a "nature miracle" fails to understand both the incident's social context and its relationship with the

Passage	Illness/Bodily Affliction	Location	Means
8:2–4	leper	open space	"touched him"
8:5–13	paralytic	open/house	word of Jesus
8:14–17	Peter's mother-in-law	house	"touched her hand"
8:23–27	the storm	open space	command
8:28–34	2 demoniacs	open space, tombs	command
9:2–8	paralytic	uncertain in Matthew	command
9:18–19, 23–26	ruler's dead daughter	house	"took her" (v. 25)
9:20–22	hemorrhaging woman	open space	woman touches Jesus
9:27–31	2 blind men	open space/house	"touched their eyes"
9:32–34	demon-possessed mute	open space	command (implied)
12:9–14	man with withered hand	synagogue	command
12:22	demoniac	open space (implied)	command (implied)
15:21–28	Canaanite woman	open space	word of Jesus
17:14–20	moonstruck boy	open space	command (rebuked demon)
20:29–34	2 blind men	open space	touch
21:14	blind and lame	temple	not stated

Table 5.2: Typology of Healing Stories in Matthew

succeeding stories of the two demoniacs (8:28–34) and the paralyzed man (9:2–8). Jesus' healing power circumscribes "all misfortune" (Pilch 1986:105).

A summary of the locations indicates the following:

1. Nine take place in open space (out of doors) (8:2–4, 23–27, 28–34; 9:20–22, 32–34; 12:22; 15:21–28; 17:14–20; 20:29–34).
2. Two are in "public" locations (synagogue/temple) (12:9–14; 21:14).
3. Two are in private settings (houses) (8:14–17; 9:18–19, 23–26).
4. One is located both outdoors and in a house (9:27–31).
5. One location is uncertain (9:2–8) even though Mark locates it in a house (Mark 2:1–12).

Men usually are healed in open space, a procedure having possible political implications (Pilch 1985:147). The hemorrhaging woman and the Canaanite woman also encounter Jesus outside the private domain of the house.

A summary of the means of healing indicates the following:

1. Six accounts entail touching, nine involve the word and/or command of Jesus, and, in one instance, the means of healing is unknown.
2. Incidents of touching probably involve purity issues (our third model of degrees of impurity).
3. The word or command of Jesus relates to the healing of paralytics, those suffering from demons, a demon-possessed mute, the man with a withered hand, and the "moonstruck" boy (our first model of spirit aggression).

Even though the healing of the hemorrhaging woman lacks multiple attestation, it belongs to the larger social profile of those Jesus heals. Deviant elements include both the woman's illness and that she is healed outside the private kinship domain.

Matthew's Redaction

In all three Synoptic accounts, the story of the hemorrhaging woman is associated with the raising of a dead girl (Matt 9:18–19, 23–26; Mark 5:22–23, 37–43; Luke 8:40–42, 49–56). Matthew's redaction, however, indicates that the woman's healing has no essential connection to the larger narrative. For example, unlike Mark and Luke, Matthew reports at the outset that the girl is dead (9:9); in Mark, she is "at the point of death" (5:23), and in Luke the girl is dying (8:42). Often overlooked, Matthew omits that the girl is "twelve years of age" (Mark 5:42; Luke 8:42), thus restricting the number twelve to the older woman. Finally, even though Jesus and the disciples follow the father to his home, all "intermediaries" are omitted. Only Jesus and the distressed person ("the two poles," Theissen and Merz 1998:284–85) are featured; there are no representatives, embassies, or opponents. The woman is alone with Jesus in open space. This may indicate her lack of a family network and/or community support (4:35). The social irony is that an intensely private and apparently gender-specific misfortune is healed outside a domestic setting. At any rate, Matthew's account can be analyzed alone.

Further, even though Matthew's tradition is drawn from Mark, his redaction is much briefer and ignores the rudeness of the disciples as it depicts Jesus in absolute control. Matthew omits the negative opinion about physicians (Mark 5:26), that the woman has heard reports about Jesus (Mark 5:27), and that she experiences healing within her body (Mark 5:29). Matthew also omits that Jesus perceives that power has gone forth from him and that, in the press of the crowd, he asks who had touched his garments (Mark 5:30). He also omits the disciples' incredulous reaction to Jesus' question (Mark 5:31), that the woman comes to Jesus in fear and trembling (Mark 5:33), and that Jesus tells her to go in peace (Mark 5:34). For some, it appears that Matthew's "meltdown" is done for theological reasons (Held 1963) and is further removed from the activity of Jesus. However, this perspective fails to understand that Matthew's redaction is related to Jesus' distinctive mission to Israel (Matt 10:5; 15:24) and that Jesus' healing activity results in praise to "the God of Israel" (Matt 15:31; see 8:11; 22:32).

Finally, does the woman perceive Jesus as a healer with magical powers? The woman "came up behind" Jesus, "touched the fringe of his garment," and thought, "if I only touch his garment, I shall be made well" (9:21; see 14:36; cf. Mark 6:56; Acts 19:12). As indicated in our first model, Matthew probably suppresses hints of magic. He omits Mark's stories of the healing of the deaf-mute (7:31–37) and the healing of the blind man at Bethsaida (8:22–26)—accounts with possible magical implications. Matthew also omits Mark's emphasis that healing power leaves Jesus' body, as Meier puts it, "almost as though it were an electric current" (1994:709). Yet the woman's behavior parallels popular beliefs about magic in agrarian societies; that is, she believes the healer's clothing has healing power, a notion repeated in 14:36 (see Acts 5:15; 19:12). If an aura of magic remains in the story it could fit either the period of the evangelist, the time of Jesus, or both.

Applying the Models of Social Domains and Degrees of Purity

What is the basis for stating that Matthew's story originates with Jesus? It is demonstrated in a combination of the woman's faith, her identity as an Israelite outcast, the location of the healing in open space, and the violation of the Second Temple's purity boundaries. These factors coalesce to validate the woman's identity as an Israelite in need of healing (Matt 10:1–16; Malina 1999b:33)—the heart of Jesus' theocratic mission to Israel. How does the evidence support these assertions?

First, in a "purity system" the physical body manifests concerns of the social body (Wright 1992:729–41). In the case of Matthew's story, the social body is the Second Temple and its far-reaching, hierarchical religious system that replicates purity expectations in the symbolic world of culture (Pilch 1981:108–13). In other words, the "symbolic universe" of the woman and her social world includes an ideological geography (Neusner 1979:105) extending from Jerusalem to Galilee. According to the Pharisees' world order, the hemorrhaging woman is "dirt." She is "out of place," not whole, imperfect (Douglas 1966:5; 1975:50–51). Her body is a bounded system. Her continuous flow of blood is proof to all who know her that she has crossed a forbidden "frontier" (Douglas 1966:115; Neyrey 1986:101). Accordingly, she is "unclean" and dangerous to the guardians of the purity system centered on the Jerusalem temple. This is true even though the text does not label her "unclean," since this would have been a common perception of the bystanders anyway (Neyrey 1986:101). This is true even though she is not the direct object of ideological confrontation. And this is true because the location of the healing in open space makes it a potential political issue. The Pharisees' core value of maintaining holiness (Lev 11:44) has been violated, their exclusive strategy bypassed (Neyrey 1988:72–82). The woman's story parallels the purity/political map of the third model.

Second, the story parallels political expectations of the model of social domains, primarily because Matthew uses the number twelve in association with Jesus' mission to Israel. "Twelve" identifies the disciples/apostles (10:1, 2, 5; 11:1; 19:28; 20:17; 26:14, 47; 26:20), whose limited mission is only to the "lost sheep of the house of Israel" (10:5) and whose destiny is to sit on twelve thrones judging the twelve tribes of Israel (19:28). "Twelve" designates the full baskets collected after the feeding of the five thousand (14:20)—probably a symbolic reference to Israel (see 19:28). Jesus could appeal to his Father, who would at once send more than twelve legions of angels (26:53). Matthew consistently uses the number twelve to reinforce Jesus' mission. Matthew's omission that the ruler's daughter is twelve years old (Mark 5:42) indicates that the number has significance only in reference to the woman. It identifies the time of her suffering (twelve years), but it also reinforces Matthew's message that the woman is an example and paradigm of the lost sheep of the house of Israel (10:6; 15:24). She is "helpless" and without a shepherd (9:36). The combination of her sickness, faith, and healing serves as a paradigm of Israel's sick condition and need of salvation before Israel's God—the basis of Jesus' historical proclamation of the kingdom of heaven (Matt 10:1–16; Malina 1999b:33). The woman's healing underscores Jesus' Israelite mission. Her paradigmatic significance as a symbol of Israel also fits the time of the evangelist.

The model of social domains demonstrates that the kinship sphere (household/family) as a plurisignificant social institution has political significance. In the woman's story in Matthew, this is indicated when Jesus addresses the woman as "daughter" (9:22). The endearing word "daughter," a tender form of recognition, is also a social metaphor that particularizes Israel (Lam 2:13; Matt 21:5). Only two times in Matthew does Jesus address women by gender—here and in the case of the Canaanite woman (15:28). The first instance designates an Israelite; the second identifies a Gentile.

By stripping away numerous Markan allusions, Matthew highlights the healing as a distinctive Israelite event that parallels the model of social domains. The woman probably is a rural Israelite expendable whose courageous initiative—her faith—makes her a symbol of Israel. If so, she represents the "house of Israel" in the new theocratic kingdom, in contrast to the house of Israel that will be left desolate (23:38). Matthew's rendition thus points in two directions: to the time of the Gospel and to the historical period of Jesus as an Israelite healer.

Conclusion—Differences That Matter

But what difference does the healing make to the woman? The woman's blood flow may have cut her off from blood ties. The healing would bring two possibilities: a return to her household or becoming one of the women at the cross, who followed Jesus from Galilee and beheld Jesus' death from a distance (27:55). At any rate, it is unrealistic, let alone anachronistic, to view her now as an autonomous woman. She belongs either to her family or to the women at the cross—or possibly both. Returning to her household would open the family to Jesus as their healer, for the household itself would be made whole. Family renewal would mean provision and protection for the woman and increased productivity for the family—essential for the subsistence of agrarian households. No longer would she be avoided for fear of the damage her own power could do before God, the crops, and family well-being (Blum and Blum 1965:33–34). The woman's good fortune would spread to her family and to other members of her community. Family and community boundaries would be restored—no longer would she be "dirt." The one boundary still violated would be the political boundary of the temple and its far-reaching establishment.

The fallout for the healer would be mixed. Among peasants, Jesus' reputation and status would be magnified. The God of Israel would be praised for his mercy (15:31). Increased authority would bind the healer's actions, teachings, and preaching. Conversely, the relationship between Jesus and the center of Judean political, economic, and religious power—the Jerusalem temple—would deteriorate (see Hollenbach 1981). The core value of God's holiness once more would have been violated, the temple-based network of control weakened, scriptural authority sullied, strong purity concerns ignored. Jesus would have crossed forbidden boundaries, and his standing with the Second Temple's power structure would be "dirt," out of place.

Works Cited

Allbaugh, Leland G. 1953. *Crete: A Case Study of an Underdeveloped Area.* Princeton: Princeton University Press.

Blum, Richard, and Eva Blum. 1965. *Health and Healing in Rural Greece: A Study of Three Communities.* Stanford, Calif.: Stanford University Press.

Douglas, Mary. 1966. *Purity and Danger: An Analysis of the Conceptions of Pollution and Taboo.* London: Routledge & Kegan Paul.

———. 1975. *Implicit Meanings.* London: Routledge & Kegan Paul.

Duling, Dennis C. 1992. "Matthew's Plurisignificant 'Son of David' in Social Science Perspective: Kinship, Kingship, Magic, and Miracle." *BTB* 22:99–116.

Elliott, John H. 1991. "Temple versus Household in Luke-Acts: A Contrast in Social Institutions." In *The Social World of Luke-Acts: Models for Interpretation*, edited by J. H. Neyrey, 211–40. Peabody, Mass: Hendrickson.

Foster, George M. 1976. "Disease Etiologies in Non-Western Medical Systems." *American Anthropologist* 78:773–82.

Hahn, Robert A. 1995. *Sickness and Healing: An Anthropological Perspective.* New Haven: Yale University Press.

Hanson, K. C. 1994. "BTB Readers Guide: Kinship." *BTB* 24:183–94.

Held, Heinz Joachim. 1963. "Matthew as Interpreter of the Miracle Stories." In *Tradition and Interpretation in Matthew*, edited by G. Bornkamm et al., 165–99. Translated by P. Scott. NTL. Philadelphia: Westminster.

Hollenbach, Paul W. 1981. "Jesus, Demoniacs, and Public Authorities: A Socio-Historical Study." *JAAR* 49:567–88.

Hull, John M. 1974. *Hellenistic Magic and the Synoptic Tradition.* SBT 2/28. Naperville, Ill.: Allenson.

Isenberg, Sheldon K. 1975. "Mary Douglas and Hellenistic Religions: The Case of Qumran." In *SBLSP 1975*, 179–85.

Isenberg, Sheldon K., and Dennis E. Owen. 1977. "Bodies, Natural and Contrived: The Work of Mary Douglas." *Religious Studies Review* 3:1–17.

Jackson, Ralph. 1988. *Doctors and Diseases in the Roman Empire.* Norman: University of Oklahoma Press.

Kee, Howard Clark. 1986. *Medicine, Miracle, and Magic in New Testament Times.* SNTSMS 55. Cambridge: Cambridge University Press.

Kleinman, Arthur. 1986. "Concepts and a Model for the Comparison of Medical Systems as Cultural Systems." In *Concepts of Health, Illness, and Disease: A Comparative Perspective,* edited by C. Currer and M. Stacey, 29–47. New York: Berg.

———. 1989. *Patients and Healers in the Context of Culture: An Exploration of the Borderland between Anthropology, Medicine, and Psychiatry.* Comparative Studies in Health Systems and Medical Care 3. Berkeley: University of California Press.

Levine, Amy-Jill. 1996. "Discharging Responsibility: Matthean Jesus, Biblical Law, and Hemorrhaging Woman." In *Treasures New and Old: Recent Contributions to Matthean Studies,* edited by D. R. Bauer and M. A. Powell. 379–97. SBLSymS 1. Atlanta: Scholars.

Malina, Bruce J. 1999a. "Assessing the Historicity of Jesus' Walking on the Sea: Insights from Cross-Cultural Social Psychology." In *Authenticating the Activities of Jesus,* edited by B. D. Chilton and C. A. Evans, 351–71. NTTS 28/2. Leiden: Brill.

———. 1999b. "Criteria for Assessing the Authentic Words of Jesus: Some Specifications." In *Authenticating the Words of Jesus,* edited by B. D. Chilton and C. A. Evans, 27–45. NTTS 28/1. Leiden: Brill.

———. 2001. *The New Testament World: Insights from Cultural Anthropology.* 3d ed. Louisville: Westminster John Knox.

Meier, John P. 1994. *A Marginal Jew: Rethinking the Historical Jesus.* Vol. 2: *Mentor, Message, and Miracles.* ABRL. New York: Doubleday.

Murdock, George Peter. 1980. *Theories of Illness: A World Survey.* Pittsburgh: University of Pittsburgh Press.

Neusner, Jacob. 1973. *The Idea of Purity in Ancient Judaism.* SJLA 1. Leiden: Brill.

———. 1978. "History and Purity in First-Century Judaism." *HR* 18:1–17.

———. 1979. "Map without Territory: Mishnah's System of Sacrifices and Sanctuary." *HR* 19:103–27.

Neyrey, Jerome H. 1986. "The Idea of Purity in Mark's Gospel." *Semeia* 35:91–128.

———. 1988. "Unclean, Common, Polluted, and Taboo." *Forum* 4, no. 4:72–82.

———. 1991. "The Symbolic Universe of Luke-Acts: 'They Turn the World Upside Down.'" In *The Social World of Luke-Acts: Models for Interpretation,* edited by J. H. Neyrey, 271–304. Peabody, Mass: Hendrickson.

———. 1995. "Miracles, in Other Words: Social Science Perspectives on Healings." Unpublished paper.

——. 1996. "Clean/Unclean, Pure/Polluted, and Holy/Profane: The Idea and the System of Purity." In *The Social Sciences and New Testament Interpretation*, edited by R. L. Rohrbaugh, 80–104. Peabody, Mass: Hendrickson.

Perdue, Leo G., et al. 1997. *Families in Ancient Israel. The Family, Religion, and Culture.* Louisville: Westminster John Knox.

Pilch, John J. 1981. "Biblical Leprosy and Body Symbolism." *BTB* 11:108–113.

——. 1985. "Healing in Mark: A Social Science Analysis." *BTB* 15:142–50.

——. 1986. "The Health Care System in Matthew: A Social Science Analysis." *BTB* 16:102–6.

——. 1991. "Sickness and Healing in Luke-Acts." In *The Social World of Luke-Acts: Models for Interpretation*, edited by J. H. Neyrey, 181–209. Peabody, Mass: Hendrickson.

——. 1992. "A Spirit Named 'Fever.'" *PACE* 21:253–56.

——. 1993. "Visions in Revelation and Alternate Consciousness: A Perspective from Cultural Anthropology." *Listening* 28:231–44.

——. 1994. "Insights and Models for Understanding the Healing Activity of the Historical Jesus." In *SBLSP 1994*, 154–77. Atlanta: Scholars.

Ross, J. M. 1978. "Epileptic or Moonstruck?" *Bible Translator* 19:126–28.

Sigerist, Henry E. 1961. *A History of Medicine*. Yale Medical Library: Historical Library 27. Oxford: Oxford University Press.

Sjoberg, Gideon. 1960. *The Preindustrial City: Past and Present.* New York: Free Press.

Smith, Morton. 1978. *Jesus the Magician.* San Francisco: Harper & Row.

Theissen, Gerd, and Annette Merz. 1998. *The Historical Jesus: A Comprehensive Guide.* Translated by J. Bowden. Minneapolis: Fortress Press.

Twelftree, Graham H. 1993. *Jesus the Exorcist: A Contribution to the Study of the Historical Jesus.* WUNT 2/54. Tübingen: Mohr/Siebeck.

Wright, David P. 1992. "Holiness (OT)." In *ABD* 3:237–49.

6

Altered States of Consciousness in the Synoptics

John J. Pilch

While he was suffering extreme pain, St. Porphyry (353–420 C.E.) had a trance in which he saw Jesus on the cross alongside the "good thief." Porphyry was moved to repeat the request and prayer of the "good" thief: "Jesus, remember me when you come in your kingly power" (Luke 23:42). Then Jesus directed the thief to descend from the cross and to console Porphyry. The thief raised Porphyry and brought him to Jesus, who came down from the cross to receive him. When Porphyry awoke from his trance, his pain was gone (Brewer 1884:325).

Others such as Pope Alexander I (118 C.E.) and St. Anthony of Padua claim to have seen Jesus as an infant or little child (Brewer 1884:59). St. Philomena (d. 320 C.E.) held the infant Jesus in her arms (Walsh 1906:1.126). William Booth, founder of the Salvation Army, claimed that he saw Jesus, who rebuked him for his "nominal, useless, lazy, professing Christian life" (Huyssen and Huyssen 1922:34). This vision led to his establishing a special mission to the poor known around the world.

Collections of reports like these are usually dismissed by contemporaries as unscientific and uncritical. Scholars tend to appeal to the psychological sciences to explore and evaluate these claims, sometimes in conjunction with theological principles. Theology admits that visions are possible in principle, but each vision has to be tested according to specific criteria; for example, is the revelation divisive or does it promote unity and growth in the Christian community (McBrien 1994:268–69; Jelly 1990)? What should one make of these visions? How should one understand visions reported in the Bible?

In general, historical-critical biblical scholars tend to be skeptical about determining the exact nature of the visions experienced by Jesus and his disciples

as reported in the New Testament. For example, with regard to the transfiguration, Barbara Reid states: "[T]he methods of historical criticism cannot provide
scientifically certain results [about the historical events of Jesus' life]"
(1993:147). Recommending a similar position for the Jesus Seminar delibera-
tions, Miller says: "I find that this story [transfiguration] contains nothing useful for reconstructing the life of the historical Jesus" (1994:219). Fitzmyer
(1981:796) and Meier (1994:972) agree, although Meier admits the possibility
of "spiritual visions" in the life of Jesus and of his disciples *in principle*.

In a previous study, I have argued that "adequate and culturally plausible explanations are just as valid as scientific certitude" (Pilch 1995:49). The culturally plausible Mediterranean scenario for understanding visions in the
Synoptic Gospels and elsewhere in the Bible is the panhuman experience
known as altered states of consciousness (ASC). Ninety percent of people on
this planet have such experiences normally and naturally. On the basis of
ethnographic data in the Human Relations Area Files (HRAF) at Yale University (http://www.yale.edu/hraf), social-scientific scholars estimate that 80 percent of the societies in the Mediterranean world had such experiences. The
percentage was at least that high in antiquity since ancient documents from the
Mediterranean world are included in the HRAF database.

Social-scientific research substantiates the universality of ASCs as an origin
for religious experience and as a foundation for some manifestations of religious behavior (Winkelman 1999: 398). Specifically, social-scientific research
indicates that ASC experiences are essential to the life and function of
shamans. These experiences are essential because they put the shaman in contact with the world of the spirit. It is also from this world that the shaman receives the power for one of his or her major functions, namely, healing.

In the Israelite tradition, the holy man (*ḥasid*; *ṣaddiq*) fits into the category
of shaman. Thus, in social-scientific terms, the Gospels portray Jesus precisely
as such a holy man or shaman who was gifted with ASC experiences, with
power to heal, and with power over spirits. By reflecting on the social-scientific
understanding of shamans and ASCs, the interpreter of the Gospels will be
able to make fresh, culturally plausible interpretations of the events such as the
visions reported about Jesus and his disciples.

Social-Scientific Concepts

Cultural anthropology and various subdisciplines such as cross-cultural psychology provide a good understanding of the concepts needed in this investigation. We rely on cross-cultural psychology because psychology and

psychiatry are monocultural disciplines too inextricably embedded in Western culture to be of significant use in analyzing the Mediterranean document we call the Bible (Pilch 1997a). Since psychology and psychiatry, from their beginnings, have focused on individuals in industrial urban societies and developed in that context, they are Western, ethnocentric, and incomplete sciences rooted in Freud and Freudian matrices. As Stannard has observed: "The time has come to face the fact that, behind all its rhetorical posturing, the psychoanalytic approach to history is irremediably one of logical perversity, scientific unsoundness, and cultural naivete. The time has come, in short, to move on" (1980:156).

In contrast, cross-cultural psychology, also known as social psychology, is "the study of similarities and differences in individual psychological functioning in various cultural and ethnic groups; of the relationships between psychological variables and sociocultural, ecological, and biological variables; and of current changes in these variables" (Berry et al. 1992:2). Exegetes, like anthropologists, are therefore obliged to pay serious attention to indigenous information about and evaluation of ASCs. We do this by constructing an applied etic (that is, outsider) perspective on the emic (that is, native) data in hopes of developing a derived etic perspective (Pilch 1997a). A derived etic perspective should accurately translate the information from the native's culture into the language and terminology of the researcher's culture.

Altered States of Consciousness

Western and Indo-European cultures offer strong cultural resistance to ASC experiences (for more on ASCs, see Pilch 1993; 1995; 1997a; 1997b). These cultures tend to consider the ASC as pathological or infantile while considering *their* own mode of consciousness as normal and ordinary. We do well to heed Tart: "Our ordinary state of consciousness is a construction, not a given, and a specialized construction that in many ways is quite arbitrary. Thus many of the values associated with it are quite arbitrary and culturally relative" (1980:245). Tart also maintains that cultural conditioning shapes the wide range of human potentials into a fixed and stable state of ordinary consciousness, which he describes as "a characteristic and habitual patterning of mental functioning that adapts the individual more or less successfully to survive in *his culture's consensus reality*" (1980:249, emphasis mine). Historical-critical biblical scholars concerned with determining factual, historical events in Jesus' life never attend to his *Mediterranean culture's consensus reality*, which is quite different from *Western culture's consensus reality*.

Krippner (1972) enumerated twenty states of consciousness: dreaming, sleeping, hypnagogic (drowsiness before sleep), hypnopompic (semiconsciousness preceding waking), hyperalert, lethargic, rapture, hysteric, fragmentation, regressive, meditative, trance, reverie, daydreaming, internal scanning, stupor, coma, stored memory, expanded consciousness, and "normal."

Cross-cultural psychologists emphasize that it is important to retain the plural "states" in the phrase "altered states of consciousness," for various kinds and degrees of altered consciousness are available in each culture and even in each subset. For instance, cross-cultural psychologists observe that most shamanic activities take place in a "nonordinary psychic state." It is usually called "ecstasy" or "trance." Both terms, however, pose problems. Ecstasy implies rapture, frenzy, euphoria, an extremely strong emotion, and, in particular, a condition in which rational thinking and self-control disappear. Some shamans do experience euphoria, but it is not the only experience. On the other hand, trance implies a hypnotic or dazed state, but this too is not evident in all shamanic activity (Townsend 1999:441–42). Therefore, Harner (1982:xvi, 20–30, 46–56) has suggested the use of the term "shamanic state(s) of consciousness" (SSC) to set shamanic experiences apart from other ASC experiences that may or may not be the same.

Harner's proposed distinction between ASC and SSC reflects two approaches among cultural anthropologists. Those who emphasize similarities across and within cultures, and who seek universalist perspectives, would speak of ASCs. In contrast, those who emphasize cultural context, specificity, and arbitrariness, and who seek a culturally specific perspective, would urge the adoption of the term SSCs. In this essay, I retain the ASC terminology.

Shamans

A simple and workable definition of "shaman" is difficult to develop. It seems preferable to present the universal nucleus of specific traits that must be present in order to speak of a shaman. Above all, the purpose of a shaman is to interact with the spirit world for the benefit of those in the material world. This is accomplished chiefly by means of ASC. According to Townsend (1999:431–32), the essential criteria of a shaman include the following characteristics. I have modified her model to match the realities that appear in the Bible. The essential criteria are:

1. Direct contact/communication with spirits. Spirits can be sentient beings (animal or humanlike spirits), forces of nature, or transcendent energy. A shaman ordinarily will have one or more special helping spirits for assistance and protection.

2. Control of or power over the spirits. A shaman controls the spirits, and not vice versa.

3. Control of the ASC, the vehicle through which the shaman contacts the spirit world. This ASC is usually called trance, ecstasy, or something similar. This is the vehicle through which the shaman engages spirits.

4. A "this-worldly" focus on the material world. A shaman uses his or her abilities for the benefit of individuals or the community and not for personal aggrandizement.

5. Sky journeys (often called "soul flight," "magical flight," or "shamanic journey"), whereby the shaman can travel through the spirit world. The shaman can travel in the spirit world while both feet are planted on the ground. Often a tutelary spirit or "familiar" helps in this journey. Similar experiences in other cultures include out-of-the-body experiences, "astral projection," and near-death or clinical death experiences (Winkelman 1999:411). In ancient literature, Odysseus and Aeneus, who were not considered to be shamans, visited the underworld.

The related criteria are:

1. In the encounter with spirits, the shaman can interact with them without fear of them possessing him.

2. Memory. The shaman remembers at least some aspects of the ASC.

3. Healing is a major focus of shamanic activity.

In this ideology, spirits are considered to cause problems in the world of human beings that can be corrected by other spirits, with the shaman acting as intermediary or broker. Thus mastery over or control of spirits, as in exorcism, is essential to a shaman.

The Call and Initiation of the Shaman

The spirits decide who will become a shaman, not the individual (see Townsend 1999:445–46). Most calls come unbidden, but the person must respond or serious problems can result. The usual sequence of becoming a full shaman, adapted from Hitchcock (1976:169) to the biblical context, is:

1. Contact with the spirit (by possession or adoption)
2. Identification of the possessing/adopting spirit
3. Acquisition of necessary ritual skills
4. Tutelage by both a spirit and real-life teacher
5. Growing familiarity with the possessing/adopting spirit
6. Ongoing ASC experiences

It is also possible that a death-rebirth or major-change symbolism moves the novice from old status to a liminal transitional position and finally to rebirth as a changed being (Hitchcock 1976:167; Townsend 1999:446).

This very brief sketch of a social-scientific understanding of shamanism and ASCs helps us to read the Synoptic Gospels and the Bible in a fresh way.

ASC Events in the Gospels

I have selected five ASC events relative to Jesus as they are presented in the Gospels and examine them briefly in the light of the above concepts.

The Baptism of Jesus
(Mark 1:9–11//Matt 3:13–17//Luke 3:21–22)

This scene can be interpreted as the call of Jesus to be a shaman or holy man. Jesus meets John the Baptist, his teacher and guide, and becomes his apprentice (Hollenbach 1982; see John 3:22–24). In an ASC, Jesus sees the Spirit (holy; or of God) descending upon him, and he hears the voice from heaven announcing a new identity: a beloved son who pleases the father.

In order to deal with spirits, the holy man must be able to "see" spirits clearly as well as other things in alternate reality. The cultural world of Jesus and his followers was permeated by spirits who regularly intervened in ordinary human life (Pilch 1999:159–64). Such spirit activity was an essential part of that belief system; hence, this event in the life of Jesus does not surprise or shock him or the first hearers or readers of the Gospel. In this scene, Jesus is adopted by God and commissioned as God's beloved Son (Neyrey 1998:110). He is called to be a shaman, a holy man, a broker on behalf of the patron/God. In the steps toward becoming a shaman, Jesus has met his guide and has been contacted by the spirit world, and the spirit has revealed its identity.

Lentzen-Deis's masterful study of the baptism of Jesus in Matthew concluded that the evangelist crafted a *Deute-Vision* for Jesus, fully resonant with the beliefs of the Israelite tradition. Yet because he did not seem to be aware of the panhuman potential for ASC experiences, Lentzen-Deis was satisfied with theological conclusions rather than seeking a culturally plausible factual experience that would underpin those conclusions.

The Testing of Jesus
(Mark 1:12–13//Matt 4:1–11//Luke 4:1–13)

In accord with Mediterranean cultural values, the honors attributed to Jesus in the baptism have to be tested. Will he really prove to be a faithful, adopted son of God? In social-scientific terms, Jesus engages in a challenge-riposte contest with the tester and wins (Rohrbaugh 1995; Neyrey 1998:115–16). He proves to be an honorable son who remains loyal to the father. The experience and successful passing of this test is also another step toward becoming a shaman: Jesus demonstrates that he has acquired the necessary ritual skills to deal with and control the spirit world.

Moreover, this scene in each of the Synoptics takes place in an ASC in which Jesus enters alternate reality. Human beings live in a single reality, the universe, which in its totality includes two dimensions: the material dimension in which we live, and the alternate reality in which spirits abide (these include deceased ancestors, spirits, and the deity). What happens in alternate reality affects material reality. While humans ordinarily do not enter alternate reality except by death or in ASC, spirits enter material reality more readily and frequently. The Bible is replete with reports of spirits interacting with human beings in material reality. Anthropologists recognize that this paradigm is found in part or whole in a wide variety of nonexclusively materialistic cultural systems (Townsend 1999:437; I have adopted the alternate position presented in 461 n. 8).

Walking on the Sea
(Mark 6:45–52//Matt 14:22–33//John 6:16–21)

Pilch (1998b) and Malina (1999) have presented a distinctively different but highly plausible cultural interpretation of this event in the life of the Mediterranean Jesus. The most recent interpretation of this pericope, by Madden (1997), bogged down in analyzing the literary form. He was unable to identify and failed to propose, in any significant way, a plausible reality behind the event during the lifetime of Jesus. Madden concluded that the event is a displaced resurrection narrative (1997:138–39; see the critical review by Mowery [1998]).

Actually, this Gospel report is a classic example of an ASC experience. Even if it strains our Western credulity to believe walking on the sea to have been an actual event in the life of Jesus, the pericope is meaningful to the original audience, *not* because of its alleged literary form, but because it reports a type of experience readily available (without the use of stimulant) to at least 80 percent of the Mediterranean population at that time.

The ASC experience normally stirs apprehension in the subject. Hence the first statement of the person in the vision is to allay this feeling ("Fear not") and to assure personal identity ("It is I"). In this story, Peter remains skeptical. Accepting Jesus' invitation to join him in the ASC experience, Peter follows Jesus' bidding and successfully walks on the sea until he "sees the wind," terminates, or steps out of the ASC and predictably begins to sink. This is intelligible in context. Peter has exited alternate reality (the ASC) and has returned to the material world, where such an activity is simply not possible. Peter transferred from one dimension of reality to another. Whether at the level of the historical Jesus or of the church's or evangelist's interpretation, the report makes perfect sense in the context of ASCs. It is a real experience of a real event in alternate reality.

The Transfiguration
(Mark 9:2–10//Matt 17:1–9//Luke 9:28–36)

The evangelists present this event after the imprisonment and death of John the Baptist. As Hollenbach has argued, Jesus began his career as an apprentice of John the Baptist, his teacher and guide into shamanism—that is, his guide into becoming a holy man in the Israelite tradition (see Pilch 1999:79–84). When John was imprisoned, Jesus faced a dilemma: what to do now? When Jesus realized that his healing powers were from God and not from the evil spirit world (Beelzebul; see Matt 12:26–28), he branched out on his own with his own disciples, some of whom transferred allegiance from John to Jesus. As opposition to him grew among his enemies, Jesus and his followers would understandably become confused and unsettled.

In the Mediterranean world of the present and of antiquity, the solution to concerns and problems often come in ASC experiences (dreams, trances, visions, and the like). The transfiguration experience does just that (see Pilch 1995). It assures Jesus of his identity and mission (beloved son), and it exhorts the disciples in their ASC to bond closer to Jesus (to listen to him more than to Moses and Elijah, that is, the Law and the Prophets).

Resurrection Appearances

The Israelite tradition fully expected that the holy man who perseveres to the end receives the reward of the righteous: resurrection and a place in alternate reality. Holy persons who inhabit alternate reality routinely make contact with humans in material reality by a variety of ASCs: dreams (for example, Asclepius to his clients); visions (God to prophets like Isaiah and Ezekiel, among others); and appearances (the risen Jesus to his followers).

How to understand such human experiences has remained a lively question to this day. A recent study by Phillip Wiebe seeks to "explore the possibility that contemporary phenomena might contribute to the understanding of the NT accounts of the post-Resurrection appearances and visions of Jesus" (1997:6). He reports nearly forty interviews, most with people in British Columbia who claimed to have had a "direct visual encounter with Jesus Christ." Then he compares these accounts with postresurrection appearances of Jesus and considers three categories of explanations: supernaturalistic, mentalistic, and physicalistic.

Supernaturalistic explanations propose that entities or forces that transcend the natural order (like angels, the Holy Spirit, God) bring about visions or appearances. Mentalistic explanations are diverse but suggest in general that mental states such as stress, wishing, expectations, or even unconscious mental states bring about apparitions or visions. Finally, physicalistic explanations link every event with the central nervous system and explain visions and apparitions as a neurophysiological function of the human organism. Wiebe concludes that the relationship between contemporary Christic visions and the reports in New Testament writings is unclear. Further, he questions the distinction many scholars commonly make between appearances (in the New Testament) and visions (postresurrection and post–New Testament experiences). Though transcendent explanations seem to prevail, they must be joined with mentalistic and physicalistic. He proposes further, refined study.

Wiebe's book gathers and reviews a significant amount of information about visions and appearances, but it is essentially a collection of data in search of a model. He does not utilize the full repertoire of historical and critical procedures typical of professional historians and interpreters of ancient documents. For instance, his analysis and evaluation of biblical evidence relies on secondary sources selectively chosen; he couples these sources with his intuitive judgments about the biblical information as he reads it. In this regard, his book is an excellent example of an imposed etic perspective on appearances and visions in human, chiefly Christian, experience. He does not develop a derived etic perspective.

The drawback of this perspective is reflected in his assessment of visions and apparitions as *"aberrant perceptual experiences"* (1997:12). When 90 percent of people have such experiences routinely, it is inappropriate to call them or anyone's similar experience aberrations in perception. Wiebe's interviews and historical reports—like the Gospels and the Bible in general—present the modern, Western reader with information about reality as the "natives" knew and experienced it. This is an emic data set.

The outsider to this native information, that is, a modern, Western reader, tries to understand it by imposing an understanding couched in modern terminology. The most appropriate terminology should be drawn from cross-cultural studies. As noted earlier, concepts from modern psychology and psychiatry are inappropriate. This is the imposed or applied etic interpretation. The researcher must go back and forth between the emic and imposed or applied etic perspectives until a good match has been made. Such a match is called a derived etic interpretation. The modern understanding is derived from rather than imposed on the ancient information from another culture. The entire process is the key challenge in cross-cultural communication and interpretation (Pilch 1996).

The majority of historical-critical biblical scholars insist that the resurrection is beyond the pale of historical investigation, but that the appearances of the risen Jesus are not (Meier 1990:1328). Pannenberg claims that the experiences of resurrection appearances reported by Paul (1 Cor 15:1–11) were not just subjective visions but, rather, objective visions, since they communicated a historical event, namely the resurrection of Jesus by God (Pannenberg 1977:95, 97, 98). In contrast, Pannenberg claims that "the appearances reported in the Gospels, which are not mentioned by Paul, have such a strongly legendary character that one can scarcely find a historical kernel of their own in them" (1977:89).

The judgments of historical-critical biblical scholars like Pannenberg are neither sufficiently historical nor critical. In a previously published study (Pilch 1998a), I demonstrated that traditional analyses of the resurrection appearances failed to take into account the social-scientific information about such experiences. The appearances are indeed ASC experiences and, therefore, quite real. The visionaries saw Jesus in alternate reality. The interpretation that the visionaries gave to these experiences was that God had raised Jesus from the dead. This is very similar to other people, even today, who have ASC experiences of recently deceased persons (see Pilch 1998a:58).

That 90 percent of the current population have such experiences routinely, without drugs or other stimulants, argues that the empirical investigation of such events, whether in antiquity or the present, is open. Investigation is open to any and all observers who, if they never had such experiences, would be willing to learn how to have them. Felicitas Goodman (1990; 1997), a pioneer in the anthropological investigations of alternate reality, has trained facilitators to assist her in offering such a learning opportunity under the auspices of the Cuyamungue Institute in Santa Fe, New Mexico. In the United States, such opportunities are also available in Columbus, Ohio, and Edgewater, Maryland, among other places.

Exegetical studies that separate auditions from visions (the spoken and visionary aspects) in these resurrection experiences are wrongheaded. Research indicates that the ASC experience itself is vacuous (Goodman 1990:17). Culture provides the content and the soundtrack. Israelites who saw Jesus in alternate reality also saw other beings and heard information that derived from their Israelite (rather than Greco-Roman) culture. For instance, they were instructed to go to Galilee, not to Delphi, Mount Olympus, or Rome.

Each resurrection appearance follows the typical pattern: The visionary sees a person whom they do not immediately recognize. The person assuages the visionary's concerns ("Fear not!") and then presents identity ("It is I"). To see Jesus in alternate reality is not surprising, but reassuring. As already noted, the Israelite tradition about holy men fully recognized a reward for righteousness in alternate reality. For instance, the righteous in alternate reality enjoy meals at golden tables that stand on three golden legs (see *Ḥag.* 14b). Hence the risen Jesus from alternate reality could eat broiled fish in material reality. The appearances convinced Jesus' followers that God was indeed pleased with him despite his ignominious death.

Finally, the appearances offer new information or a commission to the visionaries. In either case, the visionaries' doubts are removed, resolve is strengthened, and each visionary can return to undisturbed, normal life.

Conclusion

Social-scientific approaches, particularly cultural, Mediterranean, and psychological anthropology (cross-cultural psychology, social psychology) provide the biblical interpreter a distinct set of hermeneutical tools for interpreting the Synoptic Gospels and the Bible in general. Jesus clearly fits the social-scientific figure of a shaman, a holy man. In his culture, this is a *ḥasid* or *ṣaddiq* (see Pilch 1997; 1998). As such, Jesus has been properly selected, initiated, and commissioned, as the Gospels document. An essential element to the shamanic identity is the experience of ASCs. But more than this, ASCs are part and parcel of the ordinary experience of at least 80 percent of this Mediterranean population, hence Jesus' disciples—and his audience (see John 12:38–39)—are equally capable of such experiences. Cultural information interpreted by social-scientific methods strongly argues that these ASC experiences did occur in the life of Jesus and his followers, just as they continue to occur among 90 percent of people in the contemporary world.

The events in the life of Jesus and of his followers presented above are presented in emic terms in the Gospels. Cross-cultural psychology, based on a study of the world's cultures, proposes derived etic interpretations of these events by using two etic models: that of the shaman or holy man, and that of ASCs. The actuality of such experiences in Mediterranean cultures thereby makes a social-scientific interpretation of the Gospel tradition much more plausible and credible than the results of literary and redactional studies uninformed by this kind of social-scientific research.

Works Cited

Berry, John W., et al. 1992. *Cross-Cultural Psychology: Toward Applications.* Cross-Cultural Research and Methodology Series 10. Newbury Park, Calif.: Sage.

Brewer, E. C. 1884. *A Dictionary of Miracles.* London: Chatto & Windus.

Fitzmyer, Joseph A. 1981. *The Gospel according to Luke I–IX.* AB 28. Garden City, N.Y.: Doubleday.

Goodman, Felicitas. 1990. *Where the Spirits Ride the Wind: Trance Journeys and Other Ecstatic Experiences.* Bloomington: Indiana University Press.

———. 1997. *My Last Forty Days: A Visionary Journey among the Pueblo Spirits.* Bloomington: Indiana University Press.

Harner, Michael. 1982. *The Way of the Shaman: A Guide to Power and Healing.* 2d ed. New York: Bantam.

Hitchcock, John T. 1976. "Aspects of Bhujel Shamanism." In *Spirit Possession in the Nepal Himalayas,* edited by J. T. Hitchcock and Rex L. Jones, 165–96. New Delhi: Vikas.

Hollenbach, Paul W. 1982. "The Conversion of Jesus: From Jesus the Baptizer to Jesus the Healer." In *ANRW* 2.25.1, 196–219. Berlin: de Gruyter.

Huyssen, Chester, and Lucille Huyssen. 1922. *I Saw the Lord.* Tarrytown, N.Y.: Revell.

Jelly, F. M. 1990. "Visions." In *The New Dictionary of Theology,* edited by J. A. Komonchak et al., 1085–87. Collegeville, Minn.: Liturgical.

Krippner, Stanley. 1972. "Altered States of Consciousness." In *The Highest State of Consciousness,* edited by J. White, 1–5. New York: Doubleday.

Lentzen-Deis, Fritzleo. 1970. *Die Taufe Jesu nach den Synoptikern: Literarkritische und gattungsgeschichtliche Untersuchungen.* Frankfurt: Knecht.

Madden, Patrick J. 1997. *Walking on the Sea: An Investigation of the Origin of the Narrative Account.* BZNW 81. Berlin: de Gruyter.

Malina, Bruce J. 1999. "Assessing the Historicity of Jesus' Walking on the Sea: Insights from Cross-Cultural Social Psychology." In *Authenticating the Activities of Jesus,* edited by B. Chilton and C. A. Evans, 351–71. NTTS 28/2. Leiden: Brill.

McBrien, Richard P. 1994. *Catholicism.* Rev. ed. New York: HarperCollins.

Meier, John P. 1990. "Jesus." In *The New Jerome Biblical Commentary,* edited by R. E. Brown et al., 1316–28. Englewood Cliffs, N.J.: Prentice-Hall.

———. 1994. *A Marginal Jew: Rethinking the Historical Jesus.* Vol. 2: *Mentor, Message, and Miracles.* New York: Doubleday.

Miller, Robert J. 1994. "Historicizing the Trans-historical: The Transfiguration Narrative." *Forum* 10:219–47.

Mowery, Robert L. 1998. "Review of *Walking on the Sea,* by Patrick J. Madden." *CBQ* 60:769–70.

Neyrey, Jerome H. 1998. *Honor and Shame in the Gospel of Matthew.* Louisville: Westminster John Knox.

Pannenberg, Wolfhart. 1977. *Jesus—God and Man.* Translated by L. L. Wilkins and D. A. Priebe. 2d ed. Philadelphia: Westminster.

Pilch, John J. 1993. "Visions in Revelation and Alternate Consciousness: A Perspective from Cultural Anthropology." *Listening* 28:231–44.

———. 1995. "The Transfiguration of Jesus: An Experience of Alternate Reality." In *Modelling Early Christianity: Social-Scientific Studies of the New Testament in Its Context,* edited by P. F. Esler, 47–64. New York and London: Routledge.

———. 1996. "Altered States of Consciousness: A 'Kitbashed' Model." *BTB* 26:133–38.

———. 1997a. "BTB Readers Guide: Psychological and Psychoanalytical Approaches to Interpreting the Bible in Social-Scientific Context." *BTB* 27:112–16.

———. 1997b. "A Window into the Biblical World: Jesus, the Holy Man, and Nature." *TBT* 35:114–19.

———. 1998a. "Appearances of the Risen Jesus in Cultural Context: Experiences of Alternate Reality." *BTB* 28:52–60.

———. 1998b. "A Window into the Biblical World: Walking on the Sea." *TBT* 36:117–23.

———. 1999. *The Cultural Dictionary of the Bible.* Collegeville, Minn.: Liturgical.

Reid, Barbara P. 1993. *The Transfiguration: A Source- and Redactional-Critical Study of Luke 9:28-26.* Cahiers de LaRevue Biblique 32. Paris: Gabalda.

Rohrbaugh, Richard L. 1995. "Legitimating Sonship—a Test of Honour: A Social-Scientific Study of Luke 4:1–30." In *Modelling Early Christianity: Social-Scientific Studies of the New Testament in Its Context,* edited by P. F. Esler, 183–97. New York and London: Routledge.

Stannard, David E. 1980. *Shrinking History: On Freud and the Failure of Psychohistory.* New York: Oxford University Press.

Tart, Charles. 1980. "A Systems Approach to Altered States of Consciousness." In *The Psychobiology of Consciousness,* edited by J. M. Davidson and R. J. Davidson, 243–69. New York: Plenum.

Townsend, Joan B. 1999. "Shamanism." In *Anthropology of Religion: A Handbook,* edited by S. D. Glazier, 429–69. Westport, Conn.: Praegher.

Walsh, William J. 1906. *The Apparitions and Shrines of Heaven's Bright Queen.* 4 vols. New York: Cary-Stafford.

Wiebe, Phillip. 1997. *Visions of Jesus: Direct Encounters from the New Testament to Today.* New York: Oxford University Press.

Winkelman, Michael. 1999. "Altered States of Consciousness and Religious Behavior." In *Anthropology of Religion: A Handbook,* edited by S. D. Glazier, 398–428. Westport, Conn.: Praeger.

7

Jesus and the Demoniacs

Christian Strecker

At the close of January 1999, the Vatican published *De Exorcismis et supplicationibus quibusdam,* a revision of the almost four-hundred-year-old official Roman Catholic rite of exorcism in the *Rituale Romanum.* Thus, shortly before the turn of the millennium, the Catholic Church continues unwaveringly to stress the legitimacy and relevance of ecclesiastical exorcisms. Yet compared to Africa or Asia, for example, the phenomenon of spirit possession is of little significance in the everyday life of most Western people. The most recent case of exorcism to stir public discussion in Germany dates back more than twenty years to the tragic death of Anneliese Michel (Goodman 1985:114ff.). Therefore it is not surprising that the revised version of the Roman Catholic exorcism ritual seemed rather strange to the majority of the people in this country, and not only to Protestants. Yet it is possible that the Roman ritual shares discourse that, in spite of variations over the centuries, is still rooted in the exorcistic action that most scholars associate with the historical Jesus himself. The patent uneasiness about the new version of the *Rituale Romanum* seems to reflect a fundamental problem in historical-critical Jesus research. This is the difficulty of confronting and comprehending strange and unfamiliar behaviors and ways of thinking that lie at the root of our own Christian tradition. The publication of the revised exorcism rite of the *Rituale Romanum* once more calls that difficulty to our minds.

After a short consideration of the historical relevance of the New Testament material, I introduce a model that might prepare the ground for a less prejudiced approach to spirit possession. The model then provides a new evaluation of the exorcistic practice of Jesus.

The New Testament Tradition of Jesus' Exorcisms

Looking at the entire Jesus tradition in the New Testament, there are six narratives dealing with exorcisms. The oldest Gospel, the Gospel of Mark, tells about the exorcizing of a demoniac in the synagogue at Capernaum (1:21–28), about a possessed man who lived among the tombs of Gerasa (5:1–20),[1] about the daughter of a Syrophoenician woman (7:24–30), and about a boy suffering from fits (9:14–29). Furthermore, Q relates the casting out of a spirit from a mute demoniac (Q 11:14), a story that Matthew takes up again in 9:32–33. In addition to these passages, the exorcistic practice of Jesus also appears a number of times in the sayings tradition, for example, in the summary in Luke that notes Jesus' exorcizing of several women, including Mary Magdalene (possessed by seven demons; Luke 8:2). Offhand mentions of Jesus' exorcistic activity appear in other summaries (Mark 1:34, 39; 3:11–12; Luke 7:21) as well as in Jesus' message to Herod (Luke 13:32). Finally Jesus' exorcistic practice is the basis of the so-called Beelzebul controversy (Mark 3:22ff.; Q 11:15–26), a passage composed of diverse sayings that discuss the profile and implications of Jesus' exorcisms.

That the exorcistic activity of Jesus is attested by several independent strands of the Gospel tradition (Mark, Q, added material) and articulated in both major categories of forms, the sayings and the narratives, points to its historicity. In addition, other significant indications substantiate the historical probability of such activity. The charge that Jesus could exorcize because he was in league with the devil (Mark 3:22; Q 11:15) was embarrassing for early Jesus groups, hence surely not created by them. Another point supporting the historical plausibility of Jesus' exorcisms is the way they take place: there were no special magical objects (charms, magic puppets, herbs, etc.), long incantations, prayers, or laying on of hands. These accounts form a remarkable contrast to contemporary exorcisms.[2] Only the exorcisms of the Neo-Pythagorean philosopher and miracle-worker Apollonius of Tyana, active in the second half of the first century, show similar features. It cannot be excluded, however, that the reports of Philostratus, dating to the beginning of the third century, were perhaps influenced by the Gospels. Finally, it is important that numerous ancient sources—from reports in the New Testament itself (Mark 9:38; Matt 7:22; Acts 19:13–17) to sayings and incantations in the Greek magical papyri (see *PGM* IV.1231ff.)—report exorcists acting "in the name of Jesus." This leads to the conclusion that Jesus had historical impact as an exorcist.

Taking everything into consideration, there is no reason to doubt the historical fact of the exorcistic activity of Jesus—no matter what historical credibility one ascribes to the actual narratives in detail (see Meier 1994:617ff.; similarly Annen 1976:112ff.; Meier 1994:406; Twelftree 1993:130ff.; Theissen and Merz 1998:292–93). Given that Jesus practiced exorcism on the demon-possessed, how might one assess and understand this feature of Jesus' career, so unfamiliar to us today? To shed light on this question, it first seems necessary to clarify the phenomenon of spirit possession.

The Phenomenon of Possession: Performance

"Whenever the ethnologists appear, the spirits disappear from the island"—this insightful Haitian saying can be found in the German cult book *Traumzeit* by Hans Peter Duerr, a refreshingly frank and unconventional analysis of exotic, living contexts (1985:204). The fact is that scientific, rational discourse, in striving for objectivity, usually has difficulty respecting the foreign quality, the otherness, of alien societies. Often the so-called savage or primitive is quickly reduced to sameness, to "how they are just like us," thus eliminating the strangeness. The philosopher Bernhard Waldenfels emphasizes this tendency in his book, revealingly titled *Der Stachel des Fremden* (The Sting of the Strange). Waldenfels points out three fatal mechanisms of reduction that characterize Western discourse on the Other: egocentrism, logocentrism, and ethnocentrism. These features of Western science refer to the monopolization of the Other based on our modern sense of self, our subjectivity (egocentrism), our enlightened rationality (logocentrism), and our alleged cultural superiority (ethnocentrism) (Waldenfels 1990:57–71).

All three mechanisms of reduction cast their shadow on Jesus research as well, especially in the field of spirit possession and exorcism. In my opinion, it is this very field in which the ego-, logo-, and ethnocentrist qualities block access to the otherness and strangeness of alien societies. This is what Waldenfels criticizes, and this is reflected in the common tendency among exegetes to psychologize, to rationalize in a functional manner, and to pathologize the phenomena of possession described in the New Testament.

The rather recent idea of a cohesive autonomous self seems axiomatic for the majority of the exegetical scientific community. As a consequence, this self-concept is taken for granted when judging ancient persons, their ideas, and practices. Possession is explained, therefore, as a totally subjective and purely internal occurrence. This leads most biblical interpreters to employ current psychological theories as models of explanation (see Trunk 1994:13ff.; Castillo 1994). Thus, New Testament reports about demoniacs are still considered as cases of hysteria, mania, or epilepsy.[3] Lately, the model of dissociative disorders, especially that of the multiple-personality disorder, has become quite fashionable (see Weber 1999:30; Davies 1995:86ff.; Goodman 1988:15ff.). It is true that by subsuming spirit possession into the prevailing psychological discourse, modern scholars can integrate such phenomena into our modes of thinking, and thus assimilate them into our cognitive perspectives and label them in such a way that makes them seem familiar. On the other hand, this is the way in which possession becomes detached from the original, "native" experience and deprived of its culturally specific, characteristic features. The essential feature of spirit possession is possession, that is, a human being's interaction or fusion with spirits or demons, and modern psychological approaches make this essential feature fall victim to a kind of rationalization, which ultimately makes possession an irrelevant and obsolete idea. As a result, psychological models produce "experience-far concepts," as Clifford Geertz puts it (1977). Upon closer examination, this holds true in two different ways.

In the first place, psychological attempts at explanation are "experienced-far" because they are based essentially on a Cartesian, solipsistic determination of inside and outside, which does not match the mentality of the ancients. In ancient Mediterranean culture, emotions, individual competence, and personal identity were not associated with or causally located in some more or less autonomous, sharply defined, inner psychic core (Malina 2001:58–80). Thus, Plato ascribes poetic creativity to being seized by the gods, that is, to a divine influence from outside or to spirit possession (see *Apology* 22c; *Ion* 533e; *Phaidros* 244–250; Maurizio 1995:77ff.). At least since the age of Romanticism, we have been used to regarding creativity as a consequence of ingenuity. In this context, Vincent Crapanzano, noted for his research in spirit possession, has drawn our attention to the problematical shift of perspective that, due to the unquestioned concentration on the inner self, is immanent in the Western psychological patterns of interpreting possession (concerning the following explanation, see Crapanzano 1977:12–13; 1987:14). Modern Western models usually consider possession in psychoanalytical perspective as a "projection" of repressed inner emotions or conflicts onto another person—in this case, onto a spiritual being as an alter ego. Yet native reports of possession imply the opposite, since they portray scenarios of a sort of literal "introjection" (not psychoanalytically speaking): the entering and indwelling or inhabiting of a spirit from outside a person into the inner being of that individual (see Q 11:24–26). Possession as a centripetal process of cause and effect is thus reversed in the psychological interpretation into a centrifugal process. Thus the alien quality of the process, the intravening spirit, is cut out and replaced by the possessed person's own self. As a consequence, the indigenous experience of possession dissolves in the "experienced-far" psychological discourse that anesthetizes "the sting of the strange."

Further, the psychological patterns of understanding are "experience-far" with regard to a second point: their implicit identification of possession with disease. The sweeping explanations of possession as, for example, hysteria or as multiple-personality disorder (MPD) inevitably lead to a pathologizing of the phenomenon. That, even today, numerous religions and cultures differentiate between disease and possession is ignored or not taken seriously.[4] Yet even the New Testament attests to the distinction. At least the summaries of the Gospel of Mark indicate such a differentiation. Mark 1:34, for example, reads: "And he [Jesus] healed many who were sick with various diseases, *and* cast out many demons." Correspondingly, the accounts of the exorcisms and the healings in the Jesus tradition have to be distinguished as independent genres with their own motifs, as Gerd Theissen convincingly demonstrates (1983:85–94). It is true that, in the New Testament, disease can also be traced back to demons, like, for example, the fever of Peter's mother-in-law (Mark 1:29–31 par.).[5] Yet possession is not exactly the same since, in this case, the person affected is not completely occupied by a demon but only influenced by a demon through fever. Hence, this case has to be regarded as a demonic etiology of illness, not a demon possession. In this respect, too, the ancient perspective runs at cross angles to our own. Possession in the world of the New Testament is not a disease per se. On the contrary, certain diseases are looked upon as possible indications of possession. Moreover, in the words of Crapanzano, one has to ask quite generally: "What, besides a protective shield, do we gain from calling . . . an individual possessed by a spirit a paranoid, a neurotic, or an hysteric?"[6]

Anthropologist Erika Bourguignon took decisive steps in the 1960s and 1970s against the pathologizing of possession. She interpreted possession inter alia, within the neutral concept of "altered states of consciousness" that she noted in great variety throughout the world (1973; also Goodman 1988:5–6). In biblical exegesis, John J. Pilch (1996) and John Dominic Crossan (1994:87–88) have recently made use of this category. But this approach is not without its problems either, inasmuch as here, too, the psychologizing inner perspective basically remains. For when Bourguignon partially defines possession as a culturally specific interpretation of psychobiological states that ultimately are *independent* of culture and naturally accessible to all human beings, then it is obvious, at least in this respect, that she, too, is rooted fundamentally in the egocentric paradigm of modern psychology.[7] At this point, one has to ask critically: Are not altered states of consciousness culturally determined from the start, so that, separate from this cultural influence, it is impossible to conceive of them, for example, as alleged psychobiological or "natural" phenomena (Lambek 1989:37–38)?

Finally, some sociologically oriented approaches run the risk of reducing possession to a strategy of the underprivileged or of the oppressed to strengthen their self-esteem, or to protest their condition. The functionalistic theories of I. M. Lewis are an instance of such a sociological approach, welcomed by New Testament exegetes such as John Dominic Crossan and Paul W. Hollenbach, among others. In this perspective, cases of possession in Jesus' time could be attributed largely to the prevailing Roman colonial oppression in Palestine (Crossan 1994:88–89; Hollenbach 1993:123ff.; and Lewis 1989).

This interpretation might be illuminating in some ways. Yet the functional rationalism in this approach reduces the complexity of the phenomenon in an alarming way, pushing indigenous reports to the sideline as well as the beliefs and the direct experiences of the people concerned. Instead, scholars adopt a universal, functionalistic perspective, thus limiting possessed persons to the role of "*re*-actors" in an overarching structure, instead of looking on them as *real* actors in the social arena (Kapferer 1983:93–100; Boddy 1989:139ff.). To relate to the period of Jesus' activity one has to ask whether possession and exorcisms were the widespread mass phenomenon that this approach implies. Apart from the New Testament, there is comparatively little evidence for exorcisms (Kampling 1986; Trunk 1994:357).

Taking these critical remarks into consideration, what is an appropriate approach to possession? Minimally, such an approach would avoid, as far as possible, the reductionisms of Western ego-, logo-, and ethnocentrism, including the implied tendencies to psychologize, rationalize, and pathologize the phenomenon. To this end, it seems helpful to realize that the difficulty in grasping spirit possession adequately has roots in the following: it is by means of spirit possession that dichotomies between I and not-I, identity and alterity, reality and illusion, body and spirit, rationality and irrationality are destroyed (similarly, Lambek 1989:52–53). Hence a "soft" model of understanding is called for, namely a model capable of integrating paradoxical processes and factors. The thesis I propose is that an interpretation of possession as *performance* is probably the best way to meet the said requirements.[8]

On the surface, possession is nothing but odd behavior. This is also documented by the Gospels. The screaming of the possessed man in the synagogue of Capernaum (Mark 1:23–24), the uncontrollable raging and self-flagellations of the Gerasene demoniac (Mark 5:2–7), and the teeth-grinding, foaming at the mouth, and the exposure to fire and water of the boy in Mark 9:18–22 come to mind. Possession thus looks like the staging of a certain role: the possessed person activates dramatically in public the role that society regards as indicat-

ing possession. In other words, queer patterns of behavior are the public manifestation of what Vincent Crapanzano called the "possession idiom" of a society (1987:14). Possession therefore is, on the whole, an interactive process
based on and within an established cultural pattern—the possession idiom. At
this point, one notes a double feedback: the idiom determines the behavior as
much as the behavior influences and forms the idiom.

Such an interpretation of possession as performance can shed light on the
paradoxical character of the phenomenon, that is, on the dissolving of the
above-mentioned dichotomies of identity/nonidentity, reality/illusion, and so
forth. Richard Schechner, the well-known anthropologist of theater, states: "All
effective performances share this 'not–not not' quality: Olivier is not Hamlet,
but also he is not not Hamlet: his performance is between a denial of being another (= I am me) and a denial of not being another (= I am Hamlet)"
(1985:123). This holds true not only for stage performances but also for social
performances. This borderline situation, or existence, between varying identities characterizes the possessed person. Just as Olivier still may be identified on
stage, so the Gerasene remains to the shepherds an identifiable fellow citizen.
Similarly, as Hamlet appears in Olivier's person on stage, so a demon appears
in the yelling and raging of the Gerasene. Olivier and Hamlet, the Gerasene
and the demon—each enters the stage and the social arena. During the performance, therefore, the clear borders between identity and nonidentity, inside
and outside, reality and illusion are obscured. To ask whether the possessed
person is just "performing" or if a spirit-event "really" takes place, possibly in a
trance state, ultimately seems as futile as asking whether Olivier is Olivier or
Hamlet on stage. To depreciate a performance by calling it a fake or just role-
playing belies a rational dichotomization that does not do justice to the performance model and its inherent ambiguity. For it is characteristic of a
performance to absorb the performer and thus to eradicate the clear borders between performance and reality for both the performer and the audience.

A famous and much-cited example in ethnological literature may demonstrate this assimilation in the performance. It concerns a biography of a native,
written in the language of the Kwakiutl, that Claude Lévi-Strauss discusses in
his *Structural Anthropology* (1963:167–85). The biographical fragment gives us
an account of a young man called Quesalid, who made it his business to unmask the shamans of his tribe as quacks. Driven by his curiosity to find out their
dubious tricks in order to expose them later, he tried to get into closer contact
with them until, one day, he was accepted as a member of their group and got
a full training in shamanism. There, among other things, he was taught to feign
a faint, to vomit intentionally, and to charge spies with spying out patients. He
was also taught to hide a wad of down within his mouth during a healing ritual

so that, after a strong bite on his tongue, he could present it as a bloody foreign mass, ostensibly sucked from the sick patient's body. The funny thing about his schooling is that, during his attempt to unmask the shamans, Quesalid himself carried out shamanistic performances that achieved great success by spectacularly healing patients. From then on, he ranked as such an esteemed shaman that he apparently lost sight of its supposed dishonesty. Quesalid, as Richard Schechner aptly remarks, was absorbed into the field of his own performance (1985:121); due to his successful performance as a shaman, he himself became part of what he wanted to expose. Lévi-Strauss says: "Quesalid did not become a great shaman because he cured his patients, he cured his patients because he had become a great shaman" (1963:180). The performance had, so to speak, created a world of its own in which Quesalid became someone else and many patients were cured. The example demonstrates that designating such performances as deception or reality is not appropriate. A successful performance creates its own reality, thus possessing, to use a term from literary studies, an *effet de réel* (R. Barthes, following Gebauer and Wulf [1998:194], who refer to the seriousness of play).

Similarly, possession may be understood as a performance that creates a demonic reality in the sense of *effet de réel*, physically putting into action the possession idiom of a society that itself is constituted and formed by performances. In contrast to the case just mentioned, the possession performance is experienced as compulsion.[9] Approaching possession with performance theory seems the best way to shed light on the phenomenon, respecting the indigenous experience while preserving its strangeness and opacity to a scientifically justifiable degree.

The Exorcistic Practice of Jesus: Transformance

In the Gospel accounts, Jesus of Nazareth, with his exorcistic action, invades the field of possession performance. What does Jesus' action mean in terms of what has been described? That question cannot be answered easily, for, although the historicity of the exorcistic practice of Jesus is not to be doubted (see above), it is still difficult, considering the complex problems of the Jesus tradition, to know adequately the concrete historical features of Jesus' exorcisms (on this conclusion, see Meier 1994:661). Sticking to the approach taken here, I find it appropriate and useful to define exorcisms as *transformances*, that is, as transformative performances.[10] In this perspective, the ritual exorcistic actions of Jesus are regarded as performative ritual actions that bring real transformations within possessed persons and their environment. In other words, in Jesus' exorcisms possession itself undergoes a performative change. Due to this change—as we may infer from the texts at hand and the general dynamic of exorcistic processes—the identity of possessed persons is constituted anew, their ranks and positions in the social arena revised, and the cosmic order reestablished. Before taking a closer look at this subject, I make some remarks about the legitimacy of this approach.

The interpretation of exorcisms as transformances, as dramatic performances of change, is based fundamentally on the public and demonstrative character of the actions. The decisive narrative traditions agree in reporting that Jesus did not carry out the exorcisms in private, like a magician (see Graf 1996:204–5), but in public: before witnesses in the synagogue (Mark 1:21), in the presence of the shepherds (Mark 5:14, 16), or in front of a crowd (Mark 9:14–29; Q 11:14; Matt 9:33).[11] The summaries mentioned above likewise support this point, although they are admittedly of little historical relevance. In addition, the recorded confrontations of Jesus and possessed persons show a visibly dramatic character. The presence of Jesus provokes abrupt outbreaks of possession (see Mark 1:23; 5:6–7; 9:20), whereupon he starts a more or less violent conflict with the demons embodied in possessed persons (see Mark 1:25–26; 5:8–13; 9:25–26; Twelftree 1993:155–56; Theissen and Merz 1998:292–93). The demonstration quality of the exorcisms becomes more obvious as the tradition notes the admiration or acclamation of witnesses, a feature that should not be regarded solely as an element of genre, without historical relevance. All things considered, exorcisms show features of a dramatic performance, and, more exactly, of a transformance.

It well fits these sketches to assume that Jesus himself underwent a dramatic transformation during his exorcistic actions. There is something to be said for suggesting that the behavior of possessed persons was somehow mirrored in Jesus, so that his exorcistic action itself was involved in the possession idiom. Several pieces of the Jesus tradition, with negative overtones, indicate that at least some in his social circles regarded him, due to his exorcisms, as a spirit-possessed person.[12] First there is Mark 3:22, in which Jesus is accused of being possessed by Beelzebul (see Mark 3:30: an unclean spirit) and of casting out demons through Beelzebul. This invective can also be found in Q 11:19.[13] In the added material of Matthew is another identification of Jesus with Beelzebul (Matt 10:25). Moreover, shortly before the Beelzebul controversy, Mark tells us that Jesus' relatives were disconcerted by his behavior. Mark gives in *elegon gar hoti exestē* ("For they said, 'He is beside himself,'" 3:21) a formulation that fits the possession idiom. This also holds true for the accusation in John 10:20 that Jesus has gone out of his mind; the verb *mainomai* (to be mad) in this verse, as the context reveals, unambiguously stands for spirit possession.

Three passages in John, by repeated use of the expression *daimonion echei* or *echeis* ("he has/you have a demon"; 7:20; 8:48, 49, 52; 10:20, 21), make possible spirit possession of Jesus the explicit subject of discussion. One can add the New Testament tradition that Jesus spoke directly with demons, thus, so to speak, standing on the same level with them. Further, the discussion about Jesus' true identity in Mark 8:27–28 and 6:14–16 likewise recalls the possession idiom. How else should we understand the view in those passages that Jesus was John the Baptist, Elijah, or one of the prophets? Taking ethnological findings into account, the assumption that Jesus once had been possessed by a spirit himself gains in importance. Although caution is called for in filling in the blanks too rashly, it is nonetheless significant that the practice of healers and exorcists to this day is often accompanied by behavior in the possession idiom. Numerous pieces of evidence in ethnological literature document that exorcists from varied cultures derive their power, not within themselves, but from some godlike power, as "possessed beings" or "mediums."[14] This also holds true for the ancient magician with his godlike or demonic assistant, the *paredros* (see Graf 1996:93, 99).

Relative to exorcists who serve as mediums, Peter Habermehl, a religious studies scholar, has a pertinent observation: "Where the exorcist by virtue of his nature no longer invokes the godlike power, but embodies it, the procedure as a matter of consequence decreases. His powerful word, based on his own authority, or rather his sheer presence, is sufficient for banishing and conquering the field of force opposed to him" (1990:403). As already noted, the exorcistic practice of Jesus of Nazareth was similarly lacking in techniques. According to the Jesus tradition, his exorcistic action was confined essentially to the appeal to the demon to leave, the so-called *apopomē* (*exelthe ex*: "come out of" Mark 1:25; 5:8; 9:25). Apart from that, only a request for a name (Mark 5:9), an *epipompē* (the departure of demons and their entry into swine, according to Mark 5:13), and a prohibition to reenter (Mark 9:25) are mentioned. Corresponding to exorcists who function as mediums, Jesus' effectiveness, to all appearances, was due to his presence, which obviously was regarded as the presence of some higher power manifest in him. In other words, when casting out demons, Jesus of Nazareth appeared as a medium of divine power.

If all this is accurate, then the exorcisms of Jesus witness to a direct clash between the divine and the demonic—embodied in Jesus and the possessed person, and quite real in the sense of the above-mentioned *effet de réel*. This collision results in diverse transformations, notably in the order of the self, the social order, and the cosmic order. Alterations at all three levels are closely connected to and mutually affect each other.

At first, the exorcisms of Jesus destroy the demonic identity of the possessed individuals. This happens particularly in that the audience perceives the dramatic change of behavior of the possessed person, evoked by Jesus' exorcistic action, as the departure of the demonic identity, and this perception is confirmed. The behavior of the possessed person is thus cut off from the possession idiom and thereby prepared for recoding and recontextualization. That dramatic change of behavior is expressed most vividly in the narrative of the raging Gerasene, who unexpectedly shows strikingly normal behavior (Mark 5:15). It also appears in Mark 9 in the exorcism of a boy, whose explosive manner cools to such an extent that, for a moment, he even seems to be dead (9:26). Although these descriptions may be later additions, since other exorcism narratives report the shriek of departing demons in a rather general way (cf. Mark 1:26; 7:30; 9:26; Matt 9:33; Q 11:14), the character and the success of exorcisms by definition still depend heavily on such transformations of behavior. Possession ends when the corresponding performance comes to a close—this holds true for the New Testament also. That such changes of behavior are more than masquerades becomes obvious when calling to mind the close connection between performance and identity. Exorcisms, with their dramatic rupture of the possession performance, finally provide the key to a new identity. The expulsion of demons thus figures as a ritual procedure or as a passage that makes it possible to constitute a new self that no longer compulsively embodies demonic powers.

Yet what causes the disappearance of demonic identity? It is due first to the demonic self being destroyed performatively in the direct encounter with Jesus, thanks to the higher divine order embodied in him as medium. That means that, in the exorcistic performance, possessed persons are publicly and somehow empirically integrated into the change of the cosmic order that Jesus proclaims. The proclamation of the coming kingdom of God that presumably aims at a transformation of being is, so to speak, physically realized in the possessed person. The outcome is a transformance, a tangible change of reality that can be grasped by others. Accordingly, Luke 11:20, widely considered to be an authentic saying of Jesus, reads: "But if it is by the finger of God that I cast out demons, then the kingdom of God has come upon you." In the exorcisms, perceived as transformances, the kingdom of God is thus incarnated.[15] A question raised occasionally is whether the proclamation of the kingdom is embodied in the exorcisms or whether, conversely, the exorcisms are the basis for the proclamation of the kingdom. In the context considered here, the proposed alternatives are not necessary (see Meier 1994:464–65 n. 52; Kollmann 1996:186). As transformances, the exorcisms are simultaneously illustration

(*Abbild*) and archetype (*Urbild*) of the coming kingdom—the transformation of the cosmic order.

Closely connected with the transformation of the cosmic order and the transformation of the self is a third element: social transformation. Possession is in substance an interactive event, a social performance. Therefore, it is impossible to break the possession completely, unless this is done intersubjectively. I have already emphasized the important role of the public in the exorcisms of Jesus. The often emotional reaction of bystanders, repeatedly accentuated in the tradition, plays an important part in this connection. While this might be a feature of genre, it clearly expresses the social confirmation of the end of the possession. Such an act of acknowledgment inevitably includes a change in the social status of the formerly possessed person. The destruction of demonic identity calls for the person's new placement within the social arena. This aspect is clearly discernible in the narrative of the Gerasene, who returned from social isolation at the tombs to the house of his family (Mark 5:19). In the same way, the healing of muteness and deafness in Matt 9:22 and Q 11:14 indicates a reintegration into a person's normal social context. Although the historical value of those statements may undoubtedly be discussed or even called into question, social integration is one of the main features of exorcistic action. Yet at this point the Jesus tradition has an additional emphasis. The remark about the Gerasene's intention to follow Jesus (Mark 5:18) and the mention of the exorcizing of Mary Magdalene (Luke 8:2) would have us understand that the socially integrating factor of the exorcisms might also be realized through inclusion in the Jesus group. Life in that group implied abruptly giving up one's everyday life and customary social roles. In this case, the exorcistic transformance continues into a lasting break with one's customary ways of life or in a restructuring of life. This change would most forcefully reflect the transformative power of the kingdom of God.

Conclusion

The suggestion of this essay is to interpret the New Testament accounts of possession and the exorcisms of Jesus as performances, or transformances. Such an interpretation attempts to articulate and elucidate phenomena alien to us in modern discourse, yet without reducing and dominating them. In my opinion, the relative vagueness of "performance" and "transformance" turns out to be their strong point.[16] Thus, the otherness, strangeness, and opaqueness of spirit possession and exorcism can moderate the distortions threatened by other approaches. The model of performance stays in close contact with the indigenous experience, notably counteracting secondary rationalizations that trace possession and exorcisms solely to unrelated processes and structures. To interface with aesthetic categories, as this approach suggests, seems a promising attempt to include the otherness and strangeness of the Christian tradition in a way that manages to avoid, at least somewhat, the dangers of egocentrism, logocentrism, and ethnocentrism. To really make headway, though, further efforts are required.[17]

Notes

1. We leave aside whether the narrative is to be located in Gerasa; regarding the complex problems, see Meier 1994:651–52.

2. For more details on this point, see Twelftree 1993:157–65. Yet it cannot be excluded that concrete techniques of Jesus' exorcistic activity were deliberately suppressed, having been judged to be magic. For details on contemporary exorcisms, see Trunk 1994:242–410.

3. See Kollmann (1996:206), who calls the Gerasene a "deranged person" suffering from mania. According to Trunk (1994:36), Mark 9:14–29 deals "undoubtedly" with an epileptic; on the problems of this common medical diagnosis, re-projecting the modern category of epilepsy on ancient texts, see Leven 1995; see also Meier 1994:647 and Pilch 2000:19.

4. Compare Zinser 1990:131. Lambek, by means of a humorous note, calls for not associating unfamiliar behavior like possession with disease: "We might equally well ask upon observing the strange activities of joggers or poets whether their behaviour must be ascribed to illness (or therapy)" (1989:48).

5. The demonic background is due to the personification of the fever in Mark 1:30 and to the exorcistic threat in the Lukan version (Luke 4:39: *epitimaō*); on the common connection between fever and demons in the ancient world, see 4Q560 1.4; *T. Sol.* 7:6–7; *PGM* XIII.15–17.

6. Crapanzano 1977:14; regarding the fundamental problems of applying modern medical categories in New Testament exegesis, see Pilch 2000:1–17.

7. Bourguignon (1973:15–16), however, emphasizes that belief in possession may also occur in the absence of an altered state of consciousness. It may also be linked to the modification of behavior. This aspect shall be taken seriously below.

8. For interpretations of possession as performance, see Schieffelin 1985; Lee 1989:252, 257ff. See also Lambek 1989:55–56, who, however, prefers the discourse model in the end. Spanos (1989:esp. 102ff.) interprets possession as "social role enactment." Furthermore, Butler's widely noted thesis, according to which sexual identity is

performatively constructed, is illuminating at this point; see Butler 1990. Concerning the importance and variety of applications of the performance model in science and art, see, in general, Carlson 1996.

9. Kramer convincingly explicates the feeling of becoming overwhelmed during possession with the concept of *passiones* (1987:46ff.), held by Lienhardt, which strives explicitly for preserving the difference between Western psychology and indigenous cosmologies.

10. The term "transformance" is borrowed from Schechner 1990:65ff., 129ff. An interpretation of exorcisms (in Sri Lanka) as performances appears in Kapferer 1983.

11. Only the exorcizing at a distance of the Syrophoenician woman's daughter, a tradition that lacks numerous motifs of a regular exorcism, does not relate to witnesses; see on this also Meier 1994:659.

12. Similarly Crossan 1994:92–93; Davies 1995:93–104; Smith 1998:41ff. Assumptions that Jesus imitated the physical behavior of the possessed persons also appear in Sanders 1993:153. Smith 1998:127ff. goes far beyond by claiming—in connection with his "magician" thesis—that Jesus, when he was baptized, had received the Spirit as a *paredros*, even claiming that his baptism has to be understood as a magical rite of deification.

13. Here Jesus' reaction confirms the questionable impression: "But if it is by the finger of God (by the Spirit of God [Matt 12:28]) that I cast out demons, then the kingdom of God has come upon you." The term "finger of God," which derives from Exod 8:15, connotes the "origin of miracle-working power" (Theissen and Merz 1996:259) and points most likely to the manifestation of divine power in the exorcist Jesus. In Matthew's expression, "by the Spirit of God," the idea of a medial inhabitation becomes more evident. On the original wording in Q, see Meier 1994:410–11.

14. In his cross-cultural study of magic-religious practitioners, Winkelman (1992:30ff.) subsumes exorcists under the types "Shaman/Healer," "Healer," and "Medium," that is, practitioners who act in altered states of consciousness or as spirit-possessed persons; see also, in general, Crapanzano 1987:16–17.

15. On *ephthasen*, etc., pointing to an already present event, see the explanations in Kollmann 1996:183ff. and Meier 1994:412–13, 422–23.

16. See Carlson 1996:189: "Performance . . . resists the sort of definitions, boundaries, and limits so useful to traditional academic writing and academic structures."

17. The proposal here is but a first attempt to grasp alien phenomena in the New Testament based on a performance theory on which I am currently working in Germany.

Works Cited

This essay has been translated into English by Anne Drusen.

Annen, Franz. 1976. "Die Dämonenaustreibungen Jesu in den synoptischen Evangelien." *Theologische Berichte* 5:107–46.

Boddy, Janice. 1989. *Wombs and Alien Spirits: Women, Men, and the Zar Cult in Northern Sudan.* New Directions in Anthropological Writing. Madison: University of Wisconsin Press.

Bourguignon, Erika. 1973. "Introduction: A Framework for the Comparative Study of Altered States of Consciousness." In *Religion, Altered States of Consciousness, and Social Change,* edited by E. Bourguignon, 3–35. Columbus: Ohio State University Press.

Butler, Judith. 1990. *Gender Trouble: Feminism and the Subversion of Identity.* New York: Routledge. Rev. ed., 1999.

Carlson, Marvin. 1996. *Performance: A Critical Introduction.* London: Routledge.

Castillo, Richard J. 1994. "Spirit Possession in South Asia, Dissociation or Hysteria? Part 1: Theoretical Background." *Culture, Medicine, and Psychiatry* 18:1–21.

Crapanzano, Vincent. 1977. "Introduction." In *Case Studies in Spirit Possession,* edited by V. Crapanzano and V. Garrison, 1–40. Contemporary Religious Movements. New York: John Wiley & Sons.

———. 1987. "Spirit Possession." In *Encyclopedia of Religion,* edited by M. Eliade et al., 14.12–19. New York: Macmillan.

Crossan, John Dominic. 1994. *Jesus: A Revolutionary Biography.* San Francisco: HarperSanFrancisco.

Davies, Stevan L. 1995. *Jesus the Healer: Possession, Trance, and the Origins of Christianity.* New York: Continuum.

Duerr, Hans Peter. 1985. *Traumzeit: Über die Grenze zwischen Wildnis und Zivilisation.* Frankfurt: Suhrkamp. Translated by F. D. Goodman under the title *Dreamtime: Concerning the Boundary between Wilderness and Civilization.* New York: Blackwell, 1985.

Gebauer, Gunter, and Christoph Wulf. 1998. *Spiel—Ritual—Geste: Mimetisches Handeln in der sozialen Welt.* Hamburg: Rowohlt.

Geertz, Clifford. 1977. "From the Native's Point of View: On the Nature of Anthropological Understanding." In *Symbolic Anthropology: A Reader in the Study of Symbols and Meanings,* edited by J. L. Dolgin et al., 480–92. New York: Columbia University Press.

Goodman, Felicitas D. 1988. *How about Demons? Possession and Exorcism in the Modern World.* Folklore Today. Bloomington: Indiana University Press.

Graf, Fritz. 1996. *Gottesnähe und Schadenzauber: Die Magie in der griechisch-römis-chen Antike.* C. H. Beck Kulturwissenschaft. Munich: Beck. Translated by F. Philip under the title *Magic in the Ancient World.* Revealing Antiquity 10. Cambridge: Harvard University Press, 1997.

Habermehl, Peter. 1990. "Exorzismus." In *Handbuch Religionswissenschaftlicher Grundbegriffe,* edited by H. Cancik et al., 2.401–4. Stuttgart: Kohlhammer.

Hollenbach, Paul W. 1993. "Help for Interpreting Jesus' Exorcisms." In *SBLSP 1993,* 119–28. Atlanta: Scholars.

Kampling, Rainer. 1986. "Jesus von Nazareth—Lehrer und Exorzist." *BZ* 30:237–48.

Kapferer, Bruce. 1983. *A Celebration of Demons: Exorcism and the Aesthetics of Healing in Sri Lanka.* Bloomington: Indiana University Press. 2d ed., 1991.

Kollmann, Bernd. 1996. *Jesus und die Christen als Wundertäter: Studien zur Magie, Medizin und Schamanismus in Antike und Christentum.* FRLANT 170. Göttingen: Vandenhoeck & Ruprecht.

Kramer, Fritz W. 1987. *Der rote Fes: Über Besessenheit und Kunst in Afrika.* Frankfurt: Athenäum. Translated by M. Green under the title *The Red Fez: Art and Spirit Possession in Africa.* New York: Verso, 1993.

Lambek, Michael. 1989. "From Disease to Discourse: Remarks on the Conceptualization of Trance and Spirit Possession." In *Altered States of Consciousness and Mental Health: A Cross-Cultural Perspective,* edited by C. A. Ward, 36–61. Newbury Park, Calif.: Sage.

Lee, Raymond L. M. 1989. "Self-Presentation in Malaysian Spirit Seances: A Dramaturgical Perspective on Altered States of Consciousness in Healing Ceremonies." In *Altered States of Consciousness and Mental Health: A Cross-Cultural Perspective,* edited by C. A. Ward, 251–66. Newbury Park, Calif.: Sage.

Leven, Karl-Heinz. 1995. "Die 'unheilige' Krankheit—Epilepsia, Mondsucht und Besessenheit in Byzanz." *Würzburger Medizinhistorische Mitteilungen* 13:17–57.

Lévi-Strauss, Claude. 1963. *Structural Anthropology.* Translated by C. Jacobson and B. Grundfest Schoepf. New York: Basic.

Lewis, I. M. 1989. *Ecstatic Religion: A Study of Shamanism and Spirit Possession.* 2d ed. London: Routledge.

Malina, Bruce J. 2001. *The New Testament World: Insights from Cultural Anthropology.* 3d ed. Louisville: Westminster John Knox.

Maurizio, L. 1995. "Anthropology and Spirit Possession: A Reconsideration of the Pythia's Role at Delphi." *Journal of Hellenic Studies* 115:69–86.

Meier, John P. 1994. *A Marginal Jew: Rethinking the Historical Jesus.* Vol. 2: *Mentor, Message, and Miracles.* ABRL. New York: Doubleday.

Pilch, John J. 1996. "Altered States of Consciousness: A 'Kitbashed' Model." *BTB* 26:133–38.

———. 2000. *Healing in the New Testament: Insights from Medical and Mediterranean Anthropology.* Minneapolis: Fortress Press.

Sanders, E. P. 1993. *The Historical Figure of Jesus.* New York: Penguin.

Schechner, Richard. 1985. *Between Theater and Anthropology.* Philadelphia: University of Pennsylvania Press.

———. 1990. *Theater-Anthropologie: Spiel und Ritual im Kulturvergleich.* Hamburg: Rowohlt.

Schieffelin, Edward L. 1985. "Performance and the Cultural Construction of Reality." *American Ethnologist* 12:707–24.

Smith, Morton. 1998. *Jesus the Magician: Charlatan or Son of God?* 2d ed. Berkeley, Calif.: Seastone.

Spanos, Nicholas P. 1989. "Hypnosis, Demonic Possession, and Multiple Personality: Strategic Enactments and Disavowals of Responsibility for Actions." In *Altered States of Consciousness and Mental Health: A Cross-Cultural Perspective,* edited by C. A. Ward, 96–124. Newbury Park, Calif.: Sage.

Theissen, Gerd. 1983. *The Miracle Stories of the Early Christian Tradition.* Edited by J. Riches. Translated by F. McDonagh. Philadelphia: Fortress Press.

Theissen, Gerd, and Annette Merz. 1998. *The Historical Jesus: A Comprehensive Guide.* Translated by J. Bowden. Minneapolis: Fortress Press.

Trunk, Dieter. 1994. *Der messianische Heiler: Eine redaktions und religionsgeschichtliche Studie zu den Exorzismen im Matthäusevangelium.* Herders biblische Studien 3. Freiburg: Herder.

Twelftree, Graham H. 1993. *Jesus the Exorcist: A Contribution to the Study of the Historical Jesus.* WUNT 2/54. Tübingen: Mohr/Siebeck.

Waldenfels, Bernhard. 1990. *Der Stachel des Fremden.* Suhrkamp Taschenbuch Wissenschaft 868. Frankfurt: Suhrkamp.

Weber, Hartwig. 1999. "Dämonen, Besessenheit und Exorzismus im Neuen Testament und ihre Wirkungsgeschichte." *Zeitschrift für Pädagogik und Theologie* 51:19–31.

Winkelman, Michael. 1992. *Shamans, Priests, and Witches: A Cross-Cultural Study of Magico-Religious Practitioners.* Anthropological Research Papers 44. Tempe: Arizona State University Press.

Zinser, Hartmut. 1990. "Besessenheit." In *Handbuch Religionswissenschaftlicher Grundbegriffe,* edited by H. Cancik et al., 2:131–35. Stuttgart: Kohlhammer.

Social-Boundary Concerns

8

The Baptism of Jesus:
A Ritual-Critical Approach

Richard E. DeMaris

Most New Testament scholars engaged in Gospel and historical Jesus research conclude that Jesus of Nazareth underwent baptism at the hand of John the Baptizer, but they find nothing historically reliable in the events immediately following that baptism (Mark 1:9–11; cf. Matt 3:13–17; Luke 3:21–22). Many place what is reported after Jesus' baptism, explicitly or implicitly, in the category of legend (Bultmann 1963:247) or myth (Dibelius 1934:271), and they detect christological affirmations dating from a time after Jesus. However the events following Jesus' baptism are characterized, historical-critical scholarship has in effect drawn a line between the earthly action of baptism and the heavenly manifestations that result.

In contrast to historical-critical analysis of Jesus' baptism and the consensus it has reached, an assessment of historicity informed by social-scientific research takes a very different approach to the baptism and its consequences, and it reaches entirely different conclusions. Anthropological studies of possession, trance, shamanism, ecstasy, and related phenomena, all of which fall under the rubric of altered states of consciousness, document human access to such states across the globe, including the Mediterranean world, both present and past. Such ubiquity makes it plausible, even very likely, that people in ancient Palestine had visual and auditory experiences of the sort reported in conjunction with Jesus' baptism.

These same studies note that communities and individuals regularly depend on ritual activity to induce altered states of consciousness or to trigger entry into the state of possession, although spontaneous entry into such states does occur. The account of Jesus' baptism and subsequent vision belongs to this cultural pattern. From a social-scientific viewpoint, therefore, the widely attested and well-documented conjunction of ritual and entry into an altered state lends credibility to the events and their sequence in Mark 1:9–11.

What a social-scientific approach cannot determine with much certainty is the specific ritual that induced the occurrences reported in Mark 1:10–11. The account has an affinity to an established pattern of anointing and spirit possession or bestowal of God's Spirit in ancient Israelite society, and it also resembles the later experience of many entering the Jesus movement, namely, baptism's imparting of the Holy Spirit. If a ritual other than baptism triggered Jesus' altered state of consciousness, it is easy to account for displacement of that ritual by baptism in the account as it now stands.

It is also possible that Jesus entered an altered state of consciousness without any ritual prompting, as sometimes happens among populations in which such states occur. Uncertainty regarding ritual inducement means, therefore, that a social-scientific approach comes to a conclusion that turns the scholarly consensus about the historicity of Jesus' baptism and vision upside down: Jesus' baptismal vision has a stronger claim to historicity than the baptism itself.

The followers of Jesus may have introduced the baptismal rite into the story of his possession because of the stigma attached to spontaneous possession. Cultures like that of ancient Judea typically recognize both positive and negative possession and associate the former with ritual activity. Joining a baptismal report to Jesus' entry into an altered state would have identified what happened to him as positive rather than negative, that is, as possession by the Holy Spirit and not by a demon. In this case, Jesus' baptism has no claim to historicity.

The Consensus Position on Jesus' Baptism and Its Detractors

The judgment that John baptized Jesus but that Jesus' resulting vision is historically suspect goes back to the beginning of modern historical-critical study of the Gospels and has become the dominant view in the several stages of historical Jesus scholarship. We find the view expressed in the nineteenth century, in the work of David Friedrich Strauss, for example, and it continued to find strong support in the next century (1972:237–46). In the middle of the twentieth century, Günther Bornkamm noted, "His own baptism by John is one of the most certainly verified occurrences of his life. Tradition, however, has altogether transformed the story into a testimony to the Christ" (1960:54). A half-century later, during the so-called third quest for the historical Jesus, the view faces little opposition; it is very nearly an assumption. Characterizing the mainstream of contemporary scholarship, John P. Meier says this about Jesus' baptism: "[U]sually without debate it also serves as the starting point of most scholarly reconstructions of the life of the historical Jesus. With the Infancy Narratives often declared unreliable sources, writers naturally gravitate to what they almost automatically consider firm historical ground" (1991–94:2:100).

As Meier moves from Mark 1:9 to verses 10 and 11, however, he observes, "We have in the narrative of the theophany, as it now stands, a Christian 'midrash,' a learned use of various OT texts to present the reader of the gospel with an initial interpretation of who Jesus is" (1991–94:2:106). The implication of Meier's judgment is clear: theological interpretation compromises historical reliability; between Mark 1:9 and 11, historicity vanishes (see Funk and the Jesus Seminar 1998:54–55).

Opposition to this position has both a right and left wing. Scholars more inclined to trust the reliability of the Gospel narrative are ready to find some historical kernel in the narrative after Mark 1:9. If they, too, are skeptical about the reality of the theophany described there, they insist on a psychological reality behind the mythological language, namely, Jesus' realization of his true identity or sense of call to the public ministry that follows (Sanders 1993:10–13; cf. Holtzmann 1901:106).

A more serious challenge to the consensus position comes from scholars approaching Mark from a literary or rhetorical viewpoint, who doubt the historicity of both the vision and the baptism. The precursor to this approach was redaction criticism, which emerged after World War II as a corrective of, but also complement to, form criticism. If form critics assumed the Gospel writers were primarily compilers and arrangers of tradition, redaction critics considered the evangelists to be active and creative editors: "[W]hile ultimately we cannot know even the names of our authors, their backgrounds, or their careers, we must still emphasize that we are dealing with authors" (Marxsen 1969:19). Marxsen's fellow redaction critics undertook the considerable task of recovering the theological perspectives that motivated the Gospel writers' ordering and editing of sources to create their respective Gospels. The resulting scholarship underscored the liberty the Gospel writers took with traditions as they gave voice to their theology (Rohde 1968).

Such freedom creates a problem for scholars in pursuit of the historical Jesus. The assertion that the evangelists wrote from a particular theological stance, which dictated how they edited their sources, means that recovering the traditions they used becomes difficult: "If, for instance, the evangelists' work of redaction was as heavy as some would claim, our chances of recovering early forms, let alone sources, are at the mercy of so much speculation and so many unverifiable hypotheses that we are in a bad state indeed" (Neill and Wright 1988:401–2).

The path of historical inquiry became even more difficult in North America because of the direction that redaction criticism took there. Representative of this development was Norman Perrin, who noted, "Although the discipline is called redaction criticism, it could equally be called 'composition criticism' because it is concerned with the composition of new material and the arrangements of redacted or freshly created material into new units and patterns, as well as with the redaction of existing material" (1969:1). Perrin and his colleagues exhibited great sensitivity to the evangelist as both active editor and creative author, and one consequence was that their hunt for pre-Markan materials often produced negative results. A 1976 study of the Markan passion narrative, a portion of the Gospel widely thought to have well-developed pre-Markan tradition behind it, found the evangelist more often composing the narrative than editing received tradition (Kelber, ed., 1976; cf. Donahue 1973:237–40). The study concludes, "The understanding of Mk 14–16 as a theologically integral part of the Markan Gospel calls into question the classic form critical thesis concerning an independent and coherent Passion Narrative prior to Mk" (Kelber 1976:157).

If attention to the Gospel of Mark as a work of literature raises doubts about the historicity of the passion narrative, this skepticism surely extends to Jesus' baptism. For an active Gospel writer would hardly have left the baptismal scene in Mark untouched, given its prominent location in the Gospel and the theological importance of its content. Recent literary studies of Mark point to the place of the baptism and vision in the overall structure of the Gospel, their connections to other parts of the narrative, and their voicing of key Markan themes. Jesus' baptism and vision fall in the introduction or prologue of the second Gospel, and this opening section looks forward to the middle and closing of the text, even as those later sections look back to the opening of Mark (Robbins 1984:25–31; Iersel 1989:18–26, 31–42; Stock 1989:25–29, 45–57; cf. Robbins 1996:52–53). So what we have is not a simple, straightforward report about baptism and its result but a complicated and rich literary creation fully integrated with the document it introduces. Literary critics may not concern themselves with the issue of history—some would say attention to Mark's narrative world precludes questions of historicity—but the implication of their analysis is clear: the more we see the hand of the Gospel writer, the less we see of the historical Jesus.

One of the most important recent books on Mark by an American scholar, *A Myth of Innocence: Mark and Christian Origins*, shows its debt to postwar German redaction criticism and reveals a deep suspicion about recovering any history from the Gospel story. The author, Burton Mack (1988), finds the second Gospel to be largely the creation of the evangelist. Key to that creation is what Mack calls framework stories, which the evangelist ordered in a chiastic structure that gave the Gospel its shape (283, 288, 333). The stories that provide the framework for the Gospel, Jesus' baptism, transfiguration, and crucifixion, are the same three that Philipp Vielhauer placed at the center of his 1964 redactional analysis of Mark. The three, he argued, constituted an enthronement pattern that defined Mark's Christology.

Mack does not specify in his book why Jesus' baptism by John cannot be trusted as a historical event, but Leif Vaage articulates the reasons in a recent article on Jesus' baptism. He leads the reader by asking, "What if . . . we were to explore the possibility that the evangelist himself simply 'invented' this material, introducing it into his narrative of 'Jesus Christ Son of God' for a particular purpose, namely, because such a scene was somehow thought to further one or more of the Gospel's specific efforts at persuasion?" (1996:282). The baptism raises suspicions, historically speaking, because it fits the Gospel writer's rhetorical or literary strategy so well. It also embodies his theological perspective. As Vaage notes, "The 'paradoxical' characterization of Jesus in Mark as a (or the) divine 'Son of God,' who nonetheless must suffer and die in order to fulfill his ultimate destiny, is perfectly encapsulated by the opening vignette of Jesus' baptism by John and ensuing epiphany in Mark 1:9–11" (283). That is, the baptism and vision scene is one of several crucial christological recognition scenes in Mark that give voice to an important element of Markan theology, namely, reversal: the Jesus who *humbles* himself before John is *exalted* as Son of God. Because they express the Gospel writer's theological perspective so precisely, according to Vaage, neither the baptism nor what follows can be considered historically reliable (281–82, 286, 289–90).

Other analyses of the Gospel and the evangelist's purpose in composing it, although they differ from Vaage's, may lend support to his skepticism. One such interpretation comes from the attempt to make sense of, and to find a setting in life for, the notice in Jesus' arrest scene about a young man dressed in a linen cloth who sheds it to avoid arrest (14:51–52). If that young man is the same one who appears dressed in white at Jesus' tomb to announce the resurrection (16:5–7), he may well represent a baptizand in the community for whom the evangelist wrote, who would have shed his clothing and then been reclothed in white in the ancient baptismal rite (Scroggs and Groff 1973; Standaert 1978:153–68, 498–540; McVann 1994:183–90). This interlacing of the baptizand's experience entering the Jesus movement with the arrest that leads to Jesus' death and the empty tomb that signals his resurrection would constitute the evangelist's christological anchoring of community ritual: baptism as *dying* and *rising* with Christ (see Rom 6:1–11). The same intertwining of Christology and baptism occurs elsewhere in Mark, in 10:35–40 and, of course, at

John's baptism of Jesus. The Gospel's steady focus on the baptismal rite, made evident by this interpretation, makes it likelier that the Gospel writer composed or strongly shaped Mark 1:9–11. Consequently, Vaage's skepticism about the report of Jesus' baptism in Mark 1:9–11 is fully justified.

To counteract skepticism about the Markan baptismal scene, defenders of a historical baptism typically offer two arguments. One is based on how widely attested John's baptism of Jesus is in early Christian literature. Yet disagreement over how many *independent* sources exist—Mark may be the only one—weakens the argument (e.g., Crossan 1991:232 versus Meier 1991–94:2:100). The stronger argument relies on the principle of embarrassment, which is similar to Gerd Theissen's subcriterion of "tendency-resistance" under the criterion of "historical effective plausibility" (Theissen and Winter 1997:177–80, 248). John Dominic Crossan invokes the principle when he argues for the baptism of Jesus by John: "It [the baptism] also evinces a very large amount of what I term, without any cynicism, theological damage control. The tradition is clearly uneasy with the idea of John baptizing Jesus because that seems to make John superior and Jesus sinful" (1991:232). The argument goes that no scribe or writer would have added this element to the Gospel story because the baptism carries implications that are in tension with the Jesus movement's developing Christology. Hence, the baptism by John bears the mark of the earliest and most authentic stratum of material, too well accepted not to be included in some fashion, but deeply troubling to the Gospel writers. Their discomfort shows in the changes they made in their accounts (Meier 1991–94:1:168–71; 2:101; Theissen and Merz 1998:207–8).

As logical as this claim is, the case is not as clear-cut as scholars would have it. Paul Hollenbach's assertion is an example of such overstatement: "There can be no more certain fact of Jesus' life than his baptism by John. For, considering the apologetic that surrounds the event *in all four gospels* and other early Christian literature, we can be sure that no early Christians would ever have invented it" (1982:198; italics added). Apologetic editing is evident in most of the accounts, but the nature of the editing, hence the apologetic behind it, varies considerably. The Gospel of John omits the baptism of Jesus, although it describes the setting of the baptism and seems aware of Jesus' baptismal vision, presenting it as (part of) a theophany or revelation to the Baptist (1:29–34; Brown 1966:55–72). Matthew records the baptism and vision, but also reports John's hesitation to baptize Jesus and the latter's convincing reason to proceed (3:13–17; cf. *Gospel of the Ebionites* in Epiphanius, *Panarion* 30.13.7). Luke avoids having John baptize Jesus—3:20 narrates John's arrest—but records Jesus' baptism (3:21). Immediately after his baptism, Jesus prays, then the Holy Spirit descends (3:21–22).

This redactional variety suggests we should speak of embarrassments rather than embarrassment. If the elimination of the baptism from the Fourth Gospel and the hesitation added to the First Gospel are both responses to the implications of John administering a baptism of repentance for the forgiveness of sins to Jesus, what lies behind the Third Gospel's account? For Jesus to undergo a baptism for the forgiveness of sins poses no problem there. The narrative seeks instead to sever the connection between John's baptism and bestowal of the Holy Spirit (Hartman 1992:585). This aim would account for both the absence of John at Jesus' baptism and the insertion of Jesus' prayer between baptism and vision.

This interpretation of Lukan redaction finds confirmation in the portrayal of baptism in Acts. There, too, the imparting of the Holy Spirit could not be brought about by John's baptism. Luke clearly distinguished the baptism of repentance associated with John the Baptizer from the baptism with laying on of hands that bestowed the Holy Spirit, and he privileged the latter over the former (Acts 19:1–7; cf. 18:25). Most embarrassing to the third evangelist, therefore, would have been a report about John's baptism conferring the Holy Spirit—even worse if the recipient had been Jesus!

More troubling for scholars invoking the principle of embarrassment is the lack of any clear indication of it in the Gospel of Mark. The common response that Mark's "primitive" theology and "low" Christology would account for a lack of embarrassment cannot stand in the face of Mark's obvious theological sophistication. Also weak is the claim that the Gospel writer meant to divert attention from the baptism by barely reporting it but fully describing Jesus' vision, so that the implications of the baptism would shrink in the face of Jesus' exalted status. True, the subordination of John to Jesus that we find in Mark could be a way of discounting the baptism (Breech 1983:23). Still, emphasis elsewhere or introduction of an offsetting theme does not hide or nullify what the evangelist himself reports. The temptation to read the other Gospels' discomfort into Mark is great, but must be avoided.

Difficulties with finding embarrassment in Mark may hint at a problem with the principle. Embarrassment is, after all, culturally determined and highly situational, which makes it hard to detect, much less define, in foreign cultures and ancient texts (Meier 1991–94:1:170). Because of this uncertainty, I suspect embarrassment of another kind has entered the picture. Does the scholarly consensus concerning Mark 1:9–11 defend the historicity of Jesus' baptism but abandon the rest because of an embarrassment operating among modern scholars, rather than ancient writers? Are scholars ready to segregate the historical (baptism) from the mythical and ahistorical (vision-theophany) because of their own modern embarrassment about the latter?

A more immediate question, however, weighs on the Markan baptismal account: Is there any historically plausible material in Mark 1:9–11 whatsoever?

Altered-States-of-Consciousness Research

A positive reassessment of the historicity of Mark 1:9–11 depends on identifying a historically plausible sequence of events that matches the report in Mark. Those verses clearly belong together, literarily speaking, and even a form critic like Rudolf Bultmann, although he distinguished history from legend in them, saw their essential unity: "Without disputing the historicity of Jesus' baptism by John, the story as we have it must be classified as legend. The miraculous moment is essential to it and its edifying purpose is clear" (1963:247). Yet assessments like his—what Vincent Taylor called a "depreciatory estimate" (1966:158)—have fostered the division of the verses between the authentic and inauthentic.

In Bultmann's defense, his source analysis of the scene justifiably triggered skepticism on his part. He determined episodes like the baptismal vision and Jesus' transfiguration to be resurrection or postresurrection exaltation scenes (see Acts 2:32–36; Rom 1:3–4) projected back into Jesus' life (1963:250–52, 259–61). In place of such analysis, a different way of approaching so-called mythical, legendary, supernatural, or miraculous events is needed, a way that respects the integrity of the narrative and avoids what amounts to ethnocentric judgments about what the narrative reports.

Contemporary historical Jesus scholars in North America have begun to show a great interest in the world of spirit and spiritual manifestations—exorcisms, healings, and visions—that pervade the Gospel narratives.[1] Marcus Borg devoted the first half of his book, *Jesus, a New Vision: Spirit, Culture, and the Life of Discipleship*, to treatment of the world of spirit in late Israelite religion, at the time of Jesus, and to Jesus' embodiment of spiritual power (1987:25–75; cf. Borg 1994:27–28). He insists that we take Jesus' vivid sense of the spirit seriously, and he moves toward an analysis of this phenomenon that would make Jesus' experience comprehensible. Yet the comparisons he makes between spirit-filled or holy persons across cultures lack depth, and the interdisciplinary interpretive framework he introduces to characterize the spirit world and Jesus' relationship to it is inadequate. Another recent study by Harold Remus, *Jesus as Healer* (1997), would have us take healing seriously, too, as part of the historical Jesus' activity, but again he does not offer a method or model for making sense of healing in Jesus' culture.

Better attempts at describing and analyzing the spirit world and Jesus' relation to it have come from Stevan Davies and Pieter Craffert. In *Jesus the Healer:
Possession, Trance, and the Origins of Christianity* (1995), Davies brings the
cross-cultural phenomenon of spirit possession to his analysis of the historical
Jesus, and he argues that Jesus underwent possession at baptism and in episodes
in which he healed and exorcised. Unfortunately, his study is flawed by the introduction of psychological analysis to account for Jesus' possession as a response to John the Baptizer. Statements like "John . . . encourages
psychological change"; Jesus experienced "heightened life stress"; and that
Jesus underwent "alterations in ego identity" take us into psychoanalytical or
psychiatric claims that are untenable for two reasons: they are anachronistic vis-
à-vis first-century Mediterranean personalities, and they cannot be verified
from the information the Gospels provide (Davies 1995:56, 58, 118; cf. Pilch
1996:138; 1997).

Pieter Craffert is on methodologically firmer ground when he proposes that
we investigate the historical Jesus as a social type under the rubric of shamanism. First, the shamanic model is well established in anthropology, and there is
much data for comparative analysis (Townsend 1997; Atkinson 1992). Second,
the richness of the model, what Craffert calls the shamanic complex, could account for many aspects or episodes of Jesus' life that fall into the miraculous or
supernatural (1998:12–15). Third, it is possible that the analysis of Jesus as
shaman would allow fruitful comparison between Jesus and other shamanic
types in Mediterranean cultures, particularly in Greece (Burkert 1962;
1979:88–98; Dodds 1951:135–78; cf. Eliade 1961:172–73).

The fullest use of shaman type and related models in historical Jesus research has been John Pilch's application of altered-states-of-consciousness research to various episodes in the Gospels—Jesus' transfiguration, walking on
the sea, healing, and resurrection appearances—and to related phenomena described in the New Testament, such as John's visionary experience reported in
the book of Revelation (1998a; 1998b; 1995; 1993). Pilch's research lies behind
Bruce Malina's recent analysis of the book of Revelation (Malina 1995:2, 28).
Along similar lines but independently of Pilch, Philip Esler has supplied research on dissociative states to the phenomenon of glossolalia in the Jesus
movement (Esler 1992).

Altered-states-of-consciousness research examines and compares what could
variously be described as ecstatic, trance, mystical, transcendental, or visionary
experiences that pervade human cultures around the world. The rise of drug
use and the introduction of meditative techniques from South and East Asia in
the 1960s and '70s fostered an interest in such inquiry at the popular level in

Europe and North America. More important, however, was the impetus from anthropologists and other scholars who sought to counteract dismissive assessments of departures from an alert waking state as aberrant, pathological, or dysfunctional. The very wide range of conscious states that researchers have considered under the rubric of altered states of consciousness makes it difficult to define the phenomenon with precision, or to conclude with absolute certainty that we are speaking of a unified phenomenon (Tart 1980:243; Lambek 1989:38). Nevertheless, scholars have little trouble identifying a range of conscious states that reasonably fall under this category: alterations in thinking, disturbed sense of time, loss of control, change in expression of emotions, change in bodily image, perceptual distortions, changes in meaning and significance assigned to experiences and perceptions, a sense of the ineffable, feelings of rejuvenation, and hypersuggestibility (Ludwig 1968:77–83; cf. Krippner 1972).

Pilch, like Craffert, also applies the model of shaman to Jesus, joining it to his use of altered-states-of-consciousness research. Pilch finds that the Gospels' story of Jesus matches the typical shamanic biography closely, a key feature of which is the entry into an altered state of consciousness to allow journey to, or contact with, another reality, the spirit world (Winkelman 1997:394; Townsend 1997:431–32; Walsh 1989:3–5; Reinhard 1976:16; Jones 1976:29; but see Hitchcock 1976:168).

Spirit Possession and Ritual

The present study finds another manifestation of altered states of consciousness, spirit possession, a more appropriate model for the one episode of Jesus' life it treats, his baptism. The approach differs little from that of Pilch and Craffert, because shamanism and spirit possession, while different, are exceedingly similar and interrelated phenomena (Lewis 1989:8–9; Heusch 1981:152–58).[2] The use of an altered-state-of-consciousness model under the category of spirit possession begins with Erika Bourguignon's study of dissociational states (1968a). Other interpretive models could be equally applicable, such as Raymond Firth's tripartite scheme of spirit possession, spirit mediumship, and shamanism (1964:247–56; 1967:296–99). Yet Bourguignon's approach is especially useful because she looked at altered states globally. In doing so, she identified two major ways that human cultures understand altered states of consciousness (1973:13–33). The first way, trance, corresponds to shamanism and involves the temporary absence of the soul or spirit from the body and travel to, and interaction with spirits in, an alternate realm (Walsh 1993:742). The second, possession trance, involves temporary or permanent entry of a spirit into a person or persons. Bourguignon captures the difference between

these two types succinctly when she says, "The trancer sees, hears, feels, perceives, and *interacts* with another; the possession trancer *becomes* another"
(1979:261).

While these types can coexist in a culture, trance is typical of less structured, hunter-gatherer cultures and has been prominent in middle and eastern
Asia and the native cultures of the Americas (Walsh 1989:7–9). Possession
trance, on the other hand, is common to more hierarchical, horticultural, and
agricultural societies and appears frequently in sub-Saharan African, Latin
American, Afro-American, and Mediterranean cultures (Bourguignon
1968b:18–32; 1979:236, 245–65; Boddy 1994:409). The more stratified the society, the likelier it is to have possession trance as its institutionalized altered
state of consciousness.

In the typology that Bourguignon develops of institutionalized altered states
and possession beliefs, the New Testament record appears to reflect a mixed society (1973:12–22). That is, trance and possession trance coexist. Yet while soul
journeys and visits to alternate realms typical of trance do occur in the world of
the New Testament (2 Cor 12:1–4; Rev 4:1–3; 17:1–3), possession trance in
such forms as the indwelling of the Holy Spirit and demonic possession domi-
nates the narrative world of the Gospels and Acts. Whatever the exact mixture
of trance and possession trance, the New Testament spirit world confirms Bourguignon's characterization of Mediterranean cultures.

Additional research on cultures in which possession trance is the typical altered state of consciousness indicates that spirit possession is triggered by ritual
activity (Lee 1968; Bourguignon 1972; 1979:243–45; Goodman 1988a:34–38;
1988b:11, 17, 24). As Felicitas Goodman notes in her study of spirit possession
across cultures, "All religious communities where the religious trance is institutionalized have rituals to induce it, and those participating learn to react to
them. The singing of a certain hymn or chant may do it; so will clapping, dancing, drumming, rattling, turning around one's own axis, reciting a certain formula or prayer, glancing at a flickering candle or moving water, even smelling
a certain fragrance, such as incense" (1988a:37).

Jesus' baptismal scene as Mark describes it fits this sequence of features
well: the ritual action of baptism triggers spirit possession—the Spirit descending like a dove into Jesus—and altered state of consciousness—Jesus' visual and
aural encounter with the spirit world, that is, the heavens splitting and God
speaking (Mark 1:10–11). The graphic language of possession softened over
time; Luke and Matthew have the dove descending *upon* Jesus (*epi*; Matt 3:16;
Luke 3:22) instead of *into* him (*eis*; Mark 1:10; Fitzmyer 1981:484). Moreover,
Luke and Matthew eliminated Mark's striking image of the Spirit driving or

casting Jesus into the desert in the scene that follows (Mark 1:12; cf. Matt 4:1; Luke 4:1). Only the Markan version preserves the vivid description of a spirit outside Jesus entering him and subsequently controlling him.

Not every element of Mark's account, however, has equal claim to historical reliability. The basic sequence of ritual action inducing possession trance is likely, but whether John's baptism was the triggering rite is open to question. Likewise, while Jesus very probably entered an altered state of consciousness in the form of spirit possession, the features and content of what he encountered are historically less certain. Biblical scholars, as we have seen, generally dismiss the historical reliability of what happens in Mark 1:10–11 because it resonates so strongly with parts of the Israelite religious tradition, such as Genesis 22, Isaiah 42 and 64, and Psalm 2 (Mann 1986:198–210).

A social-scientific interpretation views such resonance differently. In cultures with institutionalized altered states of consciousness, those who experience them will encounter what they have been socialized to expect. In other words, the culture not only authorizes the altered state of consciousness but provides the content as well (Walsh 1993:758; Malina 1999:357). Since Jesus grew up in Israelite society, we can assume that he knew and could have drawn from the stories of his culture to articulate what happened in his possession trance.

The rich cultural heritage of the Israelite people included many occurrences of spirit possession or bestowal of God's Spirit, often preceded by ritual action. One example is Samuel's anointing of Saul, followed by the Spirit of the Lord taking possession of Saul (1 Sam 10:1–13). Fritzleo Lentzen-Deis's exhaustive study, *Die Taufe Jesu nach den Synoptikern*, offers many more examples from the various traditions represented in the Hebrew Bible (prophetic: 1970:144–46; royal: 152–56, 185–86). To the extent that these scenarios were part of Jesus' socialization, he could have experienced and articulated his own possession trance accordingly. Yet some uncertainty enters here, because those who preserved and passed on the story of Jesus' possession trance would also have been influenced by existing cultural patterns of possession trance. So while altered-states-of-consciousness research affirms the historicity of Jesus' possession trance and its ritual inducement, it cannot guarantee the historical reliability of every feature of the episode.

Another possible source for the specific features of Jesus' ritually induced possession trance was the experience of those who underwent baptismal entry into the Jesus movement. Two key features of the Markan baptismal account recur in other passages in which baptismal language appears: Spirit bestowal and filial identification. Some groups in the Jesus movement linked spirit possession or the bestowal of the Holy Spirit to baptism (Acts 2:38; 1 Cor 6:11; 12:13; 2 Cor 1:21–22), and the Markan baptismal scene mirrors this linkage.

Filial or adoption language commonly occurs in the context of baptism (Gal 3:26–29; 4:5–6; see Rom 8:14–16), as it does at Jesus' baptism, where the voice from heaven announces Jesus' divine sonship. That baptism evoked such language is not surprising, since it marked and enacted entry into the family or household of believers, or, as an anthropologist would say, into a fictive kinship network. These two common features signal to many scholars the shaping of Mark 1:9–11 according to the practice and perspective of the Jesus movement (Bultmann 1963:250–52; Percy 1953:12–13; Mentz 1960:59–69; Chilton 1998:46; Neusner and Chilton 1998:62–66). While this deduction is not beyond dispute (Beasley-Murray 1962:62–63), we must accept the possibility that some or even many details of Jesus' ritual entry into a possession trance came from the Jesus movement and thus are historically inaccurate (Marcus 1995:513).

If the rite of baptism was a feature that entered the account in its transmission, some other rite may have induced Jesus' possession trance narrated in Mark 1:10–11. The range of activities that can induce entry into an altered state of consciousness is vast. Pieter Craffert mentions sleep deprivation and solitude as common triggers (1998:8). Dietmar Neufeld's research on Mark 3:21, in which Jesus has not eaten and is reported to be out of his mind, suggests that Jesus may have used fasting to prompt his possession trances. The Lukan baptismal scene indicates that prayer could trigger possession, although that detail entered the story late (3:21).

If a rite other than baptism originally triggered Jesus' possession by the Spirit, the alteration of the report so that it conformed to the baptismal rite of the Jesus movement is understandable, since the communities of that movement preserved the Gospel story. The interpretation of Mark mentioned above, an interpretation that identified baptism as a central concern of the Second Gospel, provides an obvious motivation for altering the story (Scroggs and Groff 1973; Standaert 1978:153–68, 498–540; McVann 1994). For if the Gospel writer intertwined community baptismal practice with a narrative about Jesus, what better place to begin the story than with Jesus' baptism?

Again, while a social-scientific analysis of Jesus' baptism in Mark supports the historical reliability of the basic narrative line, that is, of ritual having triggered Jesus' altered state of consciousness, details of the story may nonetheless be unreliable, including the specific ritual that reportedly triggered Jesus' possession trance.

Uncontrolled and Controlled Possession

While the ritual inducement of Jesus' possession trance is highly likely, complete certainty in the matter eludes us, for there is a possibility that the trance was not triggered by ritual at all. Anthropological studies of cultures in which possession takes place note occasions when entry into an alternate state of consciousness happens spontaneously, involuntarily, and suddenly, apart from any ritual (Goodman 1988a:36; Bourguignon 1976:39). Such spontaneity often occurs in an individual's initial experiences of possession (Jones 1976:47; Heusch 1981:158; Lewis 1989:50). Since Jesus' baptismal vision represents the first report we have of Jesus going into a possession trance, perhaps the Spirit fell upon Jesus spontaneously. Support for this surmise comes from the immediate context in Mark, at 1:12, where the Spirit seizes Jesus and casts him out into the desert (Davies 1995:63). No ritual prompts this occurrence of possession.

However the possession trance came about, the characterization of it may have been of concern to the Jesus movement. In first-century Judean society, as in other societies where possession is common, perceptions of it varied (Bourguignon 1968b:13–15; Goodman 1988b:21). Such societies prize possession when those possessed—spirit mediums and healers, for instance—bring vital information or the power to cure illness to the community. On the other hand, societies react negatively to possession when it results in insanity or sickness (Lewis 1989:48–49; Kiev 1968; Heusch 1981:155–58). In contemporary Moroccan society, for example, we find both desirable and undesirable possession: The Hamadsha, a society of trance healers, ritually induce their own possession by music, dance, and self-mutilation, an event the public views with approval and enthusiasm. In their role as trance healers, they are vital to the therapeutic system of Moroccan society, for, among other activities, they exorcise those possessed by devils or *jinn* (Crapanzano 1973:xi–xiv, 1–11, 133–68). In the world of the New Testament, positive possession meant being filled with the Holy Spirit, but those overtaken by an unclean spirit were negatively possessed. In Jesus' case, it was evidently important to present his possession as positive, because some were ready to identify Jesus' possession as a negative instance, that is, as demon possession (Mark 3:22).

The key to distinguishing good from bad possession is the presence or absence of ritual: negative spirit possession befalls individuals and is ritually unregulated; positive spirit possession happens to individuals or groups and is ritually controlled (Lee 1968:36–41; Pressel 1977:344–45; Jones 1976:35; Lewis 1989:48–49). The regulated triggering of spirit possession in willing subjects through ritual stands in stark contrast to sudden, involuntary, spontaneous possession, regarded by most cultures as potentially harmful and dangerous (Pressel 1977:345; Garrison 1977; Oesterreich 1966:131–375). Accordingly, proof that Jesus' possession was positive and not negative came from its association with ritual activity. Otherwise, it would have been hard to distinguish the demoniac from the person possessed by the Holy Spirit. As scholars of spirit possession in patriarchal societies have noted, men who do not fit in the social order are the ones typically who became negatively possessed (Wilson: 370–71). Jesus, like the demon possessed, matches this profile: he exhibited aberrant social behavior and lived outside a typical family or kinship network (homeless, unmarried, etc.). In Israelite culture it would have been crucial, therefore, to present Jesus' possession trance not as idiosyncratic or spontaneous but as culturally patterned and ritually structured. A report that Jesus' vision resulted from ritual anointing at the hand of a prophetlike figure would have counteracted any disparaging interpretation of Jesus' possession.

If Jesus entered an altered state of consciousness without ritual prompting, then apologetic motivations probably lie behind the introduction of baptism to the possession report. Because the charge that Jesus was demon-possessed was evidently a viable way of interpreting Jesus' possession (Mark 3:22), it would have been in the best interests of the Jesus movement to attribute the possession to ritual activity. Of course, it is possible that Jesus did undergo baptism and enter an altered state of consciousness as a consequence. Uncertainty in this matter means, however, that a social-scientific approach reaches the following conclusions regarding the historicity of the Markan account of Jesus' baptism: while Jesus' visionary experience is historically very likely, the baptismal rite (or any other rite) in conjunction with it is less so.

Conclusion

The implications of anthropological research on altered states of consciousness for historical Jesus research are clear: this widespread and well-attested phenomenon, which usually comes to expression in Mediterranean societies as possession trance, provides the basis for keeping Jesus' baptism and baptismal vision together and treating the whole episode as a historically plausible account. In a culture that allowed for possession trance, as Jesus' did, individuals could certainly have experienced what the Synoptic tradition reports. Biblical scholars must, therefore, reckon with the likelihood that Jesus of Nazareth had a vision like that reported in the Synoptics.

Native inhabitants of ancient Judea were socialized to discern the nature and cause of spirit-possession episodes. They distinguished good from bad possession: they knew about the coming of God's Spirit and the rituals that signaled it, and they knew about unclean demons taking over peoples' lives. Likewise, reports about spirit possession from that culture made the same distinction. So, in the case of the good news about Jesus, the ritual triggering of his possession— through baptism or anointing at the hand of the prophetlike John—marked it as unambiguously positive. In actuality, the spirit possession of Jesus may not have followed his baptism. He may have become possessed by some other means, or he may have undergone possession spontaneously. The possibility that an apologetic is at work in the Gospel report forces us to conclude that the baptism is historically less likely than the possession-induced vision.

Whatever scholars decide about the historical reliability of the baptism and vision account generally and of its various details, this study shows that the social sciences can advance the work of historical study and are in fact indispensable to that task. If a social-scientific approach cannot always contribute to determining the historicity of an account's specific features, it is essential for identifying events and their sequence that would have been plausible in the culture of first-century Judea. Making such a determination is useful because historical reconstruction of the ancient world relies heavily on plausibility and probability to do its work and to make its case. In this circumstance, therefore, the orientation of the social sciences toward patterns and scenarios instead of specificity and detail proves to be the historian's boon rather than bane.

Notes

Thanks go to the many colleagues who have been my conversation partners as I brought my research into its present form, particularly John J. Pilch, Pieter Craffert, Dietmar Neufeld, and Robin Scroggs, my Doktorvater. My home institution, Valparaiso University, also deserves thanks for supporting my trip to Tutzing, Germany, where I presented an earlier version of this chapter at the Evangelische Akademie.

1. For a similar orientation in Great Britain, see Dunn 1975.

2. This study also differs insignificantly from Robert R. Wilson's application of altered-state-of-consciousness and spirit-possession research to Israelite prophecy (1980:33–41).

Works Cited

Atkinson, Jane Monnig. 1992. "Shamanisms Today." ARA 21:307–30.
Beasley-Murray, George R. 1962. Baptism in the New Testament. New York: St. Martin's.
Boddy, Janice. 1994. "Spirit Possession Revisited: Beyond Instrumentality." ARA 23:407–34.
Borg, Marcus J. 1987. Jesus, a New Vision: Spirit, Culture, and the Life of Discipleship. San Francisco: Harper & Row.
———. 1994. Jesus in Contemporary Scholarship. Valley Forge, Pa.: Trinity Press International.

Bornkamm, Günther. 1960. *Jesus of Nazareth.* Translated by I. McLuskey, F. McLuskey, and J. M. Robinson. New York: Harper & Row.

Bourguignon, Erika. 1968a. *A Cross-Cultural Study of Dissociational States.* Final Report, RF Project 1652. Columbus: Ohio State University Research Foundation.

——. 1968b. "World Distribution and Patterns of Possession States." In *Trance and Possession States,* edited by R. Price, 3–34. Montreal: R. M. Bucke Memorial Society.

——. 1972. "Trance Dance." In *The Highest State of Consciousness,* edited by J. W. White, 331–43. Garden City, N.Y.: Doubleday.

——. 1973. "Introduction: A Framework for the Comparative Study of Altered States of Consciousness." In *Religion, Altered States of Consciousness, and Social Change,* edited by E. Bourguignon, 3–35. Columbus: Ohio State University Press.

——. 1976. *Possession.* Chandler & Sharp Cross-Cultural Themes. San Francisco: Chandler & Sharp.

——. 1979. *Psychological Anthropology: An Introduction to Human Nature and Cultural Differences.* New York: Holt, Rinehart & Winston.

Breech, James. 1983. *The Silence of Jesus: The Authentic Voice of the Historical Man.* Philadelphia: Fortress Press.

Brown, Raymond E. 1966. *The Gospel according to John I–XII.* AB 29. Garden City, N.Y.: Doubleday.

Bultmann, Rudolf. 1963. *The History of the Synoptic Tradition.* Rev. ed. Translated by J. Marsh. New York: Harper & Row.

Burkert, Walter. 1962. "GOHS: Zum griechischen 'Schamanismus.'" *Rheinisches Museum für Philologie* 105:36–55.

——. 1979. *Structure and History in Greek Mythology and Ritual.* Sather Classical Lectures 47. Berkeley: University of California Press.

Chilton, Bruce D. 1998. *Jesus' Baptism and Jesus' Healing: His Personal Practice of Spirituality.* Harrisburg, Pa.: Trinity Press International.

Craffert, Pieter F. 1998. "Jesus and the Shamanic Complex: Social Type and Historical Figure." Paper presented at the annual meeting of the Society of Biblical Literature, Orlando, Fla.

Crapanzano, Vincent. 1973. *The Hamadsha: A Study in Moroccan Ethnopsychiatry.* Berkeley: University of California Press.

Crossan, John Dominic. 1991. *The Historical Jesus: The Life of a Mediterranean Jewish Peasant.* San Francisco: HarperSanFrancisco.

Davies, Stevan L. 1995. *Jesus the Healer: Possession, Trance, and the Origins of Christianity.* New York: Continuum.

Dibelius, Martin. 1934. *From Tradition to Gospel.* Translated by B. L. Woolf. New York: Scribner.

Dodds, E. R. 1951. *The Greeks and the Irrational.* Sather Classical Lectures 25. Berkeley: University of California Press.

Donahue, John R. 1973. *Are You the Christ? The Trial Narrative in the Gospel of Mark.* SBLDS 10. Missoula, Mont.: Scholars.

Dunn, James D. G. 1975. *Jesus and the Spirit: A Study of the Religious and Charismatic Experience of Jesus and the First Christians as Reflected in the New Testament.* Philadelphia: Westminster.

Eliade, Mircea. 1961. "Recent Works on Shamanism: A Review Article." *HR* 1:152–86.

Esler, Philip F. 1992. "Glossolalia and the Admission of Gentiles into the Early Christian Community." *BTB* 22:136–42.

Firth, Raymond. 1964. *Essays on Social Organization and Values.* LSEMSA 32. London: Athlone.

———. 1967. *Tikopia Ritual and Belief.* Boston: Beacon.

Fitzmyer, Joseph A. 1981. *The Gospel according to Luke I–IX.* AB 28. Garden City, N.Y.: Doubleday.

Funk, Robert W., and the Jesus Seminar. 1998. *The Acts of Jesus: The Search for the Authentic Deeds of Jesus.* New York: HarperSanFrancisco.

Garrison, Vivian. 1977. "The 'Puerto Rican Syndrome' in Psychiatry and Espiritismo." In *Case Studies in Spirit Possession,* edited by V. Crapanzano and V. Garrison, 383–449. Contemporary Religious Movements. New York: Wiley.

Goodman, Felicitas D. 1988a. *Ecstasy, Ritual, and Alternate Reality: Religion in a Pluralistic World.* Bloomington: Indiana University Press.

———. 1988b. *How about Demons? Possession and Exorcism in the Modern World.* FTod. Bloomington: Indiana University Press.

Hartman, Lars. 1992. "Baptism." In *ABD* 1:583–94.

Heusch, Luc de. 1981. *Why Marry Her? Society and Symbolic Structures.* CSSA 33. New York: Cambridge University Press.

Hitchcock, John T. 1976. "Aspects of Bhujel Shamanism." In *Spirit Possession in the Nepal Himalayas,* edited by J. T. Hitchcock and R. L. Jones, 165–96. New Delhi: Vikas.

Hollenbach, Paul W. 1982. "The Conversion of Jesus: From Jesus the Baptizer to Jesus the Healer." In *ANRW* 2.25.1:196–219. Berlin: de Gruyter.

Holtzmann, Oscar. 1901. *Leben Jesu.* Tübingen: Mohr/Siebeck. Translated by J. T. Bealby and M. A. Canney under the title *The Life of Jesus.* London: A. & C. Black, 1904.

Iersel, Bas van. 1989. *Reading Mark.* Translated by W. H. Bisscheroux. Edinburgh: T. & T. Clark.

Jones, Rex L. 1976. "Limbu Spirit Possession and Shamanism." In *Spirit Possession in the Nepal Himalayas,* edited by J. T. Hitchcock and R. L. Jones, 29–55. New Delhi: Vikas.

Kelber, Werner H. 1976. "Conclusion: From Passion Narrative to Gospel." In Kelber, ed., 1976:153–80.

————, ed. 1976. *The Passion in Mark: Studies on Mark 14–16*. Philadelphia: Fortress Press.

Kiev, Ari. 1968. "The Psychotherapeutic Value of Spirit-Possession in Haiti." In *Trance and Possession States*, edited by R. Price, 143–48. Montreal: R. M. Bucke Memorial Society.

Krippner, Stanley. 1972. "Altered States of Consciousness." In *The Highest State of Consciousness*, edited by J. W. White, 1–5. Garden City, N.Y.: Doubleday.

Lambek, Michael. 1989. "From Disease to Discourse: Remarks on the Conceptualization of Trance and Spirit Possession." In *Altered States of Consciousness and Mental Health: A Cross-Cultural Perspective*, edited by C. A. Ward, 36–61. Cross-Cultural Research and Methodology Series. Newbury Park, Calif.: Sage.

Lee, Richard B. 1968. "The Sociology of !Kung Bushman Trance Performances." In *Trance and Possession States*, edited by R. Price, 34–54. Montreal: R. M. Bucke Memorial Society.

Lentzen-Deis, Fritzleo. 1970. *Die Taufe Jesus nach den Synoptikern: Literarkritische und Gattungsgeschichtliche Untersuchungen*. FTS 4. Frankfurt: Knecht.

Lewis, I. M. 1989. *Ecstatic Religion: A Study of Shamanism and Spirit Possession*. 2d ed. New York: Routledge.

Ludwig, Arnold M. 1968. "Altered States of Consciousness." In *Trance and Possession States*, edited by R. Price, 69–95. Montreal: R. M. Bucke Memorial Society.

Mack, Burton L. 1988. *A Myth of Innocence: Mark and Christian Origins*. Philadelphia: Fortress Press.

Malina, Bruce J. 1995. *On the Genre and Message of Revelation: Star Visions and Sky Journeys*. Peabody, Mass.: Hendrickson.

————. 1999. "Assessing the Historicity of Jesus' Walking on the Sea: Insights from Cross-Cultural Social Psychology." In *Authenticating the Activities of Jesus*, edited by B. D. Chilton and C. A. Evans, 351–71. NTTS 28/2. Leiden: Brill.

Mann, C. S. 1986. *The Gospel according to Mark*. AB 27. Garden City, N.Y.: Doubleday.

Marcus, Joel. 1995. "Jesus' Baptismal Vision." *NTS* 41:512–21.

Marxsen, Willi. 1969. *Mark the Evangelist: Studies on the Redaction History of the Gospel*. Translated by J. Boyce. Nashville: Abingdon.

McVann, Mark. 1994. "Reading Mark Ritually: Honor-Shame and the Ritual of Baptism." *Semeia* 67:179–98.

Meier, John P. 1991–94. *A Marginal Jew: Rethinking the Historical Jesus*. 2 vols. ABRL. New York: Doubleday.

Mentz, Hermann. 1960. *Taufe und Kirche in ihrem ursprünglichen Zusammenhang*. BETTA 29. Munich: Kaiser.

Neill, Stephen, and Tom Wright. 1988. *The Interpretation of the New Testament, 1861–1986*. 2d ed. New York: Oxford University Press.

Neufeld, Dietmar. 1996. "Eating, Ecstasy, and Exorcism (Mark 3:21)." *BTB* 26:152–62.

Neusner, Jacob, and Bruce Chilton. 1998. *Jewish-Christian Debates: God, Kingdom, Messiah.* Minneapolis: Fortress Press.

Oesterreich, Traugott K. 1966. *Possession, Demoniacal and Other: Among Primitive Races, in Antiquity, the Middle Ages, and Modern Times.* New Hyde Park, N.Y.: University Books.

Percy, Ernst. 1953. *Die Botschaft Jesus: Eine traditionskritische und exegetische Unter-suchung.* LUÅ 49/5. Lund: Gleerup.

Perrin, Norman. 1969. *What Is Redaction Criticism?* GBS. Philadelphia: Fortress Press.

Pilch, John J. 1993. "Visions in Revelation and Alternate Consciousness: A Perspective from Cultural Anthropology." *Listening* 28:231–44.

———. 1995. "The Transfiguration of Jesus: An Experience of Alternate Reality." In *Modelling Early Christianity: Social-Scientific Studies of the New Testament in Its Context,* edited by P. F. Esler, 47–64. New York and London: Routledge.

———. 1996. "Altered States of Consciousness: A 'Kitbashed' Model." *BTB* 26:133–38.

———. 1997. "Psychological and Psychoanalytical Approaches to Interpreting the Bible in Social-Scientific Context." *BTB* 27:112–16.

———. 1998a. "Appearances of the Risen Jesus in Cultural Context: Experiences of Alternate Reality." *BTB* 28:52–60.

———. 1998b. "A Window into the Biblical World: Walking on the Sea." *TBT* 36:117–23.

Pressel, Esther. 1977. "Negative Spirit Possession in Experienced Brazilian Umbanda Spirit Mediums." In *Case Studies in Spirit Possession,* edited by V. Crapanzano and V. Garrison, 333–64. Contemporary Religious Movements. New York: Wiley.

Reinhard, Johan. 1976. "Shamanism and Spirit Possession: The Definition Problem." In *Spirit Possession in the Nepal Himalayas,* edited by J. T. Hitchcock and R. L. Jones, 12–20. New Delhi: Vikas.

Remus, Harold. 1997. *Jesus as Healer.* Understanding Jesus Today. New York: Cambridge University Press.

Robbins, Vernon K. 1984. *Jesus the Teacher: A Socio-Rhetorical Interpretation of Mark.* Philadelphia: Fortress Press.

———. 1996. *The Tapestry of Early Christian Discourse: Rhetoric, Society, and Ideology.* New York: Routledge.

Rohde, Joachim. 1968. *Rediscovering the Teaching of the Evangelists.* Translated by D. M. Barton. NTL. Philadelphia: Westminster.

Sanders, E. P. 1993. *The Historical Figure of Jesus.* London: Penguin.

Scroggs, Robin, and Kent I. Groff. 1973. "Baptism in Mark: Dying and Rising with Christ." *JBL* 92:531–48.

Standaert, Benoit. 1978. *L'Évangile selon Marc: Composition et Genre Littéraire.* Lire la Bible 61. Nijmegen: Stichting Studentenpers.

Stock, Augustine. 1989. *The Method and Message of Mark.* Wilmington, Del.: Michael Glazier.

Strauss, David Friedrich. 1972. *The Life of Jesus Critically Examined.* Translated by G. Eliot. Lives of Jesus Series. Philadelphia: Fortress Press.

Tart, Charles T. 1980. "A Systems Approach to Altered States of Consciousness." In *The Psychobiology of Consciousness,* edited by J. M. Davidson and R. J. Davidson, 243–69. New York: Plenum.

Taylor, Vincent. 1966. *The Gospel according to St. Mark.* 2d ed. New York: St. Martin's.

Theissen, Gerd, and Annette Merz. 1998. *The Historical Jesus: A Comprehensive Guide.* Translated by J. Bowden. Minneapolis: Fortress Press.

Theissen, Gerd, and Dagmar Winter. 1997. *Die Kriterienfrage in der Jesusforschung: Vom Differenzkriterium zum Plausibilitätskriterium.* NTOA 34. Göttingen: Vandenhoeck & Ruprecht.

Townsend, Joan B. 1997. "Shamanism." In *Anthropology of Religion: A Handbook,* edited by S. D. Glazier, 429–69. Westport, Conn.: Greenwood.

Vaage, Leif E. 1996. "Bird-Watching at the Baptism of Jesus: Early Christian Mythmaking in Mark 1:9–11." In *Reimagining Christian Origins: A Colloquium Honoring Burton L. Mack,* edited by E. A. Castelli and H. Taussig, 280–94. Valley Forge, Pa.: Trinity Press International.

Vielhauer, Philipp. 1964. "Erwägungen zur Christologie des Markusevangelium." In *Zeit und Geschichte: Dankesgabe an Rudolf Bultmann zum 80. Geburtstag,* edited by E. Dinkler, 155–69. Tübingen: Mohr/Siebeck.

Walsh, Roger. 1989. "What Is a Shaman? Definition, Origin, and Distribution." *Journal of Transpersonal Psychology* 21:1–11.

———. 1993. "Phenomenological Mapping and Comparisons of Shamanic, Buddhist, Yogic, and Schizophrenic Experiences." *JAAR* 61:739–69.

Wilson, Peter J. 1967. "Status Ambiguity and Spirit Possession." *Man* 2:366–78.

Wilson, Robert R. 1980. *Prophecy and Society in Ancient Israel.* Philadelphia: Fortress Press.

Winkelman, Michael. 1997. "Altered States of Consciousness and Religious Behavior." In *Anthropology of Religion: A Handbook,* edited by S. D. Glazier, 393–428. Westport, Conn.: Greenwood.

9

The Politics of Exorcism

Santiago Guijarro

Accusations against Jesus are frequently mentioned not only in the writings of Christian apologists, but also in the earliest strata of the Gospel tradition (Q 7:34; Mark 2:7, 16; 14:64; Matt 27:63; Luke 23:2, 5; John 10:33, 36). These accusations are a privileged starting point for the study of the historical Jesus because of their embarrassing nature, and because of their close relationship to the trial and execution of Jesus, which are among the best-documented facts of his biography. In social-scientific analysis, accusations can be described as negative labels, while titles of prominence can be identified as positive labels. Both negative and positive labels are social weapons whose purpose is to identify and control behavior that is outside the normal. Models derived from the sociological study of deviant behavior and of societal reaction to it have been applied recently by English-speaking scholars in the study of some New Testament documents (Luke: Malina and Neyrey 1991a and Richter 1995; Matthew: Malina and Neyrey 1988; Paul's letters: Richter 1995), as well as in the study of the relationships between Judaism and Christianity in the first century (Sanders 1993; Barclay 1996). German-speaking scholars have used a particular aspect of this approach for the study of the historical Jesus (Ebertz 1987; Mödritzer 1994; Theissen and Merz 1996) and the early Christian movement (Theissen 1989 and 1995; Ebertz 1992).

Following the path opened by the above-mentioned studies, I use the social study of deviant behavior to understand the cluster of sayings known as the "Beelzebul Controversy" (Matt 12:22–30 par.). In this text segment we find one of the best-attested accusations against Jesus, followed by his reaction to it. Both the accusation and Jesus' reaction are the key to interpreting his exorcisms (Yates 1977:43), an activity widely attested in the Gospel tradition (Twelftree 1993).

Pre-Easter Traditions in the Beelzebul Controversy

In the Synoptic Gospels we find four versions of the Beelzebul controversy: two in Matthew (Matt 9:32–34; 12:22–30), one in Mark (Mark 3:22–27), and one in Luke (Luke 11:14–15, 17–23). The studies of the verbal agreements among these passages have produced different proposals about the sources the evangelists used. The common view is that behind these four versions were two independent sources (Mark and Q), which Matthew and Luke used for different purposes (Sellew 1988:99–100; Oakman 1988:112–13; Boring 1992:615–16; Humphries 1993; Kollmann 1996:174; see, in disagreement, Fuchs 1980: 109–14). In these two versions we find many agreements in content and order, as table 9.1 shows:

Independent Units	Q (Luke)	Mark
1. Narrative introduction (exorcism)	11:14	3:22
2. Accusation/s	11:15	3:23–26
3. Answer A (kingdom divided)	11:17–18	3:27
4. Answer B (by the Spirit of God)	11:19–20	3:27
5. Answer C (the strong one spoiled)	11:21–22	
6. Answer D (for or against me)	11:23	3:28–30
7. Conclusion A (behavior of unclear Spirits)	11:24–26	

Table 9.1: Comparison of the Two Sources

Especially striking is the coincidence in the order of accusation (2), answers A (3) and C (5), along with the fact that the accusation and the argument developed in answer A have a similar form in both versions. These coincidences suggest that Mark and Q might depend on an earlier (oral) version. Trunk assigns (2), (3), and (5) to this common oral tradition; (1), (4), and (6) to the compositional work of Q; and conclusion A (7) to Mark (1994:89–90). This proposal basically matches other attempts to explain the composition of the Q version (Schürmann 1992:574) and its final redaction according to ancient rhetorical techniques (Crossan 1983:184–91; Humphries 1993:127–39).

This compositional process shows that Mark, Q, and the traditions behind them rely on a wider oral tradition (Sellew 1988:96–98, 102–3), witnessed by the presence of one of these sayings in the *Gospel of Thomas* (*Gos. Thom.* 35; par. Mark 3:27 and Q 11:21–22). Of special interest for our purposes are the accusation and the first three answers; thus, we concentrate our analysis in these four units to find out whether they can be assigned to the historical Jesus.

The accusation (Matt 12:24; 9:34; Mark 3:22; Luke 11:15) contains, most probably, a charge against the historical Jesus (Twelftree 1993:106; Kollmann 1996:179). In addition to Mark and Q, the charge is attested in two other independent sources: three times in John (John 7:20 and 8:48–52: *daimonion echeis* "he has a demon and is mad"; John 10:20–21: *daimonion echei kai mainetai* "you have a demon"), and once in the Sermon on the Mount (Matt 10:25: *Beelzebul*). On the other hand, it is improbable that such an accusation could have been created by the early church. Finally, this accusation refers to one widely attested activity of Jesus (his exorcisms), an activity that was not denied even by his adversaries.

Jesus' first response (Matt 12:25–26; Mark 3:23–26; Luke 11:17–18a) has a tripartite form in Mark and Matthew, and a bipartite form in Luke. The tripartite structure is characteristic of oral discourse, and we can suppose that Matthew has preserved the earliest form of this tradition (Sellew 1988:103–4). It can also be said that this saying was originally independent of the preceding accusation, both because it does not answer it directly, and because of the different name given to the prince of demons— "Satan" rather than "Beelzebul." In spite of these observations, there is no reason to challenge the assignment of this saying to the historical Jesus. The response uses a proverb of everyday wisdom. But this proverb is part of an argumentative answer to the accusation of being allied to Satan. As we see later, this kind of argument fits the social and political situation in Galilee in the time of Jesus extremely well (Oakman 1988:114–22).

The second answer of Jesus (Matt 12:27–28; Luke 11:19–20) has been almost unanimously attributed to the historical Jesus (Meier 1994:404). Both its content and form make a strong case in favor of its historicity. The kingdom of God was a central concern in the preaching of Jesus. The saying relates the kingdom's initial coming with Jesus' exorcisms, something that the early church never did. Moreover, the use of antithetical parallelism is characteristic of Jesus, and so is the use of *ekballō* ("cast out") in the context of exorcisms (Twelftree 1993:110; Kollmann 1996:182).

The third answer (Matt 12:29; Mark 3:27; Luke 11:21–22; *Gos. Thom.* 35), independently attested in the *Gospel of Thomas*, was included in the sayings cluster in the oral tradition, because we find it in Mark and in Q. Its similarity to the saying about the defeat of Satan (Q 10:18) speaks in favor of its historicity and of its relationship to the controversy concerning Jesus' exorcisms (Kollmann 1996:189–95; see also the arguments of Twelftree 1993:111–12). In both sayings, Jesus understands his mission as a struggle against Satan in order to advance the coming of the kingdom of God.

As a result of the previous analysis, we may conclude that Jesus was accused of casting out demons by the power of Beelzebul, the prince of demons, and that he answered this negative label with at least three different arguments (answers A, B, and C). From these answers, we can discern the meaning he assigned to his exorcisms. The next step is to develop a scenario that would help us understand the societal reaction that provoked the accusation against Jesus.

Societal Reaction to the Exorcisms of Jesus

The activity of Jesus as an exorcist provoked different societal reactions. Q's version of the Beelzebul controversy reports two reactions that we find frequently in the Gospels: "[T]he people were amazed, but some of them said: he casts out demons by the power of Beelzebul, the prince of demons" (Q 11:14b-15). The first reaction implies a positive interpretation of the reported exorcism, whereas the second interprets Jesus' behavior as deviant. The negative interpretation of Jesus' exorcisms is characteristic of the demonic perspective that does not differentiate very much among types of deviants (Pfohl 1985:25). Use of the sociological study of deviants can help us identify more precisely the meaning of this societal reaction and the real causes of this accusation. Among the different approaches to the study of deviants, we use the labeling theory developed by symbolic interactionists (Lemert 1967:14-22; Thio 1998:34-38). According to this perspective, public accusations are negative labels used to control behavior that some individual(s) have interpreted as negative or dangerous to society at large, or to a group within it.

Labeling Deviants

Negative labels are attached to negative deviant behavior, that is, to "vagrant forms of human activity, moving outside the more orderly currents of social life" (Erikson 1962:307). The process by which these negative labels are ascribed to such a behavior is called stigmatization, and comprises the "attaching of visible signs of moral inferiority to persons, such as invidious labels, marks, brands, or publicly disseminated information" (Lemert 1967:65). Labeling a person deviant is then a complex social process "by which the members of a group, community, or society (1) interpret behavior as deviant, (2) define persons who so behave as a certain kind of deviant, and (3) accord them the treatment considered appropriate to such deviants" (Kitsuse 1962:248). These basic definitions of labeling, deviance, and the labeling process raise questions about the social nature of deviance that can be useful in interpreting the negative reaction to the exorcisms of Jesus.

First, it must be said that deviance is a socially assessed phenomenon. What is considered deviant depends on a socially shared interpretation, so that "the deviant is one to whom that label has successfully been applied; deviant behavior is behavior that people so label" (Becker 1963:9). This means that different cultures may have different standards for interpreting and defining deviant behavior. The reason for the cultural nature of deviance is that deviant behavior can only be defined and enforced by reference to the values and rules of a given society (Becker 1963:129–34; Lemert 1967:31–32). Values and rules are related to the maintenance of social boundaries, and, for that reason, "transactions taking place between deviant persons on the one side and agencies of control on the other are boundary-maintaining mechanisms" (Erikson 1962:309–10). The values and boundaries of a society are then the framework in which deviant behavior can be understood as such. Consequently, the deviant nature of the exorcisms of Jesus and the societal reaction to them can only be understood in the context of the culture in which he and his accusers lived.

Some common traits of the Mediterranean culture affect the definition of deviance within it. First are the core values of honor and shame, which reveal a deep concern for the opinion of other people. The importance of public opinion was such that an intense process of social control was operating continuously (Malina and Neyrey 1991c:25–46). Related to these core values is the dyadic perception of the self, by which a person understands himself or herself as part of a group, particularly the kinship group. Deviance is perceived as a characteristic affecting the honor of the group, not just the individual (Malina and Neyrey 1991b:76–80). The strong-group, collectivistic quality of that society is likewise important. This quality makes social boundaries more defined and at the same time more dangerous. Such a society placed no value on innovation. For that reason, innovative behavior was considered nonconformist, and only fully conforming role performance was tolerated (Coser 1962:123–33).

Structural patterns in the deviance process and in societal reaction to it are common to different cultures. One of these is the purpose of the deviance process. The deviance process entails a degradation ceremony that effects a transformation of identity, so that "the other person becomes in the eyes of his condemners literally a different and new person. It is not that the new attributes are added to the old 'nucleus.' He is not changed, he is reconstituted. . . . the former identity stands as accidental; the new identity is the 'basic reality.' . . . The public denunciation effects such a transformation of essence," and "through the interpretive work . . . the denounced person becomes in the eyes of the witnesses a different person" (Garfinkel 1956:421–22). To be successful, the degradation ceremony must include features, such as the identification of the denouncer as a public person, whose task is the defense of suprapersonal (socially shared) values (Garfinkel 1956:422–23). Malina and Neyrey have shown that these conditions existed in the deviant career of Jesus (1988:45–46). Hence the public denunciation of Jesus can be considered a social sanction, whose purpose "is not a simple act of censure," but "a sharp rite of transition at once moving him out of his normal position in society and transferring him into a distinct deviant role" (Erikson 1962:311).

Locating the accusation of casting out demons by the power of Beelzebul within this scenario can help identify the purpose of Jesus' accusers and the nature of this accusation. Being labeled a deviant means not only being accused as a rule breaker, but receiving a deviant ontological status, which tends to make a person an outsider and to exile that person from the group. By accusing Jesus, his accusers try to assign him a new identity, a new self of a negative kind. They do this in order to neutralize his activity. Jesus' activity is perceived as negative, either dangerous for society as a whole or for the group that initiated the deviance process. The scenario suggested here has a heuristic value, because it helps ask new questions: Why were the exorcisms of Jesus so important and dangerous for his accusers? Who were the accusers? What social values or boundaries were violated in casting out demons? Only by answering these questions can we find what is behind the accusation of casting out demons by the power of Beelzebul.

The Threat of Exorcisms

The importance accusers attached to Jesus' exorcisms is striking for us, because we do not experience demon possession and exorcism in the same way as persons in antiquity. Nevertheless, close scrutiny of the Gospel tradition reveals that the exorcisms were an essential part of Jesus' activity. Some years ago, Hollenbach called attention to this fact. He noted that (a) "quantitatively the exorcisms played a large role in Jesus' career"; (b) "qualitatively . . . exorcisms figure prominently in Jesus' own understanding of his career"; and (c) "it was in connection with this particular activity that he drew upon himself the wrath of all the important public authorities of his time" (1981:568–69). In his challenging and groundbreaking study, Hollenbach proposed an interpretation of demon possession and exorcism that threw new light on the reaction provoked by the exorcisms of Jesus.

Some anthropological studies led him to discover a close relationship between demon possession and social tensions, such as "class antagonisms rooted in economic exploitation, conflicts between traditions where revered traditions are eroded, colonial domination and revolution" (Hollenbach 1981:573; see also Pfohl 1985:38–40 and Sanders 1993:133–35). Hollenbach rightly saw these instances as relevant analogies because the circumstances described are very similar to those of Israel in the time of Jesus (see, in disagreement, Davies 1995:78–81). That situation finally exploded in the Judeo-Roman war of 66–70 C.E. This structural analogy allowed Hollenbach to interpret the situation of Roman Palestine in the light of contexts in which demon possession is frequent. In these contexts, "mental illness can be seen as a socially acceptable form of oblique protest against, or escape from oppressions," and "some types of mental disorders became . . . 'cures' for, as well as symptoms of social conflict" (575). The kinds of possession described "suggest the possibility that Palestinian possession performed a similar function and occurred within a similar social and political pattern. It may have functioned as a 'fix' for people who saw no other way to cope with the horrendous social and political conditions in which they found their lot cast" (576).

Demon possession was a socially accepted way to cope with tensions, because it allowed those possessed to do and say what they could not do or say as a sane person. In the world of Jesus were two social domains: the public (political) and the private (familial), and in both were people under constraints of abusive authority. In the kinship context, persons subject to the authority of the paterfamilias, and especially women, were more likely to recur to demon possession to soften the tensions of patriarchal authority (Mark 7:24–30; 9:14–27). In the public arena, on the other hand, we are more likely to find male adults, as we do in the exorcism performed by Jesus in the synagogue of Capernaum (Mark 1:23–28), and with the Gerasene demoniac (Mark 5:1–20). Davies has stressed the importance of the exorcisms of Jesus in the kinship sphere (1995:85–86), but the public accusations against him must have been provoked by the exorcisms effected by Jesus in public.

This leads to the question of who were Jesus' accusers. Although the accusers identified in individual Gospel documents may mirror the situation of the communities for whom those documents were composed, as with the "Pharisees" of Matthew (Matt 9:34; 12:34), there are reasons for identifying them with the dominant elite of Roman Galilee or their retainers (the scribes of Mark 3:22). Accusations of madness, witchcraft, and possession are used frequently by the elites as a means of social control, especially in times of social unrest (Hollenbach 1981:577). The tradition preserved in Luke 13:31–33, which may be traced back to a saying of Jesus (Kollmann 1996:187–89), shows the hostility of Herod Antipas against Jesus. It also demonstrates that the activity for which Herod sought Jesus were his exorcisms: "Go and say to that fox: Behold, I cast out demons and perform cures today and tomorrow, and on the third day I will finish my task, but it is necessary for me to keep walking today, tomorrow, and the next day, because a prophet cannot be killed outside Jerusalem.'" An intriguing relationship among casting out demons, the hostility of Herod, and death as a prophet in Jerusalem appears in this saying of Jesus. This relationship stresses the links between the accusations against Jesus and his trial and crucifixion.

The exorcisms of Jesus were a threat first to the governing elite of Galilee and, subsequently, to the Judean elite. By interpreting the casting out of demons as a sign of the coming kingdom of God, and by making his exorcisms part of his strategy for restoring Israelite integrity, Jesus threatened the stability of the social order. The puzzling reaction of his own family, affected by gossip claiming Jesus was demon possessed (Mark 3:21; see Neufeld 1992), as well as the reaction of the townspeople after the exorcism of the Gerasene demoniac (the townspeople ask Jesus to leave their region [Mark 5:17]), reveal that his exorcisms were perceived by ordinary people as dangerous. Those reactions must be understood in connection with the accusation of the scribes (Mark 3:22) and with Herod's persecution (Luke 13:31–33). All these instances mirror the threatening consequences of Jesus' restorative activity, which had disruptive effects for the stabilized social order.

Jesus' responses to the accusation of casting out demons by the power of Beelzebul contain heavy political overtones. These responses point to how the exorcisms of Jesus were perceived by the political elite of Israel. In them, Jesus talks about a divided kingdom (Q 11:17–19), and says that the casting out of demons is part of hostilities against God's enemies and a sign of God's coming kingdom (Q 11:20). Hence his exorcisms must be interpreted as a victory over the strong man and his house (Mark 3:27).

Douglas Oakman has tried to find out "why have all of these words been attracted to this particular context?" (1988:114). He suggests that they should be located in a peasant context and in a political situation in which these statements lived on orally. According to Oakman, "[T]he conflict surrounding Beelzebul . . . underscores the political and economic dimension of demon possession. The 'demons' that the 'reign of God' is colliding with are not just 'spooks' and psychoses. There is in view here economic disprivilege, malnutrition, endemic violence, and the destruction of rural families" (115).

There may be other complementary explanations to the hostility raised by the exorcisms of Jesus, but all can be understood as arguments that underscore the exorcisms' threatening nature for the governing elite. The accusation of possession was commonly leveled at exorcists in the ancient world as well as in many preindustrial societies (Eitrem 1966:49ff.; Kolenkow 1976). Placed in their original peasant context and in the political situation of first-century Galilee, the exorcisms of Jesus reveal subversive connotations that might have been lost, in part, as his literate followers recorded his words and deeds in a new situation, in which exorcisms had different connotations (Oakman 1988:109–10). Some of these connotations can be perceived in the responses of Jesus to his accusers.

Jesus' Response to His Accusers

The analysis of the deviance process from the perspective of societal reaction permits only a partial view. Societal reaction was the focus of labeling theorists in the 1960s. But in the early 1970s, some scholars proposed a more comprehensive approach to the study of deviance, and began to consider the point of view of those labeled deviants (Mankoff 1971; Rogers and Buffalo 1974; Lipp 1977; Warren 1980). Our purpose is to unveil this point of view using two complementary perspectives: the first provided by studies of Mediterranean anthropology, and the second by a typology intended to study the strategies that those labeled deviants use to fight back.

Challenge and Riposte

The point of view of the accused is important, because it helps us understand the meaning he or she attaches to deviant behavior. This is precisely what we find in the response of Jesus to his accusers. To adequately understand Jesus' response, we need to know that, in this cultural context, both accusation and response had a particular meaning. Jesus lived in an honor culture, in which an accusation was perceived not only as an act of aggression, but also as an honor challenge. An honor challenge cannot remain unanswered, because when the person challenged does not respond, personal reputation in the eyes of the public is lost. The response of Jesus to his accusers must be understood in the challenge-and-riposte pattern characteristic of Mediterranean culture (Malina and Neyrey 1991c:29–32). In this context, his response appears as a defense of his honor and, at the same time, as an explanation of the meaning of his exorcisms.

Whatever the precise wording of the pre-Easter tradition of Jesus' first answer, the reasoning behind it is clear: the accusation is inconsistent, because Beelzebul cannot act against himself (Matt 12:25–26 par.). Jesus resorts to popular wisdom, recalling that a divided kingdom and a divided house (an extended family, most probably the ruler's family) cannot continue to exist. In the ancient world, political and familial solidarity were so highly valued that it was easy to understand Jesus' argument and its conclusion: Jesus does not belong to Satan's *basileia* ("kingdom"; see also Q 4:5–8). Consequently, his accusers lose face in the public arena and are dishonored by his wise answer. To the original audience of the Gospels, this was so evident that the author does not need to spell it out.

In the second saying (Matt 12:27–28 par.), Jesus' response goes further by making his reaction against his accusers explicit. More important, it provides an alternative explanation for his purported deviance. The verbal coincidences with the accusation (*en Beelzebul . . . ekballein . . . ta daimonia*; by Beelzebul to cast out . . . demons") makes this second response a more direct answer. The saying begins with an ad hominem argument. This argument is clear if the sons of Jesus' accusers are his own disciples. If Jesus casts out demons by the power of Beelzebul, the same can be said of them, and so the shame/deviance that his accusers want to cast on him reverts to them. But Jesus then offers a different explanation of his exorcisms: he belongs to the *basileia* of God; he is acting not on behalf of the prince of demons, but of the Spirit of God; his exorcisms reveal not an alliance with Satan, but war against him and the victory over him.

The third answer (Matt 12:29 par.) is linked to the first by the catchword "house" (*oikia*). It offers a complementary explanation: Jesus does not belong to the house of Beelzebul, but attacks that house. The reign of Satan is not divided, but under siege. The image behind this saying is that of a ruler's house attacked by a rival to the throne, an image that would have been familiar to Jesus' audience (Oakman 1988:114–17). The proverb, which may be a piece of popular wisdom, recalls another saying of Jesus that declares victory over Satan (Q 10:18). Some have seen in this saying an early account of the vision of Jesus' call by God (Theissen and Merz 1998:211–12). This perspective helps to explain the importance of the exorcisms in his public activity, and the context of his answer.

Following the challenge-riposte pattern characteristic of Mediterranean public interaction, Jesus accepts the challenge and responds to it by defeating his accusers. In so doing, he wins honor in the eyes of the public. But he does even more, since, by his responses and by the way in which he reacts to the labels tossed at him, he reveals the meaning that he attached to the acts his accusers labeled deviant. To find the meaning of Jesus' reactions, we have to place them in the context of other possible reactions, and, for that, we use the typology proposed by Rogers and Buffalo.

Strategies for Fighting Back

J. W. Rogers and M. D. Buffalo have proposed a typology to describe and classify different modes of adaptation to a deviant label. In their proposal, modes are classified according their tactical and societal relationships (1974:105–14). The tactical relationship refers to "the deviant maneuvering vis-à-vis his/her labelers in terms of attitude and action," whereas societal reaction represents the "thrust emerging from the deviant's tactic encountering societal context" (106). The authors consider three possible reactions on the part of the labeled person—assent, rejection, and exchange—and three possible societal reactions to each one of these—magnification, manipulation, and obliteration. Combining those different possibilities, in figure 9.1 they propose nine modes of adaptation to a deviant label.

	Magnification	Manipulation	Obliteration
Assent	Acquiescence	Channeling	Reinterpretation
Rejection	Repudiation	Evasion	Redefinition
Exchange	Fight	Modification	Alteration

Figure 9.2: Rogers and Buffalo's (1974) modes of adaptation to "deviant" label

In terms of tactical relationship, Jesus' three responses can be classified under rejection, because, in all, Jesus rejects the accusation of alliance with Beelzebul. But in each response we find different connotations that allow us to identify them with the three types of rejection considered in the typology.

Repudiation is the outcome when an accused deviant rejects an accusation that is coupled with societal magnification. Such rejection might be described as overt rejection of the deviant label through such claims as, "It isn't so" (Rogers and Buffalo 1974:107). The public nature of this kind of resistance to stigmatization requires considerable determination on the part of the accused. It also requires resources and power to be successful, because such a reaction effects societal magnification of the label. Jesus' answer A (kingdom divided) can be assigned to this category. His argument, based on comparisons of the divided kingdom and family, has the effect of publicly rejecting the accusation: The accusation is not true, Jesus states, because it is impossible for Satan to be against himself. This answer, like the rest, is uttered in public and, through the open rejection, magnifies the accusation.

The second mode of rejection is evasion. Evasion is the outcome when an accused deviant rejects an accusation that is coupled with societal manipulation. This mode of rejection "refers primarily to verbal manipulation as a means of defense against the imputation of deviance. The person in response rejects the label, which is manipulated to deflect to negative impact through a counter-ploy based perhaps on a differing view of reality, involving society" (Rogers and Buffalo 1974:110). Malina and Neyrey have developed this mode of reaction, including techniques of neutralization, such as: (a) denial of responsibility; (b) denial of injury; (c) denial of victim; (d) condemning the condemners; and (e) appeal to higher loyalties (1988:63–65). Most of these traits can be found in answer B ("by the Spirit of God"). Through verbal manipulation ("by Beelzebul"/"by the Spirit of God"), Jesus rejects the label of alliance with Beelzebul, but he does it in such a way that societal manipulation takes place. He begins by accusing his accusers, announcing that their own sons will be their judges. Then he appeals to a higher loyalty, ascribing his exorcisms to the power of the Spirit of God. In so doing, he implicitly denies his responsibility, and also casts his exorcisms in a positive light in which there are no victims and no injuries. This societal manipulation of the label achieves successful neutralization and, at the same time, offers a new justification of Jesus' exorcisms.

The third possible kind of rejection is redefinition. Redefinition is the outcome when an accused deviant rejects an accusation that is coupled with societal obliteration. The definitional change "is effected when that which was previously called deviant comes to be called normative. The characteristic or behavior remains the same, but society has altered its view and redefined the deviant behavior in positive terms of approval" (Rogers and Buffalo 1974:113). Redefinition is implied in answer C ("the strong one spoiled"). In this response, Jesus not only offers a different explanation of his exorcisms (as in answer B), but proposes this behavior as normative. Jesus, in fact, proposed this activity to his followers as normative behavior. They were sent by him to cast out demons (Mark 6:7), and this seems to have been his primary activity, according to the two more ancient reports of the mission charge (Q 10:17; Mark 6:13). In this core group, the meaning of Jesus' exorcisms was successfully changed; we can presuppose that this point of view was shared by those who interpreted his exorcisms in approving terms (Q 11:14b).

The identification of Jesus' three answers with the three kinds of rejection proposed in the Rogers and Buffalo typology is not an end in itself. As the authors warn, "[C]ells in a typology . . . represent only a transitional phase of theoretical endeavor," and the typology itself "implies entrances, motion within, and exits" (114). This can be also argued of our previous assignment of Jesus' different sayings. Answer A ("kingdom divided"), for example, contains an implicit condemnation of condemners (shaming them in public), which is characteristic of evasion. Answer B ("by the Spirit of God") includes some traits of redefinition, because Jesus tries to obliterate the accusation, offering an alternate explanation. Finally, in answer C ("the strong one despoiled"), one can discern features of evasion.

In any case, the basic defensive strategy of Jesus was to reject the label applied to him. In his different reactions, he did not deny his exorcisms. What he did deny was the way in which his accusers interpreted these exorcisms and the labels attached to him because of this interpretation. This is a characteristic feature of behavior that seeks political change. In fact, two of the strategies that we have identified in the sayings of Jesus (repudiation and redefinition) figure, according to Rogers and Buffalo, among the three more likely adaptations for political action labeled deviant (115). This fits strikingly well with the content of the responses, and also with the political overtones of Jesus' exorcisms, as already noted. The exorcisms of Jesus had political consequences. He and his accusers knew it. But while his accusers interpreted the exorcisms as a threat to the political order, Jesus considered them a sign of the reign of God. The main purpose of Jesus' responses was not to clarify what kind of an exorcist he was, but to make clear the cosmic and political implications of his exorcisms. Among such implications, the social restoration of the victims of social and economic tensions had a prominent place.

Contributions to the Study of the Historical Jesus

The foregoing discussion of societal reaction to the exorcisms of Jesus and of his own strategies to counter this reaction, as reflected in the Beelzebul Controversy, suggests reflections that can be helpful for the study of the historical Jesus.

The use of social studies of deviant behavior as a cognitive and heuristic tool for interpreting the deviance process of Jesus can help clarify in which sense Jesus was considered a "marginal" person. The Gospels contain a demonic interpretation of Jesus' deviance, but this kind of interpretation does not explore the historical causes and consequences. When we analyze the data of the Gospels with the tools developed for the social study of deviant behavior, new questions arise. The historical causes and consequences of Jesus' deviant activity appear more clearly.

The social study of deviant behavior has helped us discover that the accusation of possession by Beelzebul belongs to a broader strategy, whose purpose was to discredit Jesus, to declare him an outsider in his society, and to assign him a new identity. These features have raised a new set of questions, which have led us to a more concrete contextualization of Jesus' exorcisms. The analogy of the situation in first-century Palestine with that of other societies in which demon possession is frequent has been the clue to discovering that Jesus' exorcisms were perceived as threatening to the governing elite and their retainers. By casting out the demons and restoring people to society, Jesus threatened a social order in which demon possession was an escape valve. The puzzling reaction to his exorcisms from his own family, as well as from the people, the scribes, and Herod Antipas, suggests that the social reintegration of demoniacs had societal and political connotations for Jesus and for his contemporaries that are opaque to us.

The responses of Jesus to the accusation of casting out demons by Beelzebul reveal that he never accepted this interpretation. He fought it in all possible ways, trying to unveil the real meaning and purpose of his exorcisms. Coherent with his culture's perspective on nature that included nonvisible, personlike beings to explain certain events, Jesus explained that he was possessed by the Spirit of God, and that, in his dealings with those possessed by demons, he was engaged in a cosmic war against Satan. Victory over Satan was the sign of the dawning of God's rule. The sign of the coming of God's reign was the restoration to society of those at the margins. Jesus called them to be part of a new family, together with him and his followers (Mark 3:31–35; 10:28–30), and this was highly disruptive.

Works Cited

Barclay, J. M. G. 1996. *Jews in Mediterranean Diaspora from Alexander to Troyan* (323 B.C.E.–117 C.E.). Edinburgh: T & T Clark.

Becker, Howard Saul. 1963. *Outsiders: Studies in the Sociology of Deviance*. New York: Free Press.

Boring, M. Eugene. 1992. "The Synoptic Problem: 'Minor' Agreements and the Beelzebul Pericope." In *The Four Gospels 1992: Festschrift Frans Neirynck*, edited by F. van Segbroeck et al., 587–619. BETL 100. Leuven: Leuven University Press.

Coser, L. A. 1962. "Some Functions of Deviant Behavior and Normative Flexibility." In *Continuities in the Study of Social Conflicts*. New York: Free Press. 111–33.

Crossan, John Dominic. 1983. *In Fragments: The Aphorisms of Jesus*. San Francisco: Harper & Row.

Davies, Stevan L. 1995. *Jesus the Healer: Possession, Trance, and the Origins of Christianity*. New York: Continuum.

Ebertz, Michael N. 1987. *Das Charisma des Gekreuzigten: Zur Soziologie der Jesubewegung*. WUNT 45. Tübingen: Mohr/Siebeck.

————. 1992. "Le stigmate du mouvement charismatique autour de Jesus de Nazareth." *Social Compass* 39:255–73.

Eitrem, S. 1966. *Some Notes on the Demonology in the New Testament.* 2d ed. Symbolae Osloenses 20. Oslo: Brøgger.

Erikson, Kai T. 1962. "Notes on the Sociology of Deviance." *SocProb* 9:307–14.

Fuchs, Albert. 1980. *Die Entwicklung der Beelzebulkontroverse bei den Synoptikern: Traditionsgeschichtliche und redaktionsgeschichtliche Untersuchung von Mk 3,22–27 und Parallelen, verbunden mit der Rückfrage nach Jesus.* SNTSU B/5. Linz: Studien zum Neuen Testament und seiner Umwelt.

Garfinkel, Harold. 1956. "Conditions of Successful Degradation Ceremonies." *AJS* 61:420–24.

Hollenbach, Paul W. 1981. "Jesus, Demoniacs, and Public Authorities: A Socio-Historical Study." *JAAR* 49:561–88.

Humphries, Michael L. 1993. "The Kingdom of God in the Q Version of the Beelzebul Controversy." *Forum* 9:121–50.

Katz, J. 1972. "Deviance, Charisma, and Rule-Defined Behavior." *SocProb* 20:186–202.

Kitsuse, John I. 1962. "Societal Reaction to Deviant Behavior: Problems of Theory and Method." *SocProb* 9:247–56.

Kolenkow, A. B. 1976. "A Problem of Power: How Miracle Doers Counter Charges of Magic in the Hellenistic World." In *SBLSP 1976*, 105–10. Missoula, Mont: Scholars.

Kollmann, Bernd. 1996. *Jesus und die Christen als Wundertäter.* FRLANT 170. Göttingen: Vandenhoeck & Ruprecht.

Lemert, Edwin M. 1967. *Human Deviance: Social Problems and Social Control.* Englewood Cliffs, N.J.: Prentice-Hall.

Lipp, Wolfgang. 1977. "Charisma—Social Deviation, Leadership, and Cultural Change." *The Annual Review of the Social Sciences of Religion* 1:59–77.

Malina, Bruce J., and Jerome H. Neyrey. 1988. *Calling Jesus Names: The Social Value of Labels in Matthew.* Sonoma, Calif.: Polebridge.

————. 1991a. "Conflict in Luke-Acts: Labeling and Deviance Theory." In *The Social World of Luke-Acts: Models for Interpretation*, edited by J. H. Neyrey, 97–122. Peabody, Mass.: Hendrickson.

————. 1991b. "First-Century Personality: Dyadic, Not Individual." In *The Social World of Luke-Acts: Models for Interpretation*, edited by J. H. Neyrey, 67–96. Peabody, Mass.: Hendrickson.

————. 1991c. "Honor and Shame: Pivotal Values of the Mediterranean World." In *The Social World of Luke-Acts: Models for Interpretation*, edited by J. H. Neyrey, 25–65. Peabody, Mass.: Hendrickson.

Mankoff, Milton. 1971. "Societal Reaction and Career Deviance: A Critical Analysis." *SocQ* 12:204–18.

Meier, John P. 1994. A *Marginal Jew: Rethinking the Historical Jesus.* Vol. 2: *Mentor, Message, and Miracles.* ABRL. New York: Doubleday.

Mödritzer, Helmut. 1994. *Stigma und Charisma im Neuen Testament und seiner Umwelt.* NTOA 28. Göttingen: Vandenhoeck & Ruprecht.

Neufeld, Dietmar. 1996. "Eating, Ecstasy, and Expression (Mark 3:21)." *BTB* 26:152-62.

Oakman, Douglas E. 1988. "Rulers' Houses, Thieves, and Usurpers: The Beelzebul Pericope." *Forum* 4, no. 3:109–23.

Pfohl, Stephen. 1985. *Images of Deviance and Social Control: A Sociological History.* New York: McGraw-Hill. 2d ed., 1994.

Richter, Philip. 1995. "Social-Scientific Criticism of the New Testament: An Appraisal and Extended Example." In *Approaches to New Testament Study,* edited by S. E. Porter and D. Tombs, 266–309. JSNTSup 120. Sheffield: Sheffield Academic.

Rogers, J. W., and M. D. Buffalo. 1974. "Fighting Back: Nine Modes of Adaptation to a Deviant Label." *SocProb* 22:101–18.

Sanders, Jack T. 1993. *Schismatics, Sectarians, Dissidents, Deviants: The First Hundred Years of Jewish-Christian Relations.* Valley Forge, Pa.: Trinity Press International.

Schürmann, Heinz. 1992. "QLuke 11,14–36 kompositionsgeschichtlich gefragt." In *The Four Gospels 1992: Festschrift Frans Neirynck,* edited by F. van Segbroeck et al., 563–86. BETL 100. Leuven: Leuven University Press.

Sellew, Philip. 1988. "Beelzebul in Mark 3: Dialogue Story or Sayings Cluster?" *Forum* 4:93–108.

Theissen, Gerd. 1989. "Jesusbewegung als charismatische Wertrevolution." *NTS* 35:343–60.

———. 1995. "Jünger als Gewalttäter (Matt 11,12f.; Luke 16,16) Der Stürmerspruch als Selbstigmatisierung einer Minorität." In *Mighty Minorities? Minorities in Early Christianity, Positions and Strategies: Essays in Honor of Jacob Jervell,* edited by D. Hellholm, H. Moxnes, and T. K. Seim, 183–200. Oslo: Scandinavian University Press.

Theissen, Gerd, and Annette Merz. 1998. *The Historical Jesus: A Comprehensive Guide.* Translated by J. Bowden. Minneapolis: Fortress Press.

Thio, Alex. 1998. *Deviant Behavior.* 5th ed. New York: Longman.

Trunk, Dieter. 1994. *Der mesianische Heiler: Eine redaktions-und religions-geschichtliche Studie zu den Exorzismen in Matthäusevangelium.* Herders biblische Studien 3. Freiburg: Herder.

Twelftree, Graham H. 1993. *Jesus, the Exorcist: A Contribution to the Study of the Historical Jesus.* WUNT 2/54. Tübingen: Mohr/Siebeck.

Warren, Carol A. B. 1980. "Destigmatization of Identity: From Deviant to Charismatic." *Qualitative Sociology* 3:59–72.

Yates, Roy. 1977. "Jesus and the Demonic in the Synoptic Gospels." *ITQ* 44:39–57.

10

The Historical Jesus
and Honor Reversal at the Table

S. Scott Bartchy

One distinctive feature of the historical Jesus' public life was his practice of a radically inclusive, status-leveling, and honor-sharing fellowship at table as a central strategy in his announcement and redefinition of the in-breaking ruling of Israel's God. In so doing, Jesus of Nazareth presented a living parable and model of his vision of a renewed Israel. His actions profoundly challenged the inherent exclusivism and status consciousness sustained by the prevailing cultural values and social codes. In this essay, I argue that by deed and word the historical Jesus sought to undermine traditional meal practices that provided easy opportunities for males in his culture to seek honor and display their acquired or ascribed honor.

Jesus' vision of human relationships submitted to the rule of God required a reversal of expectations regarding the giving and receiving of honor.

The Significance of Shared Meals

It would be difficult to overestimate the importance of table fellowship for the cultures of the Mediterranean basin in the first century of our era. Mealtimes were laden with meanings that greatly exceeded individuals' consumption of food. Biblical exegetes owe a debt of gratitude to cultural anthropologists who have discerned that eating practices encode far-reaching messages about appropriate patterns of social relations among participants. In the words of conceptual pathbreaker Mary Douglas: "The message is about different degrees of hierarchy, inclusion and exclusion, boundaries and transactions across the boundaries" (1972:61).

Thus when we seek to enter the cultural and social world of Jesus and Paul, we will seriously misunderstand narratives and exhortations pertaining to eating if we are not acutely aware that being welcomed at a table to eat with another person had, long before the first century, become a ceremony richly symbolic of friendship, intimacy, and social unity. The extended family was the usual context in which meals were consumed. Coming together to eat became the occasion for sensing again that one was an integral, accepted part of a group. Beyond the household, people generally preferred to eat with persons from their own social class. Such meals of like with like reinforced the systems of social stratification, with the seating arrangements further signaling the relative status and honor of each guest. It was expected that meal invitations would be given to one's social, religious, and economic equals, that is, to those in a position to return the favor in a relationship of balanced reciprocity.

Even everyday mealtimes were highly complex events in which fundamental social values, boundaries, statuses, and hierarchies were reinforced. Anyone who challenged these rankings and boundaries would be judged to have acted dishonorably, a serious charge in cultures based on the values of honor and shame. Transgressing these customs consistently would make a person a dangerous enemy of social stability. As Mary Douglas has observed, a meal, which is itself an ordered system, "represents all the ordered systems associated with it. Hence the strong arousal power of a threat to weaken or confuse that category" (1972:80). There is solid evidence both for concluding that the historical Jesus did threaten the social order encoded in the meal traditions of his culture (see, for example, Bartchy 1992:797–98; Crossan 1991:341–42; Neyrey 1991) and for reconstructing the reasons for the sharply negative responses that his practice provoked.

Religious Traditions as Reinforcement for Social Codes

To illustrate the prevailing cultural values and social codes regarding meals, I have selected relevant documents from both the house of Israel (the Dead Sea Scrolls) and the early Jesus-group tradition (the *Teaching of the Twelve Apostles* [*The Didache*]). Readers and communities informed and constrained by the instructions for eating meals appearing in these documents found few if any challenges to the social codes and cultural values into which they had been socialized as children. Rather, these documents provided encouragement for traditional social practices. In particular, these writers and their readers and hearers grew up assuming that eating in a group with more or less exclusive boundaries was both proper and just, as was the reinforcement of social rank through seating order. And, at least in Roman society, social rank was displayed by differences in the quality of food offered and consumed. Everyone in that ancient world expected that meals would be exclusive occasions in which honor was given to those to whom honor was due.

So even if the community at Qumran exaggerated these values beyond the norm, it still made social sense that they only permitted those who had survived one year's residence to eat with them (1QS 6.16–17). Only those who had been granted full membership at the end of two years were permitted to partake of the "drink of the Congregation" (6.20–21). Once admitted, members guilty of slandering another member were to be excluded from the common meal for a full year (7.16).

Furthermore, a hierarchical order of honorable seating is prescribed for the participants, with those seated closest to the "anointed one of Israel" described as "the men of renown," who were to be arranged "each according to his importance, according to his station" ("Rule of the Congregation," trans. L. Schiffman, quoted in VanderKam 1994:174)

Later, near the end of the first century c.e., Jesus-group members who heeded the admonitions in the *Didache* heard these words: "Let none eat or drink of your 'Eucharist' except those who have been baptised in the Lord's name. For concerning this also did the Lord say, 'Give not that which is holy to the dogs'" (*Did.* 9.5). Here the familiar concept of an exclusive meal is reinforced by a saying of Jesus. Within the community, "the first fruit of the produce of the winepress and of the threshing floor and of oxen and sheep" should be given "as first fruits to the prophets, for they are your high priests" (13.3). Clearly there is a social hierarchy to be honored, although nothing explicit is said about seating order at the eucharistic meal.

The Historical Jesus as a Challenge to Traditional Meal Theory and Praxis

In striking contrast, many of the meal practices reported in the traditions associated with Jesus of Nazareth go against the grain of Mediterranean culture in general, and against both of these Israelite and later Jesus-group meal prescriptions in particular. Thus, to the criterion of double dissimilarity, long familiar to New Testament scholars, we should add the strong subcriterion of dissimilarity of cultural values. Application of this criterion supports the claim that deviant, inclusive, status-leveling, honor-reversing meal practices were indeed characteristic of the behavior and teaching of the historical Jesus.

The Importance of Honor—and How to Obtain It

Before turning to comments on the most extensive report of Jesus' prescription for sharing meals, namely, Luke 14, I identify five general characteristics of honor in Jesus' world:

1. Honor was the pivotal cultural value, "much like wealth in our society," as Malina notes (1993:34). Honor is the claim to social worth, especially by males, based on one's birth and one's subsequent performance, that has been and continues to be publicly acknowledged. Xenophon regarded the passion for honor and praise (*philotimia*) as the defining characteristic separating human beings from the other animals (*Hieron* 7.3 C, a dialogue version of the "wise man meets autocrat" scenario).

2. Seeking greater honor for oneself and one's family was the fundamental life task of every adult. Within all social classes, traditional male socialization produced human beings programmed to pursue a never-ending quest for greater honor and influence. Young males learned very early that they symbolized the honor of their households, and that they were obligated to defend that honor on a daily basis.

3. Among strangers and men from other families, honor could be acquired only at the expense of someone else's honor, since honor was a cultural good in limited supply. As Plutarch wrote: "As though commendation were money, he feels that he is robbing himself of every bit [of praise] that he bestows on another" ("On Listening to Lectures" 44b).

4. Correspondingly, retaliation was the only honorable response to any challenge to one's personal honor. Attempts to undermine one's honor could be expressed in almost any words, gestures, and actions. To lose honor was to be shamed, resulting in diminished worth and reputation in the eyes of one's peers (see Neyrey 1998:5–34 for an excellent overview of ancient Mediterranean honor and shame).

5. Meals were an especially prominent venue for the reassertion of one's honor and for seeking to acquire more. According to Matthew's Gospel, Jesus observed with scorn that the scribes and the Pharisees "do all their deeds to be seen by men; for they make their phylacteries broad and their fringes long, and they love the place of honor at feasts and the best seats in the synagogues, and salutations in the marketplace and being called rabbi" (23:5–7). In the absence of anthropological knowledge, exegetes have assumed that Jesus' disapproval of this behavior would have found easy resonance among the people in general.

To the contrary, men who sought the best seats and the places of honor were behaving precisely the way that their mothers and fathers had raised them to behave. By no means was such seeking for honor pharisaical. Rather, such behavior was proper and manly; it made their families proud of them. In striking contrast, Jesus' alternative vision of human relations sharply challenged such behavior. A variety of evidence suggests that the historical Jesus imagined a way of being manly that required a fundamental break with the training in honor-seeking at the core of conventional male socialization.

The Redefinition of Honor—and How to Obtain It

With these factors in mind, I direct attention to Luke 14. More than forty years ago, Burrows (1958:91) and Vögtle (1958:12–13) contrasted this passage with meal instructions in the Dead Sea Scrolls. Now, four decades later, we have a much more satisfying, because anthropologically informed, analysis by Malina and Rohrbaugh. They provide an excellent overview of the issues in their exceptionally informative and accessible Synoptic commentary (1992:364–69).

In Luke 14:7–11, our attention is directed especially to the honor-seeking behavior of the guests at a banquet to which Jesus was also invited. As Malina and Rohrbaugh observe, "[W]ho sat where at a meal was a critical statement of social relations. The practice of discriminatory seating was well known in the Hellenistic world" (1992:365). Luke's initial audience was well aware that hosts in their cultures used special care in assigning positions of honor, since one's position at the table displayed one's rank relative to the other guests, beginning at the right of the entrance to the dining area. At formal meals, the diners reclined around a central table on couches, most commonly arranged in a U-shape called a *triclinium*.

Luke 14:7–11 presents Jesus reclining (Luke's Greek implies a formal banquet setting) and teaching at the table of a Pharisee whose many guests had indeed sought the customary positions of honor. In this narrative, which is unique to Luke, Jesus shamed the guests for seeking honor and urged them to defer to others, "for everyone who exalts himself will be humbled, and he who humbles himself will be exalted" (v. 11), a saying that both Matt 23:12 and Luke 18:4 present in settings apart from meals. The critical comment on Jesus' lips echoes ancient wisdom from his tradition: "Do not put yourself forward in the king's presence, or stand in the place of the great; for it is better to be told, 'Come up here,' than to be put lower in the presence of a noble" (Prov 25:6–7).

This theme is continued in Luke's presentation of the great banquet (14:15–24), a parable from the sayings source used by both Luke and Matthew.

Jesus lured the prestige-seeking men with whom he was dining into consider-ing his parable by telling them about a man who was able to give a great dinner and to invite many guests—a man with whom they could identify. But then Jesus turned the tables on them by describing an utterly transformed social order in which the poor and outcasts are given preference, "those incapable of participating in the social games of reciprocity and status augmentation" (Green 1997:563). Jesus made clear that his own table companions under the rule of God included "the poor and maimed and blind and lame" (Matthew's version mentions "both bad and good" guests; 22:10). Jesus' undermining of conventional social codes surely provoked angry resistance from his host and his other honor-seeking guests, whom Jesus had sought to shame.

A Profound Challenge to the Elite

The structure of Luke 14 suggests further influence of the symposium genre on Luke, not only in the ambience of a dialogue (vv. 7, 12, 15) but also in the spe-cific mention of the host, the guest of honor and main speaker (Jesus), the in-vited guests, and the uninvited guests (14:13, 23, 25; 15:1) (see Bartchy 1992:798–99 and Smith 1987). For Jesus' followers, his sharp critique of con-ventional meal codes opened the door for them to practice table fellowship across status lines, and eventually across ethnic barriers as well. As Philip Esler has astutely observed, "It is surely through no inadvertence on Luke's part that the types of people specified in Lk 14:21 as replacement guests are virtually identical to the groups promised the good news in Lk 4:18 and extolled as blessed in the beatitudes in Lk 6:20–21," namely, beggars, the crippled, the blind, and the lame (1987:186).

There seems little doubt that Luke's emphasis presented "hard bread" to the elite community members among his audience. For by participating in such a socially inclusive, honor-reversing community, they placed themselves in jeop-ardy of being cut off from their prior social networks on which their own status depended. The description of invited guests who then refuse to accept the host's invitation may have been, in the words of Willi Braun, at least "partially driven by Luke's knowledge of real peer rejection and dishonour experienced by the urban rich who became members or benefactors of Christian associa-tions" (1995:110)

Later, in 22:24–27, Luke continues to focus his readers' attention on the connection between Jesus' meal practice and his reversal of honor seeking by providing a meal setting for the antihierarchical tradition found in Mark 10:35–45: "Whoever wishes to become great among you must become your servant, and whoever wants to be first among you must be slave of all" (vv. 43–44). While reclining at the Last Supper with his disciples, Jesus speaks strong words about who among them was to be regarded as the greatest (that is, the most honored), then asks: "For who is greater, one who reclines at table, or one who serves? Is it not the one reclining? But I am among you as one who serves!" With such words Luke sought to motivate his readers to sharply modify their own cultural values and traditional meal praxis.

Conclusion

In terms of the five characteristics of honor noted above, the following contrasts appear in the traditions associated with the historical Jesus:

1. Honor is still a pivotal cultural value, but now both birth honor and acquired honor have been made irrelevant. For in the name of Israel's God, Jesus gave honor to everyone, without regard for social status, personal accomplishment, purity, or health. Jesus' behavior provided the experiential base for the later Jesus-group teaching about the "grace of God."

2. Instead of seeking honor for himself, Jesus was prepared to be humiliated rather than to play the traditional male game of one-upmanship. He announced that, in his fellowship, honor is given to the merciful, to the peacemakers, and to those persecuted for righteousness' sake (for translating the Beatitudes with the term "honorable" instead of "blessed," see Hanson 1996).

3. In contrast to the prevailing assumptions about life, honor was not in limited supply for the historical Jesus. His God offered an unlimited supply of honor; in turn, those honored by God had the social resources to give honor to others without fear of diminishing their own. Jesus apparently envisioned a world of human relationships in which competition would be expressed paradoxically by seeking to excel in giving honor to each other. That Paul of Tarsus came to share this radical vision can be seen when he admonishes the followers of Jesus in Rome to "outdo one another in showing honor to each other." Such revolutionary social behavior was a central aspect of their being "transformed by the renewing of [their] minds" (Rom 12:1–16).

4. Nonretaliation thus became the only honorable response to a challenge to one's personal honor. "To him who strikes you on the cheek, offer the other also; and from him who takes away your coat do not withhold even your shirt" (the sayings source: Luke 6:29; Matt 5:39–40). Attempts to undermine one's honor were to be ignored or trumped by returning

honor for dishonor, even by blessing and praying for those who had abused and cursed you (Luke 6:28). Again, it is clear that Paul grasped this radical vision. For example, he exhorted his Roman converts: "Bless those who persecute you; bless and do not curse them. . . . Associate with the lowly. . . . Do not repay anyone evil for evil . . . but overcome evil with good" (Rom 12:14–21).

5. Meals became an especially prominent venue for this outrageous giving of honor to all, around a radically inclusive table.

Meals in Jesus' fellowship became practical parables whose meaning was as evocative as his verbal parables (which have consumed much more scholarly attention). To join in his meals consciously was, in effect, to anticipate the kingdom as it had been delineated by Jesus' teaching. Each meal was a proleptic celebration of God's kingdom. (Chilton 1996:86).

The historical Jesus' vision of human relationships submitted to the rule of God required a reversal of expectations regarding the giving and receiving of honor. By deed and word, and in the name of Israel's God, Jesus sought to undermine traditional meal practices that provided easy opportunities for males in his culture to seek honor and display their ascribed or acquired status. As 1 Corinthians 11–12 (among other passages) indicates, Paul of Tarsus sought to nurture the resocialization of his converts so that they, too, would give the greater honor to the least among them (12:24–26). "For all who exalt themselves will be humbled, and those who humble themselves will be exalted" (Luke 14:11).

Works Cited

Bartchy, S. Scott. 1992. "Table Fellowship." In *The Dictionary of Jesus and the Gospels*, edited by J. B. Green and S. McKnight, 796–800. Downers Grove, Ill.: InterVarsity.

Braun, Willi. 1995. *Feasting and Social Rhetoric in Luke 14*. SNTSMS 85. Cambridge: Cambridge University Press.

Burrows, Millar. 1958. *More Light on the Dead Sea Scrolls*. New York: Viking.

Chilton, Bruce. 1996. *Pure Kingdom: Jesus' Vision of God*. SHJ. Grand Rapids: Eerdmans.

Crossan, John Dominic. 1991. *The Historical Jesus: The Life of a Mediterranean Jewish Peasant*. San Francisco: HarperSanFrancisco.

Douglas, Mary. 1972. "Deciphering a Meal." *Daedalus* 101:61–81. Reprinted in *Implicit Meanings: Essays in Anthropology* (London: Routledge & Kegan Paul, 1975), 249–75.

Esler, Philip F. 1987. *Community and Gospel in Luke-Acts: The Social and Political Motivations of Lucan Theology.* SNTSMS 57. Cambridge: Cambridge University Press.

Green, Joel B. 1997. *The Gospel of Luke.* NICNT. Grand Rapids: Eerdmans.

Hanson, K. C. 1996. "'How Honorable! How Shameful!' A Cultural Analysis of Matthew's Makarisms and Reproaches." *Semeia* 68:81–112.

Malina, Bruce J. 1993. *The New Testament World: Insights from Cultural Anthropology.* Rev. ed. Louisville: Westminster John Knox. 3d ed., 2001.

Malina, Bruce J., and Richard L. Rohrbaugh. 1992. *Social-Science Commentary on the Synoptic Gospels.* Minneapolis: Fortress Press.

Neyrey, Jerome H. 1991. "Ceremonies in Luke-Acts: The Case of Meals and Table Fellowship." In *The Social World of Luke-Acts: Models for Interpretation,* edited by J. H. Neyrey, 361–87. Peabody, Mass: Hendrickson.

———. 1998. *Honor and Shame in the Gospel of Matthew.* Louisville: Westminster John Knox .

Smith, Dennis E. 1987. "Table Fellowship as Literary Motif in the Gospel of Luke." *JBL* 106:613–38.

VanderKam, James C. 1994. *The Dead Sea Scrolls Today.* Grand Rapids: Eerdmans.

Vögtle, Anton. 1958. *Das öffentliche Wirken Jesus auf dem Hintergrund der Qumranbewegung.* Freiburger Universitätsreden, n.s., 27. Freiburg: Schulz.

11

Jesus and the Reduction of Intergroup Conflict

Philip F. Esler

The parable of the good Samaritan (Luke 10:30–37) is one of the most cherished of all New Testament passages. The secondary literature on the parable, which forms part of the larger passage comprising Luke 10:25–37, is immense, and I will not attempt to summarize it here.[1] Many scholars regard the parable as having been uttered by the historical Jesus,[2] and I return to this issue later. In this essay, I assume that the parable is either authentic or that, even if Luke composed it (the view I prefer), he so well understood—and here passed on— the message of Jesus that perhaps it does not matter much whether it comprises Jesus' authentic words or not.

In this essay, I discuss Luke 10:25–37 within a new exegetical framework derived from social-scientific ideas relating to intergroup conflict and its reduction. Although my approach is essentially historical, in that my principal aim is to investigate the message that the passage would have communicated to its initial recipients, I am also keenly interested in the relevance that my social-scientific perspective and exegesis may have in contemporary interethnic relationships, as I indicate below. I am heartened to see that Gerd Theissen (1990) has also sought to relate the parable of the good Samaritan directly to a modern issue, namely, the current crisis surrounding the legitimacy of charitable assistance.

I employ two areas of social-scientific research to aid this historical investigation. First is anthropological research into the broad features of Mediterranean culture, which has helped generate an invaluable model for investigating the bedrock social context of biblical texts. This model is now so well known, especially from Bruce Malina's book *The New Testament World* (1981; 3d ed., 2001) and other research,[3] that I only refer to it briefly where relevant. I have recently defended the continuing usefulness of model-driven biblical research (Esler 1995:4–8; 2000). Second, and more specifically, however, I utilize a recent branch of social psychology known as social-identity theory—which forms the main theoretical perspective of my 1998 monograph on Galatians (Esler 1998:esp. 29–57)—to assist in exploring the intergroup dynamics that I argue are present in the passage. While most previous work on social identity has explored ways in which groups differentiate themselves from one another, more recent research, which I consider below, has generated an interest in ways to reduce intergroup strife.

Finally, and as intimated above, in addition to this historical investigation, I briefly suggest the relevance of Jesus' teaching—assessed in relation to these social-psychological perspectives—to one of the most troubling problems of our time, namely, intergroup conflict of the ethnic type that has recently pitted Israeli against Palestinian, Northern Irish Nationalists against Unionists, Hutu against Tutsi, Serbian against Albanian, to name only a few.

Social-Identity Theory

Social-identity theory is a branch of social psychology largely developed by Henri Tajfel (and his colleagues and students) at Bristol University in the 1970s and 1980s (see Tajfel 1969; 1972; 1978; 1981; and Tajfel and Turner 1979; 1986). Tajfel himself died in 1983, but he has left a flourishing legacy in the United Kingdom and elsewhere, especially in Europe.[4] The fundamental idea of the theory is that people obtain an important part (but not the totality) of their self-concept from being categorized as members of certain groups. To an extent, we learn who we are from the groups to which we belong.

The extent to which group membership contributes to a sense of self is affected by the level of group orientation in the ambient culture. Much research, for example that by Dutch social scientist Geert Hofstede (1980; 1994), suggests that the notably individualistic cultures of the UK, northern Europe, and North America are very unusual, with group orientation far more common elsewhere in the world. Of particular importance is that investigations by social anthropologists in the Mediterranean region over the last few decades have highlighted its collectivist nature, as one of an ensemble of related cultural features. The recent application of such findings in classical studies (Lendon 1997) and biblical research (see Malina 2001) has illustrated that the ancient Mediterranean was at least as group-oriented as the region is today. This is not to deny that we should always be alert to local variations on the overall pattern.

Central to the theory is the idea that when a specific social identity becomes salient, self-perception and conduct become stereotypical of the in-group, whereas perceptions of members of other groups become out-group stereotypical. These phenomena go hand in hand with competition between groups. Stereotyping essentially means treating all members of an out-group as if they were the same, usually accompanied by a projection of negative attitudes toward them (see Macrae, Stangor, and Hewstone 1996). Revealing illustrations of stereotypical attitudes and behavior resulting in extremes of violence, ethnic cleansing, and even genocide can be seen today in Israel, Northern Ireland, Rwanda, and the Balkans.

An in-group that regards itself as being in tension or conflict with out-groups can employ a variety of strategies, depending on how it views its power and influence in relation to those groups (Esler 1998:29–57). The processes of intergroup categorization and differentiation are more pronounced in social contexts that are collective, like the ancient Mediterranean, rather than individualist.

Judeans, Samaritans, and Social-Identity Theory

Evidence from outside the New Testament

For centuries, Judeans treated the Samaritans as a despised out-group and subjected them to the negative stereotyping discussed above, climaxing in John Hyrcanus destroying the Samaritan temple in 128 B.C.E. and Samaria itself in 107 B.C.E. Since the scope of this essay prevents a fuller exposition of this troubled history, I mention just a couple of incidents from the first century (see Anderson 1992).

In 6–9 C.E., some Samaritans secretly entered Jerusalem by night and scattered bones around the temple, thereby grossly defiling it (Josephus, *Ant.* 18.29–30). More seriously, in 52 C.E., a Galilean, one of a large number of Judeans traveling to Jerusalem for a festival, was murdered in the Samaritan village of Gema. As a result, a crowd of Judeans in Jerusalem abandoned the festival and rushed to Samaria. Some of their number attacked villages in the region of Acrabatene, southeast of Shechem, massacring the inhabitants and burning the buildings. The Romans had to stop the conflict by force (Josephus, *War* 2.232–46).

New Testament Evidence

These attitudes are reflected in the New Testament outside Luke, in Matt 10:5, when Jesus says to the crowd, "Do not go into the way of the Gentiles, nor enter a Samaritan town." Here he is presumably reflecting the standard Judean animosity to the Samaritan out-group, which associates them closely with Gentiles. To similar effect is John 4:9, in which the Samaritan woman asks Jesus,

"How is it that you, a Judean, ask me, a Samaritan woman, to give you a drink, for Judeans have no dealings with Samaritans?"

More noteworthy, however, is that Luke himself is fully aware of the bitterness of this relationship. In chapter 9 of his Gospel (vv. 51–56), not long before the Lucan Jesus tells the parable of the compassionate Samaritan, Luke narrates a remarkable incident directly on point. Because Jesus was on the way to Jerusalem, a Samaritan village would not receive him. This seems like a less serious version of events in Gema in 52 C.E. In view of the antipathy Judeans and Samaritans had for one another and the enthusiasm of his disciples for their role, their response to this rejection is not surprising: "James and John said, 'Lord, do you want us to call down fire from heaven to burn them up?'" Yet nothing could be more surprising than Jesus' brief and forceful reaction: "He turned and rebuked them." Here we have a revealing indication of Jesus' impatience with extreme forms of group differentiation, which will become even clearer in chapter 10 of Luke.

Analysis of Luke 10:25-37

The Lawyer's First Question (Luke 10:25-28)

As Theissen has rightly noted, although Luke 10:25–37 is composed of two separate pericopes, the first being the lawyer's question and the second the narrative of the Samaritan, "Both passages together form a meaningful unity in Luke" (1990:382). Accordingly, to appreciate the force of the parable at 10:30–37, it is necessary to examine both parts of this unified composition, although restrictions of space will require us to focus more on the parable itself.

Although Luke is probably using Mark 12:28–34 in the opening four verses of this passage (Salo 1991:107), he diverges from his Markan source (which ends with Jesus telling the scribe in question that he is not far from the kingdom of God [Mark 12:34]) in two revealing ways. First, he situates the exchange within a framework of conflict, which begins when a lawyer stands up testing (*ekpeirazōn*) Jesus with the question, "Teacher, what shall I do to inherit eternal life?" (10:25). This is a "challenge," the opening gambit in the social dynamic of "challenge-and-response" known to us from Mediterranean culture (Malina 2001:32–35); that is, the challenge represents an attempt to enter the social space of another, roughly one's social equal, with the aim of winning honor from the audience through success in the exchange that ensues. The lawyer (understood here not as a real individual, but as a character in a narrative, which must have made sense to Luke's audience) presumably expects that Jesus will give an unsatisfactory answer to the question, or at least an answer inferior to that which he, the lawyer, will produce. But Jesus, employing a standard tactic of challenge-and-response, instead fires back another question: "What stands written in the Law? How do you read [i.e., interpret it]?" Jesus' tone is sharp and rather dismissive: "You're a lawyer, what do you think?" This forces the lawyer to reply, which he does first by quoting Deut 6:5 and then Lev 19:18 (Luke 10:27). Jesus then seeks to end the discussion: "You have answered well; do this and you will live" (10:28). Yet this is closure with a sting, since it implies that the lawyer may not yet be fulfilling these Mosaic commandments and may not have life, meaning life in the present, not necessarily the eternal life of 10:25.[5] The conflictual nature of this exchange and the fact that it seems closely tied to this interlocutor's framework of meaning, with the lawyer, and not Jesus (as in Mark), actually citing the two halakic passages, suggests that distance exists between the Lucan Jesus and the Mosaic law.

This impression is strengthened by the second major way in which Luke diverges (or at least differs) from the Markan passage: the lawyer's question concerns the acquisition of eternal life (similar to Luke 18:18), not the identification of the most important commandment. The question as phrased in Luke most probably reflects Luke's general position on the Mosaic law. Luke is not interested in entering a debate about which provision of halakah has precedence. Salo accurately notes: "Discussion of the greatest commandment does not exist in the Third Gospel, and thus Luke does not wish to place one commandment over another" (1991:109). To consider why this is so would involve fuller discussion of Luke's attitude to the Mosaic law, which I have attempted elsewhere but which is beyond the compass of this article.[6] While the Lucan Jesus sometimes respects, sometimes transcends, and sometimes challenges the law (Esler 1987:114–18), detailed interest in the merits of one part of the Mosaic code over another is not a feature of Luke-Acts. Similarly, in the parable that follows, Luke's Jesus will, if anything, subvert the Mosaic law and the realities of group differentiation on which it was based, rather than engage in halakic interpretation.[7]

The Lawyer's Second Question and Group Differentiation (Luke 10:29)

The lawyer asks a second question: "And who is my neighbor?" (10:29). This is both a typical lawyer's question and also a second challenge to Jesus' honor. Luke's audience would assume that the lawyer, to his honor and Jesus' shame, has a good answer himself. If, compared with whatever Jesus might say, to his honor and Jesus' shame, in the agonistic nature of this exchange, announced in the word *ekpeirazōn* in 10:25.

Fitzmyer correctly notes that the implication in the lawyer's question is "Where does one draw the line?" and that, in reply, Jesus extends the answer beyond the answer given in Leviticus 19 (1985:886). But this reading does not go far enough. The legal issue posed is, "Whom are we Judeans obligated to treat as neighbors and whom are we not?" It is a boundary question of an exclusionary type. So put, it enables Judeans to determine those who fall within the obligation of the law cited from Lev 19:18 and those who do not. Whom does God require us to love as ourselves and whom are we not required to love? Or, more specifically, what is the outer limit of the people we must treat as neighbors? A common answer at this period was that "neighbor" meant fellow Israelite. After all, Lev 19:18, the source of the quoted statement, "(You must love) your neighbor as yourself," at Luke 10:27, forms part of an address that Yahweh directs Moses to give "to the whole community of the sons of Israel" (Lev 19:1–2; see Fichtner 1968:314–15).

The exclusionary nature of the issue emerges in the halakic midrashim (for an overview of this literature, see Strack and Stemberger 1991:269–99). Thus, the *Mekilta* on Exod 21:14 interprets this verse as follows: expressly stating that a serious legal consequence, capital punishment, in this case, will flow from killing one's neighbor (here, clearly an Israelite) necessarily entails that killing a non-Israelite will not trigger such a result (*Nezikin* 4.60–64; Lauterbach 1933–35:3:37).

We may assume that Samaritans would have fallen within the non-Israelite category in the first century C.E., even though they were circumcised in accordance with the Law of Moses. They were referred to as *allogenōs* ("foreigner"; Luke 17:18).

Within social-identity theory, the lawyer's question raises a key indicator for determining who is in the in-group, and thus properly treated with warmth and regard, and who belongs to the out-group, thus warranting negative attitudes. The lawyer's answer to Jesus' question in 10:29, even though he never gives it, probably would have distinguished among possible boundaries that would have filtered—from the perspective of a group-differentiating Judean—who was and who was not within the group designated "neighbor" by the law. Accordingly, while the question is a legal one—indeed, a perfectly reasonable legal question—it inevitably conveys an invitation to engage in group differentiation and stereotyping.

Jesus' Response: The Parable (Luke 10:30–35)

The traveler attacked. The precise way in which Jesus begins the parable is crucial: "A certain man (*anthrōpos tis*) was going down from Jerusalem to Jericho and he fell among bandits who stripped him and beat him and made off leaving him half-dead" (10:30). The lawyer would have considered that, in this scene-setting statement, Jesus was preparing the question, "Was this man a 'neighbor'?" so as to bring provisions of the Mosaic law, like Lev 19:18, to bear on Israelites who came upon him. Thus understood, the case was within the parameters of halakic discussion, even though the details of the situation were challenging.

As far as the lawyer is concerned, the initial (and fundamental) question is whether the man was an Israelite or not. Even though commentators often assert the man was an Israelite,[8] this is an error. Jesus' failure to specify the man's ethnicity is essential to the case he establishes and to what happens thereafter. That the man was traveling from Jerusalem to Jericho did not determine the issue, since people of all types frequented Jerusalem. But the man had been stripped; as Meggitt notes (1998:60–61), clothing was valuable, and this explains why thieves would have removed it. Yet this detail was important for two reasons.

First, it meant that an observer was now unable to decide on the victim's ethnicity by his clothing. Although this is an area needing further investigation, it seems probable that Judean and non-Judean inhabitants of first-century Palestine could be distinguished by their clothing (Bailey 1980:42–43). Second, and more important, the man's nakedness meant an observer could determine whether he was circumcised or not. If uncircumcised, he was a Greek or Roman and certainly not a neighbor; if circumcised, he was an Israelite or a Samaritan, or some other circumcising Semite. At this point, therefore, the lawyer would have imagined that an admittedly formidable case had been posed, into which various Israelites could be introduced to test the meaning of Lev 19:18.

The priest. The lawyer also would have found the next detail congenial to his habits of thought: "By chance a certain priest was traveling down that road and when he saw the man (*idōn auton*) he crossed to the other side" (10:31). Within the legal framework presupposed here, the Israelite priest, someone with more than a passing knowledge of the law, has presumably made his own estimation of whether the man was a "neighbor" or not. If uncircumcised, the man was not a neighbor, and the obligation of Lev 19:18 did not come into play. In this case, the priest was justified by the Law of Moses, in its maintenance of Israelite ethnic identity, in passing to the other side of the road. Yet even if the man were circumcised, the priest would have been uncertain whether he was Israelite and a "neighbor," or a Samaritan or some other circumcising Semite, and not a "neighbor." The priest could have reasoned to himself—arguably, if rather harshly—that he was not obliged to resolve this doubt in the man's favor and, therefore, crossed to other side of the road.

It is also possible, as Duncan Derrett (1970:208–27) and Richard Bauckham (1998), independently of Derrett, have argued, that the priest would have avoided the man because of the risk of breaking Mosaic law relating to the impurity of corpses. Bauckham's point is that the priest was in the difficult position of being subject to two laws, one to love his neighbor (Lev 19:18) and the other not to touch a corpse (Lev 21:1–4).[9] It would be sinful for the priest to infringe Lev 21:1–4, even if any ensuing impurity were ritually removed. Presumably, however, the priest could rely on the rituals of the Day of Atonement (Leviticus 16) to cleanse his sin, and this consideration might have taken some of the sting out of his dilemma. Yet one could imagine that a priest might not want to run the risk of uncleanness as specified in God's law, even if purification were possible later.

Yet Lev 21:1–4 only constitutes a prohibition (and one not specifying any penalty) on a priest incurring corpse impurity from members *of his people* (*'am* in MT and *ethnos* in the LXX), close relatives excepted (Lev 21:1). Accordingly, although Bauckham is right to raise Lev 21:1–4 as relevant to the situation as far as the priest was concerned, we need to recognize that, again, the initial issue is the ethnic identity of the injured man. The conflict of duties stemming from Lev 19:18 and 21:1–4 as proposed by Bauckham arises only if the injured man is an Israelite. If he were uncircumcised, Lev 21:1–4 was not binding on the priest. But even if he were circumcised, the priest would not have known if he was an Israelite or a Samaritan.

Other provisions existed, stating that anyone who touched a corpse, either generally (Num. 19:11) or in the open country (Num. 19:16), was unclean for seven days, although these provisions did not actually prohibit touching a corpse. This law was not restricted to Israelite corpses. A complex and expensive ritual involving the sacrifice of a red heifer, and described in Numbers 19 (see Sanders 1992:217–19), existed for the removal of such corpse impurity; it no doubt also covered any breach of Lev 21:1–4. Since the priest was traveling away from Jerusalem (probably because his time of duty in the cult was over), touching a corpse likely would have required his return to Jerusalem to undertake this ritual; he certainly would have needed to undertake it before next taking part in the temple cult. Nevertheless, since the red heifer ritual for removing corpse impurity was only a question of time, inconvenience, and expense, Luke's audience may not have regarded this a weighty reason for not coming to the man's aid.

In sum, the lawyer would have assumed Jesus had raised a very difficult set of circumstances relating to whether the priest was obliged to help the injured man or not, but yet one capable of interpretation within existing halakic discussion.

The Levite. The lawyer would have continued to think he was following the plot when he heard Jesus' next detail: "Similarly, a Levite also came upon the place and when he saw him he crossed to the other side" (10:32). The lawyer would have assumed that the Levite had, like the priest, considered the man's identity—possibly without the extra issue of Lev 21:1–4, although with the risk of corpse impurity pursuant to Numbers 19—and had come to the same conclusion. If Levites were not bound by the law in Lev 21:1–4 (probably the more likely view), the Levite would have had less reason not to help. The difference on this issue introduces a necessary novel dimension into the discussion as far as the Levites is concerned.

The Samaritan. At this juncture, Luke's lawyer thinks he is considering whether these two Israelite men, associated with the cult and therefore subject to higher legal standards than ordinary Israelites,[10] were justified in not treating the man as a neighbor. He would have been expecting the next person along the road to have been an ordinary Israelite. Up to this point, the situation Jesus poses seems one of halakic interpretation pursued in recognizable case-by-case fashion. Also underlying the discussion were fundamental notions of differentiation between Israelite and non-Israelite, which it was the whole purpose of Mosaic law to preserve.

Jesus' next statement, however, opens a hole under the lawyer's feet: "But a Samaritan traveling on the road came upon him and when he saw him he was moved with compassion" (*esplangchnisthē*; 10:33). Jesus deftly springs his trap and knocks away the implied framework of the preceding discussion—whether various Israelites could reasonably consider that they did or did not have an obligation to treat the man as a neighbor within the Mosaic law. Yet it is not simply the case that the introduction of a Samaritan means that we are no longer dealing with an Israelite in-group legal discussion. That Jesus introduces a representative of one of the hated out-groups challenges the structure of group differentiation, which the law maintained.[11] Jesus has transformed the matter under review from the meaning of particular Israelite laws to the far more fundamental issue of group differentiation and social identity. The simplicity of this move is one aspect of its genius; there is nothing artificial in posing a case in which the next passerby was a non-Israelite. Yet so natural a possibility brings chaos to the conceptual and social framework implied in the lawyer's question and in the parable itself, right up to the arrival of the Samaritan.

The Samaritan's response only compounds this challenge to group-oriented ways of dealing with other human beings. The Samaritan belonged to a group that also acknowledged the Law of Moses as *torah* within the group differentiation and stereotyping already discussed, and the Samaritan texts included Lev 19:18.[12] Thus, the Samaritan could have embarked on the same type of legal calculation as the priest and Levite. He could have asked himself, weighing the visual clues available from the man's nakedness and situation, "Is he a Samaritan—and therefore my neighbor such as to activate the obligation of Lev 19:18—or not?" Yet the text makes it plain that he did nothing of the kind. The position taken by the priest and the Levite, however legally defensible, is not part of the Samaritan's moral universe. The text does not suggest that the Samaritan's response embodied what Lev 19:18 requires. The whole issue of the obligation imposed by that part of the Mosaic law was simply immaterial to him, as the manner in which Jesus encapsulates, in 10:36, the effect of the parable confirms. For the Samaritan there was only one response, an immediate response—when he saw the man "he was moved with compassion" (*esplangchnisthē*; 10:33). It was, moreover, a compassion with few limits, as shown in the rich and loving detail that Jesus supplies in 10:34–35.

The example of the Samaritan drives one to conclude that compassion that transcends legally sanctioned ethnic boundaries and discriminations, when faced with real human need, is a superior form of human behavior than living within such boundaries. By this point, the lawyer's worldview has been radically undermined, and he has been shamed. Nevertheless, Jesus is not finished with him or the situation.

Jesus' final words with the lawyer. Even at this stage, the somewhat punch-drunk lawyer, imagining that Jesus still might be interested in his question, "Who is my neighbor?" might have supposed that Jesus would ask something like, "Given the response of the Samaritan, were the priest and Levite justified under the law in not treating the man as a neighbor?" If the Lucan Jesus really were interested in illustrating how one aspect of the law, namely the commandment to love one's neighbor, should take precedence over others, such as commandments relating to corpse impurity and so forth, this is the question Jesus would have asked. But this is not his question. He asks instead: "Which of these three men seems to you to have been a neighbor to the man who fell among the bandits?" (10:36).

Most contemporary critics notice that Jesus seems to have shifted the goalposts, moving from "neighbor" as the recipient of love to "neighbor" as its agent (Creed 1930:151; Manson [1937] 1957:263; Fitzmyer 1985:884). A social-identity approach, in light of our exegesis, allows, however, a more precise determination of what Jesus is seeking to accomplish.

In telling the parable, Jesus has refused to indulge in group differentiation and stereotyping, and has subverted these processes by exposing them as inadequate and morally inferior when confronted with a particular human need.

Yet in his question at 10:36, Jesus leaps from this particular case to the level of general principle, a principle that represents a major divergence from the

Mosaic law, not just a fresh way of interpreting it. He does this, first, by drastically overhauling the concept of "neighbor" itself. Whereas "neighbor" previously had referred, within legal interpretation, to the passive object of the group categorization process within the framework of legal interpretation, Jesus now reapplies the concept to a person who acts properly to assist someone in need. Thus Jesus gives novel meaning to a word from Mosaic law, so that it henceforth establishes a norm governing our own behavior to others, rather than differentiating, for the purpose of satisfying juridical obligation, whom we must love as ourselves and whom we do not have to love.

The articulation of this innovative view is completed in what follows. Once the lawyer has replied to Jesus' question of 10:36 with the words "the one who showed pity to him" (apparently unable even to utter the word "Samaritan"), Jesus gives him the peremptory direction: "Go, and do the same yourself" (10:37). In other words, Jesus terminates the conversation by formulating a new principle: "Act as a neighbor (in the compassionate style of the Samaritan) to people in need." "Neighbor" understood in this sense is someone who ignores group boundaries of the sort erected by the Law of Moses to assist one in need. Jesus thus calls for movement from a group-oriented to a universal ethic—and at the level of principle. The Lucan Jesus, a person who teaches with authority (Luke 4:32), thus establishes a rationale for moral obligation independent of the Mosaic law. In the group-oriented ethics of the first-century, Greco-Roman East, this was indeed a radical step.

Jesus' Approach and Social-Identity Theory

As already mentioned, recent developments in social-identity theory have detailed ways in which the extremes of negative differentiation, leading to conflict between groups, can be reduced or even eliminated. In the last major section of this article, I explore the attitude that the Lucan Jesus reveals in the parable of the good Samaritan in relation to these developments.

Crossed Categorizations

This approach to the reduction of intergroup conflict was first formalized in social-psychological terms by W. Doise in 1976, and has since been explored further by many other writers.[13] In many social situations more than one possible categorization exists for other groups, which those involved may employ. They may be classifiable in relation to ethnicity, age, class, gender, or to other available criteria, including criteria relating to the particular situation in which they find themselves.[14] In cases of crossed categorization, people sharing different category membership in one respect, which typically leads to out-group stereo-typing and bias, find themselves in the same category in another respect, so that this commonality works against the initial differentiation. In other words, Doise realized that where category systems "are orthogonal[,] then the accentuation and assimilation associated with one should effectively cancel out the same processes associated with the other" (Brown 1996:171). This situation should lead to the lessening or abolition of bias and intergroup conflict likely to be as-sociated with the initial categorization.

An example will clarify this conclusion. Doise (1976) discovered among a subject group of boys and girls that an initial tendency for children of the same gender to rate their performance more highly than those of the other gender could be counteracted by allocating half the boys and half the girls to a blue color group and half to a red color group. Thereafter, being a blue or a red rad-ically altered the children's estimation of themselves, and the previous ten-dency to assess performance on the basis of gender disappeared. Nor was it simply that one criterion for evaluation replaced the other, since children shar-ing the same gender and color rated those of the opposite gender and the other color just as favorably as themselves.

Subsequent research has tended to confirm that, in some cases, bias against those who share at least one category membership is virtually eliminated (Brown and Turner 1979; Vanbeselaere 1991). This result has potential for public policies aimed at reducing intergroup bias and strife, for example, in places such as Northern Ireland, since it suggests that persistent prejudice be-tween groups will be reduced if we arrange crossed categorizations. Crossed categorization should be borne in mind by all those seeking to reconcile war-ring groups. On the other hand, happy results do not always follow. After all, there was a major war between Iraq and Iran in the 1980s, although most of the participants shared a Shiite Islamic religious affiliation (though Iraqi leader-ship was Sunni).

The parable of the good Samaritan may be interpreted within this frame-work, although I propose that crossed categorization is not as suitable for the purpose as other areas of social-identity theory. Two relevant categories apply to the four main actors in the narrative (I omit, for this analysis, the bandits and the innkeeper). The first category is ethnicity, with the victim of unspecified ethnicity, the priest and the Levite being Judean, and the fourth a Samaritan. The second category consists of their status as persons traveling alone on a dan-gerous road, which covers all four. As for the Samaritan, his membership in a particular ethnic category, which normally would result in hostility and preju-dice toward the half-dead man if he knew or suspected the victim belonged to an out-group, is orthogonal to and is arguably canceled out by the fact that they are travelers on a dangerous road. Yet it is clear that crossed categorization is hardly a powerful factor. Two other people who could have acted on the shared status fail to do so. One out of three is not an impressive experimental result.

While analyzing the parable in this perspective does highlight the characters' shared status as solitary travelers, there is another reason against making too much of it. The text, after all, tells us that the Samaritan was motivated by compassion (*esplangchnisthē*; Luke 10:33). In other words, the notion of crossed classification, which is reasonable from an etic or social-scientific viewpoint, does not quite match the main emic (that is, indigenous) concept employed, even if there is no sharp rift between these conceptions. While possible that the Samaritan's sense of facing the same dangers as the injured man played a role in his response, the author chooses to characterize the Samaritan's action as motivated by compassion, something lacking in the priest and the Levite, even though they also were in the category of single travelers on a dangerous road.

Recategorization

The second means whereby categorization can assist in reducing bias is recategorization. This refers to the redefinition of a conflict situation so that those initially perceived "as members of the outgroup can be subsumed into a new and larger category and thereby be seen as ingroup members" (Brown 1996:173; also see Turner 1981). Unlike crossed categorization, in which two categorizations cancel each other out, we are dealing here with a sense of belonging (at least for some purposes) to a third group. This phenomenon is reasonably well attested. In his classic 1952 study, for example, R. D. Minard showed that black and white coal miners, usually in conflict with one another above ground, left such animosity behind when underground, where their common category membership as miners became salient. The usefulness of persuading members of previously competing groups that they now belong to a single superordinate group has also been demonstrated empirically by Gaertner et al. (1993). Although these results are encouraging, the real difficulty is the seeming unlikelihood that an attitude change will necessarily carry over from the members of two groups brought together in this way to members of the out-group not yet encountered (Brown 1996:174–75). When, in his Letter to the Galatians, Paul turns from his stereotyping attack on the Israelite out-group (see Esler 1998) to characterize the unity of his congregations, he often engages in recategorization. A revealing example is Gal 3:27–28: "For as many of you as were baptized into Christ have put on Christ. There is neither Judean nor Greek, there is neither slave nor free, there is neither male nor female; for you are all one in Christ Jesus."

But it is less clear that this strategy helpfully characterizes the attitude of the Lucan Jesus in the parable of the good Samaritan. The most prominent common or superordinate categorization shared by all the actors in the drama is that of human being. If Jesus had devised a parable in answer to the lawyer's question that illustrated that "neighbor" simply means human being, such an approach would represent recategorization. It would also have constituted a direct response to the lawyer, even if one with which the lawyer would have strongly disagreed.

Yet this is not the route Jesus takes. First, the point of the story is not that the Samaritan, alone of the three passersby, recognizes the injured man as a member of some superordinate category and treats him accordingly. Rather, the Samaritan disregards the issue of which of the three possible categories (Gentile, Judean, Samaritan) encompasses the injured man. Second, Jesus transforms the concept of "neighbor" from the recipient of compassion to the agent of such compassion. Perhaps, at a deep level, we might concede that a notion lurks that our common human status makes us eligible to receive acts of kindness, but Luke does not articulate such a notion here.

Decategorization

A third approach to reducing intergroup strife is to lessen the emphasis on categoric judgment by dissolving the problematic boundaries altogether. If this happens, participants in social interactions will be less attentive to group-based, that is, stereotypical, information about others and more interested in the idiosyncratic features of each individual (Brown 1996:175–76). In this view, repeated person-to-person contact is likely to disconfirm negative stereotypes of the out-group. That is, the information we obtain from members of an out-group by meeting them can sometimes (but not always) undermine the usefulness of our preexisting stereotypical attitudes. This can lead to permanent change in our attitude to members of the out-group (Brewer and Miller 1984:288–99; Bettencourt et al. 1992; Miller, Brewer, and Edwards 1985).

Although there is much to recommend this work, and it is supported by the theoretically and empirically sophisticated research of Cook (1962; 1978), there is doubt as to how far positive attitudes about some out-group members will extend to the out-group's general membership. Cook thought that some type of "supplementary influence" might be needed to promote the generalization of newfound positive regard to other members of the groups from which the individual comes (1978:103).

At this point, it is worth mentioning one other approach to reducing intergroup conflict that is closely related to decategorization—the contact hypothesis (Brown 1996:181–83). Initially set out by Allport (1924), but extensively developed by Tajfel and other researchers in the social-identity field (Cook 1978; Hewstone and Brown 1986; Hewstone 1996), its premise is that the best way to reduce tension and hostility between groups is to have them come into contact with one another under appropriate conditions (Brown 1996:181). Literature on the contact hypothesis also reveals the difficulty of generalizing changes of attitudes and abolition of stereotypes from participants in a specific contact situation to other situations (Brown 1996:182–85).

As far as the parable of the good Samaritan is concerned, however, it is enough to note that the Lucan Jesus is concerned with this issue: how decategorization effected through a single interpersonal contact can be generalized beyond those caught up in the contact's dynamics. This is achieved in part, as already noted, by moving the focus from "neighbor" as the passive object of the group categorization process to "neighbor" as a person who acts properly (and compassionately) to assist someone in need (Luke 10:36). Thus the Lucan Jesus promotes a vision of human agency that extends beyond this narrative. But even more significant is the exchange that follows Jesus' question to the lawyer in 10:36: "[The lawyer] said, 'The one who showed mercy to him.' Jesus replied, 'Go yourself, then, and do likewise'" (10:37).

Whereas Jesus could have broken off the conversation with the lawyer's answer, that he continues with this injunction suggests a concern with doing more to generalize the Samaritan's behavior beyond the facts of that particular story. As already noted, Jesus utilizes the Samaritan's compassion to generate a new principle of moral behavior.

Conclusion

Gerd Theissen and Annette Merz have argued that the parable of the good Samaritan is authentic (1998:339). They suggest that it shows an Israelite perspective on the Samaritans as aliens, a view unlikely to have come from Luke. While I would like to believe the parable is authentic, I doubt that this can be demonstrated. Luke elsewhere reveals such interest in the Samaritans, both in the special material in his Gospel (9:51–56; 17:11–19) and in Acts (8:4–25), that it is hard to avoid the conclusion that, in this parable, he is taking up cognate issues. Moreover, something like the message that I have argued is found in the parable appears elsewhere in his double work. Thus there is a close parallel between the dissolution of social categories evident in the Samaritan's behavior and the attitude Peter attributes to God in Acts 10:34–35: "Truly I perceive that God shows no partiality, but in every nation anyone who fears him and does what is right is acceptable to him."

In other words, the Lucan advocacy for breaking down divisions between Judeans and Gentiles (especially through joint table fellowship; Esler 1987:71–109) is so similar to what the parable of the good Samaritan teaches about reducing divisions between Judeans and Samaritans that it is difficult to make a strong argument for authenticity.

In the end, however, I doubt this judgment really matters. We first can say that Luke well understood the message of Jesus as it revealed itself most particularly in his undoubtedly historical practice of breaking down other forms of social categorization by, for example, dining with sinners and tax collectors. Therefore, might we say that this is the sort of parable Jesus would have been happy to proclaim even if, in fact, he did not?

There is no denying that, in our world, modern yet still riven by the murderous consequences of ethnic division, the brilliant solution the parable proposed to much the same problem in the ancient Mediterranean suggests that this Jesus (Lucan or not) continues to speak to us with considerable power. There is perhaps no better proof of this than the ease with which the parable's strategy can be accommodated to important social-scientific research.

Notes

The initial version of this essay was presented at the "Jesus in New Contexts" conference at Tutzing, Bavaria, on 27 June 1999. Later versions were delivered at the Society of New Testament Studies conference in Pretoria on 5 August 1999 (at a joint session of the Luke-Acts and socio-rhetorical criticism seminars) and at the St. Mary's College Graduate Seminar on 1 December 1999. A detailed exposition of my views on the parable was published in *Biblical Interpretation* (2000:325–57), and I am grateful to its publisher Brill Academic Publishers, Leiden, for agreeing to the publication of this abridged form. I am also most grateful to those present on the three occasions I presented the paper orally for helping me to develop my approach, but especially to Professor Gerd Theissen after Tutzing and to my St. Mary's colleague, Professor Richard Bauckham. Responsibility for the views expressed here, however, is mine alone.

1. For a spread of views and useful bibliography, see Bauckham 1998; Crossan 1974; Fitzmyer 1985:882–90; Jülicher 1910; Lambrecht 1981:56–84; McDonald 1996; Schneider 1977:245–49; Wiefel 1987:206–11; and Zahn [1920] 1988:427–35.

2. Such as Lambrecht 1981:68–70 and Theissen and Merz 1998:339. Earlier in his career, John Dominic Crossan argued for the parable's authenticity (1991:xxxiii), but now considers this is hard to demonstrate (1991:449).

3. See Esler 1994:19–36 and the essays in Neyrey 1991; Esler 1995; Malina 1996; and Rohrbaugh 1996.

4. See Hogg and Abrams 1988 and the essays and bibliographies in Robinson 1996 and Worchel et al. 1998.

5. While many commentators assume that "you shall live" in Luke 10:28 is equivalent to "find eternal life," and thus echoes v. 25 (so Fitzmyer 1985:881), Bailey has demonstrated that this is an unjustified assumption (1980:38): Jesus is actually saying, "Do this and you will come alive." Jesus does not expressly endorse the view that those who adhere to the Mosaic law will find *eternal* life—a point I missed previously (Esler 1987:115).

6. See Esler 1987:110–30. For other discussions of this subject, see Salo 1991; Jervell 1979:133–51; Wilson 1983; and Blomberg 1984.

7. Accordingly, while agreeing with Richard Bauckham's view (1998) that issues of halakic interpretation arise in considering the attitudes of the priest and Levite to the injured man, I do not consider that the parable as a whole deals with how the law should be interpreted or that it presents Jesus as involved in legal interpretation.

8. So Zahn [1920] 1988:432, while Wiefel (1987:210) says he was probably a Judean.

9. Bauckham suggests that, although the man is described as "half-dead," the priest ran the risk that he would die when he went to help, or that it was impossible to ascertain whether he was alive or dead without coming so close—even without actual physical contact—that he would incur the corpse's impurity if the man were dead (1998:477–78).

10. The priest and the Levite would have been held to higher legal standards because of their connection with the cult and their expertise in interpreting the law (Sanders 1992:170–83).

11. Theissen's interesting suggestion that a tradition of altruistic help among Samaritan people possibly underlies the choice of the Samaritan (1990:388–89) seems to rest on an insufficient evidentiary basis and clashes with the very unflattering way that the Samaritans are treated shortly before, at Luke 9:51–56.

12. Although the Samaritans used a text of the Pentateuch slightly different from the Judeans, there is no difference between them as far as loving one's neighbor in Lev 19:18 is concerned; see Sadaqa and Sadaqa 1964:27.

13. For example, see Deschamps and Doise 1978; Brown and Turner 1979; Brewer et al. 1987; Diehl 1990; Hagendoorn and Henke 1991; Vanbeselaere 1991; Hewstone, Islam, and Judd 1993; Brown 1996; and Migdal, Hewstone, and Mullen 1998.

14. In the literature, situational categories are less common than those that preexisted the social interaction in question. But they do occur, as in the experiment conducted by Deschamps and Doise (1978), in which the two categorizations were gender and the allocation to subjects of a blue or red pen.

Works Cited

Allport, Floyd. 1924. *Social Psychology.* Boston: Houghton Mifflin.

Anderson, Robert A. 1992. "Samaritans." In *ABD* 5:940–47.

Bailey, Kenneth J. 1980. *Through Peasant Eyes: More Lucan Parables, Their Culture, and Style.* Grand Rapids: Eerdmans.

Bauckham, Richard. 1998. "The Scrupulous Priest and the Good Samaritan: Jesus' Parabolic Interpretation of the Law of Moses." *NTS* 44:475–89.

Bettencourt, B. A., et al. 1992. "Cooperation and the Reduction of Intergroup Bias: The Role of Reward Structure and Social Orientation." *Journal of Experimental Social Psychology* 28:301–9.

Blomberg, C. L. 1984. "The Law in Luke-Acts." *JSNT* 22:53–80.

Brewer, M. B., and N. Miller. 1984. "Beyond the Contact Hypothesis: Theoretical Perspectives on Desegregation." In *Groups in Contact: The Psychology of Desegregation,* edited by N. Miller and M. B. Brewer, 281–302. New York: Academic.

Brewer, M. B., et al. 1987. "Social Identity and Social Distance among Hong Kong Schoolchildren." *Personality and Social Psychology Bulletin* 13:156–65.

Brown, R. J., and J. C. Turner. 1979. "The Criss-Cross Categorization Effect in Intergroup Discrimination." *British Journal of Social and Clinical Psychology* 18:371–83.

Brown, Rupert. 1996. "Tajfel's Contribution to the Reduction of Intergroup Conflict." In Robinson 1996:169–89.

Cook, S. W. 1962. "The Systematic Analysis of Socially Significant Events." *JSI* 18:66–84.

———. 1978. "Interpersonal and Attitudinal Outcomes in Cooperating Significant Events." *Journal of Research and Development in Education* 12:97–113.

Creed, John Martin. 1930. *The Gospel according to St Luke.* Macmillan New Testament Commentary 3. London: Macmillan.

Crossan, John Dominic. 1991. *The Historical Jesus: The Life of a Mediterranean Jewish Peasant.* San Francisco: HarperSanFranciso.

———, ed. 1974. *Semeia 2: The Good Samaritan.* Missoula, Mont.: Scholars.

Derrett, J. Duncan M. 1970. *Law in the New Testament.* London: Darton, Longman & Todd.

Deschamps, J.-C., and W. Doise. 1978. "Crossed Category Memberships in Intergroup Relations." In Tajfel 1978:141–58.

Diehl, M. 1990. "The Minimal Group Paradigm: Theoretical Explanations and Empirical Findings." In *European Review of Social Psychology,* edited by W. Stroebe and M. Hewstone, vol. 1. 263–292. Chichester, England: Wiley.

Doise, W. 1976. *L'articulation psychosociologique et les relations entre groupes.* Brussels: de Boeck. Translated under the title *Groups and Individuals: Explanations in Social Psychology.* Cambridge: Cambridge University Press, 1978.

Esler, Philip F. 1987. *Community and Gospel in Luke-Acts: The Social and Political Motivations of Lucan Theology.* SNTSMS 57. Cambridge: Cambridge University Press.

———. 1994. *The First Christians in Their Social Worlds: Social-Scientific Approaches to New Testament Interpretation.* London: Routledge.

———, ed. 1995. *Modelling Early Christianity: Social-Scientific Studies of the New Testament in Its Context.* New York and London: Routledge.

———. 1998. *Galatians.* NTR. London: Routledge.

———. 2000. "Models in New Testament Interpretation: A Reply to David Horrell." *JSNT* 78:107–13.

———. 2000. "Jesus and the Reduction of Intergroup Conflict: The Parable of the Good Samaritan in the Light of Social Identity Theory." *BibInt* 8:325–57.

Fichtner, Johannes. 1968. "*Plēsion* in the LXX and the OT." In *TDNT* 6:312–15.

Fitzmyer, Joseph A. 1985. *The Gospel according to Luke X–XXIV.* AB 28A. New York: Doubleday.

Gaertner, S., et al. 1993. "The Common Ingroup Identity Model: Recategorization and the Reduction of Intergroup Bias." In *European Review of Social Psychology*, edited by W. Stroebe and M. Hewstone, 1:1–26. Chichester, England: Wiley.

Hagendoorn, L., and R. Henke. 1991. "The Effect of Multiple Category Membership on Intergroup Evaluations in a North-Indian Context: Class, Caste, and Religion." *BJSP* 30:247–60.

Hewstone, M. 1996. "Contact and Categorization: Social-Psychological Interventions to Change Intergroup Relations." In Macrae, Stangor, and Hewstone 1996:323–68.

Hewstone, M., and R. Brown, eds. 1986. *Culture and Conflict in Intergroup Encounters.* Oxford: Blackwell.

Hewstone, M., M. R. Islam, and C. M. Judd. 1993. "Models of Crossed Categorization and Integroup Relations." *Journal of Personality and Social Psychology* 64:779–93.

Hofstede, Geert. 1980. *Culture's Consequences: International Differences in Work-Related Values.* Beverly Hills, Calif.: Sage.

———. 1994. *Cultures and Organizations—Software of the Mind: Intercultural Cooperation and Its Importance for Survival.* London: HarperCollins.

Hogg, Michael A., and Dominic Abrams. 1988. *Social Identifications: A Social Psychology of Intergroup Relations and Group Processes.* London: Routledge.

Jervell, Jacob. 1979. *Luke and the People of God.* Minneapolis: Augsburg.

Jülicher, Adolf. 1910. *Die Gleichnissen Jesu. Erster Teil. Die Gleichnissen Jesu im Allegemeinen.* 2d ed. Tübingen: Mohr/Siebeck.

Lambrecht, Jan. 1981. *Once More Astonished: The Parables of Jesus.* New York: Crossroad.

Lauterbach, Jacob Z. 1933–35. *Mekilta de-Rabbi Ishmael: A Critical Edition on the Basis of the Manuscripts and Early Editions with an English Translation, Introduction, and Notes.* 3 vols. Philadelphia: Jewish Publication Society of America.

Lendon, Jon E. 1997. *The Empire of Honour: The Art of Government in the Roman World.* Oxford: Clarendon.

Macrae, C. N., C. Stangor, and M. Hewstone, eds. 1996. *Stereotypes and Stereotyping.* New York: Guildford.

Malina, Bruce J. 1996. *The Social World of Jesus and the Gospels.* New York and London: Routledge.

———. 2001. *The New Testament World: Insights from Cultural Anthropology.* 3d ed. Louisville: Westminster John Knox.

Manson, T. W. [1937] 1957. *The Sayings of Jesus: As Recorded in the Gospels according to St. Matthew and St. Luke.* London: SCM.

McDonald, J. I. H. 1996. "The View from the Ditch—and Other Angles: Interpreting the Parable of the Good Samaritan." *SJT* 49:21–37.

Meggitt, Justin J. 1998. *Paul, Poverty, and Survival.* Edinburgh: T. & T. Clark.

Migdal, M. J., M. Hewstone, and B. Mullen. 1998. "The Effects of Crossed Categorization on Intergroup Evaluations: A Meta-Analysis." *BJSP* 37:303–24.

Miller, N., M. B. Brewer, and K. Edwards. 1985. "Cooperative Interaction in Desegregated Settings: A Laboratory Analogue." *JSI* 41:63–79.

Minard, R. D. 1952. "Race Relationships in the Pocahontas Coal Field." *JSocSci* 8:29–44.

Neyrey, Jerome H., ed. 1991. *The Social World of Luke-Acts: Models for Interpretation.* Peabody, Mass.: Hendrickson.

Robinson, W. Peter, ed. 1996. *Social Groups and Identities: Developing the Legacy of Henri Tajfel.* Oxford: Butterworth-Heinemann.

Rohrbaugh, Richard L., ed. 1996. *The Social Sciences and New Testament Interpretation.* Peabody, Mass.: Hendrickson.

Sadaqa, Avraham, and Ratson Sadaqa, eds. 1964. *Jewish and Samaritan Versions of the Pentateuch: Leviticus.* Jerusalem: Rubin Mass.

Salo, Kalervo. 1991. *Luke's Treatment of the Law: A Redaction-Critical Investigation.* Annales Academiae Scientiarum Fennicae Dissertationes Humanarum Litterarum 57. Helsinki: Suomalainen Tiedeakatemia.

Sanders, E. P. 1992. *Judaism: Practice and Belief, 63 BCE–66 CE.* Philadelphia: Trinity Press International.

Schneider, Gerhard. 1977. *Das Evangelium nach Lukas: Kapitel 1–10.* 2d ed. ÖTNT 3. Gütersloh, Germany: Gütersloher.

Strack, H. L., and G. Stemberger. 1991. *Introduction to the Talmud and Midrash.* Translated by M. Bockmuel. Minneapolis: Fortress Press; Edinburgh: T. & T. Clark.

Tajfel, Henri. 1969. "Cognitive Aspects of Prejudice." *JSI* 25:79–97.

———. 1972. "La catégorisation sociale." In *Introduction à la Psychologie Sociale*, edited by S. Moscovici. Vol. 1. 272–302. Paris: Larousse.

———. 1981. "Social Stereotypes and Social Groups." In *Human Groups and Social Categories: Studies in Social Psychology*, edited by H. Tajfel. 144–167. Cambridge: Cambridge University Press.

———, ed. 1978. *Differentiation between Social Groups: Studies in the Social Psychology of Intergroup Relations*. London: Academic.

Tajfel, Henri, and J. C. Turner. 1979. "An Integrative Theory of Intergroup Conflict." In *The Social Psychology of Intergroup Relations*, edited by W. G. Austin and S. Worchel. 33–47. Monterey, Calif.: Brooks-Cole.

———. 1986. "The Social Identity Theory of Intergroup Conflict." In *Psychology of Intergroup Relations*, edited by S. Worchel and W. G. Austin. 7–24. Chicago: Nelson-Hall.

Theissen, Gerd. 1990. "Die Bibel diakonisch lesen: Die Legitimitätskrise des Helfens und der barmherzige Samariter." In *Diakonie — biblische Grundlagen und Orientierung: Ein Arbeitsbuch zur theologischen Verständigung über den diakonischen Auftrag*, edited by G. K. Schäfer and T. Strohm, 376–401. Veröffentlichungen des Diakoniewissenschaftlichen Instituts an der Universität Heidelberg 2. Heidelberg: Heidelberger Verlagsanstalt.

Theissen, Gerd, and Annette Merz. 1998. *The Historical Jesus: A Comprehensive Guide*. Translated by J. Bowden. Minneapolis: Fortress Press.

Turner, John C. 1981. "The Experimental Social Psychology of Intergroup Behaviour." In *Intergroup Behaviour*, edited by J. C. Turner and H. Giles, 66–101. Oxford: Blackwell.

Vanbeselaere, N. 1991. "The Different Effects of Simple and Crossed Categorizations: A Result of the Category Differentiation Process or Differential Category Salience." In *European Review of Social Psychology*, edited by W. Stroebe and M. Hewstone, 1:247–78. Chichester, England: Wiley.

Wiefel, Wolfgang. 1987. *Das Evangelium nach Lukas*. Berlin: Evangelische Verlagsanstalt.

Wilson, Stephen G. 1983. *Luke and the Law*. SNTSMS 50. Cambridge: Cambridge University Press.

Worchel, Stephen J., et al., eds. 1998. *Social Identity: International Perspectives*. London: Sage.

Zahn, Theodor. [1920] 1988. *Das Evangelium des Lukas: Mit einem Geleitwort von Martin Hengel*. Wuppertal: Brockhaus.

The Plague of Uncleanness?
The Ancient Illness Construct "Issue of Blood"
in Luke 8:43-48

Annette Weissenrieder

Illnesses are not invariable throughout history. The way a sick body is viewed is not constant over different periods of time. Rather, it is always influenced by the cultural codes associated with various illnesses at a particular time.[1] In Judaism, this is especially true with regard to the illness constructs for "leprosy" and "issue of blood," which play a role in the stories of the Synoptic Gospels. In the Judaic context, these constructs are associated with implications of medical, ritualistic, and social origin. In today's exegesis, "leprosy" and "issue of blood" are cited as paradigms for uncleanness. It is often argued that normal or "harmless" (Wohlhers 1999) bodily functions are identified as unclean—either arbitrarily or with misogynistic intent—and used as grounds for social exclusion or equation with the dead. Jesus, so runs the argument, by touching the leper and the hemorrhaging woman critiques this marginalization (Bovon speaks of a "critique of the Law" [2002:338]).

I intend to show that the author of the Gospel of Luke rejects the ritualistic implications of the illness in favor of a medical interpretation. *Jesus functions as a "healer" of both physical and social bodies.*

Almost no interpretation of Luke 8:43–48 has managed to avoid analysis of previous tellings, even though this analysis is often not acknowledged as a separate step in the process. Of primary interest is the irregular female issue of blood described in Leviticus 15 (LXX) as ῥύσις αἵματος (lit. flow of blood). If Leviticus 15 is included in the interpretation, the text functions as evidence of the woman's illness. This is supported first by the fact that no ancient author uses exactly this terminology to describe menstruation (Selvidge 1989:619; Vogt 1993:113ff.). Furthermore, the text assigns no precise meaning to the actual illness or to its classification in medical terms (Hengel and Hengel 1980:338–39), although "gonorrhea-blood-pus-issue" is referred to based on Leviticus 15. In this context, the woman's illness is analyzed as *gender-specific*.[2] This brings a far-reaching exegetical consequence: through the illness, the woman's uncleanness is implied,[3] which, in turn, supplies a *thanatological* dimension. At the same time, the exegetical argumentation to support these conclusions is often circular: if Leviticus 15 is the only reference, the ancient medical texts lose their relevance and the hermeneutic appears clear: *Jesus calls into question and overrides the Israelite law of purity.*

The first question I consider concerns the implications of Leviticus 15's portrayal of the irregular issue of blood. Second, I examine the illness as described in medical texts. Finally, I focus on signs indicating an illness and the associated thanatological dimension in Luke 8:43–48.

Leviticus 15 and the Communicability of *Ṭum'ah* (Uncleanness)

The woman's illness, described as an issue of blood, is more closely defined with the term ῥύσις αἵματος, which we encounter in Leviticus 15 (LXX).[4] Leviticus 15 is part of the so-called Purity Code, which applies to individual Israelites in fundamental life situations. Individual norms governing cleanness and uncleanness are used here in a purely functional role. Above all, they define a human being's capacity for ritual (see Batmartha 1995). The Purity Code is framed by two literary sections dealing with sacrifices and feast days (chaps. 1–10: instructions for priests and rituals; chaps. 16–27: orders for all of Israel). As a model for the theme of cleanness and uncleanness, Leviticus 15 deals with genital emission. Here, for the priest's benefit, it concentrates on the recognizable signs of cleanness and uncleanness in the (sick) person, and implicitly, on the protection of the community. First, Leviticus 15 briefly describes emissions of the male genitals, then discusses female issues of blood.[5] The following thematic areas are addressed: (1) normal and abnormal discharges; (2) communicability of the *ṭum'ah*; and (3) the period of separation. The text addresses various implications, although the *medical implication*, with the description of abnormal discharges, stands out. The text describes discharges in men that are caused by illness (vv. 2–3) and irregular issues of blood in women (vv. 25ff.). The LXX uses various terms for regular *and* irregular issues of blood: ῥύσις αἵματος (Lev 15:25); ἡ ῥέουσα αἵματι (Lev 15:19); η ῥύσις (Lev 15:1.19.25ff.); ῥέω (Lev 15:25); and πηγῆ τον αἵματος, αἱμορρούσῃ (Lev

15:33). Accordingly, no terminological difference between regular and irregular issues of blood can be inferred; the distinction between the two forms seems unclear. This point of view reflects the general understanding one finds in ancient medical texts concerning issues of blood.

Ritualistic implications in the Purity Code are directed primarily toward priests. At 15:14–15 and 29–30, restrictions concerning atonement for the two diseased emissions are roughly parallel. The period of separation for an uncleanness acquired through another person (vv. 4–8, 10–11, 19, 21ff., 27) or caused by pollution (vv. 16–17), lasts until the evening. Insofar as a man's diseased discharges and a woman's irregular issue of blood are placed on the same level, the period of separation for both occurrences covers the length of the illness plus seven days (vv. 13, 18).

Social implications concern communicability. In the case of a man infected with a venereal disease, every uncleanness—with the exception of pollution—is communicable: objects as well as people may be contaminated. Objects capable of being contaminated include, above all, clothing and surfaces for sitting and lying down (vv. 4, 9, 12, 17, 20, 26), whose uncleanness can then be transferred to third parties (vv. 5–6, 10, 21ff., 27). Further, rules of contamination for a man are transposed to an irregularly bleeding woman: "Every person whom she touched or who touched her becomes unclean" (Fander 1990:52; also Bovon 1989:447). Although scholars repeatedly cite Lev 15:19 as the basis for their argument regarding various forms of uncleanness in the Synoptic pericopes examined in this essay, the Levitical text furnished in support of the argument's conclusion relates only to an issue of blood occurring in regular cycles: "And the woman whosoever shall have an issue of blood, when her issue shall be in her body . . . everyone that touches her shall be unclean until evening" (Lev 15:19 LXX).

At this point, the text assumes a twofold transferal of uncleanness: the contamination of people *and* of objects on which the (sick) woman sits and lies. The modalities mentioned demonstrate a tendency toward intensification, since a distinction has otherwise been made between the contamination of people and that of objects. This distinction is now pointed out clearly by offering a further reference to an irregularly bleeding woman. It is acknowledged that "all the days of the issue of her uncleanness shall be as the days of her separation"; however, the additional remark "everyone that touches her shall be unclean until evening" lacks the case of the irregularly bleeding woman. Leviticus 15 assumes only the *"simple" contamination* of the objects on which the irregularly bleeding woman sits and lies. Specific mention of the contamination of people does not appear here. Only the secondary contamination of objects is noted explicitly. Later Israelite texts do relate the contamination of objects to that of people, with particular reference to this text, but to cite those exegetical conclusions in relation to either the Levitical or Synoptic texts under investigation would be to argue anachronistically.

What are the consequences of this reading of Leviticus 15 for the interpretation of Luke 8:43–48? The majority of commentaries have used the aura of uncleanness surrounding the bleeding woman as a starting point. Her condition is analyzed in the context of how she contaminates Jesus. But if the previous analysis is taken into account, this interpretation is not justified: close reading of Leviticus 15 indicates that Jesus was not risking contamination by being touched by the hemorrhaging woman, since the Levitical text in question distinguishes between contamination of people and objects when referring to irregularly menstruating women. From the perspective of Leviticus 15, Jesus is not affected by a communicable *ṭum'ah* from the bleeding woman. Therefore, in my opinion, if we are to make sense of the Synoptic pericope we must look outside Leviticus 15 (LXX) to a broader Hellenistic context. Focusing solely on Leviticus 15, as contemporary exegetes are wont to do in trying to clarify the sociocultural variables, will not support the conclusions usually drawn.

The Illness Construct and Ancient Professional Medicine

In chapter 9 ("De Sanguinis Fluore") of *Tardarum passionum II*, Caelius Aurelianus defines an issue of blood as an "outflow of blood from a hidden part" of the body (2.9.117; on ancient professional medicine, see Horstmanshoff 1990). Aurelianus distinguishes between correct and incorrect usage of the term "issue of blood" in the medical texts of his time. A correct use would describe a flow from close to the surface of the body. In contrast, he identifies an incorrect application of the term as one referring to an "ascending" (2.9.119) flow from the lung or stomach (2.9.119).[6] Aurelianus lists the causes (2.9.118) of an issue of blood as a blow or a fall, crying out loudly, carrying a heavy load, severe vomiting, or the result of chronic hemorrhoids. Soranus and the Hippocratics also recognize other causes such as fever, or an issue of blood as a phenomenon specific to women.

The location of the issue of blood is not very specific. According to Aurelianus, blood can flow from a wide variety of places in the body (2.11.127). For example, he mentions the top of the throat (2.11.128), the trachea (2.11.129), the lungs (2.11.130), the liver, the spleen, and the large vein connected to the spine (2.11.132). Soranus, Pliny, and the Hippocratics also mention the *regular issue of blood* in women.

For the most part, the four types of explanations in the medical texts of the Hippocratics, Soranus, Caelius Aurelianus,[7] and Pliny can be categorized as follows:

1. *Issue of blood as the result of ruptured veins.* The Hippocratics recognize a flow of blood (ῥύσις αἵματος), caused by the bursting of veins in connection with fever, although most of the examples are found in the so-called Coa presagia "Fever, redness of the face, severe headache and pounding pulse—it is these symptoms that mostly lead to hemorrhage . . ." (*Coa* 1.138, also 130). The Hippocratics explain these symptoms as arising from the body's attempt to reestablish an equilibrium in the bodily fluids and to cleanse the body. Heat is released by means of an issue of blood. After Caelius Aurelianus, a similar concept is supported by the followers of the Asclepiades (*Tardarum passionum* 2.10.124). Here an issue of blood is also understood as a therapeutic evacuation for cleansing the body.

2. *Issue of blood as the result of injury, decay, and tearing of tissues.* This form of blood issue, identified by Caelius Aurelianus as *flux sanguinis*, refers to internal injuries in the body that only become visible due to an issue of blood. The consistency of the issue of blood—whether it is clear blood (2.11.126) or a puss-like fluid (2.11.127)—are clues to a correct diagnosis.

3. *Issue of blood as the result of strenuous movement during pregnancy.* A ῥύσις αἵματος also appears in Soranus's gynecological works in reference to pregnancy. In the section "The care of women who have conceived," Soranus outlines three time periods in the care of a pregnant woman: (a) preservation of the implanted sperm; (b) "alleviation of possible accidents"; and (c) development of the embryo and easing the birth process. Under the first point he explains:

> For the seed is evacuated through fright, sorrow, sudden joy and, generally, by severe mental upset; through vigorous exercise, forced detention of the breath, coughing, sneezing, blows, and falls, especially those on the hips; . . . through want, indigestion, drunkenness, vomiting, diarrhea; by a flow of blood from the nose, from hemorrhoids or the other places; through relaxation due to some heating agent, through marked fever, rigors, cramps and, in general, everything inducing a forcible movement by which a miscarriage may be produced. (Soranus, *Gyn.* 1.46)

The Hippocratics also recognize a connection between an issue of blood and an aborted pregnancy (*Coa* 2.522).

4. *Blood issue in relation to regular female issues of blood.* The phrase ῥύσις αἵματοσις used at various points in the Corpus Hippocraticum and by Pliny and Soranus to refer to the regular female period. However, the images presented in the different texts differ from present-day knowledge of menstruation. *Coa* 2.163 describes: "Pounding in the head with ringing in the ears points to a hemorrhage or to menstruation; especially when severe heat descends down the spine. . . ." The body is seen as a shell within which various fluids are moving. Even from a distance—from an opposing part of the body—a stimulus can redirect an excess of fluid on a path that would not appear to be harmful. Today's common understanding of the inside of the body as containing a bloodstream or vessels did not exist for the ancients. The interior of the body was like an unstructured, osmotic space. For today's readers, the idea that a woman's issue could exit the body through different openings may seem strange. In *Aphor.* 5.32–33, it is written that "an issue of blood from the nose is a good thing, when female bleeding does not occur (αἵματος ῥύσις)." Pliny, too, groups nosebleeds and menstruation together in a way that seems curious to us. "The red seeds of the peony stops flows of blood; the same effect lies in the roots of the peony. The famous Klymenos agree totally, whether blood flows from the nose or the abdomen or the uterus" (*Nat. hist.* 26.131). Here the term for an issue of blood is *sanguis profluctio*, which corresponds to the Vulgate. This is supported by the idea of the equilibrium of bodily fluids, which, in line with ancient understanding, can also be maintained by blood flowing out of different parts of the body. Menstrual blood could exit through various openings: this belief is confirmed by Duden for the period until the mid–eighteenth century (1987:145–62). Possible exits were defined as the mouth, nose, ears, skin, and uterus.

Flux sanguinis or ῥύσις αἵματος is thus quite common terms in ancient medicine. Its is used in reference to widely varying symptoms of illnesses, all of which seem to have a similar cause: a disturbance in the equilibrium of fluids. For many ancient physicians, the study of fluids represented a fundamental means of explaining the etiology of diseases. According to this model, the human body functions according to an equilibrium of fluids, of which four are commonly named: blood, phlegm, and yellow and black bile. A person is healthy as long as the fluids are correctly balanced. Conversely, illness is identified as a lack or an excess of one of the fluids: in the case of the woman with an issue of blood, an excess of blood.

If one extends this inquiry to include other terms for an issue of blood, the focus falls particularly on the *irregular female issue of blood* that suggests itself in the background of Leviticus 15.

In the chapter "On Female Discharge" of the third book of his *Gynaeciorum*, Soranus discusses various physicians' opinions on issues of blood. Most of these physicians' works have not been preserved, but Soranus's version offers a good look at the discussions of antiquity. Alexander Philalethes defines the "female issue" as "an increased flow of blood through the uterus over a protracted period." It remains unclear whether Philalethes could be referring here to a continuous issue of blood lasting for twelve years. Demetrius defines the issue of blood as "a flow of fluid matter through the uterus over a protracted period since the flux may not be sanguineous only, but different at different times" (*Gyn.* 3.43). He does not attribute the issue exclusively to the uterus; rather, he includes the entire body when he claims that "one kind comes from the whole body, another from the uterus, and a third from some other part" (*Gyn.* 3.43). This statement corresponds to the results of the analysis of the term ῥύσις αἵματος, that blood can flow out of different openings in a woman's body. The important factor seems to be only that blood flows. Soranus himself defines an issue of blood as "a chronic rheum of the uterus where the secreted fluid is perceptibly increased" (*Gyn.* 3.43). He identifies symptoms of an issue "from the fact that the genital parts are continually moistened by fluids of different color, and the patient is pale, wastes away, lacks appetite, often becomes breathless when walking, and has swollen feet" (*Gyn.* 3.43). The Hippocratics also paraphrase irregular issues of blood with a form of ῥέω ("to flow") or ῥύσς ("flow"), sometimes combined with αἷμα ("blood"). Here, too, the term can be seen as a simple paraphrasing. "A red [= blood] issue occurs," write the Hippocratics, "following a fever, but more often after a miscarriage; however, it also occurs after the retention of the monthly flow, if this, having been blocked, suddenly breaks through. It also occurs after a birth" (Corpus Hippocraticum *Mul.* 2.110). According to this definition, an issue of blood can be interpreted as an internal flow that leaves the body unexpectedly. Issues leaving the body could also then be defined as a release, since they also have the effect of cleansing the body—except when they continue for long periods of time.

Blood issues of every sort are the subject of the second book of *De mulieribus*.[8] The term "issue" is variable and only more specifically defined through description. Thus, the word seems to be a paradox in and of itself, since an internal issue often becomes evident through the fact that it "freezes" or appears very suddenly. The term can be applied to pain that occurs with an internal issue, or to different issues such as menstruation, white or red issue, or to seeping wounds. Hence the word "issue" combines subjective impressions and descriptions with complex meanings. Yet another point becomes clear in this brief overview: an issue is associated with various symptoms, which makes the already loose concept of internal issue open to interpretation. The gravity of the irregular female issue of blood depends on the symptoms accompanying the illness, for example, shortness of breath, irregular pulse, invariability in sensory perception, or numbness in the body (Föllinger 1996). The simple label "issue of blood," then, is not sufficient to assess the severity of the illness.

The Illness Construct "Issue of Blood" in Luke 8:43–48

That issues of blood appear in the medical texts of antiquity is indisputable, even though, in contemporary exegesis on the Lucan pericope, there is no reference to them. The relevant question for the exegesis of Luke 8:43–48 is whether the author used Leviticus 15 as a reference point—which could then be seen as a vote in favor of the text's orientation to the Israelite discussion of cleanness and uncleanness—or if, on the other hand, the author is referring back to ancient medical science.

Use of the terms "issue of blood" (ῥύσις αἵματος) (Mark 5:25; Luke 8:43–44; cf. Lev 15:19, 25) and "touch" (ἅπτομαι) (Mark 5:27f.; Luke 8:44ff.; cf. Lev 15:7, 19, 27) speaks for accepting the text as part of an Israelite discussion on cleanness and uncleanness. Leviticus 15 could then function as a reference for Luke 8:43–48. This conclusion, however, is contradicted by the fact that the terminology of cleanness characteristic of Leviticus 15 and of the entire Purity Code, κάθαρσις/ἀκαθαρσις (Lev 15:20–27), is not used here (see Kahl 1995). Neither the expiatory sacrifice nor the rules of restriction are themes. Whatever relevance Leviticus 15 may have had, therefore, for the hemorrhaging woman of Luke 8:43–48, Luke's complete disregard of its semantic frame indicates that purity and uncleanness are not determinative sociocultural categories in the proper historical interpretation of this pericope.[9]

Nevertheless, questioning an analysis of the text against the background of the Purity Code seems debatable when one considers the use of αττομαι. The LXX reference to the issue of blood, connected with the reference to touching, recalls the semantic frame of reference of cleanness and uncleanness. Bovon concludes: "Her condition is all the more dramatic because her discharge of blood renders her ritually unclean and thus socially isolated. Contact with her is forbidden by the law. Thus the word ἅπτομαι ('to touch') is key here." (Bovon 2002:337). In Luke 8:43–49, however, the touching does not appear in the context of restrictions, nor is there mention of a priest who points out the

woman's cleanness. Rather, a semantic opposition is created between divine reality and human reality. Within human reality, an "issue of blood" is described
as a chronic illness, which brings massive economic consequences: the sick
woman is impoverished. As described by the few witnesses in Luke, the consulting physicians were unable to heal her. The divine reality is represented by
Jesus' extraordinary power (8:46), which was released with the touching of his
garment. The divine power, which brings healing through touch (Luke 5:13)
or by word (Luke 5:17, 24), is plausible within the context of Luke's Gospel.
That this is a case of divine reality is also made believable through the reaction
of the surrounding witnesses: they are "amazed" (5:26) Thus the text does not
lead us to consider the influence of the Purity Code on the hemorrhaging
woman or on Jesus being touched by her. This is not the woman's concern, nor
is it the concern of Jesus or, evidently, of the crowd around them. What does
shed light on this text, however, are the medical texts we have been examining.

First, it is striking that, in contrast to Mark's version, Luke does not include
two crucial points that would permit an interpretation in the sense of the Purity
Code. According to Mark 5:29, the woman felt that she was healed of her
"plague" (μάστιξ), an expression repeated with emphasis in 5:34. The author
of Mark also reports in 3:10 that many sick people wished to touch Jesus. On
the other hand, the term is only used once in Luke (7:21), in which plagues are
listed along with a general description of illnesses and the healing of evil spirits. If one considers the usage of μάστιξ in the LXX, Ps 38:8 stands out in particular. In verses 4, 6, and 8, various symptoms are listed that are also named in
the context of "leprosy": no "soundness in my flesh," the "wounds stink" and
"are corrupt." In verse 12, the social consequences of the illness are reported:
the people nearest to the speaker stand aloof because of the plague, that is, at a
distance. This distance could certainly indicate a social and local isolation like
that mentioned in Luke 17:12. Accordingly, the term "plague" may be interpreted as terminology that differs from other disease constructs, at least those associated with uncleanness in the Purity Code. In Leviticus 15, this term is not
applied to an irregular "issue of blood." This expansion of the meaning occurs
for the first time in 4Q274. Central to this text is a code of behavior for illnesses
identified with uncleanness, such as discharges and issues of blood. Plague is
explicitly mentioned in relation to "a woman suffering from her menstruation,"
thus equating the flow of blood with a plague.

Therefore, it is at least possible that the omission of the word "plague" could
stem from the fact that its use would point to the disease construct for an issue
of blood that characterizes the Purity Code and, with it, Leviticus 15. Significantly, therefore, far from invoking Leviticus 15 as the backdrop for understanding this pericope, our author wishes to avoid this association.

This theory is further supported by a second conspicuous omission: Luke does not mention the source of the issue of blood, which Mark describes with "fountain of her blood"—πηγὴ τον αἵματος. In Lev 12:7 (LXX), this phrase appears as the source of an issue of blood in the context of instructions for women who have given birth. It is the equivalent of "uterus" in Hebraic texts that also deal with medical problems (see Preuss [1911] 1992). If the author of Luke is avoiding this term, which is indigenous to the Purity Code, then this in turn represents a conscious decision in terms of understanding the illness. He avoids any reference to the code of purity. Could it be that he intends instead to follow the ancient medical understanding of the illness? The etiology of the issue of blood does not appear to be important to him, otherwise he would have left the gender-specific references in the text or even have emphasized them. As it is, it is simply clear that blood is flowing. In this way, the author of Luke reduces his statement to the case history of an issue of blood, and thereby to an ancient construct of the body and illness that centers on the equilibrium of fluids.

By neglecting to use the terms that Mark employs—"plague" and "fountain of her blood"—as well as those indicating cleanness and uncleanness, the author does away with the fundamental references to the Purity Code of Leviticus 12–15 and concentrates solely on the issue of blood as an indicator of illness and the social consequences that accompany it.

If the author of Luke has made the signs of disease the focal point, the second essential question becomes that of the *severity of the illness*. Unfortunately, the majority of ancient medical texts do not offer precise answers to this question. In the introduction to his ninth chapter dealing with issues of blood, Caelius Aurelianus describes the following: "An outflow of blood from a hidden part [of the body] can often lead to an improvement in health, but can just as often be highly dangerous. In some cases, it can lead to immediate death, if the body becomes weakened by an excessive issue [of blood]. In other cases, death comes in the final phase [of the illness], when consumption develops or when an internal wound fails to heal" (*Tardarum passionum* 2.9.117). This statement is supported by similar terminology from the physicians of antiquity. A variety of terms are employed interchangeably to describe regular and irregular issues of blood. For example, the Hippocratics mention "female flow" (*Aphor.* 173) and "flow", Soranus describes regular and irregular issues of blood with "female flow" (*Gyn.* 2.41, 43), and Pliny treats the following terms as equivalent: *profluvium* (*Nat. hist.* 26.160) and, more frequently, *sanguis profluvia* (26.131, 133); *fluctiones mulierum* (21.123); and *profluvia feminarum* (27.103; 29.9). None of these expressions refers to the etiology or pathogenesis of the illness. They simply describe the facts without evaluating them. Therefore, the term ῥύσις αἵματος (flow of blood) by itself does not indicate an illness. The severity of the disease is not linked to the term "issue of blood;" rather, it is determined by a series of other criteria, for example, the heaviness of the blood flow or the duration. The duration of the illness is reported in Luke 8:43–49, as well as in Mark, to be twelve years.[10] In addition, the texts mention the physicians the woman has consulted and the hopelessness of a cure. If the inclusion of the illness's duration in the text seems unusual to today's readers, the perspective shifts when one considers that, according to the Corpus Hippocraticum, an exact record of the length of an illness was of great relevance to the case history. The duration of illnesses is mentioned often in the seven books of "On Epidemics," in which the duration of an illness is an essential part of the chronicles of illness. In such references, the number of weeks, months—or, very occasionally, years—are seen as signs of intensification of the illness and of the imminence of death. If a physician diagnoses a patient as being near death, the therapy is discontinued. The patient is already considered to be dead.

In light of this understanding, an illness lasting twelve years (Luke 8:43) would signal incurability and imminent death. The mention of physicians, which covers just a few lines of text, can then be seen as part of this line of thinking.

By avoiding references to the Purity Code of Leviticus 15 and the associated focus on the indicators of illness, the author emphasizes the thanatological dimension. In other words, the interest is in the degree of illness and not—as is often assumed in exegesis—in uncleanness. Christologically, the Lukan Jesus removes the "plague" of illness rather than the plague of uncleanness.

A further measure of support for this thanatological reading may be found in the narrative composition. The relevance of the community and the function of the individual within the community form the background for the following considerations. If disease is interpreted within a thanatological framework, and met with a dimension of death of whatever nature, the idea concealed behind this interpretation is that life in its fullest sense is only possible within a community (Janowski 1995:163). Therefore, *only the community can guarantee subsistence to the individual,* both economically and socially (with a different emphasis, see Hasenfratz 1984). Both aspects are illustrated with the reference in Luke 8:43 to the unsuccessful visits to the physicians. On the one hand, in the context of ancient medicine, the futility of the visits points to the termination of medical help, which underlines the incurable nature of the illness. On the other hand, the bleeding woman's livelihood is consumed due to the consultation. Both of these results could be interpreted as the sphere of death. Illness can be defined as *a loss of function in the social body.* However, it would be an oversimplification of this point to infer the woman's exclusion from society on the basis of illness. After all, it is significant that the woman with the issue of blood steps forth out of a crowd and attains healing within the obscurity of the multitude, v. 45; v. 47). One should consider the connotation of the crowd in Luke's Gospel: it distinguishes itself in that it can be interpreted as a "summoned gathering of Jesus' close relatives" (Bovon 2002:336–37 n. 31). If the woman with the issue of blood lingers within this group, this could indicate her affiliation with the crowd of believers. An analogy to Jairus's daughter—whose healing forms the framing story here—and her membership in a family could then be constructed. The transformation of the bleeding woman and her state of privation, however, is set in motion not by an intermediary, but by the woman herself.

This transformation is particularly made clear through the *verbs of movement:* while the people are depicted as waiting (v. 40), verbs of movement are repeatedly applied to the woman (v. 44; v. 47; v. 47; v. 48). The verbs are accompanied by details that express a paradox, that the woman approached from "behind him"[11] and "hid." One could speak of a "paradoxical integration." The central point is not exclusion from the community, but the lack of functionality imposed on the woman due to her long-term illness and absence of hope for a cure.[12] The bleeding woman's lack of function stands out in contrast to Jairus, who, as the ruler of a synagogue and a homeowner (v. 41), represents various aspects of belonging. Second, the transformation is also indicated through the *verbs of speech* repeatedly applied to Jesus. Before the healing, the verbs of speech function as a sign of the seclusion of the incident for the people and the disciples (vv. 45–46), and verify the incident's visibility for Jesus; afterward, the verbs function as the expression of positive change. Not Jesus and the disciples, but the people, are named as the forum for the proclamation of the woman's healing (v. 47). This is striking when one takes into account the forum in Mark 5:33 for the speech to the healed woman: Jesus. The triumph over the presence of death in Luke occurs, in the end, through the integration of the bleeding woman into the community, when Jesus makes her his daughter (v. 48). Not only is her relationship to Jesus implied. Amid the crowd, the healed woman is given a function as the daughter of Jesus, which amounts to a repeal of her "paradoxical integration."

Conclusion

In the Gospel of Luke, medical and social implications take on greater importance than the ritualistic implications. Jesus appears as a healer. At the center of the story in 8:43–48 is the healing of an illness that has moved the woman into the realm of the dead; the story represents healing of the physical as well as the social body. In contrast, in Mark's Gospel, Jesus fills more of a priestly function. The central point is the plague of uncleanness, which does not, however—as is often assumed—refer to a contamination of uncleanness through touch.

1. The theme in Luke 8:43–48 is not the plague of uncleanness, but the "plague" of illness, which causes the bleeding woman to enter the realm of the dead. The theme of cleanness and uncleanness professed by the implied reference to Leviticus 15 is consciously avoided. The focus is not on Jesus' questioning or even overriding of the Israelite law of purity, but on overcoming the sphere of death, which the woman has entered because of her illness. Two consequences of the dimension of death are mentioned: the *economic implications* and the *"paradoxical integration."* The triumph over the dimension of death comes through the healing power of Jesus and through the woman's assignment as a daughter of Jesus.

2. After analysis of Luke's text, the *etiology of the issue of blood* remains obscure when viewed against the background of ancient professional medicine, since the author does not mention the "fountain of her blood." On the one hand, an issue of blood can indicate a serious internal illness that accompanies an injury or a rupture of tissues. On the other hand, an issue of blood is identified as the cause of a miscarriage, or it can represent a therapeutic evacuation to restore the equilibrium of body fluids. Additionally, the Hippocratics, Soranus, and Pliny use the term "issue of blood" in the sense of menstruation, which can exit the body through various openings.

3. The reporting of the duration of the illness—twelve years—and the mention of supposed attempts at healing by various physicians make it likely that the issue of blood would have been classified as a *severe illness*.

4. Up to now, exegetes have analyzed the issue of blood—above all in feminist discussions—as a *gender-specific illness*. The omission of the etiology of the issue of blood, specifically of "the fountain of her blood"—as the uterus is also called in the Hebrew texts (e.g., Leviticus 15)—makes a gender-specific interpretation no longer inevitable. Omission of the term "plague," which, in the Purity Code in Leviticus, is applied to leprosy, also points away from Leviticus 15 as a frame of reference. Finally, recoding the semantic frame of reference for "touch," and avoidance of the terms cleansing/defilement—also missing from Mark's text—speak against the connotations of uncleanness.

Notes

1. Since this essay does not use social-scientific method, I do not make use of the distinction suggested by Pilch and his anthropological sources (2000:93) between disease as a "biomedical" and illness as a "sociocultural perspective." Even the medical point of view is not free of cultural and social constructs, although this may be an irrelevant observation.

2. Compare most recently Pilch (2000:96–97), who notes that Luke reports only men having leprosy and only women with an "issue of blood."

3. This connotation is also assumed when a psychosomatic cause is suspected as the etiology of the illness, as in Fenner 1930:45ff.

4. Leviticus 15 presents a kind of abstract, an extremely brief summary of information relating to an irregular issue of blood. Whether rules against contamination or contact already existed in the first century c.e.—as *m. Zabim* 2:14 or *m. Nid.* 3:2 suggest—is not as clear to me as it seems to Fander (1990:193). Compare also the remarks of Cohen (1991:278ff.), who assumes that rules against contact with bleeding women, and their exclusion from the synagogue, would not have been plausible before the sixth or seventh century.

5. At the level of content, a concentric structure is evident. See Milgrom 1991:905.

6. Aurelianus explains the incorrect identification thus, in *Tardarum passionum* 2.9.120: "But when one considers the differentiation of the names, the Greeks identified these things [ascending and descending] the other way around: they speak of *anagōgē* [ascending], which specifically differentiates an issue [of blood] from a lower to a higher area" (translation mine).

7. A large part of Soranus's medical discourse has only been preserved through Caelius Aurelianus's Latin version, recorded in the sixth century.

8. Writings from the gynecological texts of the Hippocratics have been considered, although without reference in the analysis of Grensemann 1982.

9. Kahl (1995:66–67) assumes that the author of the Gospel of Mark must have been familiar with the rules for priests and with restrictions connected with the sickness of "leprosy," which would have also been relevant in this area. This assumption is only partially helpful when applied to Luke, although, on the whole, Luke 5:12–16 maintains the style of Mark's text. In Luke, the interpretation of "leprosy" as unclean is not questioned; nevertheless, a recoding of the semantic frame of reference takes place.

10. In several stories in Luke, the duration of an affliction is pointedly emphasized, for example, in the case of the "bent" woman (13:11) and of the possessed man from the country of the Gadarenes, where the illness is assumed to have been present for a long time (8:27, 29).

11. The use of "behind" is also central in the appearance of the "woman . . . who was a sinner" in Luke 7:36-50.

12. One could also speak of a paradoxical integration in reference to the people healed in the synagogue, who are lingering there with nothing to do before they are healed. Compare, for example, Luke 4:33ff. and 6:6–11.

Works Cited

Batmartha, Ina J. 1995. "Machen Geburt und Monatsblutung die Frau 'unrein'? Zur Revisionsbedürftigkeit eines missverstandenen Diktums." In Schottroff and Wacker 1995:43–60.

Bendz, Gerhard, and I. Pape, eds. 1990. *Caelii Aureliani: Celerum Passionum Libri III. Tardarum Passionum Libri V, Teil I.* Berlin: Akademie.

Bovon, François. 2002. *Luke 1: Luke 1:1—9:50.* Translated by C. Thomas. Hermeneia. Minneapolis: Fortress Press.

Burguière, Paul, et al., eds. 1988–94. *Maladies des femmes (Soranos d'Éphèse).* 3 vols. Paris: Les belles lettres.

Cohen, Shaye J. D. 1991. "Menstruants and the Sacred in Judaism and Christianity." In *Women's History and Ancient History*, edited by S. B. Pomeroy, 273–99. Chapel Hill: University of North Carolina Press.

Dietz, Friedrich Reinhold, and Valentin Rose, eds. 1882. *Sorani Gynaeciorum vetus translatio latina nunc primum edita cum additis graeci textus reliquiis a Dietzio repertis atque ad ipsum Codicum Parisiensem nunc recognitis.* Bibliotheca scriptorum Graecorum et Romanorum Teubneriana. Leipzig: Teubner.

Duden, Barbara. 1987. *Geschichte unter der Haut: Ein Eisenacher Arzt und seine Patientinnen um 1730.* Stuttgart: Klett-Cotta. Translated by T. Dunlap under the title *The Woman beneath the Skin: A Doctor's Patients in Eighteenth-Century Germany* (Cambridge: Harvard University Press, 1991).

Fander, Monika. 1990. *Die Stellung der Frau im Markusevangelium: Unter besonderer Berücksichtigung kultur- und religionsgeschichtlicher Hintergründe.* Münsteraner theologische Abhandlungen 8. Altenberge: Telos.

Fenner, Friedrich. 1930. *Die Krankheit im Neuen Testament.* Untersuchungen zum Neuen Testament 18. Leipzig: Hinrichs.

Föllinger, Sabine. 1996. "Σχετλια δρωσι: 'Hysterie' in den hippokratischen Schriften." In *Hippokratische Medizin und antike Philosophie*, edited by R. Wittern and P. Pellegrin, 437–50. Medizin der Antike 1. Hildesheim: Olms Weidmann.

Grensemann, Hermann. 1982. *Hippokratische Gynäkologie: Die gynäkologischen Texte des Autors C nach den pseudohippokratischen Schriften De mulieribus I, II und De sterilibus.* Wiesbaden: Steiner.

Hasenfratz, Hans-Peter. 1984. "Die Toten Lebenden: Religionsphänomenologische Studie zum sozialen Tod in archaischen Gesellschaften." *HR* 23:387–89.

Hengel, Rudolf, and Martin Hengel. 1980. "Die Heilungen Jesu und medizinisches Denken." In *Der Wunderbegriff im Neuen Testament*, edited by A. Suhl, 338–73. Wege der Forschung 295. Darmstadt: Wissenschaftliche Buchgesellschaft.

Horstmanshoff, H. F. J. 1990. "The Ancient Physician: Craftsman or Scientist?" *Journal of the History of Medicine*. 45:176–97.

Janowski, B. 1995. "Dem Löwen gleich, gierig nach Raub: Zum Feindbild in den Psalmen." *EvTh* 55:155–73.

Jones, W. H. S., ed. [1931] 1959. *Hippocrates*. Vol. 4. LCL. London: Heinemann.

Kahl, B. 1995. "Jairus und die verlorenen Töchter Israels: Sozioliterarische Überlegungen zum Problem der Grenzüberschreitung in Mk 5, 21–43." In Schottroff and Wacker 1995:61–78.

Kapferer, Richard, ed. 1927–49. *Die Werke des Hippokrates: Die Hippokratische Schriftensammlung in neuer deutscher Übersetzung*. Stuttgart: Hippokrates-Verlag.

König, R., and G. Winkler, eds. 1973–. *C. Plinius Sekundus d.Ä.: Naturalis historise libri XXXVII. Naturkunde lateinisch-deutsch*. Darmstadt.

Littré, Emile, ed. 1961–63. *Oeuvres complètes d'Hippocrate*. 10 vols. Amsterdam: Hakkert. Reprinted, 1973–91.

Milgrom, Jacob. 1991. *Leviticus 1–16*. AB 3. New York: Doubleday.

Neusner, Jacob. 1976. *A History of the Mishnaic Law of Purities*. Pt. 15: *Niddah*. SJLA. Leiden: Brill, 1976.

Pilch, John J. 2000. *Healing in the New Testament: Insights from Medical and Mediterranean Anthropology*. Minneapolis: Fortress Press.

Preuss, Julius. [1911] 1992. *Biblisch-talmudische Medizin: Beiträge zur Geschichte der Heilkunde und der Kultur überhaupt*. Reprint, Farnborough: Gregg.

Schottroff, Luise, and Therese Wacker, eds. 1995. *Von der Wurzel getragen: Christlich-feministische Exegese in Auseinandersetzung mit Antijudaismus*. BibIntSer 17. Leiden: Brill.

Selvidge, Marla J. 1990. *Woman, Cult, and Miracle Recital: A Redactional-Critical Investigation on Mark 5:24–34*. Lewisburg, Pa.: Bucknell University Press.

Temkin, Owsei. 1991. *Soranus' Gynecology*. Baltimore: Johns Hopkins University Press.

Vogt, Thea. 1993. *Angst und Identität im Markusevangelium: Ein textpsychologischer und sozialgeschichtlicher Beitrag*. NTOA 26. Göttingen: Vandenhoeck & Ruprecht.

Wohlers, M. 1999. "Aussätzige reinigt" (Mt 10,8): Aussatz in antiker Medizin, Judentum und frühem Christentum." In *Text und Geschichte: Facetten theologischen Arbeite aus dem Freundes- und Schülerkreis. Dieter Lührmann zum 60. Geburtstag*, edited by S. Maser and E. Schlarb. Marburger theologisher Studien 50. Marburg: Elwert.

Politics and Political Religion

13

The Political Dimension of Jesus' Activities

Gerd Theissen

How political was Jesus? This question often implies another question that has immediate relevance. How political is the Christian church, and how political should it be? These questions are quite distinct, yet not unrelated. The first focuses on the political dimension of Jesus' activity; it is an academic question reflecting interest in historical knowledge. The second question looks to contemporary political responsibility reflecting practical interest. Both questions are interdependent, since if we demonstrate a political dimension in Jesus' activity, we may heighten Christian awareness of the political dimension of religion and of a responsible attitude in politics.

To return to the original question: How political was Jesus? The answer depends on the concept of politics on which we base our discussion. Politics may be understood in a broad or narrow sense. In antiquity, people understood politics in a broad sense only. According to Aristotle, the objective of politics is to realize the idea of a good life within a *polis*, the Greek city. This concept is normative. It implies standards for a successful life—the goal of politics. In modern times we often encounter a narrower concept of politics that states that politics is the art of gaining and maintaining power. This concept implies no normative objective. It was Machiavelli who developed this idea in the beginning of modern times (Sellin 1978:790). But his concept is not the prevailing modern concept of politics either. The broader understanding is still in vogue. In German, unlike English, the word *Politik* refers to (1) "polity" in the sense of the political institution, society, its structure and its political system; (2) "politics" as the process of achieving some collective objective in conflict situations; and (3) "policy" as the goals and values that are to be achieved (Münkler 1997:1). While "polity" (the political institution) and "policy" (goals and values) refer to politics in the broad sense, "politics" (process of gaining and holding control) points to the narrower usage that I prefer here. This is the normal English usage. For if we employ the broader meaning, there is no doubt that Jesus' activities include a political dimension, since politics and ethics, policies and political structures cannot be separated. Yet if we ask, "How political was Jesus?" we usually look to the narrow concept of politics, that is, to Jesus' concern to gain and hold domination. With this meaning in mind, we may ask: Was Jesus executed as a political rebel? Did he and his disciples plan a revolution? Did they sympathize with resistance movements? What did Jesus teach about the use of force?

One major objection to the application of the narrow concept of politics in discourse about Jesus is that the broad concept prevailed in antiquity. There is no doubt that Jesus is a representative of the ancient world. Should we not analyze his world with the help of categories that existed in his world? Does the narrow understanding of politics not suggest an anachronistic separation of religion and politics in antiquity? Does not the narrow understanding neglect normative goals and religion? And is not this neglect a specifically modern phenomenon? True, some would hold that the separation of religion and politics had already begun in antiquity—in Israelite and early Jesus groups—but that it manifested itself only in modern times. In antiquity, nobody could imagine politics without religion, and neither did Israelite or early Jesus groups. Do we unconsciously project modern structures onto the ancient world when we deal with the relationship between Jesus and politics as if religious proclamation and politics were two separate domains? In what follows, my preference is for the narrow definition of politics, and the reason is that, if there is a connection between Jesus and politics in the narrow sense, we can a fortiori assume such a connection between Jesus and politics in the broader sense. Ultimately we gain a better view of how politically oriented Jesus was in the broader sense of politics.[1]

Let us start with some definitions of politics, power, violence, and domination. They are based on definitions by Max Weber, the early twentieth-century social philosopher. Weber defines politics as "striving for participation in power or to influence the distribution of power, both between states and between the groups of human beings within a state" (1976:822; 1964:167–85, 506). He thus opts for the narrow understanding of politics. Yet he also demands of politicians an ethic of responsibility (*Verantwortungsethik*) that looks to public welfare.[2] In doing so, he combines the narrow definition of politics with the broader. But at the center of all politics he sees the distribution of power. What is power?

Weber defines power as "every opportunity to realize one's own will within a social relation regardless of the basis for this opportunity," that is, regardless of whether power is based on force or legitimation.[3] The exercise of power always confronts human beings with demands and promises (in case the demands are fulfilled). In principle, there are three ways to realize one's will (see Etzioni 1968:357–58 for these distinctions):

1. *Utilitarian power.* We can gain the support of other people by evoking expectations of advantages, if they fulfill our will. Usually this happens by paying money. But natural products or other forms of support may be means to gain such power. Even far-reaching promises of future (religious) salvation may be subsumed under utilitarian power. This way of having effect on others is done by inducement.

2. *Coercive power.* Power can be based on force, which injures or threatens to injure health, life, possession, and liberty. Political power is characterized by the ability to wield the negative sanction of force. Therefore, politicians always strive to gain control over the coercive apparatus of the state, especially over the police and the military. It is a modern development to grant the state a monopoly over the legitimized exercise of force. Yet, in the long run, no state can sustain itself on force alone.[4] This way of having effect on others is done by force.

3. *Persuasive power.* We can get other people to obey our will by convincing or persuading them. Persuasion is involved in every legitimate exercise of power, because it is characteristic of legitimate power that a ruler's authority is internally accepted by those who are ruled. This way of having effect on others is done by influence.

Power is governance inasmuch as a ruler's command is accepted by the ruled as a legitimate exercise of power. Governance implies "the opportunity for a given order to be obeyed by a defined group of persons" (Weber 1976:28). The struggle for political power is therefore not only a struggle for materialistic advantages and for the control of armed force. It is, to a great extent, a struggle for the legitimation of the exercise of power, especially for the power to promulgate legitimate laws and edicts. In his sociology of domination, Weber distinguished among three forms of authority that legitimize human domination.[5] All these forms of legitimation can reduce the display of power within relations of domination:

1. *Charisma* may be defined by the fact that authority is accepted without force, even when dominant traditions and institutions are opposed to charismatics.

2. *Tradition* (e.g., dynastic descent) effects acceptance of authority and no force is necessary.

3. *Bureaucracy* legitimizes its authority by rules designed to reduce arbitrary domination.

The result is that, in all these cases, certain individuals or role incumbents have an increased opportunity for exercising power. These are charismatic "leaders," dynastic rulers, or bureaucratic administrators. Evidently, the more legitimacy power has, the more it can renounce the exercise of force and the threat of force as sanction. In other words, the more one motivates people to do something by persuasion, the more one can renounce inducement and force. Now we can state that we encounter with Jesus a special way of exercising power:

1. We do find elements of utilitarian power. Jesus employs inducement. He promises salvation—partly in the present in the form of miracles and a meal community, partly in the near future as participation in the kingdom of God.
2. We find no coercive power, but a clear rejection of the application of force. Yet the endurance of violence (passivity in face of violence) plays a crucial role. Charismatics like Jesus are often successful because they risk becoming the victims of violence and aggression. Charisma is established by self-stigmatization (Mödritzer 1994; for a critique of Weber's view of charisma and its application to the story of Jesus, see Malina 1984). The charismatic takes the role of an outsider who has no real chance to gain social acceptance by the majority. Yet in this role he exercises much more power. If he survives the refusal of the majority, this survival provides the basis for increased influence on his adherents—without exercise of force or compulsion.
3. The most important aspect of Jesus' exercise of power is persuasion. By basing all power on the power of the kingdom of God, he based his power on the central conviction of the Israelite community—in the faith in the one and only God of Israel. All the influence he exerts on other people is legitimated by this faith. Moreover, symbols have a remarkable importance in his activity. Consider how much legitimacy derived from the possession of symbols like crown and scepter! The politics of power based on force applied by soldiers and the police is complemented by the use of symbols, that is, by political symbolic actions (see Dörner 1995). Jesus was a master not only at inventing parabolic short stories, but also at performing political symbolic actions.

Having made these distinctions,[6] we may put forward the following theses, which will be supported by arguments in the course of this essay.

1. Jesus evoked political expectations. In his environment, he elicited the hope that he might eventually be the ruler as the Messiah. He had effect on people by the expectation of salvation that his activity attracted, and therefore he was crucified on the grounds of a political accusation, of his being the king of the Judeans, Israel's Messiah. This does not imply that he believed himself to be the messianic ruler, but neither did he clearly deny the messianic expectations he had aroused.

2. In tension with the first thesis, Jesus refused force and coercion. He thus opposed a constituent element of all politics. In the end he was the victim of political force: he was crucified by a Roman governor. He had a negative or hostile attitude toward the exercise of power by force.[7] We find him, especially in the Sermon on the Mount, to represent a nonpolitical ethical awareness (*Gesinnungsethik*).[8] However, there is more.

3. The contradiction between expectations of Jesus as a political ruler and his nonpolitical attitude to the use of force cannot be resolved by the widespread assumption that Jesus himself was not politically oriented, but that he was crucified because of a political misunderstanding. In fact, Jesus preferred a way of ruling that reduced the use of force. This was his politics by symbols. It should be emphasized that, by itself, politics by symbols does not exclude force. It is possible, with the help of political symbols, to stir up sentiment in favor of the use of force. But the means used to increase the use of force are in fact nonviolent in this case. So far as there is an opportunity to employ those means, they can likewise be used to reduce coercion.

4. The fourth thesis sets this politics of curtailing force within the traditions of antiquity. The result represents a humane ideal of domination, which in antiquity demanded the self-limitation of power. It is a characteristic of the Jesus tradition to use the ideal of the humane ruler as an ideal for the ethic of common people. The charisma of Jesus—his nonrational radiance and ability to attract and attach persons to himself—is based on the fact that he let other people participate in his "sovereignty."

I want to contrast the thesis of a political misunderstanding of Jesus' activity with my thesis of a politics of symbols without coercion. This politics is formed by an alternative ancient ideal of sovereignty and makes this ideal accessible to everybody. We then encounter a political paradox, since there is no politics without latent exercise of physical coercion. Yet all civic efforts in politics aim at reducing and subduing coercion in politics. Jesus takes a part in the history of these efforts.

All research on the historical Jesus is inhibited by uncertainty. All Jesus traditions are subject to questions of authenticity. We cannot discuss this subject here. But even if we had room to do so, we would never come to the end of the discussion. Therefore, one may read the following exposition as an analysis of the oldest Jesus traditions—and leave open the question whether these oldest Jesus traditions are stamped by the profile of a historical figure or by the imagination of early Jesus groups. Yet a simple consideration makes it plausible that the action of the historical Jesus presupposes a political framework. Despite all skepticism, we can be certain about two key events: the baptism of Jesus in the beginning of his career and his crucifixion at the end of his life.[9] Whatever is preserved of authentic Jesus traditions must be placed between these two key facts. Both have been an embarrassment for early Jesus groups. Jesus' baptism suggested that Jesus considered himself a sinner, who needed remission of his sins by baptism, and that he was subordinated to John the Baptist.[10] Even more offensive was the cross. It is difficult to proclaim someone who suffered the ignominious death of the cross as a God-given savior. Both key facts have something to do with politics. Jesus started as a disciple of John the Baptist, who was killed early on for political reasons (Josephus, *Ant.* 16.116–19). And Jesus also ended as a criminal—charged on the grounds of his claim to be the king of the Judeans, striving for political power. Since these key facts cannot be interpreted without taking their political dimension into consideration, can we then imagine that Jesus' actions between these key events were totally nonpolitical? We should rather ask: in what sense were his actions political?

Jesus and the Expectation of His Messianic Rule

Among the last generation of historical-critical exegetes, there was a near consensus that Jesus did not consider himself a Messiah. Jesus' disciples were the first to call him Messiah when the resurrected Jesus appeared to them. In the last few decades, historical research has pointed out that we cannot speak of *the* Messiah in Judaism, because we encounter very different expectations concerning the Messiah, which were not at all shared by all Israelites (Charlesworth 1992; see the essays in *Jahrbuch für biblische Theologie* 8 [1993]). It strikes us all the more that early Jesus groups nearly unanimously called Jesus "Messiah" (in Greek: *Christos*).[11] Even Josephus refers to him as the "one called *Christos*" (*Ant*. 20.200). The Greek version, "Christ," came to be treated as a proper name, yet the label did radiate a numinous aura of being "anointed."[12] It is also striking that, among early Jesus groups, the title "Christ" was always understood as a designation for a royal Messiah, the "king of the Judeans," and not for a prophetic or priestly Messiah.[13] This is not at all self-explanatory, because the term "Messiah" did not a priori designate "royal Messiah."

It seems probable that Jesus did not claim to be the Messiah. But, during his lifetime, others did consider him the Messiah. He encountered the expectation and the hope that he would be the royal Messiah, the future ruler of Israel. The confession of Peter may have a historical core. It is no retrospective anachronism of post-Easter faith.[14] Some arguments in favor of its authenticity may be summarized as follows.

There are no examples of a person becoming a Messiah because he looked like a Messiah, but there are instances of persons being proclaimed Messiah by other people during their lifetime. In the same way, as Peter declared Jesus to be Messiah, Rabbi Akiba declared Bar Kochba to be Messiah (*y. Ta'an*. 4.68d). Josephus considered Emperor Vespasian to be the fulfillment of messianic hopes (*War* 3.401–2). The pseudo-messiahs of Mark 13:21–22 are proclaimed Messiah by others. "Look, here is the Christ!" or "Look, there he is." Why should not the adherents of Jesus have proclaimed him Messiah? This is all the more likely since, in the Gospels, the title "Messiah" is always used by other people, only rarely by Jesus himself.[15] Typically, others apply this title to Jesus. As we have said, there are many instances of this phenomenon. But there are no examples of a person designated Messiah thanks to being raised from the dead and/or appearing to others after a resurrection from the dead.

As far as the messiahship of Jesus is concerned, there is a consensus in the Gospel story among both adherents and opponents of Jesus. Peter, as the spokesman of the other disciples, confesses that Jesus is the Messiah (Mark 8:29). When Jesus entered Jerusalem, the common people expect him to usher in the "kingdom of our father David" (Mark 11:10). The Romans crucify Jesus as the "king of the Judeans," an affirmation that the Judeans in the passion narrative echo as "Messiah of Israel" (Mark 15:26, 32). The inscription on the cross (or on the crucified) may be historical. If adherents and opponents agree, we may be close to the historical truth.

We know of popular expectations at the time, specifically of people who longed for an Israelite monarchy. Yet we are not sure whether such popular Israelite monarchs were called Messiah or called themselves messiah. In the war of the robbers in 4 B.C.E. (Josephus, *Ant.* 17.269–85), Athronges appeared as such a popular king, whereas Judas, the son of Hezekiah or Judas Galilaios, was more of a teacher who wanted to promote theocracy, but not his own kingdom (*War* 2.56). It is historically probable that comparable expectations arose during Jesus' lifetime.

Since Jesus was confronted with messianic expectations from his own disciples, he had to deal with the expectations of a political messiah who would liberate Israel. It is possible that he rejected such an expectation. There is something interesting about the conjecture that the recognition of Jesus' messiahship and his statement about Satan belong together in Mark 8:29 and 33. Still, it is only a conjecture.[16] The connection between acknowledgment and refusal does not necessarily imply that Jesus refused the title of Messiah as such. What he explicitly refuses is the earthly mind of Peter: "Get behind me, Satan! For you are not on the side of God, but of man" (Mark 8:33).

We know of no suffering Messiah in pre-Christian Israel. This view is supported by the New Testament. The disciples of Emmaus expect a savior and first learn that the Messiah must suffer when they encounter the risen Jesus (Luke 24:26, 46). Their expectations were transformed only after Easter. If the traditional idea of Messiah designated a Messiah who did not suffer, then it is much more likely that Jesus was accorded the title of Messiah before Easter, that is, when his disciples and other contemporaries could hope for a victorious Messiah in an earthly sense. For what would motivate them to transfer the title of victorious king to Jesus after Easter, after the cross had destroyed hope of earthly victory? And why should they transform the category of a nonsuffering, victorious Messiah into a role that combines suffering and messiahship?[17] It is much more plausible that the title of Messiah was accorded to Jesus during his career and that the title played a part in his trial and subsequent passion. This may explain the inherent connection between messiahship and suffering in the earliest Jesus-group traditions, since this connection cannot be deduced from pre-Jesus traditions. The traditional notion of a victorious Messiah was not transformed into that of a suffering Messiah before Jesus' trial and execution (see *Psalms of Solomon* 17 and 18 from the middle of the first century B.C.E.).

If Jesus' adherents hoped that he were a royal Messiah, this, at the time, clearly would have been a political expectation. According to Psalms of Solomon 17, the Messiah was to be a Davidic king who would expel all aliens from the land of Israel. Since Jesus was charged as Messiah and executed as such, we may at least conclude that he did not dissociate himself from this messianic hope. If he had articulated this position before hostile witnesses, Jesus' followers would have had to deal with this problem. I am convinced, therefore, that Jesus consciously refused to dissociate himself from the messianic expectations that the people and his disciples entertained. Yet does this mean that Jesus welcomed these expectations?[18] Did he claim to be the Messiah? He did, in fact, expect the kingdom of God—but did he not dream of a kingdom of his own? Significantly, he refused the use of force, and force is part and parcel of the role of a political ruler.

Jesus' Refusal of the Politics of Physical Force

There are many intimations in the Jesus tradition that Jesus refused force. While there is consensus in this regard, that this refusal of force has been articulated with political categories has not been underscored. The directives of the Sermon on the Mount charging the disciples not to resist evil and to love enemies are often considered nonpolitical (Weber 1964:173–74). Yet, in an indirect way, love of enemies is very political. It is a protest against the differentiation between enemies and friends—a differentiation that Carl Schmitt considers the principle of all politics (1927). Jesus presumably speaks not only of personal enemies, but of all enemies, including national enemies (Horsley [1986], however, argues that the statement indicates only personal enemies). Some observations may support this proposal for broader political implications:

  1. The command to love enemies is directed to a group, since it is formulated in the plural. The command to love one's neighbor uses the singular (see Lev 19:18). We read: "*You* have heard that it was said, '*You* shall love *your* neighbor and hate *your* enemy'"—all forms in the singular (Matt 5:43). The passage does not continue with, "But I say to you: Love your [singular] enemies"; instead, Matthew shifts to the plural: "Love your [plural] enemies!" The shift to the plural is due to Matthew's combining the secondary antithetical form of this command with the substance of the command. But what can we say about the pre-Matthean tradition and perhaps about Jesus' own words? There, too, the plural is striking. As a rule, the admonitions in wisdom literature are formulated in the singular. This is also true for the admonitions to love one's enemy in Prov 25:21: "If your [singular] enemy is hungry, give him bread to eat; and if he is thirsty, give him water to drink" (see Rom 12:20; note also the singular formulation in the covenant, concerning an enemy's cattle: Exod 23:4–5). If Jesus were thinking exclusively of a personal opponent and an enemy in village life, the singular would have fit much better.

2. The command to love one's enemies presupposes that the addressed enemies have power. They can persecute. This is why Matthew adds:
". . . and pray for those who persecute you!" (5:44). The word "persecution," as it is used in Matthew, always implies an element of force.[19] We
are dealing with the enemies of the Christians, and these enemies possess
means of compulsion; that means that they exercise political power either
directly or indirectly. But again we must consider that only Matthew adds
the word "persecute" (cf. Luke 6:27). Again we have to ask: what can we
say about the pre-Matthean form of the tradition on the love of enemies?
How did Jesus understand this love of enemies? Or, more exactly, what
did the addressees of his preaching most likely understand by "love of enemies"? In exegetical literature, we sometimes find the idea of a distinction between a personal opponent (*echthros* or *inimicus*) and an enemy of
the state (the *polemios, hostis*),[20] and that the Jesus tradition uses the word
for personal opponents (*echthros*). But in the *Assumption of Moses*, a writing (re)published shortly before Jesus' public activity, the enemies are
clearly non-Israelites. "National" (i.e., ethnic) enemies are also enemies
(*echthroi*) in the hymn of Zechariah (Luke 1:74).

One question regarding latent tendencies in Jesus to employ force does
recur. But the few frequently mentioned hints in this direction are not convincing. I pick three of these hints: Jesus' disciple named Simon the Zealot, the
incident of the two swords, and the so-called cleansing of the temple.

It is true that a follower of Jesus is named Simon the Zealot (Luke 6:15; Acts
1:13). But even if his epithet pointed to *the* Zealots (who, according to Josephus, appeared forty years after Jesus and defended the temple of Jerusalem),
we could not conclude that Jesus' adherents were Zealots in the sense of those
armed rebels. If one member in a group is called "the Arab," we can assume
that all others are not Arabs. If one is called "the Zealot," we may equally be
sure that all the others were not Zealots.

Then there is the tradition of the two swords (Luke 22:38). The passage in
question deals with mitigating the strict equipment rules for disciples in Luke
9:3 and 10:4. It is Jesus himself who corrects the rules. Instead of renouncing a
staff, as they had been told in Luke 9:3, the disciples should now have a sword
(Mark 6:8 concedes at least a staff). The Essenes also concede the sword as
equipment for a journey (Josephus, *War* 2.125–26). When viewed in the context of the revised equipment rules, the mention of two swords in Luke 22:38
must have a similar meaning. Henceforth, specifically in the time of Luke, the
Jesus-group missionaries should not travel like defenseless beggars. In addition,
we may assume an apologetic concern. It is only in the Gospel of Luke that

Jesus is charged before Pilate with stirring up a rebellion: "We found this man perverting our nation and forbidding us to give tribute to Caesar, and saying that he himself is Christ, a king" (Luke 23:2). The reader of Luke should know in advance how absurd these charges are. As far as the payment of taxes is concerned, the reader knows from the discussion on taxes in Luke 20:20–26 that this charge is unjustified. As far as rebellion is concerned, the reader should infer from the statement about the two swords that these were all the arms the disciple possessed. Nobody can stir up a rebellion with two swords. At the same time, these two swords explain why Jesus was "reckoned with transgressors" (Luke 22:37 = Isa 53:12). Luke is aware of a possible political misunderstanding of Jesus' project.

Moreover, the so-called cleansing of the temple depicts Jesus using force. But the scene does not portray an attempt to incite political revolt. Rather, it describes a prophetic symbolic action, imparting the message that this temple will be destroyed and a new temple will arise in its place. In carrying out their symbolic actions, Israel's prophets likewise behaved in ways that would otherwise be judged reprehensible. Hosea, for example, had to marry a prostitute and an adulteress. When Jesus employs force in a prophetic symbolic action, he does not sanction coercion, any more than Hosea, when he marries an adulteress, advocates adultery. With his provocative action, Hosea sought to demonstrate that the God of Israel is faithful even to an unfaithful people. When he disturbed the temple routine, Jesus wanted to announce judgment on the temple and proclaim the hope for a new temple in place of the old.

In conclusion, Jesus surely renounced the use of force. He rejected this essential means of political governance. At the same time, he evoked expectations of his being a messianic ruler with political power, and that is why he was crucified. There is a contradiction in these inclinations. Political power is always based on sanctions of force. Can we explain this contradiction with the assumption that Jesus was thoroughly nonpolitical, even to the degree that he was not aware of the incompatibility of nonviolence and political rule? Or did his society, both adherents and opponents, misunderstand him?

Jesus and Political Misunderstanding

The thesis that Jesus was misunderstood politically is widespread, and one example is enough to illustrate the point.

His [Jesus'] whole message entailed a rejection of the violence and nationalism implied in the popular understanding of the title. Yet his words and deeds incited

in the people a vivid expectation that he might, after all, be one who would deliver Israel. There is a deep irony here. One might almost see Jesus as a victim
crushed between the jaws of opposing historical forces. He rejected the way of violent revolution and so disappointed the hopes of many of his own followers; but
because he excited—perhaps contrary to his own intention—messianic hopes,
he was executed by the authorities as a potential danger to the stability of the social order. (Hays 1996:164)

Is such a political misunderstanding plausible in the historical context?
There are two comparable instances to note. First is the Josephus' depiction of
John the Baptist. When compared with the image in the Gospels, Josephus' report may hint at political misunderstanding (Hays 1996:165). The second comparable instance is the statement of Josephus about the rebellious leader Judas,
son of Hezekiah (reported both in *War* and somewhat differently in *Antiquities*). These accounts show that a charismatic figure like Jesus, who proclaimed
God's rule, could be thought to harbor personal ambitions for rulership.

In the case of John the Baptist, the Gospels represent him as a prophet who
proclaims the coming of God (or of a messianic figure) as judge. John criticizes Herod Antipas because of Herod's illegal marriage to the divorced wife of
Herod's brother. As a result, John is executed. Josephus, however, attributes
the execution of John the Baptist to political motives: "When others too joined
the crowds about him, because they were aroused to the highest degree by his
sermons, Herod became alarmed. Eloquence that had so great an effect on
mankind might lead to some form of sedition" (*Ant.* 18.118). Herod orders the
Baptist killed for political reasons. There is no doubt that the Gospels represent the Baptist far less politically than Herod Antipas saw him, according to
Josephus. Should we conclude that Herod misunderstood the Baptist's political orientation, while the Gospels represented him correctly as a nonpolitical
figure? It may have been the other way around. In the Gospels, the political
dimension of the historical Baptist has disappeared.[21] We have to be aware that
political tendencies in Jesus' action may also have faded in the Gospel
traditions.

The second comparable instance has not been discussed so far. In both *War*
and the *Antiquities*, Josephus sketches the political career of Judas, the son of
Hezekiah. In both writings, he portrays him as a political rebel, who, together
with other rebels, plunged the country into a war after the death of Herod the
Great. But Josephus makes a significant distinction. According to *War*, Judas attacked all who strove for rulership (2.56), but, twenty years later in the *Antiquities*, Josephus states that Judas himself strove for rulership. In other words,
Josephus attributes to Judas precisely that ambition that was opposed previously

in *War*. He describes this ambition in both cases with words from the root
"strive": *zēloō* (cf. "he strove for royal honor," *Ant.* 17.272). If we attribute to this
Judas the teaching ascribed to Judas the Galilean (both persons may even be
identical),[22] we can explain Josephus's differing viewpoints. Judas the Galilean
was a teacher with radical theocratic ideas. His objective was the rule of God,
and his credo was that God alone should rule, not the Romans. He strove for
God's rule, not for his own rule. Therefore he opposed all others who vied for
their own rule. In the *Antiquities*, Judas the Galilean is placed among claimants
to the throne who are all contending for their own power, because the people
did not have a king. At first, Judas kept other claimants at bay by his virtue, but
later, Josephus reports, he strove for kingship, "a prize that he expected to obtain not through the practice of virtue but through excessive ill-treatment of
others" (*Ant.* 17.277). Here we observe a transformation of a rebel who fights
for God's rule to a rebel who himself wants to rule. Is it possible that a similar
transformation applied to Jesus? Jesus proclaimed the kingdom of God, and
this was interpreted as his attempt to install himself as ruler. If Josephus misunderstood one of the leaders of the revolt in this way, how much more likely
would it have been for Pilate to have misunderstood Jesus in the same way?
There is, of course, an important difference: Judas the Galilean fought for
God's rule,[23] Jesus proclaimed God's rule. But was Jesus' proclamation of God's
kingdom nonpolitical because the kingdom of God was not to be realized by
force? How then was it to be realized? The answer to this question lies in Jesus'
political symbols.

Jesus and the Political Strategy of Symbols

Let us return to the categories that I developed in the beginning. Governance
or ruling is the exercise of power not only by force, but also by legitimacy and
symbols. The more that power is based on legitimacy and the more that it is
supported by convincing symbols, the less this rule has to be gained and maintained by physical coercion. Did Jesus dream of a way of ruling minimized
force with the help of maximized legitimacy and a politics of symbols?

The historical period of Jesus was full of conflict expressed in political symbols (Theissen 1997b). Herod Antipas called his capital Tiberias, built it on a
cemetery, and erected images of animals in his palace. Pilate tried to introduce
shields with emblems of Caesar into Jerusalem, and he minted coins with symbols of Roman cults. At the same time, prophets appeared among the people,
and these prophets performed or announced symbolic actions that protested
the acculturation to an alien culture.

Just before the public career of Jesus, John the Baptist proclaimed a single baptism that was to clear the country and the people of all impurity. This contrasted with the brazen manner in which Herod Antipas offended the laws of purity when he built his capital (*Ant.* 18.36–38). The tensions between Antipas and the Baptist are well known and culminated in the Baptist's execution.

Some time after Jesus' death, a Samaritan prophet (*Ant.* 18.85) promised to rediscover the vessels of the temple hidden by Moses on Mount Gerizim. With this, the dream of a revival of native worship was revived. This gesture contrasts with the Roman cultic instruments that Pilate stamped on his coins. Is it by accident that this Samaritan prophet was also killed by Pilate?

The events connected with the Baptist and the Samaritan prophet provide the time frame within which Jesus of Nazareth functioned. He performed some actions that may have had symbolic political meaning. In what follows we cannot discuss whether the respective Jesus traditions have a historical core or not. This remains controversial. But what is true or untrue for Jesus is in any case valid for Jesus traditions, even if these traditions are unhistorical.

In his exorcism, Jesus experiences a breakthrough of the kingdom of God. Usually the kingdom of God implies a victory over the Gentiles. But here it is a victory over demons. But is it not the alien powers that are latent in the demons? One of these demons proudly calls himself "Legion" (Mark 5:9), in a story that contains many fictional elements.

When Jesus appoints the twelve disciples to govern Israel, he appoints an antigovernment standing over against other governmental structures, both against the remnants of the autonomous Judean administration, with the high priest as its center, as well as against the governmental structure of the Roman province. Common people are appointed rulers over restored Israel (cf. Mark 3:13–19 and par.; Matt 19:28–29 and par.).[24]

As he enters Jerusalem, Jesus is hailed as "king" or as representative of the "kingdom of our father David." This story, whether historical or not,[25] stands in antithesis to the entry of the prefect at all great temple feasts (Duff 1992; Kinman 1994; 1995). It underscores expectations of native rule—the rule of *our* father David.

When Jesus performs the cleansing of the temple as a symbolic prophetic action to announce its forthcoming destruction, this action, too, protests the rule of the priestly aristocracy. And it is understood as a protest. Jesus deprives the temple of religious legitimacy. His cleansing of the temple leads to his interrogation before the Sanhedrin, as noted in the passion narrative.

These two symbolic actions, the entry into Jerusalem and the cleansing of the temple, intimate a conflict with both the political and the religious system of power. Even if neither system is attacked in a direct way, they are both deprived of legitimacy (Theissen 1997a).

Let us summarize our preliminary results. Even if Jesus did not plan a revolt with force, it is basically not a misunderstanding when his followers and adversaries assumed that Jesus envisaged political goals. Jesus refused the use of force, but he was probably a master of symbolic actions in the political arena. Just as he was very creative in formulating pertinent parables, he was likewise equally creative in devising relevant symbolic prophetic actions. In fact, some of them have a direct political target. Must we then say that he *was* a ruler, but a ruler who paradoxically sought to renounce force? Can we imagine such a figure in the ancient world? This question leads us to our last point.

Jesus and His Alternative Ideal of Rulership

Jesus took up an ancient humane ideal of governance and transformed it into an ideal for his adherents. This was the ideal of governance without coercion and compulsion. I demonstrate this ideal in three items of tradition: in the command to love one's enemy, in the admonition to rule by service, and in the beatitude of the peacemaker. In all these instances, we can find traces of a transformed ancient ideal of governance.

The love of enemies is based on the political ideal of a humane ruler who treats his opponents generously (Schottroff 1975). The nearest analogy to the command to love enemies can be found in a maxim attributed to the Spartan king Ariston. Someone had praised the principle of his predecessor, that a good king must do good things to his friends and bad things to his enemies. Ariston is said to have answered: "How much better, my friend, is it, to do good to friends and to make enemies into friends" (Plutarch, *Moralia* 218A). This humane kingly ideal also existed in Israel. The *Letter of Aristeas* contains many sayings on the necessity of self-limitation of royal power and of a king's mildness when dealing with adversaries. The Jesus tradition takes up such lore, but makes it accessible to common people. Common people without political power should behave like rulers, who have more advantages than disadvantages through generosity. They should, therefore, practice love of enemies, the "clemency of Caesar," and they will be called "sons of God"—just like ancient rulers. That this usage of the title "son of God" is paralleled only in wisdom literature fits this picture, because the wise person is king. There is more political substance in this supposedly nonpolitical protest than there might appear at first glance,[26] but it is a political stance of obvious and explicit nonuse of force. It is a sort of antipolitics.

Such an antipolitical stance toward politics is explicitly formulated in the passage concerning the Zebedees. Here Jesus says to his disciples: "You know that those who are supposed to rule over the Gentiles lord over them, and their great men exercise authority over them. But it shall not be so among you; but whoever would be great among you must be your servant, and whoever would be the first among you must be slave of all" (Mark 10:42–44). Here Jesus explicitly contrasts the prevailing harsh ideal of ruling by repressive power with a way of ruling that should be practiced among his disciples, a way of ruling that takes on the form of slave service (Wischmeyer 1999). In antiquity there is indeed a tradition of a humane ruler, who considers his rule a way of service or of slavery. King Antigonos Gonatas is said to have admonished his son: "Do you not know that kingship is an honorable slavery?" (Aelian, *Varia Historia* 2.20). Of course it is a political fact that common people take on the role of humane rulers in the Jesus tradition. This means rule without compulsion and coercion.

Finally, we consider the beatitude about peacemakers: "Blessed are the peacemakers, for they shall be called sons of God" (Matt 5:9). This is also paralleled by statements on rulers and kings (this is the thesis of Windisch 1925). When the belligerent king Demetrios Poliorketes entered Athens in 291/290 B.C.E., he was greeted with the following words: "You, son of the mighty God," and they bade him: "Above all make peace, my dear, for you are Lord" (*FGH* 76 F 13). Rulers are called "son of gods"—and we equally find evidence for the term "peacemaker." Dio Cassius calls Caesar a "peacemaker" (*eirēnopoios*, 44.49.2). In the inscription of Priene, Augustus is called the one "who finished the wars and shaped peace."

If we look at the traditions in antiquity, we may distinguish two variations on this humane ideal of a ruler: on the one hand, to rule is considered a kind of service and slavery, and, on the other hand, the ruler is to have humility. Some of the most important evidence is cited below (see also Seeley 1993 and Windisch 1925).

Rulership as a Kind of Slavery

Plato, who died in 348/347 B.C.E., provides the earliest evidence of the topos that rulers are actually servants: "And those who are termed 'magistrates' I have now called 'ministers' (*hypēretas*) of the laws, not for the sake of coining a new phrase, but in the belief that salvation, or ruin, for a State hangs upon nothing so much as this. For wherever in a State the law is subservient and impotent, over that State I see ruin impending; but wherever the law is lord over the magistrates (*despotēs tēn archontēn*) and the magistrates are slaves of the law (*archontēs douloi tou nomou*) there I descry salvation and all the blessings that the gods bestow on States" (*Leg.* 4.715c–d). Antigonas Gonatas, who died in 239 B.C.E. and was a friend of the Stoic philosopher Zenon and the Cynic Bion, gave his son the admonition and maxim that "kingship is an honorable slavery," as noted previously (Aelian, *Varia Historia* 2.20). In the second half of the first century C.E., Seneca takes up this topos in his programmatic writing on the kindness and mildness of a ruler (*On Clemency*), addressed to Nero. He says that rulership is a "noble slave service" (*Clem.* 3.6.1 = I.viii.1), but he reinterprets the idea. The ruler cannot do all that a private person is allowed to do:

> You think that it is a serious matter to deprive kings of the right of free speech, which belongs to the humblest man. "That," you say, "is servitude, not sovereignty." What? Are you not aware that the sovereignty is ours, the servitude yours? . . . How many things there are which you may not do, which we, thanks to you, may do! It is possible for me to walk alone without fear in any part of the city I please, though no companion attends me, though I have no sword at my house, none at my side; you, amid the peace you create, must live armed. You cannot escape from your lot; it besets you, and whenever you leave the heights, it pursues you with its magnificence. In this lies the servitude of supreme greatness — that it cannot become less great (*Est haec summae magnitudinis seruitus non posse fieri minorem*); but you share with the gods that inevitable condition. For even they are held in bondage by heaven, and it is no more lawful for them to leave the heights than it is safe for you; you are nailed to your pinnacle.

Theophylactus Simocatta (who lived 610–641 C.E.) provides the last evidence for the topos in question (1.1.17).

Rulership as a Way of Displaying Humility

This topos can be found both in Greek and biblical traditions. Xenophon wrote shortly after the death in 360 B.C.E. of Agesilaus, the last Spartan king to be able to practice power politics on a broad scale. "He was never arrogant, but always reasonable; at least if he showed his contempt for the haughty, he was humbler (*tapeinoteros*) than the common man" (*Agiselaus* 11.11). Such ideas are echoed much later. Plutarch writes in the first century C.E. about Epameinondas, the commander of Thebes (fourth century B.C.E.), that he appeared in public very modestly (*tapeinos*) after his victory over the Spartans; Epameinondas explained his behavior with the following consideration: "Yesterday I felt myself much more proud than was justified; therefore today I chastise the lack of moderation of my rejoicing" (*Apophthegmata* 11.193a). To be *tapeinos* is something like being penitent. But as victorious commander he could afford such a public "self-deprecation." It did not do any harm to him. We find comparable ideas in the biblical tradition as well. Deutero-Zechariah is a reaction to the campaign of Alexander the Great (333 B.C.E. and following); the work contrasts the great conqueror with the ideal of the humble king,

Deutero-Zechariah's conscious counterimage to Alexander (Knauf 1994:177), whose conquest of Tyre is presupposed in Zech 9:1–17.

> Rejoice greatly, O daughter of Zion!
> Shout aloud, O daughter of Jerusalem!
> Lo, your king comes to you;
> triumphant and victorious is he,
> humble and riding on an ass,
> on a colt the foal of an ass.

This ideal of a "humble" king underwent continued changes in Israelite thought. *The Letter of Aristeas* at the end of the second century B.C.E. describes an Israelite-Hellenistic ethic for a ruler. It reflects the absolutist Hellenistic ideal of a ruler on the one hand, yet shows typical biblical corrections: The ruler is only a human being, not the epiphany of a God. He is advised to be humble according to God, who exalts and humbles. The king asks how he could gain acceptance in exile: "If you put yourself on the same level as all men, he answered, and if you appear to be rather more inferior to your host than superior. Also God is accepting, according to his nature, of what is humbled and men are friendly to those who are inferior" (§257). A similar answer is given to the question of the gentile king who asks how to avoid pride: "If he maintains equality and remembers always that he is ruling human beings as a human being. And God destroys the proud, but exalts the merciful and the humble" (§263).

At the time of early Jesus-group consolidation, Dio Chrysostom, who died in about 120 C.E., outlines another impressive ideal of a humane ruler in four of his speeches on kingship. Dio Chrysostom was banned under Domitian and had lived as an itinerant orator and philosopher for nearly fourteen years. Only under Nerva (98 C.E.) or Trajan (99–117 C.E.) was he allowed to return to Rome. He considered Trajan to be the realization of his ideal of a humane ruler:

> Then, the care bestowed on his subjects he does not consider an incidental thing or mere drudgery, when weighed down, let us say, by cares, but as his own work and professions. . . . it is only when he helps men that he thinks he is doing his duty, having been appointed to this work by the greatest god, whom it is not right for him to disobey in aught nor yet to feel aggrieved, believing as he does, that these tasks are his duty. (*Or.* 3.55)

This conception of government is characterized by care for the weak:

Once more, you see that God has everywhere appointed the superior to care for and rule over the inferior: skill, for instance, over lack of skill, strength over weakness, and for the foolish he has made the wise to have care and thought, to watch and plan; and with all these responsibilities governing is by no means easy; nay, it is laborious and does not get the greater share of relaxation and ease, but rather of care and toil. (*Or.* 3.62)

But this is the best illustration: You see how greatly the sun, being a god, surpasses man in felicity and yet throughout the ages does not grow weary in ministering to us and doing everything to promote our welfare. For what else would one say that the sun accomplishes throughout the ages except what man stands in need of? . . . Verily one might say that he endures a servitude most exacting; for, if he were to be careless but for a moment and leave his appointed track, absolutely nothing would prevent the whole heavens or on earth, and the whole sea from going to wrack and ruin. . . . (*Or.* 3.73–75)

Conclusion

We can now summarize our argument. Jesus was faced with popular expectations that he should be the messianic ruler. He contradicts such expectations by refusing a politics based on the use of force. Instead he employs symbolic actions to have political effect. Notably, he transfers hopes of rulership to his disciples. They are not only to rule over the twelve tribes of Israel, but are to live up to the ideal of a humane rulership. They are to be tribal kings who are generous to their enemies and who consider their rule as a service and an occasion for peacemaking—and all this in spite of the fact that they are common people. This program does not establish the rule of Jesus, but the rule of God: God's kingdom.

All this does not solve the basic conundrum of humane rulership. Without a system of power ready to apply sanctions of force, it is impossible to realize appropriate collective goals. But by applying force, even the noblest goals are always compromised. Jesus and his movement envision a humane rulership, and Jesus expects that God will establish this rulership. Only God can realize a way of ruling without the use of force and coercion. This process is as nonviolent as the growth of plants. Yet Jesus and his adherents did not espouse political quietism. They do not remain passive. They participated in the realization of the kingdom of God by an explicit renunciation of force, by political symbolic actions, and by an in-group exercise of humane rulership.

Thus we are faced with a basic political conundrum. Without politics there is no foundation for a good life, as Aristotle has clearly seen. But politics always entails a struggle for power and the maintenance of power. This is what Machiavelli taught. Political power is always based on a latent exercise of force—and force corrupts. As Lord Acton put it: "Power corrupts; absolute power corrupts absolutely." Jesus was confident that the power of absolute reality (namely, the power and kingdom of God) could resolve this conundrum. In anticipation of God's rule, he was active in a political sense. In his action we recognize the goal of all civil politics, which is to diminish and to tame political force and to limit the power of the powerful. This is to be accomplished by the participation of powerless common people and by a balance of power. Jesus' political activity aims at minimizing force. It seeks attention with the help of legitimating and delegitimating political symbolic actions. And it seeks to exalt the powerless as agents of power. His project had a political dimension, and this is true even if we define politics according to its narrow, normal English, sense.

Notes

This article is dedicated to Ulrich Duchrow. He has shown, in an admirable way, how to be a Christian and how to engage in politics. Christianity and responsibility for the world is not only the title of his *Habilitationsschrift*, published in 1968, but also his life maxim. See Duchrow.

1. A decision in favor of the broader sense of "politics" is made by Borg 1994; see the chapter "Jesus and Politics on Contemporary Scholarship" (97–126): "If 'politics' is used in the narrow sense, then Jesus was basically nonpolitical. A few scholars since Reimarus have argued that Jesus sought a change in government by inciting a political rebellion against Rome, but their arguments have not persuaded many. Moreover, it seems evident that Jesus did not seek a position of governmental power or to reform governmental policy. Yet, as I shall argue, Jesus both challenged the existing social order and advocated an alternative; his challenge involved social criticism, an alternative social vision, and the embodiment of that vision in the life of a community. This is 'political' in the broad sense of the word. Indeed, in this broader sense, much of the biblical tradition is political" (98).

2. Max Weber combines this narrow concept of politics with a broader concept when he makes a case for why politicians should have an ethics of responsibility. He integrates normative elements into his notion of political action, for an ethics of responsibility is neither mere ethical awareness (*Gesinnungsethik*) nor utilitarian ethics, but combines both: normative aims and the relevance of what can practically be realized (see Weber 1964).

3. One is not a sharp alternative to the other, because legitimate force also exists. In a modern state, the state has a monopoly over the legitimate exercise of force.

4. Talleyrand is credited with having said, "You may do many things with bayonets, but you cannot sit on them."

5. Beside these three forms of legitimate rule, sometimes he mentions a fourth form, democratic rule.

6. In order to analyze the relation between Jesus and politics, N. A. Røsæg (1990) uses four categories: (1) demands/benefits, (2) sanctions, (3) personal positions (institutions, roles), and (4) ideology (the issue of legitimacy) (see p. viii). If we relate these to our categories, we may say: (1) benefits correspond to utilitarian power; (2) sanctions correspond to coercive power; (3) persons and roles are created by different forms of exercising rule, by charismatics, dynastic rulers, and bureaucrats; and (4) ideology is persuasive power and serves the legitimization of rule. For a fuller four-category model of effectiveness in social interaction, based on Talcott Parsons, see Malina 1986:68–97.

7. The different variants of the thesis that Jesus was a rebel who planned an armed revolt should be shelved. For a discussion, see Bammel 1984.

8. This is the famous judgment of Max Weber in his essay (1964): "If as a consequence of the non-worldly love ethic it says: 'do not resist evil with force,' for the politician, the contrary is valid: 'you shall forcefully resist evil,' otherwise you are responsible for evil gaining control. He who wishes to act according to the ethic of the Gospel should abstain from strikes because they are force; let him join the yellow trade unions. But most of all, let him not speak of revolution." Weber distinguishes between two forms of ethics: first the ethics of the Sermon on the Mount as an ethical consciousness, which does not take into account the real consequences of one's deeds, and, second, an ethic of responsibility, according to which one is responsible for the consequences of one's actions.

9. Scriba introduces the "evaluation of data" (*Datenauswertung*) as a criterion, that is, the evaluation of some key facts that are historically valid, such as Jesus' baptism and crucifixion (1998).

10. Compare the apologetic motifs in the story of Jesus' baptism in Matt 3:13–17: The Baptist refuses to baptize Jesus, because he needs to be baptized by Jesus. In the *Gospel of the Ebionites* (fragment 5), the Baptist prostrates himself before Jesus. In John 1:29–34, Jesus comes to the Baptist with sin—but these sins are not his own sins, but the sins of the world. We do not read anything about a baptism with water. In the *Gospel of the Nazarenes* (fragment 2), Jesus denies explicitly that he depends on baptism to get remission of sins (Theissen and Merz 1998:207).

11. The *Gospel of Thomas* is an exception. The term "Messiah" is missing in this gospel. This absence should not be overestimated, since this term is used by other people in the other Gospels and not by Jesus, and since the *Gospel of Thomas* contains only sayings of Jesus (no stories about him).

12. This numinous aura is due to the fact that, in antiquity, the idea of closeness existed between anointed things or persons on the one hand and gods on the other hand. See especially Karrer 1991.

13. The Gospels understand the Messiah as a royal Messiah, because (1) they connect the Jesus tradition and the title of a son of David, and (2) they presuppose Jesus' royal messiahship in the passion narrative. The Jesus tradition would never have represented Jesus as son of David without further argument, if the royal character of his messiahship had not been presupposed as a matter of course (see Rom 1:3–4; Mark 10:47–48). In the passion narrative, *Christos* (= Messiah) is synonymous with "king." Jesus confesses to his judges in the Sanhedrin that he is "Christ, the Son of the Blessed" (Mark 14:61–62); he is interrogated by Pilate as a "king" (15:2ff.). The crowd mocks the crucified as "Christ, king of Israel" (Mark 15:32 par.). Here the royalty of the Messiah is also presupposed as a matter of course and need not be explained.

Karrer says that being the anointed one connotes closeness to God comparable to proximity to the Holy of Holies, for the Holy of Holies is also called "the anointed" (according to Dan. 9:24–27 LXX) (1991). It is true that, at the time, the term "anointed" suggested nearness to God. Jesus as the anointed Messiah is the king of Israel, who is near to God—in contrast to all the godless rulers. But nevertheless he is a king.

14. That is the thesis of Bultmann (1919–20). How healing leads to political expectations has been demonstrated by Hollenbach (1981).

15. There are only a few exceptions: (1) two sayings of the earthly Jesus: the admonition to support disciples, because they belong to the Christ (Mark 9:41 without parallel), as well as Jesus' discussion about the son of David (Mark 12:35 with parallels), where Jesus is speaking of the Messiah in general; (2) words of the exalted one, who teaches his disciples that the suffering of the Messiah was necessary (Luke 24:2, 46) or who summarizes in the so-called high priestly prayer his message and the Jesus-group faith in retrospect (John 17:3). The high priestly prayer relates to the time before the passion, as far as the external situation is concerned, but the prayer is expressed after he has quit the world (see John 17:11).

16. The thesis of an original connection between the confession of Peter and his rebuke as Satan can be supported by the following arguments: (1) They are also connected in variations of this tradition. In John 6:66–71, Peter expresses his acknowledgment not as a confession to the Messiah, but in general terms. The saying on Satan immediately follows the confession, but is referred to Judas Iscariot. The parallel in the *Gospel of Thomas* echoes Jesus' rejection in reaction to the confession of Thomas: "I am not your master, because you drank [and] became drunk from the bubbling spring which I have measured out" (*Gos. Thom.* 13). Then Jesus takes Thomas aside and speaks three words to him. After Thomas returns to the other disciples, he says about these words: "If I tell you one of the words that he said to me, you will take up stones

[and] cast [them] at me, and a fire will come forth from the stones [and] will burn you up" (*Gos. Thom.* 13). Jesus' rejection of Thomas is transformed into a refusal of the other disciples, anticipated by Thomas. (2) The separation of the confession of Peter and the reprimand as Satan can be explained as Markan redaction, if we consider Jesus' command to be silent (Mark 8:30) and the first prediction of his suffering (Mark 8:31) as Markan insertions. Both have further parallels in the Gospel of Mark, which lead us to suppose that Mark himself has formulated them or that he has inserted a tradition into this context. The thesis of an original connection between Peter's confession and his reprimand as Satan is advocated chiefly by Dinkler (1964) and Hahn (1963:226–30).

17. We encounter this combination in both the passion narrative and in the pre-Pauline formulas. Compare Rom 5:8, 6; 14:15; 1 Cor 8:11; 1 Thess 5:10; Gal 2:21; and 1 Cor 15:3b–5.

18. Hengel is of the opinion that Jesus considered himself to be the Messiah (1992).

19. Compare "persecute" in Matt 10:23 and 23:34. Persecution implies the expulsion from one town to the other. In 23:34, the verb stands next to "kill," "crucify," and "scourge."

20. See Foerster 1964:811: *echthros* rather designates "personal opponent." But both *echthros* and *polemios* are synonyms in the late writings of the LXX (see 1 Macc 14:31, 34, etc.).

21. John's criticism of the marriage of Herod Antipas had a political dimension and effect on foreign and domestic politics. The marriage with Herodias had disastrous consequences for foreign relations. Since Herod Antipas planned to repudiate his first wife, a princess of the Nabateans, she escaped to her father, who later inflicted a heavy defeat on Antipas. The people interpreted this defeat as God's revenge, because Antipas had killed John the Baptist. The people were aware of the connection between the marriage, which the Baptist had criticized, and the military defeat of Antipas. Even more dangerous were the internal consequences. The Herodians (at least Herod's wife, Herodias) fell into disrepute for breaking with Israelite traditions. The Baptist articulated dissatisfaction with the Herodians, which was widespread among the people. Josephus also severely criticizes Herodias because of her marriage. Compare Theissen 1991:81–97.

22. Hengel (1989) argues in favor of an identification of Judas, the son of Hezekiah, and Judas the Galilean. Rhoads argues against the identification (1976:50–51).

23. But Judas the Galilean was chiefly a teacher. Josephus calls him a *sophistēs*, a teacher (*War* 2.118) who founded a new philosophy (*Ant.* 18.9). Josephus stresses his teachings and does not know anything of warlike actions. We hear of his violent death only from Acts 5:37, where we read explicitly that his adherents were dispersed. All this

information is compatible with a nonviolent movement. But in this case we would have to make a strong distinction between Judas the Galilean and Judas, the son of Hezekiah, who undoubtedly was involved in armed resistance, which means that they cannot be identical. Rhoads especially has tried to restrict the significance of Judas the Galilean by showing that he was a rather isolated teacher in Israel (1976:47–60).

24. E. P. Sanders is correct when he defends the authenticity of the saying on the Twelve (1985:98–106). If we date it to the post-Easter period, it is very unlikely that all the Twelve, including Judas Iscariot, had been assigned such an honorific position in the new world.

25. Two arguments are usually brought against the historicity of this passage: (1) The entry of a messianic king may be developed from Zech 9:9. (2) There is the question why the Romans did not intervene. There is no doubt that the motif of the miraculous finding of an animal that could be used for riding was added and is thus secondary. But this does not speak against the historicity of the passage. The legendary expansion of the passage about Jesus' baptism by the voice from heaven does not speak against the historical fact that Jesus was baptized. Nor does the eclipse of the sun speak against the historicity of Jesus' crucifixion. The entry into Jerusalem happened in public, unlike many other events. And it is doubtful whether the Romans were able to recognize a pilgrim, who perhaps rode on an ass, as a messianic claimant. They were not that familiar with the symbolic language of Israel.

26. It may be due to this potential political aspect of the commandment to love one's enemies that it could develop in modern times into the concept of a "reasonable love of enemies" (C. F. von Weizsäcker)—a love of enemies that also opposes the political "principle of friend and enemy."

Works Cited

Bammel, Ernst. 1984. "The Revolution Theory from Reimarus to Brandon." In *Jesus and the Politics of His Day*, edited by E. Bammel and C. F. D. Moule, 11–68. Cambridge: Cambridge University Press.

Borg, Marcus J. 1994. *Jesus in Contemporary Scholarship*. Valley Forge, Pa.: Trinity Press International.

Bultmann, Rudolf. 1919–20. "Die Frage nach dem messianischen Bewusstsein Jesu und das Petrus-Bekenntnis." ZNW 19:165–74. Reprinted in *Exegetica: Aufsätze zur Erforschung des Neuen Testaments*, 1–9. Tübingen: Mohr/Siebeck, 1967.

Charlesworth, James H., ed. 1992. *The Messiah: Developments in Earliest Judaism and Christianity*. Minneapolis: Fortress Press.

Dinkler, Erich. 1964. "Petrusbekenntnis und Satanswort: Das Problem der Messianität Jesu." In *Zeit und Geschichte: Dankesgabe an Rudolf Bultmann*, 127–53. Tübingen: Mohr/Siebeck. Reprinted in *Signum Crucis: Aufsätze zum Neuen Testament und zur christlichen Archäologie*, 283–312. Tübingen: Mohr/Siebeck, 1967.

Dörner, Andreas. 1995. *Politischer Mythos und symbolische Politik: Sinnstiftung durch symbolische Formen am Beispiel des Herrmannsmythos.* Opladen: Westdeutscher.

Duchrow, Ulrich. 1983. *Christenheit und Weltverantwortung: Traditionsgeschichte und systematische Struktur der Zweireichelehre.* 2d ed. FBESG 25. Stuttgart: Klett-Cotta.

Duff, Paul B. 1992. "The March of the Divine Warrior and the Advent of the Greco-Roman King: Mark's Account of Jesus' Entry into Jerusalem." *JBL* 111:55–71.

Etzioni, Amitai. 1968. *The Active Society: A Theory of Societal and Political Processes.* London: Macmillan.

Foerster, Werner. 1964. "*Echthros.*" In *TDNT* 2:811–15.

Hahn, Ferdinand. 1963. *Christologische Hoheitstitel: Ihre Geschichte im frühen Christentum.* FRLANT 83. Göttingen: Vandenhoeck & Ruprecht. Translated by H. Knight and G. Ogg under the title *The Titles of Jesus in Christology: Their History in Early Christianity.* New York: World, 1969.

Hays, Richard B. 1996. *The Moral Vision of the New Testament — Community, Cross, New Creation: A Contemporary Introduction to New Testament Ethics.* San Francisco: HarperSanFrancisco.

Hengel, Martin. 1989. *The Zealots: Investigations into the Jewish Freedom Movement in the Period from Herod I until 70 A.D.* Translated by D. Smith. Edinburgh: T. & T. Clark.

———. 1992. "Jesus, der Messias Israels: Zum Streit über das 'messianische Sendungs-bewusstsein' Jesu." In *Messiah and Christos: Festschrift D. Flusser,* edited by I. Gruenwald et al., 155–76. Tübingen: Mohr/Siebeck.

Hollenbach, Paul W. 1981. "Jesus, Demoniacs, and Public Authorities: A Socio-Historical Study." *JAAR* 49:567–88.

Horsley, Richard A. 1986. "Ethics and Exegesis: 'Love Your Enemies' and the Doctrine of Non-Violence." *JAAR* 54:3–31

Karrer, Martin. 1991. *Der Gesalbte: Die Grundlagen des Christustitels.* FRLANT 151. Göttingen: Vandenhoeck & Ruprecht.

Kinman, Brent. 1994. "Jesus' 'Triumphal Entry' in the Light of Pilate's." *NTS* 40:442–48.

———. 1995. *Jesus' Entry into Jerusalem in the Context of Lucan Theology and the Politics of His Day.* AGAJU 28. Leiden: Brill.

Knauf, E. A. 1994. *Die Umwelt des Alten Testaments.* NSK.AT 29. Stuttgart: Katholisches Bibelwerk.

Malina, Bruce J. 1984. "Jesus as Charismatic Leader?" *BTB* 14:55–62.

———. 1986. *Christian Origins and Cultural Anthropology: Practical Models for Biblical Interpretation.* Atlanta: John Knox.

Mödritzer, Helmut. 1994. *Stigma und Charisma im Neuen Testament und seiner Umwelt: Zur Soziologie des Urchristentums.* NTOA 28. Göttingen: Vandenhoeck & Ruprecht.

Münkler, Herfried. 1997. "Politik/Politologie." In *TRE* 27:1–6.

Rhoads, David M. 1976. *Israel in Revolution, 6–74 CE: A Political History Based on the Writings of Josephus*. Philadelphia: Fortress Press.

Røsæg, N. A. 1990. "Jesus from Galilee and Political Power: A Socio-historical Investigation." Diss. theol., Oslo.

Sanders, E. P. 1985. *Jesus and Judaism*. Philadelphia: Fortress Press.

Schmitt, Carl. 1927. "Der Begriff des Politischen." *Archiv für Sozialwissenschaft und Sozialpolitik* 58:1–33.

Schottroff, Luise. 1975. "Gewaltverzicht und Feindesliebe in der urchristlichen Jesustradition, Mt 5,38–48 / Lk 6, 27–36." In *Jesus Christus in Historie und Theologie: Neutestamentliche Festschrift für Hans Conzelmann zum 60. Geburtstag*, edited by G. Strecker, 197–222. Tübingen: Mohr/Siebeck.

Scriba, Albrecht. 1998. "Kriterien der Jesus-Forschung: Darstellung und Kritik mit einer neuen Rekonstruktion des Wirkens Jesu." Diss. theol. habil., Mainz.

Seeley, David. 1993. "Rulership and Service in Mark 10:41–45." *NovT* 35:234–50.

Sellin, Volker. 1978. "Politik." In *Geschichtliche Grundbegriffe*, 4:789–874. Stuttgart: Klett-Cotta.

Theissen, Gerd. 1991. *The Gospels in Context: Social and Political History in the Synoptic Traditions*. Translated by L. Maloney. Minneapolis: Fortress Press. Originally published as *Lokalkolorit und Zeitgeschichte in den synoptischen Evangelien: Ein Beitrag zur Geschichte der synoptischen Tradition*. NTOA 8. Göttingen: Vandenhoeck & Ruprecht, 1989.

———. 1997a. "The Ambivalence of Power in Early Christianity." In *Power, Powerlessness, and the Divine: New Inquiries in Bible and Theology*, edited by C. L. Rigby, 21–36. Scholars Press Studies in Theological Education. Atlanta: Scholars.

———. 1997b. "Jesus und die symbolpolitischen Konflikte seiner Zeit: Sozialgeschichtliche Aspekte der Jesusforschung." *EvTh* 57:378–400.

Theissen, Gerd, and Annette Merz. 1998. *The Historical Jesus: A Comprehensive Guide*. Translated by J. Bowden. Minneapolis: Fortress Press.

Weber, Max. 1964. "Der Beruf zur Politik." In *Soziologie: Weltgeschichtliche Analysen. Politik*, edited by J. Winckelmann, 167–85. 3d ed. KTA 229. Stuttgart: Kröner.

———. 1976. *Wirtschaft und Gesellschaft: Grundriss der verstehenden Soziologie*. 5th ed. Tübingen: Mohr/Siebeck.

Windisch, Hans. 1925. "Friedensbringer—Gottessöhne: Eine religionsgeschichtliche Interpretation der 7. Seligpreisung." *ZNW* 24:240–60.

Wischmeyer, Oda. 1998. "Macht—Herrschaft und Gewalt in den frühjüdischen Schriften." In *Recht—Macht—Gerechtigkeit*, edited by J. Mehlhausen, 355–69. Veröffentlichungen der Wissenschaftlichen Gesellschaft für Theologie 14. Gütersloh: Kaiser.

———. 1999. "Herrschen als Dienen—Mk 10,41–45." *ZNW* 90:28–44.

14

The Political Jesus:
Discipleship and Disengagement

T. Raymond Hobbs

This essay is intended as a prelude to exegesis and historical investigation. As its title clearly indicates, it is inspired by the book written by John Howard Yoder, *The Politics of Jesus*, a work that has appeared in two editions, in 1972 and 1994.

Yoder's book was extremely popular—a socially significant fact. This popularity was matched by an intense interest, in the years between the first and second editions, in the relationship of Jesus to politics. In those years and since, numerous books produced in biblical studies, inside the academy, also betray an interest in the topic.

The social situation of first-century Palestine, as offered in numerous volumes since the early 1970s—Theissen (1978; 1987; 1992), Horsley (1988; 1995), Oakman (1986), Crossan (1989; 1991), Fiensy (1991), and, more recently, Hanson and Oakman (1998)—is basically agreed upon. There are, of course, differences in interpretation among these and other writers, but what Lenski described as an "advanced agrarian economy"—with its accompanying graphic representation—is a good descriptive and analytical model for the region and the period. It is a "useful" model (Elliott 1993:40–48; Barrett 1996:214).

In almost all of these analyses, insufficient notice is taken of the dominant institution of the army—the Roman citizen-army and auxiliary militia—that was present in force in the region. Although the early days of Roman control were "fluent and changeable" (Millar 1993:24), the nature of the control became more organized and widespread. Within a few decades, the legionaries and the unknown number of auxiliary militia in the region had become the face of the empire that most of the inhabitants saw and experienced (Millar 1993:33).

This essay is an invitation, against this backdrop, to an examination of the ministry of Jesus in a light that has, to date, been rather underexposed.

Master Narratives and Conceptual Metaphors

The Role of "Master Narratives"

Halvor Moxnes has reminded us of the role of "master narratives" underlying much of modern Jesus research (Moxnes 1998). Drawn from modern historical research, the notion of "master narrative" (sometimes called a "metanarrative," or "metadiscourse") is a complex ideological or conceptual framework within which historical and archaeological data are placed and understood. It functions in an almost unconscious mode, much like the social scientist's "model," and indeed has been depicted in this way by historians like Berkhofer (1998). The recognition of the "master narratives" is such that Lori Rowlett has commented that "an argument could be made that the field of biblical studies needs to include among its axiomatic assumptions that our own historical context inevitably plays a part in the way we read" (1996:25; see also Elliott 1995:37).

Historian David Lowenthal has established the lines of an extremely important debate, between what he labels "history" and "heritage." For Lowenthal, heritage is

> the tendency to domesticate history for a personal or selfish purpose. In domesticating the past we enlist it for present causes. Legends of origin and endurance, of victory or calamity, project the present back, the past forward; they align us with forbears whose virtues we share and whose vices we shun. We are apt to call such communion history, but it is actually heritage. The distinction is vital. History explores and explains pasts grown ever more opaque over time; heritage clarifies pasts so as to infuse them with present purposes. (1998:xv)

"Heritage," he states elsewhere, "is not an inquiry into the past, but a celebration of it, not in an effort to know what happened but a profession of faith in a past tailored for present purposes" (1998:x). The notion of heritage is closely akin to what the late Moses Finley called the "teleological fallacy" (1980:17).

Whereas heritage is always teleological and personal, history carries within it a certain anonymity, in the sense that it is owned by no one, whether victor or victim, and it is always incomplete. If heritage is a domestication of the past, then history is a discovery of the alien nature of the past. Historical study then compels the investigator to confront challenges, surprises, disappointments, joys, and sadness, and refuses to be seduced by that most Western of narrative clichés (i.e., a "master narrative"), the "Happy Ending."

In a similar fashion, there is an anonymity to the historical Jesus. He comes to us as one unknown—if not as a phantom walking on the sea then as one who refuses to fit into ready-made molds, whether it be the rebel, the conformist, the religious reformer, the peace activist, or the politician. As with the crowds in Mark's Gospel, the historian of Jesus and the Jesus movement must always be prepared to be amazed and to confess that we never saw anything like this (Mark 2:12).

Robert Berkhofer suggests, "[M]ost (all?) of what is presented as (f)actuality is a special coding of the historian's synthetic expository texts, designed to conceal their highly constructed basis. . . . That such coding is conventional also means that it is arbitrary" (1997:149–50). I understand the "highly constructed basis" of which Berkhofer writes to be identical with the "master narrative," or what Berkhofer himself labels "metanarrative." But "master narratives" are not purely random, nor are they neutral. They, like other elements, are cultural artifacts born in the matrix of the author's own social and cultural context. They therefore provide a potentially interesting area for examination.

Conceptual Metaphors

The historian's focus on the past was once assumed to be clear. Now the focus has become fuzzy, forcing the historian to align the instruments of observation (the constructed, rhetorical nature of our knowledge) more carefully and, incidentally, to pay more attention to them (Kellner 1998:134). Like all others, historians are the subjects of "socialization," in which "the history of social relations enters into people's understanding of themselves and of the world they live in" (Toren 1996:514). Involved in socialization is the transmission of cultural values, understandings of the nature of the universe/world, the language used, the myths retold, and the way in which these are all embedded in social systems. Lakoff and Johnson complement this with the notion of the "conceptual system," which "plays a central role in defining our everyday realities" (1988:3). The conceptual system is learned, constructs our social realities, is often unconscious, is betrayed by language, and, importantly, is metaphorical. Such constructs of reality are akin to, if not identical with, the "metanarratives," or "master narratives," of the historian, or the "metadiscourse" of the anthropologist, in that they provide a conceptual and ideological framework within which data and experiences can be understood.

In his book *Imagined Communities: Reflections on the Origin and Spread of Nationalism* (2d ed., 1996), Benedict Anderson concludes with reflection on

"The Biography of Nations" (204–7). Such biographies, he suggests, are not written in the conventional sense from parents or grandparents to children, that is, "down time," through a long, progressive chain of begettings (205), but "up time." "This fashioning . . . is marked by deaths, which in a curious inversion of conventional genealogy, start from an originary present," and grab hold of elements of the past "wherever the lamp of archaeology casts its fitful gleam" (205). It is the perpetual domestication of the past from which we find it hard to escape—that is, from Lowenthal's notion of "heritage." Reflection on our own "national histories" and the way in which they are presented will substantiate this observation.

Reflections on Anomalies in the Debate

The Nature of "Politics"

Calling Jesus "political" (Yoder) begs certain historical questions. In Western writing on political science since the 1950s, terms like "political culture" have come into the vocabulary, indicating a broadening of the notions of politics, the practice of politics, and the subject for political analysis (Kavanagh 1972; Rosenbaum 1975; Femia 1993). Added to this trend are notions of the "politicizing" of knowledge (Foucault 1980), and interpreting all human relationships not only as engagements of power, but as engagements in which both sides, regardless of their standing, can do something about power (Coulson and Riddell 1980).

If Aristotle's profile of politics and political activity held any authority in the ancient Mediterranean world, then politics was what happened in cities, among property-owning males. In the Roman world of the first century C.E., politics was, by extension, what happened in Rome. Broadly speaking, it was the manipulation of power by an elite, and subsequently the exercise of power over imperial subjects. In Bailey's words: "The nation . . . becomes an arena in which the nobles fight it out with one another for a position at the top of the highest accessible heap. . . . The state from this elevated point of view was not the entire population, but only those who governed" (1991:111–12). The idea that individuals in the first century, at the farthest reaches of the empire, had political power, or could exercise such power in any meaningful way, is suspect. Their role can only be understood this way if politics is broadened to include many modern Western notions, such as the relation of the individual to society.

Within cultural anthropology of the first-century Mediterranean world, the common division between political and family life for the average person (Hanson and Oakman 1998; Pilch 1993) would support my point that Jesus was probably not involved in politics, in the sense of his time. There were examples of family intrigue and jostling for control within the family. Such cases can properly be called "political" from our later, Western perspective. But whether they would have been understood in this way in the first century is another point. Those who did practice power politics in the Mediterranean world were treated with the utmost suspicion (Herzfeld 1991:20, 27; Bailey 1971:303), a point, I think, reflected in Jesus' comment on the leadership styles among the "rulers of the nations" (Matt 20:25; Luke 22:25). It is to the same "rulers of the nations" to whom Jesus is handed over for trial (Matt 20:19).

Lenski in Reverse

One of the most popular macrosocietal models in current discussion of the first-century world of early Christianity is that of Gerhard Lenski, called the "advanced agrarian society" (1984; see figure 2.4, p. 36 above). Its familiar shape—that of an ancient bottle with a broad base and narrow top—is determined by two axes: the distribution of power and the size of the population strata. Dominant in the image is the size of the population. I suggest that this interest in demographics (i.e., numbers) reflects Western values. It is a static image and offers little explanation of how power and honor were distributed and enforced in the ancient Mediterranean world.

In the light of ancient Mediterranean terms and values, the shape of the model, though not its basic presentation, would change. What Westerners perceive as the powerless masses, thus concentrating on the large numbers in society's lower strata, were of little or no concern to the ancient politician. From Aristotle on, the masses at the lower end of the social scale were understood, not as a result of imbalance in the distribution of wealth and power, but as a fact of nature. The task of those at the top who had been endowed, again by nature, with the gift of leadership (they were the true political animals) was to control the masses below and to the advantage of those at the top. This was an idea common in European thought until Hobbes (1651). This "equilibrium" was maintained through the manipulation of the agents of power—primarily the army—and the members of the "lower class" would see themselves overshadowed by a vast umbrella of power, against which they were completely powerless (see figure 2.4, p. 36).

The "High Center" and Porous Borders

The frequently used term "marginalized" to describe the recipients of Jesus' words and acts of kindness demonstrates the strength and ubiquity of the model of "center and periphery" (Shils 1982; Champion 1989:2–5). On a large scale, the metaphor helps in describing the structure of Roman imperial rule. There was a strong center, and a distant border controlled from the center. This use of the model was fully exploited by Liverani in his studies on Assyrian imperial rule (1979) and became the subject of an important historical and archaeological symposium (Champion 1989).

The elements of the model, center and periphery, are relative (Douglas and Wildavsky 1983:120), with the observer supplying values to give the model shape. Shils' exposition (1982), dependent on a consensus around central values, betrays its Western interest in numbers, and is based on the assumption that the "mass" has a political voice. Benedict Anderson makes the following observation on "pre-modern" societies:

> Kingship organizes everything around a high centre. Its legitimacy derives from divinity, not from populations, who, after all, are subjects, not citizens. In the modern conception state sovereignty is fully, flatly, and evenly operative over each square centimetre of a legally demarcated territory. But in the older imagining, where states were defined by centres, borders were porous and indistinct, and sovereignties faded imperceptibly into one another. (1996:19)

This observation is important. Palestine, because of the nature of its geography, and its position at the "distant periphery" (Braudel 1972:355) of the Roman Empire, constituted one of its most porous borders. But, precisely because of this fact, the military presence in the region was massive. Its presence had grown since the first occupation, and it is estimated that, by the middle of the second century, more than one-third of the Roman Army was stationed in the Roman Near East (Millar 1993:4).

The Role of the "Lower Classes"

I do not want to offer a detailed picture of "lower classes" (a loaded term) in first-century Palestine. Instead, I sketch something of their political significance. I do this by drawing upon ethnographies of such classes in recent historical and anthropological literature. I begin with an important quotation from James Scott's recently published monograph, *Seeing Like a State: How Certain Schemes to Improve the Human Condition Have Failed* (1998). Scott's observations are helpful and appropriate:

> The pre-modern state was, in many crucial respects, particularly blind; it knew precious little about its subjects, their wealth, their landholdings and yields, their location, their identity. It lacked anything like a detailed "map" of its terrain and

its people. It lacked for the most part a measure . . . that would allow it to translate what it knew into a common standard necessary for a synoptic view. (1998:2)

What Scott then offers in detail is what empires did to make the "unread-
able" outposts of the empire "legible." It was a process of simplification, seen
most clearly in the construction of road systems that, in reality and symboli-
cally, straightened out old paths and redefined ancient towns and cities as centers of communication and control. This control, again, was exercised
primarily through the army. The so-called lower classes would have consisted
at least of slaves, peasants, and bandits.

Slaves. The Roman Empire, and its dependent client states, were
slave societies, seen as part of the natural order (Aristotle, *Politics* 1.5). The
term "slave" is multifaceted, including galley rowers and miners as well as estate managers and police forces. One element these groups had in common
was lack of citizenship, and, therefore, lack of legal status. It was not so much
their labor that they offered, but themselves (Finley 1980:68); they were
bonded to slave owners by "faithfulness." The relationship went beyond the
normal relationships of respect, duty, and honor in a hierarchical society (Finley 1980:103–6). This is a phenomenon reflected in the parable of the talents
(Matt 25:14–30). It is generally accepted that slaves' wide variety of occupations
and their spread over large geographical areas precluded organized outbursts
based on the fact that they were slaves. For a fuller exposition, I defer to Finley's
exposition of slavery in his *Ancient Slavery and Modern Ideology* (1980).

Peasants. I take for granted that the majority of Galilee's population
at the time of the Gospel story consisted of peasants. I also take for granted the
generally accepted image of the peasant as

> any rural cultivator who is low in economic and political status. Low economic
> status denotes little access to economic inputs (capital, land, knowledge); little
> control over the management of these inputs (what to cultivate, when to work);
> and little control over output and its distribution between the factors of produc-
> tion. Low political status, likewise, denotes little access to political inputs (such
> as votes); little control over the management of political affairs (over elected or
> appointed officials); and little control over the output of the political system (i.e.,
> the content of political decisions). (Landsberger and Hewitt 1970:561)

This depiction is based on twentieth-century peasantry. I suspect that the lot of the first-century peasant was much worse (see Rowlandson 1996).

Within the study of peasantry as background to the Gospels, aspects of peasant life—their deprivation and hardships, to name two—have rightfully been stressed. I wish to look at other "anonymous" aspects of peasant life that have not received as much attention.

Almost all studies on peasant life in the nineteenth and twentieth centuries mention passivity as the peasants' noteworthy characteristic. Well-known studies of "limited good" (Foster 1965) or "the bad life" (Bailey 1971) have stressed this feature. This passivity is not to be regarded as laziness—often a stereotyped view of peasantry. Passivity is a survival strategy based in peasants' sound understanding of themselves as what Hobsbawm calls the basic type of humanity, and as radically different from nonpeasants, whom they approach, if at all, with intense distrust.

> The major difference lies not in the theoretical aspirations of the peasantry, but in the practical political juncture in which they operate. It is the difference between suspicion and hope. For the normal strategy of the traditional peasantry is passivity. It is not an ineffective strategy, for it exploits the major assets of the peasantry, its numbers and the impossibility of making it do some things by force for any length of time, and it also utilizes a favourable tactical situation, which rests on the fact that no change is what suits traditional peasantry best. (Hobsbawm 1998a:149)

This notion of the peasant's passivity is widespread in the literature, and I add to the list Landsberger and Hewitt (1970), Feder (1971), Shanin (1971), Pearse (1975), Lenski (1984), Scott (1998), and Baker (1997:6).

Closely related to the notion of passivity is a corresponding lack of political will, that is, a will to change the system. This, too, is a widely recognized phenomenon in peasant studies. Hobsbawm, in his essay on peasants and politics (1998a), observes that while the potential power of the peasantry (i.e., their numbers) is massive, peasant political activity is "quite unrealistic" (155) because of a perception of weakness and inferiority, the lack of a suitable armed force (unless raised by outside forces), and the nature of the peasant economy. "The cycle of their labours shackles them to their fate" (156). Elsewhere he states: "The sense of the constant potential or actual confrontation of force may perhaps derive from the very exclusion of the traditional peasantry from the official mechanisms of politics" (159). Of course, these writers are dealing with nineteenth- and twentieth-century peasantry and politics. One can only assume that, in preindustrial societies, the lot of the average peasant was the same, if not worse.

Political significance should not be read into all lawless, rebellious action (Chabal 1992:95).

> Not all banditry and delinquency have deep political relevance, and it would be otiose to read political statements in every utterance and action of the disenfranchised. Whether such utterances and actions are politically meaningful depends in part on the self-consciousness of those who profess and utter them, and in part on the perception of those in high politics. (Baker 1997:12–13)

Pearse, in concert with this view, notes that the political options for peasantry are few. In his examination of Latin American peasantry, Pearse concludes that the only viable political alternative for peasants is a movement organized "from above." But, unfortunately, such a movement "is the expression of the forces of incorporation emanating from the centre; it is the form given to a new system of political and commercial manipulation" (1975:188). The benefits of such an involvement move outside the peasant group, and are almost always viewed with the peasant's inherent suspicion.

A third element of peasant life consists of the numerous strategies of survival developed by peasantry in an oppressive and exploitative system. What the first-century Mediterranean peasant would know of Rome would be taxation, and the threat of force. These make up "the sense of the constant potential or actual confrontation of force" as a determining feature of peasant life and action, Hobsbawm notes. He further states: "For most of the soil-bound peasants the problem is not whether to be normally passive or active, but when to pass from one state to the other. . . . Broadly speaking, passivity is advisable when the structure of power . . . is firm, or closed" (1998a:157–58). Peasants certainly would have understood the truism, on the lips of Jesus, that they who live by the sword shall perish by the sword (Matt 26:52). In other words, the chances of a successful change in the system are virtually nil, especially if one has to contend with the real power of the army as imperium. Accommodation, rather than open resistance, is the "better part of valor" (Shanin 1971:238–60), an opinion endorsed by Bailey, who states: "Peasants live out their lives devising ways to protect themselves and their households from the predatory incursions of the state, while the state is organized, albeit inefficiently, to extract as much as it can from its peasants" (1993:113). Bailey has coined a perceptive phrase to describe how peasants (in this case, in India) deal with potentially disastrous conflict, "the civility of indifference" (1996).

Bandits. The phenomenon of banditry, or what Hobsbawm chooses to call "social banditry," has become an important element in discussions of the historical Jesus. The essay by K. C. Hanson in this volume (see chap. 15, "Jesus and the Social Bandits") summarizes much of the debate in an extremely help-ful way and establishes the most important categories of the discussion. I do not need to rehearse well-known material. I am trying instead to give a stronger voice to some of the implied features of studies on banditry.

Hanson has drawn together an impressive lexicon of terms in ancient litera-ture, which is most valuable. Of necessity, the sources refer to military activity against outlaws. Banditry, like beauty, is in the eye of the beholder, and I be-lieve it is helpful to understand the language according to how those in power label deviance. In an ordered society, deviants are "out of place." The guardians of order, the beneficiaries of order, and those that support them affix such la-bels in the interests of maintaining proper societal boundaries (Pfohl 1985; Schur 1971:100–114; see also figure 14.1). This has been demonstrated with moving effect by Richard Moore in his study of persecution in late medieval Europe (1987).

The use of terms like "bandit" in Josephus and in other ancient writers should be seen in a broader context than simple historical description. While the need for enemies is common (Bailey 1998), the faces of those enemies are drawn from a universal bestiary (Keen 1986; Hobbs and Jackson 1991). Com-menting on a more modern phenomenon, Bailey suggests: "In politics the nor-mal route to uncalculating solidarity, the readiness to give one's all to the cause, is not so much love of the cause; it is the propensity to hate those who are pre-sented as the cause's enemies" (1998:xii). Labels like "bandit" and "terrorist" have often been used in military history as justifications for repressive action against certain segments of society, often by armies of occupation, a point con-ceded by Isaac (1990). In fact, the disappearance of the term in Josephus, once the war has begun, is noteworthy (*War* 2.253). "Bandits" it seems are responsi-ble for the start of the war and the general unrest that preceded it. In describ-ing two of the major sieges of the war outside Jerusalem, namely Gamla (4.4) and Masada (7.288–416), Josephus reserves remarkably restrained language for the defenders, who are elevated to *sicarii*, and takes pains to depict their "fights to the death" as an unavoidable, but nevertheless noble, gesture, almost gladia-torial in its expression. Such ennobling of an enemy (often to boost one's own reputation) is common.

In his study of banditry in Bengal during the latter half of the eighteenth century, Ranjit Sen distinguishes between mass robbery and social unrest on the one hand—a common feature of life, it seems—and banditry on the other (1988:45–47). "Banditry is sustained by its own motive, the motive of loot for

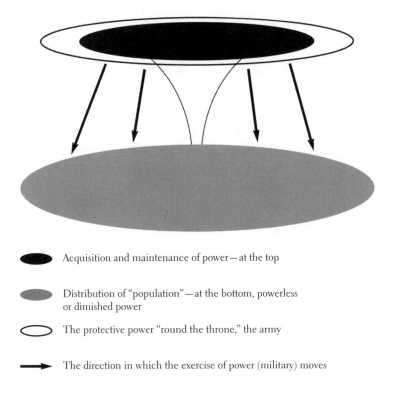

Acquisition and maintenance of power—at the top

Distribution of "population"—at the bottom, powerless or dimished power

The protective power "round the throne," the army

The direction in which the exercise of power (military) moves

Figure 14.1: Redesign of the elements of the Lenski model of "advanced agrarian society

individual sustenance or the sustenance of a group" (46). Mass robbery, such as the looting of a merchant's house at midnight by three hundred rather unorganized men, is a sign of social unrest and widespread need, and, in the case studied, was not related to banditry at all. Yet British reports of such incidents consistently refer to the lawbreakers as "dacoits" or "bandits," without discrimination. To use the unimaginative language of sociology, this is an example of "societal reaction perspective" (Pfohl 1985:283–330).

For Hobsbawm, "social bandits" represented forms of prerevolutionary (prepolitical) social protest—befitting the writer's Marxist perspective. Like labels applied to deviants, "social banditry" is a construct based on social values and becomes a term of legitimation. "Social banditry" as expounded is a cultural artifact, a way of seeing, and perhaps even an expression of hope. As if to reinforce this noble and romantic image, there is frequent appeal to the archetypical social bandit, Robin Hood (Isaac, Hobsbawm, Horsley, Hanson). The allusion is very revealing. The Robin Hood envisaged is the Robin Hood of myth and legend, not of history. The popular image of a rejected nobleman fighting on behalf of peasants against cruel overlords is just that, an image, and states more of the ideals and ideology of the seventeenth- and eighteenthcentury balladeers than the realities. Hobsbawm I think came close to this truth when he spoke more of "Robin Hoodism" than about a historical character, Robin Hood.

The recently established historical and textual project on Robin Hood, sponsored by Purdue University and the University of Wales, Cardiff, has produced a different image of the man. The scholars involved state: "In the early texts, Robin is a yeoman, not a nobleman; he is English by birth, not Saxon; he is from Barnsdale, Yorkshire, not Sherwood Forest in Nottinghamshire; he does not have a girlfriend named Marian; he does not live in the time of King Richard; and he does not 'rob the rich to give to the poor.' At times Robin is . . . impetuous, hot tempered, a poor loser, a highway robber, a philanderer, and a murderer," T. H. Olgren, Project Coordinator, http://www.sla.purdue.edu/ medieval-studies. Peasant support of such men and their gangs is sporadic at best, but never constant. Peasants would have as much to fear from bandit gangs as from Roman revenge on the gangs' supporters, as the Egyptian evidence strongly suggests.

Involvement of the military. A feature of most, if not all, studies on the historical context of Jesus is worthy of comment. That is the absence of discussion on the involvement of the Roman army and of the locally raised militias in the society of the day.

Whether by direct Roman control, or by local control, military power (not independent of political power)—that is, the face of the empire—was widespread and inescapable. Its role was important, its presence ubiquitous, and its control near absolute. Every aspect of "civilian" life was, in some measure or other, under the control of the military. The Egyptian papyrological evidence presents a situation that might be typical of the Roman Near East. It reveals an institution involved in local and city administration; economic life—especially the collection and control of taxes; security, with the attempts to control the "porous borders" of the empire; and internal justice, acting as magistrates in village, town, and city disputes over a wide range of civilian life (assault, property damage, theft, fraud, breaking of contracts, and even spousal abuse). By the second century, most of these roles were the prerogative of a locally stationed centurion, who became "a vital means of interaction between the people and the state" (Alston 1995:87).

Beyond this, the army's presence in certain areas also was meant as a deterrent against local banditry, for which Egypt and the Levant were notorious

(Alston 1995:81–86). There is no evidence to show that such bandits were widely supported or encouraged by the agricultural workers from whom they stole their provisions. The few cases recorded of this happening were dealt with in a brutal manner. What is known is that, by early in the second century, large tracts of the fertile Delta had been abandoned and neglected, the villagers having been driven away by the raids of bandits (Alston 1995:83–84). Given the passive tendencies of peasants, and their precarious existence in such a volatile climate, it seems more likely that they would have preferred the regular and predictable abuse of the oppressive system under which they lived, moved, and had their being, rather than the irregular, chaotic, and disruptive abuse and exploitation that would have come from bandit raids.

I spend some time on this topic to broaden the debate on the "politics of Jesus." The presence of the Roman army and its auxiliaries in Palestine in such numbers and with such power is a result of the militarization of traditional Mediterranean society under the Romans. Thus far in the literature I have noticed little attention to this phenomenon, and, where it is noticed, it is seen in terms of a fundamentally Newtonian model—for every action there is an equal and opposite reaction. This idea, along with the notion of the development from simplicity to complexity, has been a "master discourse" of much social anthropological literature, particularly from the 1960s and early 1970s. One result of the application of this "master narrative" is that anthropologists have viewed primary elements of social change as violent outbursts, usually by revolutionary bandits. This is the dominant characteristic of Hobsbawm's model of "social banditry" (1959), later taken up by Wolf (1969).

Of great value for New Testament studies are explorations of the role of participants in situations of dominance and resistance (Miller 1995; Rowlands 1995; Tilley 1995). While it is true that military organizations can become agents of dominance, and occasionally spark violent reaction, also noticeable is that, in situations of dominance, the dominance itself can be maintained through peaceful means. The majority of the population is not necessarily bludgeoned into submission, but can accept the dominance through simple compliance with its demands (Miller 1995:63). This again is not an unconscious reaction, but a reasoned reaction based on notions of the greater good. It is, in fact, a conscious strategy of survival. Relationships of dominance are not simply those of an active agent set against a passive subject. As Miller suggests: "The reflexive definitions and perspectives of both sides of the relationship must be ascertained and understood in relation to each other" (1995:64).

In the overall picture, the observer's (i.e., historian's) skill is not in setting the scene intuitively as one of continual tension and undeclared revolution, but in detecting when, and under what circumstances, the equilibrium between dominators and resisters is deliberately upset. On the other side, the military has to justify to itself and its rulers at what times tension is increased, and when further repression is justified. What often happens is that the tension is explained and the repression rhetorically justified in typical military and political discourse (Jahangir 1989:319). This justification ranges from drawing attention to broader questions of societal stability to apocalyptic warnings of total destruction and structural decay if things go too far.

In the case study examined by Jahangir, "there is ample evidence which points to the fact that the peasants are aware of the[se] happenings: misdeeds of the influential, corruptive practices and exploitation. This awareness is internalized by the peasants, since they are afraid of repression" (1989:316).

> [B]ehind the peasants' conduct on the public stage is an anger that is quite as intent on mitigating and denying the claims made by the dominant class as open rebels. Far from false consciousness, Scott finds a penetrating understanding by them of what is being done to them. That they quite deliberately avoid confrontation is precisely because, as the weak, they could not survive the ferocious response it would provoke. Their tactics, therefore, employ everyday but largely hidden responses. (Baker 1997:6)

Defiance does not then become the most important weapon against the dominators. The peasant can react with other methods. "The social order [is] confronted with sarcasm, with more social knowledge and cunning, as well as with defiance in certain circumstances" (Jahangir 1989:318). The key is when to use the appropriate method. A task for the observer is to determine which method of resistance is in use and when.

The "Strategy" of Jesus and the Jesus Movement

I note first three elements in Jesus' career worthy of comment, then I offer a model of human behavior that I think is consistent with Jesus' attitude and utterances. In the Gospels, those with whom Jesus has immediate contact are the villagers, the scribes, and Pharisees (representatives of Jerusalem, or an alternative "religious" group). These groups are at an intermediate stage of dominance. It is not until the end of the Gospel story that Jesus interacts with the powerful political authorities. But the precise nature of this involvement is ambiguous. One should note the nature of the accusations and the ambivalent attitude of Pilate to the proceedings of the trial.

Absence of a Program of Manumission

In the Gospels, we note the absence of manumission for slaves. Yet slavery becomes a conceptual metaphor for the ongoing life of the Jesus community. Second only to the army in number, although by no means organized, slaves made up an enormous segment of the Roman social structure. A program of social change (if such a thing could have been envisaged) would have involved dealing with slavery. Yet the world waited another seventeen centuries for an antislavery movement to be remotely inspired by Christian ideals.

Economic "Program"

We are all deeply indebted to Doug Oakman and his analysis of the economic situation of first-century Palestine (1986), and I have no wish to quarrel with the analysis. But I do raise one nagging question, and that is whether the assumed trust Jesus places in the "middleman" to bring social and economic change is, in fact, misplaced. I would ask further whether the supposed ability of the middleman to effect economic change is based on a realistic evaluation from a Mediterranean point of view.

The parable in Matt 25:14–30 reflects the household manager's role as one of acquiring goods for the household (Aristotle, *Politics* 1.9). But, in the ancient economy, such managers lacked political power to change the system. Landowning was a prerequisite for politics. As the parable demonstrates, the results of an attempt to change the system (if that is what it really is) are immediate and mean arbitrary dismissal if the household managers do not support the new system. The "whistle-blower" is a viable concept only if the manager has access to (1) publicity, (2) a network of like-minded partners, and (3) power. Outside the system, he has none of these capabilities. This manager, it seems, fell victim to the "one who has power to kill the body" (Matt 10:28).

The scenario envisaged depends on the conceptual metaphor of "organization as machine," in which the failure of one part means the breakdown of the whole. The manager, by "putting a wrench in the works," would have shut down the entire system. An alternative and more appropriate metaphor, however, is "organization as body," which is a more flexible metaphor. Within this metaphor, we have it on authority (Matt 18:7–9) that offensive parts of the body can be removed—through "excommunication," banishment, or other symbolic forms of amputation. It is a painful procedure, but a necessary one. In this parable, the corrupt manager receives his expected reward. As I outline below, this bleak portrayal of the current system is consistent with how the notion of "carnival" relates to disengagement.

Lack of Military Action

Remarkably, the Gospels lack even a hint that Jesus developed a political strategy that took into account the military realities. The few references that could be interpreted in this way are ambivalent and open to a variety of interpretations. The military, as posited above, was the dominant face of Roman power in Palestine. If analogies with Egypt hold, Roman soldiers were the enforcers of stability and order, involved in local government to the lowest level and, when necessary, in suppression of social disorder. They were not a "separate" institution of the imperial structure, but the only face of the empire that most of its subjects saw.

Yoder and others have interpreted this lack of a military agenda among Jesus and his followers as an endorsement of a deliberate antimilitaristic stance, that is, as pacifism. The conclusion is poorly supported and thoroughly anachronistic. I would argue that, in first-century Palestine, "social change" had to involve, at some stage or other, a violent confrontation with the military powers. Social change and violence were inseparable. Lack of interest in this approach among the Jesus group suggests an alternative strategy.

Model of Disengagement

Sketch of the Model

To understand some of the anomalies detected above, I turn to "disengagement," which is becoming a more common idea in social-science literature. Broadly speaking, disengagement is "an inevitable process in which many of the relationships between a person and other members of a society are severed, and those remaining are altered in quality" (Cumming and Henry 1961:210). Disengagement consists of an individual's or group's social and psychological withdrawal from an "engagement" with others, or with society. Many have seen disengagement in terms of its active or passive characteristics, and, in most of its realizations, there is a near-universal understanding of the process as negative.

The concept is used commonly of the passive process of aging, in which a reduction of life activities and of ego energy is the inevitable outcome. The aging person disengages unwillingly from society into an amorphous limbo to await the next step, death (Cumming 1968; Cumming and Henry 1961; Kastenbaum 1979; Tallmer and Kutscher 1984). Within educational theory, the term is used of what was once labeled "dropping out," especially among students of color in a predominantly white environment (Sefa Devi 1998), or of privileged white students who maintain an attitude of entitlement without the necessary sense of obligation. It is said that such students have disengaged from the rigors of the traditional educational process. In other words, they do not do assignments, or they cheat on them (Flacks and Thomas 1998). A more neutral understanding of disengagement occurs in the breakup of relationships in Western society; such breakup, in true Western fashion, is done with as much benefit to either side as possible (Cahn 1987). In legal studies, a lawyer, through fear of recriminations, or charges of conflict of interest, will disengage from, or drop, a client. The most positive and, indeed, the most consistent use of the term is in military affairs, when an army, division, brigade, regiment, company, or platoon "disengages" the enemy by withdrawal or retreat (Hinter-hoff 1959 is the classic statement).

In more recent years, the term "disengagement" has been used to describe organizations, inspired by religious or other ideologies, that have withdrawn from larger society to form their own system, consistent with their cognitive world. Historically, such volunteerism has been seen to result from conscious decisions made in the spirit of freedom of thought, worship, or speech. The label attached to such groups is the Enlightenment-influenced label of "dissent." Prominent in the study of such groups has been the work of Bryan Wilson (1966, 1967, 1973, 1976, 1982, 1990).

Active disengagement is understood as the conscious, rational, and deliberate withdrawal from a previous engagement with society or with another. The resultant dissent is understood to have been inspired by rational debate over ideas or worldviews (e.g., the "apocalyptic"). But disengagement is a much more complex social phenomenon. It is not merely a matter of reasoned opinion, but involves notions of criticism (of the larger group) alongside notions of self-interest and self-preservation. It is, therefore, a strategic position that needs further understanding. I suggest that beneath or even in place of what others have called the "political" position of Jesus, which appears to be one of continuous social criticism, might be a concern for the preservation of the group he formed and for the continuation of its values.

In his 1993 work, *The Kingdom of Individuals: An Essay on Self-Respect and Social Obligation*, Bailey developed a clear model of disengagement (figure 14.3). The model does not excise "unsuitable" aspects of the subject matter. This model comes from the domain of oppression and potential conflict, and, in the way Bailey constructs it, is an unusual model for Westerners to accommodate. Western consumer culture is used to the language of equality and equal rights, which are cultural artifacts. This culture tends to have three strategies of dealing with conflict; in descending order of importance, these are (1) conflict resolution, (2) conflict management, and (3) conflict containment. Each strategy admits the failure of the previous one. There is a fourth strategy

1. Disengagement always involves a conflict of moralities, a potential argument about where one's duty lies; the conflict is usually shaped as obligation to one's self versus duties owed to the organization.
2. The interaction that gives rise to disengagement is always between unequals. From one perspective, in other words, one partner has no hope of winning.
3. The organization is not only superior in power to the group, but also, by definition, intent upon the group's exploitation.
4. Disengagement is not the same as open protest. It is either covert, concealed from authorities, or camouflaged so that, even though authorities suspect its presence, they cannot easily take action against it.
5. Disengagers are never social reformers with a conscious political intent, or dissidents armed with programs of their own. The disengager's intention is not to change the status quo but to exploit it, and to preserve a private space that the organization cannot intrude upon.
6. Disengagement, to be successful, develops a mind that can operate beyond the larger organization—an active, independent mind capable of presenting issues or problems.

Figure 14.2: Bailey's model of disengagement (1993)

that disengagement addresses, and that is to live with the conflict, but not to let it affect life unless absolutely necessary. In another context, Bailey called this strategy "the civility of indifference." Turner's processual four-stage "social drama" of (1) breach, (2) crisis, (3) redressive action, and (4) reintegration (1974) touches on the same attitude. The last of Turner's categories sometimes involves a legitimation of social schism, that is, the ability to live without what Westerners adore, namely, "closure." These are, as we appreciate, cultural positions and ideals.

Bailey's model of disengagement has six primary characteristics. It is clear that, as Bailey expounds, disengagement is not an ascetic withdrawal from life and conflict. It is, instead, an attitude of a small, threatened group toward a larger, all-powerful, and all-pervasive group and/or dominant ideology. It is a pragmatic and a strategic response; it is, at root, subversive. Disengagers use the language of the larger group and subvert it ("antilanguage"). Disengagers present an image of compliance that masks strong disagreement. Disengagers seek to survive and to protect their way of life in the context of an alien, dominant group. Such a strategic response is consistent with what have been identified as dominant peasant attitudes (Bailey 1996:126, 129–30).

Since Bailey wrote, much more work has been done on political disengagement, especially in postcolonial peasant societies. Most helpful is a concise paper by Bruce Baker that surveys and evaluates research and outlines a much more comprehensive model (1997). Baker's model, unlike Bailey's, deals with levels of disengagement, including "social power," "unacceptable power," "political society," and/or "civic society." No one form of disengagement is thoroughly consistent and unitary. Anomalies in attitudes and actions persist even among the most radical groups. Baker calls this "straddling." But, as he suggests, "straddling is no more than the recognition that some powers are beneficial and to be engaged, and some powers are detrimental and to be disengaged from" (1997:11). To accommodate this contradiction, Baker examines the foundational strategy or value of the nonelites, which guides them in a variety of circumstances. This value, he suggests, is self-preservation. The model then becomes more flexible, and therefore more comprehensive, allowing for differing historical circumstances and differing reactions from individual groups. It also provides evidence for a variety of types of disengagement that groups can adopt. In many ways, Baker's model has the adaptability, scope, and usefulness of the grid-and-group model that Bruce Malina (1986) has developed from the observations of Mary Douglas.

First, Baker sketches nine "disengagement phenomena" that observers have considered (figure 14.3, on next page). The nine are migration; anti-establishment activity; localized autonomy; counterculture movements; economic separation; selective evasion of control; abandonment of culture; nonparticipation in formal politics; and nonparticipation in informal politics. One advantage of such a comprehensive list is that it moves investigation beyond the overworked dualities of traditional cultural analysis, such as "church" and "sect."

The typology of Baker's model (figure 14.5, on next page) has one axis, withdrawal strategy, accommodating variations in the level of disengagement of a group, movement, or individual. These levels are autonomy; avoidance and deception; and indifference. These levels are not necessarily linked to specific groups, but can also characterize a single group in different circumstances. Along another axis, with the heading "Arenas of Domination" (I would prefer "Domains of Action"), Baker places the four notions of territorial politics, economic politics, institutional politics, and cultural politics. The intersection of these axes results in twelve aspects of disengagement.

In addition, Baker attempts to evaluate the degrees of political disengagement in a society, and to link them with (ideal) types of "members" of that society (figure 14.5, on next page). On two intersecting axes of acceptance and rejection, and high and low levels of participation, he plots a range of "civic" activities embodied by the civic, voting, spectator, apathetic, hostile,

1. *Migration* to escape a hostile power
   a. External
   b. Internal
2. *Anti-establishment activity*, a rejection of legitimacy and/or attempted overthrow
   a. Organized and armed conflict/rebellion
   b. Spontaneous violence/riots/sabotage
   c. Passive resistance
3. *Localized autonomy*
   a. Secession
   b. Theocratic communities
   c. Urban "no-go" areas
4. *Counterculture movements*—"spiritual" exit by traditional, secular, or religious groups
5. *Economic separation* from political control
   a. From supervised production/distribution (nonformal economy)
   b. From recorded production/distribution (informal economy)
6. *Selective evasion of control*
   a. Abuse of tax/benefits system
   b. Opportunism (shirking, foot-dragging, false compliance, feigned ignorance)
7. *Abandonment of culture*
   a. Of civic values (pursuit of public good at the expense of purely individual ends)
   b. Of civic virtues (interpersonal trust, respect, tolerance)
8. *Non-participation in formal politics*
   a. No part in voting
   b. No part in petitions, demonstrations, personal contacts
9. *Non-participation in informal politics*
   a. Do not follow public affairs
   b. Nonmembership in associations with political content or communal activity

Figure 14.3: Proposed disengagement phenomena (Baker 1997:28)

or rebellious "citizen." This chart I find tautological and less useful than Baker's other illustrations.

A distinct advantage of Baker's model, if used in Jesus research, is that it displaces the dominant discussion about the political role and status of the poor

Withdrawal Strategies	Territorial Politics	Economic Politics	Institutional Politics	Cultural Politics
Autonomy	• Permanent exile • Internal safe haven	• Nonformal economy	• Establishment of no-go-areas • Passive resistance	• Counterculture beliefs and communities
Avoidance and Deception	• Maroonage • Border-hopping • Go underground	• Informal economy • Opportunism • Labor evasion	• Non-registration	• Underground community • Secret society
Indifference	• Political nomadism	• Question Begging	• Non-participation in elections, lobbying, campaigning	• Self-encapsulation • Rejection of civic values and virtues • Not member of associations
	Arenas of Domination			

Figure 14.4: Baker's typology of disengagement (1997)

and dispossessed—which, however noble an endeavor, is a distinctly modern (i.e., post-Victorian), Western obsession (Himmelfarb 1994). It rescues the debate from numerous "teleological fallacies" (Finley 1981:17), which assume that Jesus had the same concerns about the shape and function of society as the modern social activist. To find out whether such an assumption is true is the goal of exegesis. That it is true is an act of faith, not the result of historical investigation.

Jesus and Disengagement

It is important to outline the relevance of Baker's model for reading the Gospels. At this stage, it is impossible to link all the strategies and domains that

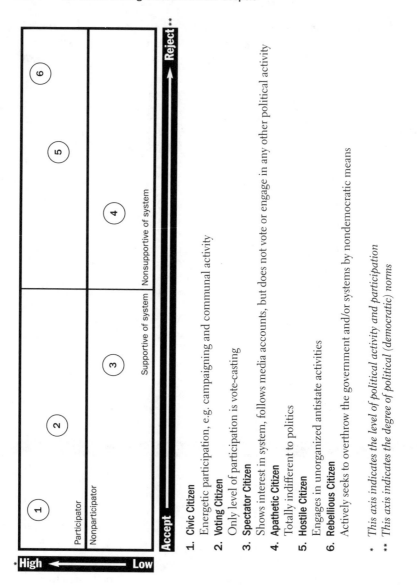

Figure 14.5: Degrees of political disengagement (Baker 1997). Disengagement is a move from 1 and 2 to 3, 4, 5, or 6.

Baker describes with the life and career of Jesus as presented in the Gospels. That work has just begun. But the introduction of this model establishes an agenda for investigation of the Gospels within modern Jesus research.

Looking at the broad picture, categories in the typology often seem to fit aspects of the life and career of Jesus as presented in the Gospels, without narrowing him and his group to one strategy or tactic. To return where I began, for Yoder's influential book the sine qua non of Jesus studies was that Jesus was a political being, that he was deeply concerned about responding in an original way to the sociopolitical environment of his day, and that, because of this, he is relevant for social ethics in the modern world (Yoder 1994:11). In this belief, of course, Yoder is not alone. Yoder's understanding is not value-neutral, but is understood in ways which I suggest Jesus might not recognize. By "political," Yoder means participatory in the structures of power. By "response," he means critical and public evaluation with an intention to change. By the "sociopolitical environment," he understands a social situation characterized by imbalance, based on numerical distribution of society's goods.

The relationships between Jesus and his social environment are subtle, and the more tools developed and used in understanding human behavior in such contexts, the clearer—or, perhaps, the more complex—the picture becomes. The anthropological model of disengagement is one model to help us understand the complexity.

Closely linked to the idea of disengagement is the anthropological concept of societal "inversion." Inversion highlights elements of a society that contain the seeds of a society's own destruction; these elements are sometimes ridiculed, or even portrayed in public fashion. This feature is certainly relevant to studies of peasant attitudes. Anthropologists have taken one of two approaches to inversion. On the one hand, inversion is seen as depicting the shadow side of a society—heaven and salvation, counterbalanced with hell and damnation, in some religious ideologies. Some Indian priests, for example, at certain ceremonies practice the antithesis of proper Hindu ideals by eating forbidden food. Such an action perhaps represents what a society may become without its established order.

But others have also noted that inversion is often used to highlight the structures of society in a grotesque way. Most common in the Mediterranean world is the carnival. Stanley Brandes' study of "Giants and Big-Heads" in Monteros society (1980:17–36) is such a case. Brandes points out that the values behind such a ritual expression are common in agrarian societies around the Mediterranean. Such values include fear of exploitation and of dominance and submission. Such a strategy—whether enacted in carnivals or through more subtle means, like public debate—can be the partner of disengagement, and, under a mask of humor, it contains the utmost seriousness. Both strategies—disengagement and carnival/inversion—contain the crucial element of subversion. This may be recognized as the conceptual foundation of comedy. "Carnivalesque practices thus attempt to invert consciousness, to render ridiculous what has become normative, to show turbulence and negation beneath conformity, to emerge as spirits of protest against the perceived sickness of society" (Strathern 1996:169).

Conclusion

I have suggested a model that will enable fresh analysis of Jesus and his relationship to "political activism" or "social change." Such notions, though noble, are anachronistic. I have introduced the model of disengagement as a possible tool to interpret the Gospel material, and briefly allied this model to the notion of social inversion. Together these strategies involve, among other things, a flattery of the authorities, the stealing of language ("antilanguage"), the development and nurture of an inner group, and avoidance of unnecessary trouble. The strategy is one of survival within an oppressive system, and not without criticism of that system. I do not claim that such a model provides an eternal and comprehensive clue to understanding the Gospels. But in offering this model I suggest that it is useful, a criterion to which all models can only aspire.

Works Cited

Adas, Michael. 1981. "From Avoidance to Confrontation: Peasant Protest in Pre-Colonial and Colonial South-East Asia." *CSSH* 23:217–47.

Alston, Richard. 1995. *The Soldier and Society in Roman Egypt: A Social History.* London: Routledge.

Anderson, B. 1996. *Imagined Communities: Reflections on the Origins and Spread of Nationalism.* 2nd ed. London: Verso.

Appelbaum, Shimon. 1978. "Judaea as a Roman Province: The Countryside as a Political and Economic Factor." In *ANRW* II.8:355–96. Berlin: de Gruyter.

Bailey, F. G. 1971. "The Peasant View of the Bad Life." In *Peasants and Peasant Societies*, edited by T. Shanin, 299–321. Harmondsworth, England: Penguin.

———. 1991. *The Prevalence of Deceit.* Ithaca, N.Y.: Cornell University Press.

———. 1993. *The Kingdom of Individuals: An Essay on Self-Respect and Social Obligation.* Ithaca, N.Y.: Cornell University Press.

———. 1996. *The Civility of Indifference: On Domesticating Ethnicity.* Ithaca, N.Y.: Cornell University Press.

———. 1998. *The Need for Enemies: A Bestiary of Political Forms.* Ithaca, N.Y.: Cornell University Press.

Baker, Bruce. 1997. *The Nature of Disengagement from Political Authority.* Occasional Papers of the African Studies Centre 3. Coventry, England: School of International Studies and Law.

Bammel, Ernst, and C. F. D. Moule, eds. 1984. *Jesus and the Politics of His Day.* Cambridge: Cambridge University Press.

Banfield, Edward C. 1958. *The Moral Basis of a Backward Society.* Chicago: Free Press.

Bar Tal, D. 1980. "The Masada Syndrome: A Case of Central Belief." In *Stress and Coping in Time of War,* edited by N. A. Milgram. New York: Brunner.

Barrett, Stanley. R. 1996. *Anthropology: A Student's Guide to Theory and Method.* Toronto: University of Toronto Press.

Berkhofer, Robert F. 1997. "The Challenge of Poetics to [Normal] Historical Practice." In *The Postmodern History Reader,* edited by K. Jenkins, 139–57. London: Routledge.

Brandes, Stanley H. 1980. *Metaphors of Masculinity: Sex and Status in Andalusian Folklore.* Philadelphia: University of Pennsylvania Press.

Bratton, M. 1989. "Beyond the State: Civil Society and Associated Life in Africa." *World Politics* 41:415ff.

Braudel, Fernand. 1972. *The Mediterranean and the Mediterranean World in the Age of Philip II.* Translated by S. Reynolds. Vol. 1. New York: Harper & Row.

Broughton, T. R. S. 1933. "The Roman Army." In *The Beginnings of Christianity.* Pt. 1: *The Acts of the Apostles,* edited by F. J. Foakes-Jackson, 427–45. London: Macmillan.

Cahn, Dudley D., Jr. 1987. *Letting Go: A Practical Theory of Relationship Disengagement and Reengagement.* Albany: State University of New York Press.

Carney, T. F. 1974. *The Shape of the Past: Models in Antiquity.* Lawrence, Kans.: Coronado.

Carp, Frances. 1972. *Retirement.* New York: Behavioral Publications.

Chabal, Patrick. 1992. *Power in Africa: An Essay in Political Interpretation.* New York: St. Martin's.

Champion, T. C., ed. 1989. *Centre and Periphery: Comparative Studies in Archaeology.* London: Unwin Hyman.

Cohen, R. 1980. "Resistance and Hidden Forms of Consciousness Amongst African Workers." *Review of African Political Economy* 19:8–22.

Coulson, Margaret A., and Carol Riddell. 1980. *Approaching Sociology.* London: Routledge & Kegan Paul.

Crossan, John Dominic. 1989. *Jesus: A Revolutionary Biography.* San Francisco: Harper & Row.

———. 1991. *The Historical Jesus: The Life of a Mediterranean Jewish Peasant.* San Francisco: HarperSanFrancisco.

Cumming, Elaine. 1968. *Systems of Social Regulation*. New York: Atheron.

Cumming, Elaine, and William E. Henry. 1961. *Growing Old: A Process of Disengagement*. New York: Basic.

Douglas, Mary, and Aaron Wildavsky. 1983. *Risk and Culture: An Essay on the Selection of Technological and Environmental Dangers*. Berkeley: University of California Press.

Elliott, John H. 1993. *What Is Social-Scientific Criticism?* GBS. Minneapolis: Fortress Press.

Evans, Richard J. 1997. *In Defence of History*. London: Granta.

Feder, Ernest. 1971. *The Rape of the Peasantry: Latin America's Landholding System*. New York: Doubleday.

Feld, Maury D. 1977. "A Typology of Military Organization." In *The Structure of Violence: Armed Forces and Social Systems*, 31–69. Beverly Hills, Calif.: Sage.

Femia, Joseph V. 1993. "Political Culture." In *The Blackwell Dictionary of Twentieth-Century Social Thought*, edited by W. Outhwaite et al., 475–77. Oxford: Blackwell.

Fiensy, David A. 1991. *The Social History of Palestine in the Herodian Period: The Land Is Mine*. SBEC 20. Lewiston, N.Y.: Mellen.

Finley, M. I. 1980. *Ancient Slavery and Modern Ideology*. Harmondsworth, England: Penguin.

———. 1983. *Politics in the Ancient World*. Cambridge: Cambridge University Press.

———. 1985. "War and Empire." In *Ancient History: Evidence and Models*, 67–87. New York: Viking.

———. 1986 "Anthropology and the Classics." In *Uses and Abuses of History*, 102–19. London: Hogarth.

Flacks, R., and S. L. Thomas. 1998. "Among Affluent Students: A Culture of Disengagement." *The Chronicle of Higher Education*, 27 November.

Foster, George M. 1965. "Peasant Society and the Image of the Limited Good." *American Anthropologist* 67:293–310.

Foucault, Michel. 1980. *Power/Knowledge: Selected Interviews and Other Writings, 1972–1977*. Edited by C. Gordon. Translated by C. Gordon et al. New York: Pantheon.

Freyne, Sean. 1989 "Bandits in Galilee: A Contribution to the Study of Social Conditions in First-Century Palestine." In *The Social World of Formative Christianity and Judaism*, edited by J. Neusner et al., 50–68. Philadelphia: Fortress Press.

Goldsworthy, Adrian Keith. 1996. *The Roman Army at War, 100 BC—AD 200*. Oxford Classical Monographs. Oxford: Clarendon.

Halliday, M. A. K. 1978. *Language as Social Semiotic: The Social Interpretation of Language and Meaning*. London: Arnold.

Hanson, K. C., and Douglas E. Oakman. 1998. *Palestine in the Time of Jesus: Social Structures and Social Conflicts.* Minneapolis: Fortress Press.

Harries-Jenkins, G., and Charles C. Moskos. 1981. "The Armed Forces and Society." *Current Sociology* 29:1–170.

Herzfeld, Michael 1991. *The Poetics of Manhood: Contest and Identity in a Cretan Mountain Village.* Princeton: Princeton University Press.

Himmelfarb, Gertrude. 1994 "The Mischievous Ambiguity of the Word 'Poor.'" In *The Demoralization of Society: From Victorian Virtues to Modern Values,* 125–42. New York: Vintage.

Hinterhoff, Eugene. 1959. *Disengagement.* London: Stevens.

Hirschman, Albert O. 1970. *Exit, Voice, and Loyalty: Responses to Decline in Firms, Organization, and States.* Oxford: Oxford University Press.

———. 1978–79. "Exit, Voice, and the State." *World Politics* 31:94ff.

———. 1993. "Exit, Voice, and the Fate of the GDR: An Essay in Conceptual History." *World Politics* 45:173ff.

Hobbs, T. R., and P. K. Jackson. 1991. "The Enemy in the Psalms." *BTB* 21:22–29.

Hobsbawm, Eric R. 1959. *Primitive Rebels: Studies in Archaic Forms of Social Movement in the Nineteenth and Twentieth Centuries.* New York: Norton.

———. 1998a. "Peasants and Politics." In *Uncommon People: Resistance, Rebellion, and Jazz,* 146–65. London: Weidenfeld & Nicholson.

———. 1998b. "Peasant Land Occupations." In *Uncommon People: Resistance, Rebellion, and Jazz,* 166–90. London: Weidenfeld & Nicholson.

Horbury, William. 1984. "Christ as Brigand in Ancient Anti-Christian Polemic." In *Jesus and the Politics of His Day,* edited by E. Bammel and C. F. D. Moule, 183–96. Cambridge: Cambridge University Press.

Horsley, Richard A. 1988. *Jesus and the Spiral of Violence: Popular Jewish Resistance in Roman Palestine.* Minneapolis: Fortress Press.

———. 1995. *Galilee: History, Politics, People.* Valley Forge, Pa.: Trinity Press International.

Isaac, Benjamin. 1990. *The Limits of Empire: The Roman Army in the East.* Oxford: Clarendon.

———. 1994. "Bandits." In *ABD* 1:575–80.

Isaacman, A. 1990. "Peasants and Social Protest in Africa." *African Studies Review* 33:43ff.

Jahangir, Borhanuddin Khan. 1989. "Violence and Consent in a Peasant Society." In *Domination and Resistance,* edited by D. Miller et al., 316–24. London: Allen & Unwin.

Janowitz, Morris, ed. 1981. *Civil-Military Relations: Regional Perspectives.* Beverly Hills, Calif.: Sage.

Janowitz, Morris, and Roger W. Little. 1975. "Primary Groups and Military Effective-
    ness." In *Sociology and the Military Establishment*, 93–115. Berkeley, Calif.: Sage.
Jenkins, Keith, ed. 1997. *The Postmodern History Reader*. London: Routledge.
Kastenbaum, Robert, ed. 1979. *Between Life and Death*. New York: Springer.
Kavanagh, Dennis. 1972. *Political Culture*. London: Macmillan.
Keen, Sam. 1986. *Faces of the Enemy: Reflections of the Hostile Imagination*. San
    Francisco: Harper & Row.
Kellner, Hans. 1998. "Language and Historical Representation." In *The Postmodern
    History Reader*, edited by K. Jenkins, 127–38. London: Routledge.
Kennedy, David L., ed. 1996. *The Roman Army in the East*. JRASup 18. Ann Arbor:
    JRA Press.
Kyrtatas, Dimitris J. 1987. *The Social Structure of the Early Christian Communities*.
    London: Verso.
Lakoff, George, and Mark Johnson. 1980. *Metaphors We Live By*. Chicago: University
    of Chicago Press.
Landsberger, Henry A., and C. N. Hewitt. 1970. "Ten Sources of Weakness and Cleav-
    age in Latin American Peasant Movements." In *Agrarian Problems and Peasant
    Movements in Latin America*, edited by R. Stavenhagen, 559–85. Garden City,
    N.Y.: Doubleday.
Lemarchand, Rene. 1992. "Uncivil States and Civil Societies." *Journal of Modern
    African Studies* 30:187ff.
Lenski, Gerhard E. 1984. *Power and Privilege: A Theory of Social Stratification*. 2d ed.
    Chapel Hill: University of North Carolina Press.
Liverani, Mario. 1979. "The Ideology of the Assyrian Empire." In *Power and Propa-
    ganda: A Symposium on Ancient Empires*, edited by M. T. Larsen, 297–312.
    Copenhagen: Akademisk.
Lowenthal, David. 1998. *The Heritage Crusade and the Spoils of History*. Cambridge:
    Cambridge University Press.
Malina, Bruce J. 1986. *Christian Origins and Cultural Anthropology: Some Useful
    Models*. Atlanta: John Knox.
Malina, Bruce J., and Jerome H. Neyrey. 1988. *Calling Jesus Names: The Social Value
    of Labels in Matthew*. Sonoma, Calif.: Polebridge.
Migdal, Joel S. 1974. *Peasants, Politics, and Revolution: Pressure toward Political and
    Social Change in the Third World*. Princeton: Princeton University Press.
Millar, Fergus. 1993. *The Roman Near East, 32 BC–AD 337*. Cambridge: Harvard
    University Press.
Miller, Daniel. 1995. "The Limits of Dominance." In Miller et al., eds. 1995:63–78.
Miller, Daniel, et al., eds. 1995. *Domination and Resistance*. London: Allen & Unwin.
Moore, R. I. 1987. *The Formation of a Persecuting Society: Power and Deviance in
    Western Europe, 950–1250*. New York: Blackwell.

Moxnes, Halvor. 1998. "The Historical Jesus: From Master Narrative to Cultural Context." *BTB* 28:135–49.

Oakman, Douglas E. 1986. *Jesus and the Economic Questions of His Day.* SBEC 8. Lewiston, N.Y.: Mellen.

Pearse, Andrew. 1975. *The Latin American Peasant.* Library of Peasant Studies 1. London: Cass.

Pelikan, Jaroslav. 1985. *Jesus through the Centuries: His Place in the History of Culture.* San Francisco: Harper & Row.

Pfohl, Stephen. J. 1985. *Images of Deviance and Social Control: A Sociological History.* New York: McGraw-Hill.

Pilch, John J. 1993. "Power." In Pilch and Malina 1993:139–42.

Pilch, John J., and Bruce J. Malina, eds. 1993. *Biblical Social Values and Their Meaning.* Peabody, Mass.: Hendrickson.

Putnam, Robert D. 1993. *Making Democracy Work: Civic Traditions in Modern Italy.* Princeton: Princeton University Press.

Rich, John, and Graham Shipley, eds. 1993. *War and Society in the Roman World.* Leicester-Nottingham Studies in Ancient Society 5. London: Oxford University Press.

Roman, P. M. 1967. *Organizational Structure: The Emeritus Professor.* New York: Knopf.

Rosenbaum, Walter A. 1975. *Political Culture.* Basic Concepts in Political Science. London: Nelson.

Rothschild, Donald, and Naomi Chazan, eds. 1988. *The Precarious Balance: State and Society in Africa.* Boulder, Colo.: Westview.

Rowlands, Michael. 1995. "A Question of Complexity." In *Domination and Resistance,* edited by D. Miller et al., 29–40. London: Allen & Unwin.

Rowlandson, Jane. 1996. *Landowners and Tenants in Roman Egypt: The Social Relations of Agriculture in the Oxyrrhyncite Nome.* Oxford Classical Monographs. Oxford: Oxford University Press.

Rowlett, Lori L. 1996. *Joshua and the Rhetoric of Violence: A New Historicist Analysis.* JSOTSup 226. Sheffield: JSOT Press.

Schur, Edwin M. 1971. *Labeling Deviant Behavior: Its Sociological Implications.* New York: Harper & Row.

Schwartz, Rosalie. 1989. *Lawless Liberators: Political Banditry and Cuban Independence.* Durham, N.C.: Duke University Press.

Scott, James C. 1985. *Weapons of the Weak: Everyday Forms of Peasant Resistance.* New Haven: Yale University Press.

———. 1998. *Seeing Like a State: How Certain Schemes to Improve the Human Condition Have Failed.* New Haven: Yale University Press.

Sefa Devi, G. J. 1995. *Drop Out or Push Out? The Dynamics of Black Students' Disengagement from Schools.* Toronto: Ontario Institute for Studies in Education.

Sen, Ranjit. 1988. *Social Banditry in Bengal: A Study in Primary Resistance, 1757–1793*. Calcutta: Ratna Prakashan.

Shanin, Theodor. 1971. "The Peasantry as a Political Factor." In *Peasants and Peasant Societies*, edited by T. Shanin, 238–63. Harmondsworth, England: Penguin.

Shils, Edward. 1982. "Center and Periphery." In *The Constitution of Society*, 93–109. Chicago: University of Chicago Press.

Spencer, J. 1996. "Peasants." In *Encyclopedia of Social and Cultural Anthropology*, edited by A. Barnard and J. Spencer, 418–19. London: Routledge.

Stambaugh, John E., and David L. Balch. 1983. *The New Testament in Its Social Environment*. LEC 2. Philadelphia: Westminster.

Stern, Menachem. 1974a. "The Province of Judaea." In *The Jewish People in the First Century*, edited by S. Safrai et al., 1:308–76. CRINT. Philadelphia: Fortress Press; Assen: Van Gorcum.

———. 1974b. "The Reign of Herod and the Herodian Dynasty." In *The Jewish People in the First Century*, edited by S. Safrai et al., 1:216–307. CRINT. Philadelphia: Fortress Press; Assen: Van Gorcum.

———. 1975. "The Reign of Herod." In *The World History of the Jewish People*. Vol. 7: *The Herodian Period*, edited by M. Avi-Yonah, 71–123. New Brunswick, N.J.: Rutgers University Press.

Strathern, Andrew J. 1996. *Body Thoughts*. Ann Arbor: University of Michigan Press.

Stuart, P. H. 1997. "Did Specialization Result in Social Work's Disengagement from the Poor?" Unpublished paper, School of Social Work, University of Alabama, Tuscaloosa.

Tallmer, Margot, and Lillian G. Kutscher, eds. 1984. *The Life-Threatened Elderly*. New York: Columbia University Press.

Theissen, Gerd. 1978. *Sociology of Early Palestinian Christianity*. Translated by J. Bowden. Philadelphia: Fortress Press.

———. 1987. *In the Shadow of the Galilean: The Quest of the Historical Jesus in Narrative Form*. Translated by J. Bowden. Philadelphia: Fortress Press.

———. 1992. *Social Reality and the Early Christians: Theology, Ethics, and the World of the New Testament*. Translated by M. Kohl. Philadelphia: Fortress Press.

Thomae, Hans, and George L. Maddox, eds. 1982. *New Perspectives on Old Age*. New York: Springer.

Toren, Christina. 1996. "Socialization." In *Encyclopedia of Social and Cultural Anthropology*, edited by A. Barnard and J. Spencer, 512–14. London: Routledge.

Tripp, L. 1998. "Community in America." http://condor.stcloudstate.edu/~ltripp/Mindi Schultz. html.

Turner, Victor. 1974. *Dramas, Fields, and Metaphors: Symbolic Action in Human Society*. Ithaca, N.Y.: Cornell University Press.

Watson, G. R. 1969. *The Roman Soldier.* Aspects of Greek and Roman Life. Ithaca, N.Y.: Cornell University Press.

Wilson, Bryan R. 1966. *Religion in a Secular Society: A Sociological Comment.* London: Watts.

―――. 1967. *Patterns of Sectarianism.* London: Heinemann.

―――. 1970. *Religious Sects: A Sociological Perspective.* New York: World.

―――. 1973. *Magic and the Millennium: A Sociological Study of Religious Movements of Protest among Tribal and Third-World Peoples.* San Francisco: Harper & Row.

―――. 1976. *Contemporary Transformations of Religion.* Oxford: Oxford University Press.

―――. 1982. *Religion in Sociological Perspective.* Oxford: Oxford University Press.

―――. 1990. *Social Dimensions of Sectarianism: Sects and New Religious Movements in Contemporary Society.* Oxford: Clarendon.

Wolf, Eric R. 1969. *Peasant Wars of the Twentieth Century.* San Francisco: Harper & Row.

Yoder, John H. 1994. *The Politics of Jesus.* 2d ed. Grand Rapids: Eerdmans.

15

Jesus and the Social Bandits

K. C. Hanson

> As *against a bandit, have you come out with swords and*
> *clubs to capture me?*
>   —Mark 14:48

The rhetorical question that Jesus asks in Mark 14:48 (par. Matt 26:55; Luke 22:52) raises several questions for the modern reader:

- What does *lēstēs* ("bandit") actually mean, and what sort of bandits were operating in ancient Palestine, and the Mediterranean in general?
- Why does Jesus associate the antagonism to bandits with elite authorities?
- Why does the term *lēstēs* appear in other Jesus sayings as a poignant metaphor (Matt 21:13; Luke 10:30; John 10:1, 8)?
- What is the significance of Jesus being crucified between two bandits (Mark 15:28) and the Fourth Gospel's identification of Barabbas as a *lēstēs* (John 18:40)?

In this study I pursue answers to these questions, and, in so doing, I build on earlier studies to construct a model of social banditry. Specifically, I want to (1) provide the word fields in Hebrew, Greek, and Latin; (2) broaden the base of parallel ethnographies; (3) articulate a more nuanced model of banditry; (4) organize the ancient data in a way that makes it more accessible; and (5) provide translations and interpretations of the biblical evidence in the Gospels.

The Word Fields

In Hebrew, the root *gnb* covers the broad range of stealing (Exod 22:2–8). But using Exod 21:16 and Deut 24:7, Albrecht Alt deduced that, in the Decalogues, *gnb* seems to connote kidnapping specifically (Exod 20:15; Deut 5:19). And the root *gzl* implies violent seizure in robbery, plunder, or confiscation (Judg 9:25b). The general term *gedud* ("band") is used often of military squads, but several times with the specific sense of "a bandit band" (1 Kings 11:23–24). (See also *me'arebim*, "ambushers" [Judg 9:22–25]; *mirmah*, "fraud" [Zeph 1:9; Ps 55:11]; *'šq*, "defraud" [1 Sam 12:3–4].) In rabbinic documents (e.g., the Mishnah), the term *lista'ah* (pl. *listîm*) is obviously a loanword from the Greek *lēstēs* (*m. Ber.* 1:3; *m. Šab.* 2:5).

But note that one of the most startling cases of social banditry in the Old Testament, that of David with his band of debtors and dispossessed, does not use technical terms: "And everyone who was oppressed, and everyone who was in debt, and everyone who was embittered rallied to him [David]; and he became their chieftain (*śar*). And there were about four hundred men with him" (1 Sam 22:2).

The Greek terms *kleptēs* and *lēstēs* are closely related, both having to do with taking possession of goods to which one has no right in law. The New Testament usage of *kleptō* is broad, describing common thievery (John 12:6), housebreaking (Matt 6:19–20; 24:43), or sheep stealing (John 10:1). *Lēstēs*, on the other hand, is a term covering bandits, pirates, and raiders, including what anthropologists call "social banditry," which I will define shortly (see Luke 10:30, 36). But the closeness of the two Greek terms is seen in John 10:1 and 10:8, where they are parallel. So while these two terms may be distinguished, they could also be used as synonyms; clearly, both literary and social contexts are necessary to distinguish between them in the ancient documents (see Rengstorf 1967).

In Greek literature, papyri, and inscriptions, several forms of *lēstēs* appear. The following are the primary forms, listed along with representative citations (see LSJ 1046; Moulton and Milligan 1930:375; Shaw 1993b:204): *archilēstarchēs*, "bandit chieftain" (Josephus, *War* 1.204; 2.253); *lēstarchēs*, "bandit chieftain" (Plutarch, *Crass.* 22); *lēstarchia*, "bandit leadership," "bandit hideout" (Strabo, *Geography* 14.1.32); *lēsteia*, "banditry," "piracy" (Philo, *Flaccus* §5); *lēstēs*, "bandit," "pirate" (Sir 36:26; Matt 26:55; 2 Cor 11:26; Josephus, *Ant.* 14.159); *lēstrikos*, "bandit," "pirate" (Josephus, *War* 1.305); *lēstrion*, "bandit band" (Josephus, *War* 1.398; *Ant.* 14.160; 15.344–45); *leia*, "booty"

(Josephus, *Ant.* 18.353; Herodotus 2.152); *lēstopiastēs*, "bandit police" (*P.Fiorentini* 2.181)

The Latin forms of *latro-* ("bandit/pirate") are broad terms (like their Greek counterparts) covering: mercenary soldiers, bandit bands, pirates, and frontier raiders. The primary nouns are *latro*, "hired servant," "mercenary soldier," "bandit," "pirate" (Cicero, *De Officiis* 2.11.40); *latrunculus*, "bandit," "freebooter" (Cicero, *Prov. Cons.* 7.15); *latrocinium*, "mercenary service," "banditry," "piracy," "bandit band" (Cicero, *Cat.* 2.1.1); *latrunculator*, "one who judges bandits" (*Digest* 5.1.61).

A Definition of Social Banditry

This brings us to defining more closely what we mean by the social-scientific (etic) category of "social banditry." Hobsbawm defines it as follows:

> It consists essentially of relatively small groups of men living on the margins of peasant society, and whose activities are considered criminal by the prevailing official power-structure and value-system, but not (or not without strong qualifications) by the peasantry. It is this special relation between peasant and bandit which makes banditry "social": the social bandit is a hero, a champion, a man whose enemies are the same as the peasants', whose activities correct injustice, control oppression and exploitation, and perhaps even maintain alive the ideal of emancipation and independence. (1973:143)

Social banditry, then, is a category of peasant brigands or bandits who primarily attack the urban elite or rural estate holders and are supported by village peasants. These bands arise in agrarian societies as a function of jarring imbalances in the social equilibrium: the inequitable exercise of law, economic pressures, land confiscations, famine, shifts in hierarchy, and so on. Robin Hood in English legend is the most famous case (but see Hobbs, pp. 260–61 above). Social bandits are one form of rural protest, and they are distinctly "prepolitical" in form. They differ from common thieves and robbers by virtue of their social protest and popular support (Stegemann and Stegemann 1999:173–78).

> As individuals they are not so much political or social rebels, let alone revolutionaries, as peasants who refuse to submit, and in doing so stand out from their fellows, or even more simply men who find themselves excluded from the usual career of their kind and therefore forced into outlawry and "crime." *En masse*

they are little more than symptoms of crisis and tension in their society. . . . Banditry itself is therefore not a programme for peasant society, but a form of self-help to escape it in particular circumstances. (Hobsbawm 1981:19)

Sant Cassia's definition reveals further important elements:

I consider banditry to be a consistent, relatively long-term flouting of the laws of the state by groups of individuals. They are so supported by a local population or potentates, either spontaneously or through a complex combination of covert and overt threats and incentives, that their betrayal to the state's agents conflicts with dominant grassroots moral sentiments. Banditry may be polyvalent or even disemic and may encompass diametrically opposed sets of values: violence and generosity, secrecy and openness, and incorporation in an exclusion from the moral community. (1993:773)

These definitions articulate a relationship among the state's ruling elite, local elites, the peasantry, and bandits, who feel they have no choice for survival but attack on the elites' resources: travelers, caravans, estates, and occasionally cities themselves. Sometimes local elites and estate holders find bandits to operate in their interests, and so protect them. At the core of this relationship is the bandits' sense that they have been treated inequitably. Fundamentally, the bandits' goal is not the toppling of regimes, but subsistence after having lost access to the "limited goods" of honor, justice, land, and goods (for analyses of limited good, see Foster 1967b; Malina 1993:90–116). Augustine elegantly describes the irony of the relationship between rulers and bandits and pirates:

And thus justice having been removed, what are kingdoms but large-scale bandit bands? And what are bandit-bands but small-scale kingdoms? [A bandit band] is composed of men, ruled by the authority of a leader, bound together by a social contract; the booty is divided by an agreed-upon principle. If this evil increases, by the admittance of destructive men—to such a degree that it controls regions, sets up homebases, occupies cities, subjugates peoples—it more obviously takes on the name "kingdom," because it is now openly conferred upon it—not by the absence of ambition, but by adding impunity. Indeed, it was an elegant and accurate response given to Alexander the Great by a pirate who had been seized. For when the king asked the man what he meant by his hostile control of the sea, he insolently answered, "The same as you by seizing the whole earth; but because I do it with a small ship, I am called a 'bandit'; when you do it with a great fleet, [you are called] 'Emperor.'" (De Civitate Dei 4.4; my translation)

Thucydides also provides an excellent emic description highlighting both the violence and the acquisition of honor for bandits and pirates:

> For in early times the Hellenes and the barbarians of the coast and islands, as communication by sea became more common, were tempted to turn pirates (*lēsteian*) under the conduct of their most powerful men; the motives being to serve their own cupidity and to support the needy. They would fall upon a town unprotected by walls, and consisting of a mere collection of villages, and would plunder it; indeed, this came to be the main source of their livelihood, no disgrace being yet attached to such an achievement, but even some glory. An illustration of this is furnished by the honor with which some of the inhabitants of the continent still regard a successful marauder (*lēstai*). . . . The same rapine prevailed also by land. (*The Peloponnesian War* 1.5; Crawley 1952:350 [Greek added])

An Egyptian edict from 210–214 C.E. regarding the capture of bandits indicates the ongoing problem and the difficulty of getting cooperation from the peasantry:

> Baebius Juncinus to the *stratēgoi* of the Heptanomia and the Arsinoite nome, greeting. I have already ordered you in an earlier letter to search out bandits (*lēstēn*) with all care, warning you of the peril of neglect; and now I wish to confirm my resolve by an edict in order that all the inhabitants of Egypt may know that I am not treating this duty as an issue of secondary importance, but offer rewards to those of you who cooperate and threaten with punishment those who choose to disobey. This edict I want publicly displayed in both the capitals and the most conspicuous places of the nomes; penalties and peril are awaiting you if in the future any criminal is able to use violence without detection. I wish you good health. (*P.Oxy.* 1408; Hunt and Edgar 1934:114–17)

This edict may also indicate the symbiotic relationship between local villagers and the social bandits, as articulated in Hobsbawm's definition.

Peasants and Peasant Resistance

Before proceeding, it is necessary to pause and define "peasant," since this definition affects the whole analysis. The issue of definition has generated a great deal of discussion. Some anthropologists have defined peasants in terms of culture, and some in terms of economics or production. Some have defined the term narrowly (agriculturists only) and others more broadly (agriculturists, artisans, pastoralists, fishers, etc.). For brief discussions of some of the issues, see Wolf (1966), Foster (1967a), Thorner (1968), Shanin (1987), and Oakman (1991, 1992). In general, we may describe "peasants" as having the following characteristics:

- They are village-based, agrarian producers, primarily (but not necessarily limited to) farmers.
- They form part of a larger society and are included within a state, usually with elites in preindustrial cities.
- Their residence, labor, and production are organized primarily through kinship ties.
- The elites hold power over the peasantry and extract the peasants' "surplus" through taxes, tolls, tribute, rents, conscripted labor, and control of commodities.
- Patron/broker/client and "fictive kinship" relations play important societal roles.
- Peasant culture is characterized by a heavy reliance on tradition and slow change.

For overviews of peasants in the Roman Empire and in Roman-era Palestine, see Rohrbaugh (1978:29–41); Goodman (1982); Oakman (1986:17–91; 1991); Fiensy (1991:75–153); Kolendo (1993); Garnsey (1994); Herzog (1994:53–73); and Stegemann and Stegemann (1999:79–96).

But the question may be asked: Given the character of peasant societies, where does social banditry fit in the larger picture? James C. Scott has been most influential in articulating how peasants deal with the larger society, and with the elites in particular (1977a; 1977b; 1985; 1990). Typically, peasants have devised a number of responses to elites' pressures, expectations, and extractions of the peasant "surplus" through taxes, tolls, tribute, rents, conscripted labor, and control of commodities. Scott identifies "foot dragging, dissimulation, false compliance, pilfering, feigned ignorance, slander, arson, sabotage" as common modes of resistance (1985:29). Herzog adds outright dissembling/lying (1995). These strategies are all meant to avoid direct confrontation in most cases.

But what shape do peasant confrontations take? At the bottom of the scale might be isolated acts of refusal, retaliation, and violence. When these start to take on group definition, new options emerge. "Social banditry" arises when peasants who cannot maintain their honor and social standing are labeled as serious "deviants" by the elites: when they fail to pay their taxes, are involved in violence or homicide, and so on; this is a prepolitical phenomenon (that is, it has no political agenda or focus). Hobsbawm identifies a variation on banditry that he labels "haidukry" (after the Balkan brigands of that name). These are bandits who become "institutionalized" because it simply pays better than working the land (Hobsbawm 1973:154–56). Rebellion and revolution is another form resistance may take. But this is a truly political form of protest; it assumes a focus, an agenda, and an alternative to the dominant social system—even if it is simply to pull the system down.

Social bandits practice a form of "establishment violence" (see Seland 1995). Note Malina's definition: "The violence exerted in establishment violence is socially unendorsed coercion directed by private persons against one another or against the regime. And *coercion* here is behavior intended to harm a person or a person's values" (1994:56). That is, the violence bandits practice in stealing, kidnapping, murder, and so on has no official sanction. Building on the model of Rosenbaum and Sederberg (1976), Malina identifies three basic types of establishment violence: crime-control, social-control, and regime-control (1994:56–57). The social bandits fit the second type: social-control vigilantism is "establishment violence directed against people believed to be competing for or advocating a redistribution of values within the system" (57). Malina goes on to say: "In this [conflict-approach] perspective, establishment violence may be considered as a process by means of which moral entrepreneurs seek to defend boundaries by exerting control over those who threaten those boundaries (= self-help justice and peace maintenance)" (65).

As Hobsbawm and Horsley have both shown (see below), these are historical processes, and should not be considered static entities. A peasant who has a disjunctive experience may be joined by others and form a bandit band (see 1 Sam 22:2; Josephus, *Ant.* 18.314–16). And a bandit band may be swept up in a peasant revolt: for example, the bandits who joined in the first Judean revolt (Josephus, *War* 4.135–61; see Horsley 1981), and Pancho Villa, who joined with the Zapatistas in the Mexican Revolution (see Hobsbawm 1973:157).

Social Banditry: History of Research

Hobsbawm's Contribution

Eric Hobsbawm has rightly been called "the father of bandit studies." His foundational work (1959; 1973; 1981) provided the first real social analysis of this phenomenon; he articulated the earliest definitions (see above) and erected the cross-cultural comparative framework, focusing especially on Spain, Italy (and its major islands), the Balkans, and Carpathia. Besides the definition of social bandits, Hobsbawm distinguishes them from common thieves, frontier raiders, Mafia-style organizations, and revolutionaries. Hobsbawm outlines his own model of social banditry in four points:

1. The bandits' violations are not considered crimes or unjustified by their fellow peasants.
2. They share their stolen gain with fellow peasants.
3. They limit their use of violence.
4. They represent the interests of peasant justice against elite justice. (1973:143–44)

Hobsbawm may be critiqued on a few of his points: He has been unclear about his definition of "peasants" and the relationship of banditry to peasantry (O'Malley 1979:490–91). His description of social banditry as manifested solely in preindustrial and precapitalist societies is also questionable. His own data for the nineteenth and twentieth centuries provide adequate evidence against this proposition (O'Malley 1979:491–92). He has minimized the ways in which bandits sometimes prey upon the local peasantry and thus weaken group solidarity (Blok 1972:496). He uses terms such as "millenarian" and "apocalyptic" without sufficient definition. In recounting tales of social bandits he often fails to provide sustained analysis, especially as it pertains to the particularities of culture.

Horsley's Contribution

Richard Horsley's work has been important to the analysis of social banditry in both biblical documents and Josephus' works (1979; 1981; 1988; 1995; Horsley and Hanson 1988). It is he who first brought the work of Hobsbawm to bear on the Gospels and Josephus. He has also made good use of the comparative data to ask fresh questions and bring nuance to the analyses of the ancient documents. Especially helpful is his exposure of the ideological stance of Josephus and other literary elites who wrote about bandits. Horsley has also astutely analyzed the way in which social banditry fit into the larger social fabric of first-century Palestine and social protests. Building on the work of Morton Smith (esp. 1971), Horsley reshaped the discussion about the relationship among bandits, popular kingship, the Sicarii, the Zealots, and the Fourth Philosophy. In particular, he demonstrated how several of the bandit bands shifted from banditry to revolution midway through the first Judean revolt (ca. 67 C.E.).

It is also noteworthy that Horsley (especially in his later works) overviews Palestinian politics and political economy in order to supply the context of social banditry. Rather than a simplistic, one-cause explanation, Horsley emphasizes that bandits arose in Roman-era Palestine in response to the numerous up-heavals in society. He identifies the following key issues:

- the imperialistic incursion of the Romans into Palestine in 63 B.C.E. (*War* 1.131–58);
- the civil war between rival Hasmonean factions (Antigonus and Hyrcanus II);
- the inconsistent policies of the Roman governors (e.g., Pilate, Cumanus, Albinus);
- the major Palestinian famines in 25–24 B.C.E. and 46–48 C.E.;
- the compounding of tithes, Herodian taxes, and Roman tribute (e.g., *Ant.* 14.202–3; 18.274);
- the questionable legitimacy of the priestly aristocracy (namely, non-Zadokites);
- the polarization of rich and poor (e.g., *Ant.* 20.180).

One can only benefit from the contributions these two have made.

Social Banditry: Creating a Model

Based on comparative data—from both the Roman era and more modern manifestations—as well as numerous analyses from the past thirty-five years, I articulate my understanding of the context, operation, organization, and outcomes of social banditry by creating a model.

A. Context
1. Social banditry is a *rural phenomenon* appearing in peasant/agrarian societies.
2. It usually appears when *the social equilibrium is upset in drastic ways*; peasants are under increased pressure due to:
   a. Ecological factors: drought, famine, plague.
   b. Political-economic factors: increased taxation, land confiscation, political disruption, and inequitable exercise of authority.
3. *Rule by a foreign power* (or "colonialism") is often at the root of bandits' disaffection with the power structures.
4. The state administration is too *inefficient* to deal adequately with the bandits swiftly.

B. Operation

5. The bandits are *labeled deviants by political authorities* (often for minor infractions), isolated, and hunted down as a threat to the state and political-economic stability; but the peasant population considers them honorable.
6. The bandits are often *supported by the local peasants* because of general peasant disaffection and the sense that the bandits stand against injustice.
7. While hiding from authorities, bandits usually *stay close to their home villages.*
8. Besides providing *an outlet for peasant disaffection,* bandits often provide tangible goods, protection, or redress of injustices for their villages.

C. Organization of Bandit Bands

9. They are held together by *the prestige of the leader.*
10. They are primarily *composed of young, unmarried males* (but whole families may sometimes be included).
11. They are usually limited to *groups of 15–40 members* due to organizational difficulties; but, in unusual circumstances, bands may be larger.

D. Outcomes

12. They are usually *limited in duration:* either they get caught and are punished, or the authorities lose interest.
13. Social banditry is usually *an ineffective strategy* for bringing about long-lasting change because:
    a. They do not originally form for political purposes.
    b. They lack the size and organization to pressure the authorities.
    c. Old and new oppressions coalesce to keep them isolated.
14. Bandits often *look for opportunities to be reintegrated* into the mainstream of peasant society.
15. The bandit bands may be *utilized (or co-opted) by local elites* for their own purposes, especially as mercenaries.
16. The bandits may become *haiduks* ("institutionalized" outlaw bands).
17. In unusual circumstances, the bandit phenomenon may accompany, or be integrated into, a full-scale *peasant revolt* (e.g., the first Judean revolt).

Figure 15.1: Context, operation, organization, and outcomes of social banditry

After one creates a model of social banditry, it may also be helpful to enunciate how it compares and contrasts with other forms of attack and stealing:

Social Banditry in the Gospels

Prepolitical				Political	
common thievery	social banditry	haidukry	frontier raiding	rebellion (sporadic)	revolution (sustained)
individuals	small groups			large groups	

Figure 15.2: Forms of attack and stealing by individuals and groups

I now turn to analyzing the evidence from the Jesus tradition. The object is to see in what ways the comparative evidence and the model may help in translating and interpreting these passages. In surveying the major Gospel commentaries, one finds little help for interpreting these passages.

Mark 11:17 (par. Matt 21:13; Luke 19:46; see John 2:16)

"He said to them, 'It is written, "My house shall be called a house of prayer"; but you have made it a "cave of bandits" [*splēlaion lēstōn*]!'" This saying juxtaposes phrases from Isa 56:7d and Jer 7:11a (both readings corresponding to the LXX). In his angry critique of the money changers and animal sellers in the temple precincts, Jesus uses antithetical parallelism to compare what is going on to a cave of bandits. This is a phrase that would have resonance for both Jesus' Judean and Galilean audiences. Herod the Great—who had renovated and expanded the Jerusalem temple—had made his initial reputation by rooting out a band of Galilean bandits from their caves (Josephus, *War* 1.304–13 // *Ant.* 14.420–31). The source of Jesus' anger about the temple situation has been a highly disputed topic. But Eppstein (1964) has posited a convincing scenario based on rabbinic sources. The animals were normally sold and the money changing handled across the Kidron Valley in the marketplace set up under the olive trees. When the sellers had given refuge to the Sanhedrin, who were involved in a dispute with Joseph Caiaphas (the high priest), Caiaphas retaliated by bringing in outside animal sellers and money changers and setting them up within the temple precincts. Presumably this would have allowed the priestly elites to take "kickbacks" from the sellers given precedence. If this scenario holds up, Jesus' outrage is targeted at the priestly elite, who were taking financial advantage of a political dispute. The chaos generated by the buying, selling, and changing had become a disruption to the sacred space. The chief

priests, who would later send troops to arrest Jesus "as a bandit," are here identified by Jesus as outlaws and bandits in a negative sense.

Jesus' action, then, constitutes an act of "establishment violence" (see
above). Since Jesus was not a priest and did not belong to the temple police, he
did not have the official sanction for such action. His violent response may be
characterized as "social-control vigilantism," with Jesus acting as a "moral en-
trepreneur" (see Malina 1994:56–57, 63–65), parallel, then, to the social bandits. Jesus' moral outrage, flare of temper, and physical acts are all in keeping
with Mediterranean cultural expectations. As Philo states:

> But if any members of the ethnic group betray the honor of the One, they should
> suffer the most severe penalties. . . . All who have zeal for virtue should be per-
> mitted to exact the penalties spontaneously and with no delay, without bringing
> the offender before jury or council, or any kind of magistrate at all, and give full
> range to the emotions which possess them, that hatred to evil and love of God
> which urges them to inflict punishment without mercy on the impious. (Philo,
> *Special Laws* 1.54; see Seland 1995:103–36 for discussion)

Jesus' saying is consistent with Augustine's later juxtaposition of "kingdom"
and "bandit band" (see above). Elite entrepreneurs (like the Jerusalem high
priestly families) would like to think that they are superior to the bandits who
live in caves and extract money and goods through force. Jesus' critique makes
it clear that he thinks the distinction is illusory. This saying is reminiscent of an
earlier Judean critique of the Jerusalem high priesthood from the Qumran
community. Referring to one of the Hasmonean high priests, the Habakkuk
pesher says: "He robbed and hoarded the wealth of the violent men who re-
belled against God. And he seized the wealth of the peoples, so that he heaped
sinful culpability upon himself" (1QpHab 8.11–12; see also 4 Macc 4:3,
15–18; Hanson and Oakman 1998:135–36). And speaking of Cypriot sentiments in the 1930s, Sant Cassia makes a comparison similar to that of Jesus:
"Politicians prey on their co-nationals, instead of representing them, much like
the bandits who grew fat on stolen meat and women" (1993:792).

I agree with Horsley that three recurring interpretations of Jesus' temple action are based on false assumptions and are not tenable, namely, (1) Jesus was
making an "eschatological" statement by defending the right of Gentiles to be
in the temple; (2) Jesus was purifying the temple cult; and (3) Jesus was attacking ritual forms in favor of a "spiritual" mode of religion (Horsley 1987:297).
But based on the interpretation above, I disagree with Horsley's conclusion:
"Jesus' demonstration in the Temple was a prophetic act symbolizing God's imminent judgmental destruction, not just of the building, but of the Temple sys-

tem" (1987:300). If Eppstein points us in the right direction, Jesus had a much more limited point to make. This does not detract from his deed as a prophetic symbolic action, but the act does take on less grandiose dimensions. My own hypothesis is that the temple action and the associated sayings were given a broader interpretation in the post-70 era.

Mark 14:48 (par. Matt 26:55; Luke 22:52)

"In that hour, Jesus said to the crowds, 'As against a bandit [*lēstōn*], have you come out with swords and clubs to capture me? Daily I sat in the temple, and you did not seize me.'" In this poignant rhetorical question, Jesus ridicules the crowds (Greek *ochloi*; read "posses" or "mobs"). They have come after him with large numbers and are armed as if ready for violent resistance. As made clear by the evidence adduced in preceding sections, the Hasmoneans, Herodians, local authorities, and Roman governors all had difficulty keeping a lid on social banditry; but they knew how to respond violently to bandits. Jesus' rhetorical question articulates how ludicrous it was for the priests' posse to confuse him with an armed social bandit. One might also emphasize that Jesus identifies the typical response from elites who perceive that their interests are threatened. Jesus' words and deeds were perceived as a fundamental challenge. The crowds also come to take him under cover of darkness, which itself indicates their lack of moral authority.

Mark 15:6–15
(par. Matt 27:15–26; Luke 23:13–25; John 18:29—19:16)

"But among the rebels in custody there was one named Barabbas who had committed murder" (15:7). Mark and Luke indicate that Barabbas (some manuscripts read "Jesus Barabbas") was involved in some sort of Jerusalem uprising and a "homicide" (*phonos*); John identifies him as a "bandit" (*lēstēs*; John 18:40). It is impossible to pinpoint exactly, from such meager information, where Barabbas fit socially. But we may say that John's identification of him as a bandit is not at odds with the Synoptics. His planned crucifixion along with two other bandits would fit this characterization. Matthew emphasizes his reputation, which coincides with the importance of bandit leaders' reputations for attracting a band. Biblical translators have often rendered *episēmion* negatively as "notorious" (RSV, NRSV, NIV); but the KJV "notable," NEB "notoriety," and TEV "well-known" are less judgmental. The Greek term simply indicates wide reputation, depending on context for valuation. If one characterizes Barabbas as "notorious" or "infamous," it would be difficult to explain the popular support for him among the masses. But we learn from cross-cultural studies that it is commonplace for social bandits to be popularly revered. That "the

chief priests and elders" (Matt 27:20) could influence the crowd to choose
Barabbas for release might seem ludicrous to a modern reader—a murderer
over a holy man? But this fails to take into account the way that social bandits
often captured the interest and support of the common folk. If one follows
Luke's characterization—that Barabbas is connected with Jerusalem—it may
modify our view of him as a traditional social bandit. Myers wants to contrast
Jesus, confused with a rural social bandit by the Judean authorities, and Barabbas, who represents the urban *sicarius* (1988:387). But just because Eleazar,
the bandit chieftain, was involved in a violent incident in Samaria did not
mean he was not a social bandit. As Horsley has shown, the Sicarii did not
emerge until more than twenty years later, in the mid-50s (Josephus, *War*
2.254–56; see Horsley 1979; 1987:39–40).

Mark 15:28 (par. Matt 27:38; Luke 23:33b; see John 19:18)

"Then two social bandits [*lēstai*] were crucified along with him, one on the
right and one on the left." More than the other passages, this one highlights the
necessity of employing models in translation and exegesis. The translations
"thieves" (KJV), "robbers" (RSV, NIV), "rebels" (SV), and "revolutionaries"
(NAB) each misleads the modern reader (for "bandits," see NEB, TEV, NRSV,
REB, and NJB). If these men were common thieves or robbers they would have
been forced to make restitution—twofold, fourfold, or fivefold, depending on
the items and their disposition (e.g., *m. B.Qam.* 7:1–5; Josephus, *Ant.* 20.215).
The translations "rebels" and "revolutionaries" mislead in another direction. As
Hobsbawm and Horsley make clear, banditry is a *prepolitical* phenomenon.
Only in rare cases do bandits get swept up into revolutionary situations. "Social
bandits" makes the most sense in this situation: they are crucified as enemies of
the state, but not because they have fomented revolution. The threat they pose
is to the political economy: attacking estates, cities, tax collectors, government
officials, travelers, and so on, and other forms of disruption.

Josephus makes it abundantly clear that the state (Hasmonean, Herodian,
Roman) handled social bandits either by killing them in battle, executing
them, or deporting them:

- Hezekiah was captured by Herod the Great and executed (*War* 1.204).
- Some of the "Galilean cave bandits" were killed in battle, while others
  were burned in their caves (*War* 1.304–13).
- Asinaios was poisoned by treachery (*Ant.* 18.352); Anilaios, his brother,
  and his men were ambushed and killed by the Parthians (*Ant.* 18.370).
- Tholomaeus was executed (*anaireitai*) by the Roman governor Fadus
  (*Ant.* 20.5).

- The Roman governor Felix captured Eleazar son of Dinai and his band, and he deported them to Rome in order to put them on display (*War* 2.253).
- The bandits Felix crucified were innumerable (*War* 2.253).

Conclusion

The analysis of social banditry is important for our study of both the sayings of Jesus and the events surrounding his death. The full implications of the work done by Hobsbawm and Horsley have not been integrated into New Testament research. I have attempted to demonstrate that social banditry needs to be taken more seriously in our translations and interpretation of the Gospels. Constructing a model of social banditry is a necessary task in interpreting the social milieu of first-century Palestine and the context of Jesus. I have also attempted to expand the range of the comparative material to include the whole circum-Mediterranean. Other regions, such as colonial Africa and South America, will also be fruitful areas in which to gain data for our models. Finally, it is hoped that my model provides a more dynamic sense of the elements of social banditry.

Works Cited

Austen, Ralph A. 1986. "Social Bandits and Other Heroic Criminals: Western Models of Resistance and Their Relevance." In *Banditry, Rebellion, and Social Protest in Africa*, edited by D. Crummey, 89–108. Portsmouth, N.H.: Heinemann.

Blok, Anton. 1972. "The Peasant and the Brigand: Social Banditry Reconsidered." *CSSH* 14:494–503.

Burian, J. 1984. "*Latrones:* Ein Begriff in römischen literarischen und juristischen Quellen." *Eirene* 21:17–23.

Crawley, Richard, trans. 1952. *The History of the Peloponnesian War.* Great Books of the Western World 6. Chicago: Encyclopedia Britannica.

Crummey, Donald, ed. 1986. *Banditry, Rebellion, and Social Protest in Africa.* Portsmouth, N.H.: Heinemann.

Eppstein, Victor. 1964. "The Historicity of the Gospel Account of the Cleansing of the Temple." *ZNW* 55:42–58.

Fiensy, David A. 1991. *The Social History of Palestine in the Herodian Period: The Land Is Mine.* SBEC 20. Lewiston, N.Y.: Edwin Mellen.

Foster, George M. 1967a. "Introduction: What Is a Peasant?" In *Peasant Society: A Reader*, edited by J. M. Potter et al., 2–14. Boston: Little, Brown.

———. 1967b. "Peasant Society and the Image of Limited Good." In *Peasant Society: A Reader*, edited by J. M. Potter et al., 300–323. Boston: Little, Brown.

Freyne, Seán. 1988. "Bandits in Galilee: A Contribution to the Study of Social Conditions in First-Century Palestine." In *The Social World of Formative Christianity and Judaism: Studies in Tribute to Howard Clark Kee*, edited by J. Neusner et al., 50–68. Philadelphia: Fortress Press.

Gallant, T. W. 1988. "Greek Bandits: Lone Wolves or a Family Affair?" *Journal of Modern Greek Studies* 6:269–90.

Garnsey, Peter. 1994. "Peasants in Ancient Roman Society." *JPS* 2:221–35.

Giardina, Andrea. 1983. "Banditi e santi: Un aspetto del folklore gallico tra tarda antichite medioevo." *Athenaeum* 61:374–89.

Goodman, Martin. 1982. "The First Jewish Revolt: Social Conflict and the Problem of Debt." *JJS* 33:417–27.

Hanson, K. C., and Douglas E. Oakman. 1998. *Palestine in the Time of Jesus: Social Structures and Social Conflicts*. Minneapolis: Fortress Press.

Herzog, William R., II. 1994. *Parables as Subversive Speech: Jesus as Pedagogue of the Oppressed*. Louisville: Westminster John Knox.

———. 1995. "Dissembling, a Weapon of the Weak: The Case of Christ and Caesar in Mark 12:13–17 and Romans 13:1–7." Paper delivered at the Context Group annual meeting, Portland, Oregon, March.

Hobsbawm, Eric J. 1959. "The Social Bandit." In *Primitive Rebels: Studies in Archaic Forms of Social Movement in the Nineteenth and Twentieth Centuries*, 13–29. New York: Norton.

———. 1972. "Social Banditry: Reply." *CSSH* 14:503–5.

———. 1973. "Social Banditry." In *Rural Protest: Peasant Movements and Social Change*, edited by H. A. Landsberger. New York: Macmillan.

———. 1981. *Bandits*. Rev. ed. New York: Pantheon.

———. 1985. "History from Below—Some Reflections." In *History from Below: Studies in Popular Protest and Popular Ideology in Honour of George Rudé*, edited by F. Krantz, 63–73. Montreal: Concordia University Press.

Horsley, Richard A. 1979. "Josephus and the Bandits." *JSJ* 10:37–63.

———. 1981. "Ancient Jewish Social Banditry and the Revolt against Rome." *CBQ* 43:409–32.

———. 1987. *Jesus and the Spiral of Violence: Popular Jewish Resistance in Roman Palestine*. San Francisco: Harper & Row. Reprinted Minneapolis: Fortress Press, 1993.

———. 1988. "Bandits, Messiahs, and Longshoremen: Popular Unrest in Galilee around the Time of Jesus." In *SBLSP 1988*, 183–99. Atlanta: Scholars.

———. 1995. *Galilee: History, Politics, People*. Valley Forge, Pa.: Trinity Press International.

Horsley, Richard A., and John S. Hanson. 1985. *Bandits, Prophets, and Messiahs: Popular Movements at the Time of Jesus*. Minneapolis: Winston. Reprinted Harrisburg, Pa.: Trinity Press International, 1988.

Hunt, A. S., and C. C. Edgar. 1934. *Select Papyri*. Vol. 2: *Non-Literary Papyri; Public Documents*. LCL 282. Cambridge: Harvard University Press.

Isaac, Benjamin. 1984. "Bandits in Judaea and Arabia." *Harvard Studies in Classical Philology* 88:171–203.

———. 1992. "Banditry." In *ABD* 1:575–80.

Kolendo, Jerzy. 1993. "The Peasant." In *The Romans*, edited by A. Giardina, translated by L. G. Cochrane, 199–213. Chicago: University of Chicago Press.

Koliopoulos, J. 1979. *Brigands with a Cause*. Oxford: Oxford University Press.

Landsberger, H. A. 1973. "Peasant Unrest: Themes and Variations." In *Rural Protest: Peasant Movements and Social Change*, edited by H. A. Landsberger, 1–64. London: Macmillan.

MacMullen, Ramsay. 1966. *Enemies of the Roman Order*. Cambridge: Harvard University Press.

Malina, Bruce J. 1986. "Interpreting the Bible with Anthropology: The Question of Poor and Rich." *Listening* 21:148–59.

———. 1987. "Wealth and Poverty in the New Testament and Its World." *Int* 41:354–67.

———. 1993. *The New Testament World: Insights from Cultural Anthropology*. Rev. ed. Louisville: Westminster John Knox.

———. 1994. "Establishment Violence in the New Testament World." *Scriptura* 51:51–78.

Moulton, James Hope and George Milligan. 1997. *The Vocabulary of the Greek Testament: Illustrated from the Papyri and Ohter Non-Literary Sources*. Peabody, Mass.: Hendrickson. (Reprint from 1930 edition.)

Myers, Ched. 1988. *Binding the Strong Man: A Political Reading of Mark's Story of Jesus*. Maryknoll, N.Y.:Orbis.

Oakman, Douglas E. 1986. *Jesus and the Economic Questions of His Day*. SBEC 8. Lewiston, N.Y.: Edwin Mellen.

———. 1991. "The Countryside in Luke-Acts." In *The Social World of Luke-Acts: Models for Interpretation*, edited by J. H. Neyrey, 151–79. Peabody, Mass.: Hendrickson.

———. 1992. "Was Jesus a Peasant? Implications for Reading the Samaritan Story (Luke 10:30–35)." *BTB* 22:117–25

O'Malley, Pat. 1979. "Social Bandits, Modern Capitalism, and the Traditional Peasantry: A Critique of Hobsbawm." *JPS* 6:489–501.

Rengstorf, K. H. 1967. "*Lēstēs.*" In *TDNT* 4:257–62.

Rosenbaum, H. Jon and Peter Sederberg, eds. 1976. *Vigilante Politics.* Philadelphia: University of Pennsylvania.

Rhoads, David. 1976. *Israel in Revolution, 6–74 C.E.: A Political History Based on the Writings of Josephus.* Philadelphia: Fortress Press.

Rohrbaugh, Richard L. 1978. *The Biblical Interpreter: An Agrarian Bible in an Industrial Age.* Philadelphia: Fortress Press.

Rosenbaum, H. Jon and Peter C. Sederberg. 1976. *Vigilante Politics.* Philadelphia: University of Pennsylvania Press.

Sant Cassia, Paul. 1993. "Banditry, Myth, and Terror in Cyprus and Other Mediterranean Societies." *CSSH* 35:773–95.

Scott, James C. 1977a. *The Moral Economy of the Peasant: Rebellion Subsistence in Southeast Asia.* New Haven: Yale University Press.

———. 1977b. "Protest and Profanation: Agrarian Revolt and the Little Tradition [2 parts]." *Theory and Society* 4:1–39; 211–46.

———. 1985. *Weapons of the Weak: Everyday Forms of Peasant Resistance.* New Haven: Yale University Press.

———. 1990. *Domination and the Arts of Resistance: Hidden Transcripts.* New Haven: Yale University Press.

Seland, Torrey. 1995. *Establishment Violence in Philo and Luke: A Study of Non-Conformity to Torah and Jewish Vigilante Reactions.* Bi 15. London and New York: Brill.

Shanin, Teodor. 1987. "Introduction: Peasantry as a Concept." In *Peasants and Peasant Societies: Selected Readings,* 1–11. 2d ed. Oxford: Blackwell.

Shaw, Brent D. 1984. "Bandits in the Roman Empire." *Past and Present* 102:3–52.

———. 1990. "Bandit Highlands and Lowland Peace: The Mountains of Isauria." *Journal of the Economic and Social History of the Orient* 33:199–233; 237–70.

———. 1993a. "The Bandit." In *The Romans,* edited by A. Giardina, 300–341. Translated by L. G. Cochrane. Chicago: University of Chicago Press.

———. 1993b. "Tyrants, Bandits, and Kings: Personal Power in Josephus." *JJS* 44:176–204.

Smith, Morton. 1971. "Zealots and Sicarii: Their Origins and Relations." *HTR* 64:1–19.

Stegemann, Ekkehard W., and Wolfgang Stegemann. 1999. *The Jesus Movement: A Social History of Its First Century.* Translated by O. C. Dean Jr. Minneapolis: Fortress Press.

Thorner, Daniel. 1968. "Peasantry." In *International Encyclopedia of the Social Sciences,* edited by D. L. Sills, 11:503–110. New York: Macmillan.

Wolf, Eric R. 1966. *Peasants.* Foundations of Modern Anthropology Series. Englewood Cliffs, N.J.: Prentice-Hall.

16

The Jesus Movement and Network Analysis

Dennis C. Duling

Gerd Theissen is well known for his view that the Jesus movement was a Palestinian "renewal movement" composed of socially uprooted, wandering charismatics who left their villages, homes, families, relatives, wealth, and safety to
pursue a radical lifestyle of voluntary poverty, and who were supported from
time to time by local sympathizers in the Galilean villages (1978:31–95). In
this study, I try to illumine Theissen's insight from the perspective of social network analysis. Such analysis has been used for analyzing certain Jesus groups
after his death (for research, see Duling 1999:156b); however, it has not been
used to analyze the historical Jesus and his disciples in Galilee.

My thesis is that network analysis will help conceptualize what Theissen
calls Jesus' geographical and social context and Jesus' social relationships
(Theissen and Merz 1998:162–239). I develop two important dimensions, the
spatial network and the personal network. I try to shift Jesus' primary spatial environment to the Lake of Galilee, a position I reinforce with settlement archaeology and a Dead Sea analogy. I then develop the view that Jesus' personal
network was what network analysts call an "Ego-centered network."

Social Network Analysis

Social network analysis came into its own with J. A. Barnes's seminal study in
1954 of the Norwegian island of Bremnes. Barnes used the traditional social-
anthropological concepts "geographical proximity" and "the workplace," but
he conceived them as "social fields." He then developed a third social field that
overlapped and cut across the other two.

The third social field has no units or boundaries; it has no coordinating organization. It is made up of the ties of friendship and acquaintance, which everyone growing up in Bremnes society partly inherits and largely builds up for himself. . . . Each person is, as it were, in touch with a number of people, some of whom are directly in touch with each other and some of whom are not. . . . I find it convenient to talk of a social field of this kind as a *network*. The image I have is of a set of points some of which are joined by lines. The points of the image are people, or sometimes groups, and the lines indicate which people interact with each other. (Barnes 1954:42–43)

Network analysts since Barnes credit him with developing what had been a useful metaphor into a method for analyzing social relationships. Berkovitz even claimed that Barnes created a "paradigm shift" in the social sciences (1982). At the least, Barnes pushed the analysis of social networks forward with specific concepts. Others have applied network analysis to Mediterranean, rural, and Third World contexts (Befu 1962; Pospisil 1964; Boissevain 1973; 1974).

I elaborate later on social network concepts. At this point I emphasize only Barnes's most basic image, dots connected by a line.

━━━●━━━━━━●━━━

This visualization had been developed in mathematical graph theory (Ore 1990), but Barnes now applied it to *social* networks: the dots, or "nodes," were *persons*.

It has become common in network analysis to begin with a sketch of the geographical and cultural context (e.g., Boissevain 1973) and then to turn to social relationships. In this study, then, I focus first on the *spatial* network. I then return to the *social* network.

The Spatial Network

GALILEE AS A REGION

In modern archaeology, "regionalism" or "settlement archaeology" can be defined as an archaeological/anthropological method that excavates a number of sites, alternating with field surveys, in a larger geographical region. Its aim is to shed light on surviving literary evidence about that region, and thus its history (e.g., Meyers 1976; 1985). Modern "regionalists" (my designation) agree with the ancients that Galilee is a geopolitical region that can be divided into three subregions: *Upper Galilee, Lower Galilee,* and the valley, which I call the *Valley-Lake Region* (e.g., Josephus, *Ant.* 5.63; *m. Šeb.* 9:2; Meyers 1979:694).

POPULATION CENTERS: SOME THEORY

Graph theorists argue that, at physical, natural points, one location emerges with the ability to control the flow of goods, services, and information in exchange networks. Peregrine, for example, has theorized about the prehistorical Cahokia people of the United States in relation to the confluence of the Mississippi, Missouri, and Illinois Rivers and their tributaries. His key mathematical concept is "point centrality," that is, that central point at which goods and services are most effectively exchanged (1991:67–69).

Central-place theorists also hold that regions have major centers that specialize in goods and services. These places are encircled by a hierarchy of smaller towns and villages, giving the central place a minimum market necessary to operate ("threshold"), within a radius ("range") within which people are willing to travel (Christaller 1966; Vogeler 1996).

Finally, some urbanologists maintain that villages and city form an "urban system" with goods and services flowing from the periphery to the center. This system has a corresponding social-structural stratification (urban elites and village nonelites) and a corresponding unequal distribution (Oakman 1986; Rohrbaugh 1991:130–33). These three distinct but overlapping perspectives are illustrated with figure 16.1:

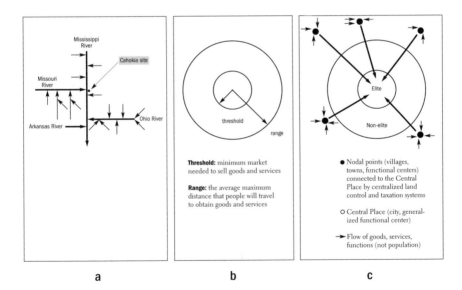

Figure 16.1a: Graph theory (Peregrine 1991: 69)
Figure 16.1b: Central-place theory (Vogeler 1996)
Figure 16.1c: Urban-systems theory (Rohrbaugh 1991:132)

Regionalists agree with the ancients that Upper Galilee contained networks of "village clusters"; they posit the same for the Valley-Lake Region (Meyers and Strange 1981:42–46). The villages in these clusters operated like nodal points, and often one town was central.

Here I concentrate only on Galilean population centers in the Valley-Lake Region (see, further, Duling 1999). These centers provided physical nodes for Jesus' social networks.

Gospel Population Centers in the Valley-Lake Region (Inside Galilee)

As some forty-five Gospel references to boats and fishing (Rousseau and Arav 1995:25) and multiple attestation of certain lake towns indicate, Jesus and his followers were active in the Valley-Lake Region. Here I note the towns and their significance.

Capernaum. Archaeologists identify Capernaum, mentioned more than any other Galilean town (sixteen times) except Nazareth, with Tell Hum on the northwest shore of the Sea of Galilee. Recent population estimates suggest that it was a village (Reed 1992). Excavations indicate the possibly of a first-century C.E. "(house-) synagogue" and "St. Peter's house" (Corbo 1992:867–68; 1993; for skepticism, see Horsley 1996:113 and Strickert 1998:22–28). Most important, Capernaum was a fishing town. Excavations suggest the remains of an ancient harbor complex (Nun 1988:24–26; 1999:24–28); a building with pools, probably a fish market (Tzaferis 1983:201; see the comment about Coracin fish in Josephus, *War* 3.519–20); and fish-hooks in "St. Peter's house" (Meyers and Strange 1981:60). Perhaps Levi's toll-booth (Mark 2:14) was related to the fishing trade (so Hanson 1997:103). Strategically located, this minor central place was "a natural selection for Jesus' headquarters" (Meyers and Strange 1981:26).

Chorazin. The town (Khirbet Karaze? Q 10:13–15) lies about four kilometers northwest of Capernaum on a plateau from which one can view the lake. It adds to the general impression of Jesus' activity in the Valley-Lake Region. Unfortunately, nothing of archaeological value from the first century C.E. has yet been discovered (Yeivin 1987).

Gennesaret. This was another village on the lake associated with the Jesus movement and fishing (Mark 6:53 = Matt 14:34; Luke 5:1), located on the hill above an anchorage. This anchorage had at least two breakwaters about four to five meters wide, extending into the lake about seventy meters (Nun 1988).

Magdala. Another lakeside fishing town (Strange 1992; Aviam 1997), Magdala is mentioned in the Gospels only in connection with Mary Magdalene (Sawicki 2000), unless Magadan in Matt 15:39 (Mark 8:10: Dalmanutha) is Magdala. It lies about five kilometers south of Capernaum. Evidence for Magdala's connections with boating and fishing is abundant. Josephus calls the town Taricheae, Greek for "salted fish" (*Ant.* 20.159); the Talmud calls it Migdal Nunya or Nunayah (Aramaic: "tower of fish"; *b. Pesah.* 46). The town had wood stores, ships, and shipyard workers (Josephus, *War* 3.462–542). Archaeological discoveries include open docks with a small building; a sheltered harbor basin; a pier; a mooring stone; lead weights for nets; a net needle; a first-century mosaic of a five-person boat ("the Migdal boat"; Nun 1999:26); boat parts similar to those of the "Galilean boat," which had wood from trees near Magdala (Wachsmann 1995). Thus Magdala was a boat-building and fish-processing center (Rousseau and Arav 1995:27). Josephus also indicates that Magdala had an abundance of artisans (*War* 3.462–70). Did Jesus the artisan ever work in the fishing "industry" there?

Gospel Population Centers in the Valley-Lake Region (Outside Galilee)

Bethsaida. Of lakeside towns where Jesus was active, Bethsaida ranks second only to Capernaum (Q 10:13–15; Mark 8:22–26; Luke 9:10; John 6:1–21 [but see 6:17]; 1:44; 12:21; see 1:43). In 30 c.e., Herod Philip transformed the village into a *polis* and renamed it "Julias" in honor of Augustus's wife (Josephus, *Ant.* 18.28; *War* 2.168); there he died and was buried (*Ant.* 18.108).

Bethsaida is, after much debate, now known to be et-Tell, about three kilometers north of the lake (Arav and Freund 1995; Arav 1999; Arav, Freund, and Schroder 2000). *Beth-tzaida* means "house of fishing" or "house of the fisherman" (Strickert 1998:47). Uncovered there is "the best selection of [fishing] equipment from any site around the Sea of Galilee" (Strickert 1998:49). Discovered in one of several houses were fishing hooks, lead and basalt net weights, lead and basalt line sinkers, a bronze sail needle (15 cm.), stone anchors, implements probably used for fish processing, a fisher's trademark seal, and a broken jar handle on which was etched a Roman-period iron anchor. This house was probably a fisherman's house (Strickert 1998:68–69). Rabbinic stories also associated Bethsaida with fish (*y. Šeqal.* 6.2, 50c; *Sifre Devarim* 4.39).

Gergesa (Gerasa/Gadara). According to Mark 5:1–20, the demons exorcised by Jesus entered swine that stampeded down a cliff into the lake. "Gergesa," usually identified with modern El Koursi on the eastern side of the lake, best fits the swine story. It is at the lakeside, and it has a steep cliff. Third-century church fathers located the "swine miracle" here (Tzaferis 1989:46–48). Gergesa appears to have had a harbor with a breakwater, a pier, and a fish market; one hundred lead sinkers were found near a public building with a mosaic floor, which was probably an administrative center for the anchorage and the fish market. Nun argues that the Gergesa anchorage existed in the first century (1988:6–9; 1999:20–23); other scholars are more skeptical (e.g., Rousseau and Arav 1995:98b).

ROADS AS PHYSICAL LINKS BETWEEN CENTRAL PLACES

I have briefly described the lakeside villages important to Jesus' physical and social network. I add more anchorages below. First, however, I address more issues of theory.

Ze'ev Safrai develops a network schematic for road networks in valleys between Palestinian villages. It consists of dots and links (1994:223, 279–84). Safrai argues that there were two major types of ancient Palestinian "trade networks." One type has a central place (model A) or, viewed from a slightly different perspective, two central places and an axis road between them (model F); the second type, which he calls a "net system," has no central place (models B–E; model C collapses his models B and E). In a slight modification (figure 16.2), I represent the secondary village roads with broken lines.

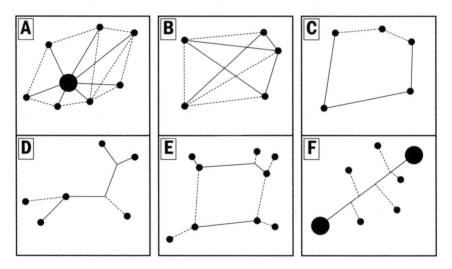

Figure 16.2: Safrai's road-network types (slightly modified)

Safrai concludes that, in Roman Palestine, the "net system" (B–E) was predominant. Yet some of his other statements suggest that his central-town model, or some mixture of the central town and net system, is appropriate (1994:268, 276, 278). This conclusion is more in line with graph theory, central-place theory, and urban-systems theory. Safrai also distinguishes between

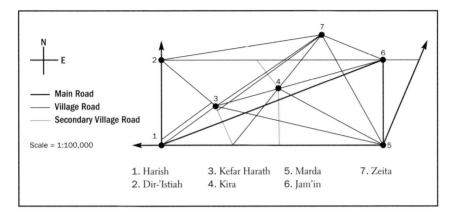

N
— E

—— Main Road
—— Village Road
········· Secondary Village Road

Scale = 1:100,000

| 1. Harish | 3. Kefar Harath | 5. Marda | 7. Zeita |
| 2. Dir-'Istiah | 4. Kira | 6. Jam'in | |

Figure 16.3: Safrai's schematic: Harish, Samaria (1994:279, fig. 59)

"road" and "secondary road," so that a schematic of Harish, Samaria, can be portrayed as in figure 16.3.

I now focus on the Roman roads as "links" in a network. It needs to be emphasized that knowledge about Roman roads has changed dramatically in recent years. First, a branch of the Via Maris from Caesarea Philippi south came down the *east* side of the Jordan Rift (Graf, Isaac, and Roll 1992:783a, 785a). It went to Bethsaida, Hippos, and Sennabris at the lake's tip, then either further south or back north to Tiberias on the western shore. A branch of the Via Maris also came down the *west* side of the Jordan Rift to Chorazin and Capernaum, Gennesaret, Magdala/Taricheae, and, again, Tiberias. A link was also built between Capernaum and Bethsaida, thus creating a road that encircled the lake.

The Romans also built three major east-west roads in the Galilean valleys from the Jordan Rift to the Mediterranean Sea. The first major road went westward from Bethsaida to Ptolemais-Akko. The second went westward from Tiberias to Sepphoris, and then either northwest to the sea or southwest through Legio-Capercotani to the sea (see Matt 4:15 [Isa 9:1–2]; Aharoni et al. 1993). The third ran westward from Bethshean-Scythopolis to Legio-Capercotani, and on to the sea. Caution is required. No milestones on these roads have been discovered prior to the reign of Claudius in 41–54 c.e. (Graf, Isaac, and Roll 1992:785b). Nonetheless, there were earlier Iron Age roads (Dorsey 1991). Thus, there was an extensive road network in Lower Galilee and the Valley-Lake Region. Kloppenborg Verbin offers the map in map 16.1, which does not show secondary roads.

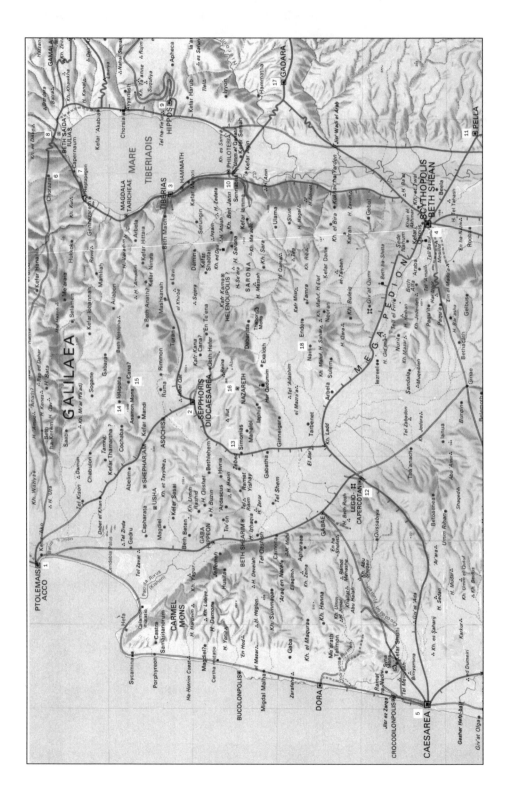

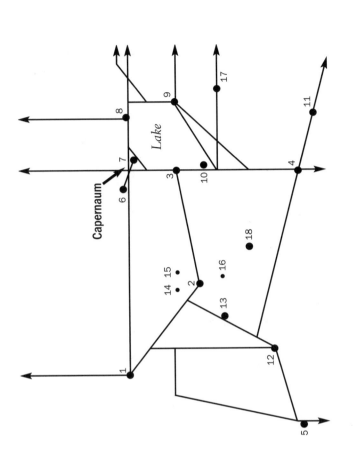

Key: Maps 16.1 and 16.2

1. Ptolemaus-Acco
2. Sepphoris
3. Tiberias
4. Scythopolis-Beth Shean
5. Caesarea Maritima
6. Chorazin
7. Capernaum
8. Bethsaida
9. Hippos
10. Sennabris
11. Pella
12. Legio-Capercotani
13. Simonias
14. Jotapata
15. Cana
16. Nazareth
17. Gadara
18. Nain

Map 16.2: Roman road networks

Map 16.1: Roman Galilee: Iron Age roads and Roman roads (opposite page)

If we graph the major road system according to the models of Safrai, it would look like map 16.2.

For my purposes, it is important to see that Capernaum (7) and Bethsaida (8) are strategically located at north-south and east-west crossroads and on the lake.

The "Lake Networks"

I now return to the Jesus movement's activity in the Valley-Lake Region. Map 16.3 shows the six lakeside towns and Chorazin.

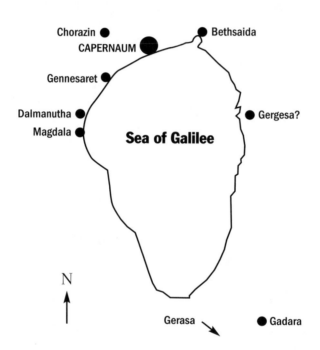

Map 16.3: Major Markan lake towns

If we graph the sailing lanes, or links, along with the major Roman roads only in these towns, it would look like map 16.4.

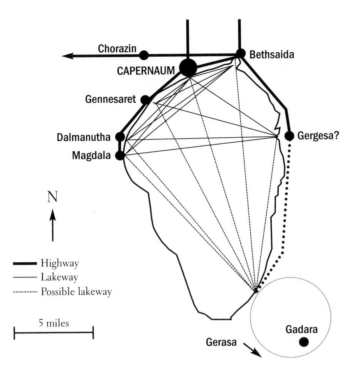

Map 16.4: Lake links and major Roman road links among Galilean lake towns in the Gospels

SMALL FISHING HARBORS AND ANCHORAGES

There were also numerous small fishing harbors and anchorages around the lake. Their purpose was especially to protect fishermen from bad weather (Nun 1988; 1999; Strickert 1998:34). Map 16.5 shows them.

It is not certain that every small port and anchorage can be dated to the first century (so Arav in a personal communication). Yet many existed. Trade and communication routes across and around the lake were, in all likelihood, quite dense in the first century.

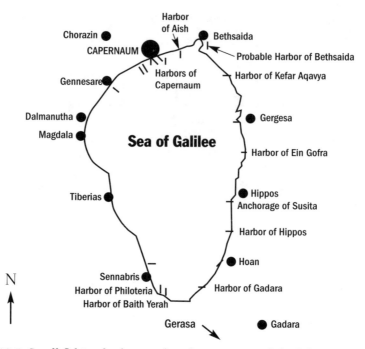

Map 16.5: Small fishing harbors and anchorages around the lake

An Analogy: Village Networks around the Dead Sea

The notion of central places and village networks, and of the physical links between them, in the Galilean Lake-Valley Region has support from the early-
second-century C.E. Babatha archive (Isaac 1992; Lewis 1994). Babatha was a
moderately wealthy, propertied widow from the Dead Sea port of Maoza (Aramaic *Machoza'* = "harbor") at the southern end of the Dead Sea. It belonged
to the district of Zoara, which was in the Roman province of Arabia. Her legal
problems centered on getting sufficient funds from her son's guardians. She ap-
pealed to the governor and the council. Although she paid her taxes in the regional financial center, Rabbat-Moab in the district of Zoara, she had to settle
legal problems at distant Petra.

Among Babatha's witnesses are apparent friends, neighbors, and acquaintances, as well as Roman officials. The surviving documents offer evidence of
bilingual or multilingual Judean scribes functioning in lower-level Roman administration. They not only reveal central administrative centers, but networks
of cities and villages (Maoza; En-gedi; Mazraa, near Livias), as well as families,
around and near the Dead Sea (Saldarini 1998:96). This picture is, of course,
contrary to the usual image of the region around the Dead Sea as a "wilderness."

The Social Network

I have already noted that Barnes developed the social network into a method of analysis. Now I briefly describe social network concepts and their application.

Foundational Concepts

"Activity fields." These are contexts in which persons who have some-thing in common relate; such contexts include one's family or neighborhood, common friends or gender, and similar age, education, and work (Jay 1964), as well as "categorical orders" such as race, ethnicity, and status (Mitchell 1973:20).

Limiting analysis. In theory, it is possible to analyze every person (an "infinite network") and every social link between them (a "total network"), and thus to construct an unlimited, all-inclusive, universal network (an "un-bounded network") (Mitchell 1969; 1973; Whitten and Wolfe 1973). In prac-tice, network analysts limit the number of persons (a "finite network") and their links (a "partial network"), and thus construct a limited network (a "bounded network," although even bounded networks are usually somewhat porous [Scrinivas and Béteille 1964:165–66]).

Criteria of Analysis

There are two types of criteria for analysis, "structural" and "interactional." Some analysts, especially those who oppose structural functionalism, argue that the analyst should begin with interactional criteria; for clarity, I begin with structural criteria.

Structural criteria. Structural criteria of analysis refer to the *form* a net-work takes. This form is configured by "the extent to which people who all know one person also happen to know one another" (Mitchell 1974:288). There are four structural criteria.

1. *Size.* Size is the most important structural criterion, although it is not calculated mathematically. *Generalization:* Larger networks provide possibilities for more interactions, but they also have potential for more interpersonal conflict.
2. *Density ("connectivity").* Density refers to "the ratio of actual existing links to the total number of possible links" (Mitchell 1974:288). Density is either "high" ("close-knit") or "low" ("loose-knit"). Using NA as the

total number of links in the network and N as the total number of persons, here is a mathematical formula for density: $\frac{100\ NA}{\frac{1}{2}[N(N-1)]}$

Figure 16.4 is a six-node network with "symmetrical" links (equal exchange between persons of equal status):

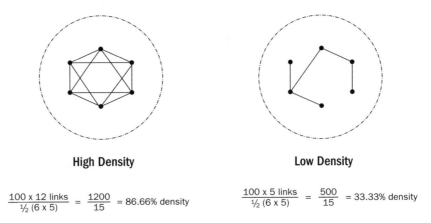

High Density   **Low Density**

$\frac{100 \times 12\ \text{links}}{\frac{1}{2}\ (6 \times 5)} = \frac{1200}{15} = 86.66\%$ density

$\frac{100 \times 5\ \text{links}}{\frac{1}{2}\ (6 \times 5)} = \frac{500}{15} = 33.33\%$ density

Figure 16.4: High and low densities of symmetrical links in a six-node network

High density allows for greater communication and usually involves relationships between persons based on more than one activity field. High density also fosters increased social conformity, thus the development of norms and attitudes. Yet it tends to aid the ability to recruit persons and mobilize support (Stark 1996), a point also made in "social movement theory" (Morris and Mueller 1992).

3. *Centrality and prestige.* Centrality is measured by the number of ties one member has with other members in the network. Focal persons have more prestige and tend to form "third-party links." In "Ego-centered networks" (see below), focal persons are more intimate with the person around whom the network is formed.

4. *Clustering.* Clustering is the degree to which certain members are more closely linked to each other than to other members of the network. Clusters tend to form cliques.

Interactional criteria. These add a more dynamic, personal dimension to the analysis, a dimension that includes possibilities for understanding both network development and conflict between its members.

1. *Uniplexity/multiplexity.* In "uniplex" relationships, network members relate on the basis of only *one* activity field, for example, family. They are "single-stranded" relationships (represented graphically by one line). In "multiplex" relationships, network members relate on the basis of more than one activity field; they are "many-stranded" relationships (represented graphically by two or more lines). *Generalizations:* Multiplex relations exhibit (a) greater accessibility to persons in the network, but also to greater influence or social pressure; and (b) stronger trust, friendship, and intimacy (Boissevain 1974:32). Such relations usually create "strong ties" between network members.

2. *Content of the links (exchange).* Content refers to *what* is exchanged in the network. Network analysts who analyze "social support" note various types of exchange: (a) material support, (b) emotional support, (c) information, and (d) companionship (Walker, Wasserman, and Wellman 1994:56–57). Social movement theorists add political support to this list (Morris and Mueller 1992). Content also implies reciprocity and gift-giving (Malina 1986:101–11 Stansell 1999): balanced reciprocity (equal in kind); negative reciprocity (receiving more than one gives); generalized reciprocity ("the recipient giving the original helper other kinds of aid"); and "network balancing" (repaying a gift by offering social support to *others* in the network) (Wellman, Carrington, and Hall 1988:167).

Directional flow ("paths"). Directional flow refers to the direction in which the exchange takes place, that is, who gives and who receives. *Generalization:* Equal exchange usually implies equal social status and power ($X \leftrightarrow Y$); unequal exchange usually implies unequal social status and power (either $x \leftarrow Y$ or $X \rightarrow y$). Directional flow can also imply reciprocity.

Frequency and duration of interaction. Frequency of interaction refers to the number of contacts between networked persons; duration refers to their length. *Generalization:* Frequency usually implies what is sometimes called "reachability" or "adjacency" (see below). It can affect the quality of the links, that is, the type of exchange. Duration of interaction is usually an index of intimacy or "strong ties"; yet, there can also be "strength in weak ties" (Granovetter 1982).

The Faction Coalition

According to Boissevain, coalitions, in contrast to "corporations" (institutions), are informal (1968). They emerge especially when there is social unrest, sometimes reflecting it, sometimes contributing to it, sometimes both. They are unstable alliances. Their members come together for a limited time and utilize each other's resources to achieve some particular purpose. Thus, individual identities and commitments are not totally lost (Boissevain 1974:170).

Boissevain analyzes several coalition subtypes. One is the "faction": "[A] faction is a coalition of persons (followers) recruited personally, according to structurally diverse principles by or on behalf of a person in conflict with a person or other persons, with whom they were formerly united over honor and/or control of resources" (1974:192; see Malina 1988a; 1988b).

This definition stresses the following aspects: (1) factions are ideological, political, and in conflict with both the established authorities and rival factions, with whom they compete for access to scarce resources; (2) the desirability of a strong leader who has more resources (e.g., the "propensity to coordinate," that is, the ability to use followers to achieve desired ends); (3) the existence of members who come from different activity fields; (4) the leader's ability to recruit followers personally.

The Faction as an Ego-Centered Network

One way to "limit the analysis" is to focus on the faction, which is also an "Ego-centered network." An Ego-centered network is a personal network with a focal person or "Ego" at its center and lines that radiate outward to connect Ego with other persons, called "alters." Relationships with Ego (faction leader) are said to be "asymmetrical" (directional flow is primarily one way, from Ego to alters), and can be illustrated by a "star sub-graph" (Ore 1990), figure 16.5.

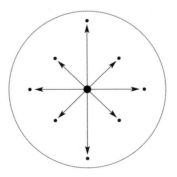

Figure 16.5: A star subgraph

Ego-centered networks are normally composed of persons from different activity fields; thus, they are termed "*structurally* diverse." Relationships between "Ego" and alters vary in intensity according to "interactional criteria"; thus, they are termed "*qualitatively* diverse." These concepts can be illustrated graphically by placing the star subgraph inside "zones of intensity" (see figure 16.6).

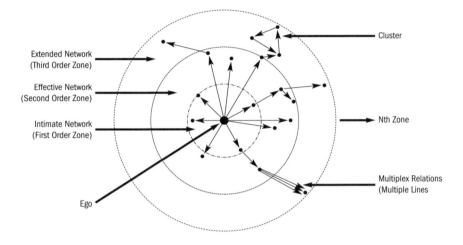

Figure 16.6: An Ego-centered network

In Ego's *intimate* network, alters are said to be "adjacent to" Ego; that is, they interact closely with Ego. In Ego's *effective* network, alters are important but not as close to Ego. They are acquaintances—"friends of friends"—with whom Ego interacts less intimately or frequently. In Ego's *extended* network, alters are not adjacent to Ego. They are unknown, distant, but potentially knowable "friends of friends of friends." Adjacency to Ego can also be expressed as "path-distances" or "reachability," that is, the distance from Ego to alter, which can be represented graphically by line length (Berkowitz 1994:487).

The above Ego-centered network example stresses size (small), density (relatively low), centrality and prestige of one person (Ego), direction of flow (from Ego to alters), reachability (short and long path-distances represented by short and long arrows), clustering (upper-right grouping of nodes), and multiplexity (lower-right group of multiple lines). It does not show interactive criteria such as content (what is exchanged), frequency or duration of interaction, or network development over time.

The faction as an Ego-centered network has been used to analyze coalitions in *modern* Mediterranean society (e.g., Boissevain 1974:170–205). Such a society, it can be argued, has a closer "fit" with ancient, collectivist Mediterranean society than with modern, individualistic Euro-American society (Malina and Neyrey 1991:69–72).

The Jesus Movement:
An Ancient Mediterranean Ego-Centered Social Network

Theissen and Merz's recent analysis of the Jesus movement's structure sees it as a series of concentric circles:

> The pervasive power of [Jesus'] charisma is indicated by his ability to attract community sympathizers and move larger crowds beyond his close circle of followers. As a result there develops around the *primary charismatic* [Jesus] three concentric circles: first, a small staff of *secondary charismatics* consisting of the followers of Jesus (especially the circle of the Twelve); second, a wider circle of community sympathizers without whose support no charismatic movement can exist, that is, the circle of people who, unlike Jesus' closest disciples, did not abandon house and home. While they continued their observable way of life as before, such *tertiary charismatics* can be distinguished from *the people as a whole,* namely, those people who listened to Jesus—perhaps were attracted to him—but did not become his sympathizers and active supporters. (1998:217; translation adapted and italics mine)

Graphically, Theissen's model can be depicted as in figure 16.7.

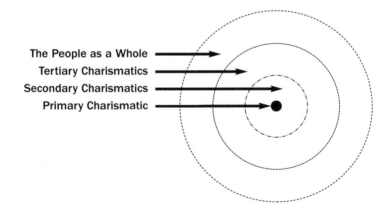

Figure 16.7: Theissen and Merz's Jesus-movement model

Theissen's concentric-circle model of the Jesus movement is very similar to the analytical model of a finite, partial, bounded Ego-centered network in Mediterranean society. The primary charismatic corresponds to Ego. The secondary charismatics, tertiary charismatics, and "the people as a whole" roughly correspond to Ego's intimate network, effective network, and extended network. This correlation can be developed in detail.

Jesus emerged in a time of social unrest in Roman-Herodian Palestine. Earlier, he had been part of the Baptizer's circle. Then he struck out on his own. He migrated to the Valley-Lake Region and, there, near a strategically located, minor central place, Capernaum, personally and publicly recruited his faction (see Duling 2000b), mainly from people around the lake. The language of recruitment is "call" and "follow." The texts are often Markan, but such "following" persons also appear in Q, and the Markan pattern is similar in Matthew and Luke. It should be noted, however, that there is a different recruitment pattern in the Gospel of John (compare John 1:39–46 to Mark 1:21; Duling 2000b).

From the perspective of network analysis, Jesus is Ego, in the center of his own network. He "desires to win" recruits; develops great resources and the "propensity to coordinate"; comes into conflict with the authorities and rival factions; and competes with other factions (Boissevain 1974:192–200).

According to Theissen, Jesus recruited secondary charismatics, both men and women. They were "fishermen and farmers," that is, people from the peasant strata of Lower Galilee and especially from the Valley-Lake Region. He chose from them twelve disciples (Meier 1997a). Their role as judges at the end of time is implied by Jesus' saying that the Twelve would sit on (twelve) thrones and judge the twelve tribes of Israel (Matt 19:28; Luke 22:30). I would add that three disciples—Peter, James, and John—seemed to form a core within the faction (e.g., Mark 1:29; 5:37, 40; 9:2; 13:3; 14:33) and that Peter probably had the highest status among them. Theissen denies that the movement was a hierarchy; rather, the Twelve were a "representative popular rule" that symbolized a renewed Israel (Theissen and Merz 1998:216). In my view, however, this fictive family was not totally "egalitarian" (Duling 1997:126). Although the presence of women contributed to the group's deviance—the traditional household was no longer the norm—it appears nonetheless that the movement retained a degree of male dominance (also Stegemann and Stegemann 1999:386). The males were competitive (Mark 10:35–45; see Boissevain 1974:196), and Peter may have already surfaced as a focal person within the network (Peter mentioned in Mark, 24 times; in Matthew, 23 times; in Luke, 17 times; in John, 25 times).

From the perspective of an Ego-centered network, the secondary charismatics are alters. They represent at least two "activity fields," family and work;

in the Gospel of John there are also friends. The network is small. The number twelve as a "collective symbol" introduces one kind of "ideological or moral content" that is exchanged (Boissevain 1974:196–97). These alters have the most frequent and lasting interaction with Ego, thus the greatest "adjacency" and "reachability." They have centrality and prestige. At least three alters form a "cluster"; they also form third-party links, and certain tasks are delegated to them. Higher and lower statuses create competition, as is normally the case (Boissevain 1974:198). One major problem in a network is that, as the network expands, Ego spends increasing time and resources holding it together in the face of competition from alters. Such an intimate network would look like figure 16.8.

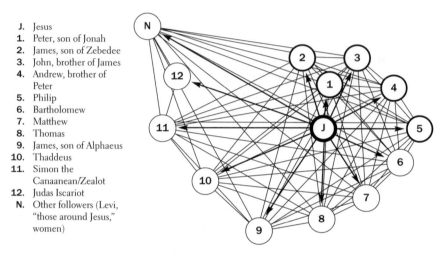

J. Jesus
1. Peter, son of Jonah
2. James, son of Zebedee
3. John, brother of James
4. Andrew, brother of Peter
5. Philip
6. Bartholomew
7. Matthew
8. Thomas
9. James, son of Alphaeus
10. Thaddeus
11. Simon the Canaanean/Zealot
12. Judas Iscariot
N. Other followers (Levi, "those around Jesus," women)

Figure 16.8: Jesus' intimate network (first-order zone)

Theissen's tertiary charismatics, that is, the community sympathizers in the villages, remained at home and adhered to traditional household norms and values. Nonetheless, they provided various kinds of support for the itinerant radicals. They received the message of salvation, liberation, and the act of healing; they returned food and shelter and "moral support."

In network analysis, the tertiary charismatics generally correspond to Ego's effective network in the second-order zone. They are "friends of friends"—usually known to Ego, but less adjacent. They are outside the intimate network. The content of the exchange is spiritual-political and material, consisting of hope and hospitality. Insofar as they are unknown to Ego initially, they can be imagined as overlapping Ego's more distant extended network. However, they are best seen as part of the effective network.

According to Theissen, there was a third group, "the people as a whole." They were, at least in the early part of the Gospels, "the crowds" (Mark 2:4) or sometimes "a large multitude" (Mark 3:8). These are also seen in the Markan language of "call" and "follow" (e.g., Mark 5:24; 8:34; 3:7; see Mark 10:32; 11:9). There were also individuals from the crowds who "followed" (Mark 10:52; 14:51). They might have become part of Jesus' closer circle. However, most remained anonymous (see 9:40).

In network analysis, such largely anonymous persons would normally form Ego's extended network, or third-order zone. They are "friends of friends of friends," unknown to Ego, but can be helpful at a distance.

Illustration: Natural Kinship in Ego's Most Intimate Network

In social-scientific terms, the Jesus movement was a "fictive kin" movement: ties with family and friends were being broken. Nonetheless, certain kinship ties remained, as later developments of the network indicate, and, indeed, these ties became critical for recruitment. I cannot analyze all ties in this essay; therefore, I limit myself to Jesus and to what was probably the most important cluster in his intimate network. I attempt to develop a rather extensive kinship network in relation to Jesus' family, although I fully recognize that not all pieces of the kinship puzzle are known.

The Joseph family (and the Zechariah family). The Lukan tradition makes a kinship link between John and Jesus through the Zechariah and Joseph families, which, together, suggest family networks.

The Gospels do not portray Jesus' kin, during his public life, as his declared followers (Mark 3:31; John 7:5), although, in the Fourth Gospel, his mother is said to have been present at the crucifixion (John 19:25; Bauckham 1990:13, 15; see now Bauckham 2000). This portrait conforms to Jesus' fictive kin movement. Two points need to be added: both the tradition of James as a central person in the Jerusalem network and the sociological theory that new religious movements, once established, grow more rapidly through family and friend networks (Duling 2000b), suggest the necessity of relating the Joseph family to other parts of the Jesus network, at least over time. In brief outline, the relationships would look like figure 16.9.

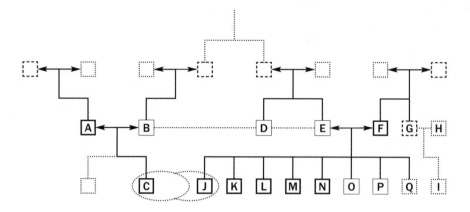

Figure 16.9: Kinship links in the Joseph family (and Zechariah family)

A. Zechariah, husband of Elizabeth (B) and father of John (C) (Luke 1:5–67; 3:2).
B. Elizabeth (B), wife of Zechariah (A), mother of John (C), perhaps kin of Mary (D) (Luke 1:5–79).
C. John, son of Zechariah (A) and Elizabeth (B), perhaps kin of Jesus (J) and his brothers and sisters (K–Q).
D. Sister of Mary (John 19:25 ["his mother's sister"]).
E. Mary, wife of Joseph, mother of at least six children, perhaps kinswoman of Elizabeth (Matthew 1–2; Luke 1–2; Mark 3:31 = Matt 12:46 = Luke 8:19; 6:3 = Matt 13:55; John 2:1–5, 12; 6:42; 19:25–27; Acts 1:14; cf. *Gospel of the Nazarenes* 2).
F. Joseph, husband of Mary, father of at least six children (Matthew 1–2; 13:35; Luke 1–2; 3:23; 4:22; John 6:42).
G. Clopas, Joseph's brother? (John 19:25; Luke 24:18; Hegesippus in Eusebius, *Hist. eccl.* 3.11; 3.32.6; 4.22.4 [Bauckham 1990:17]).
H. Mary of Clopas, probably Clopas's wife (John 19:25).
I. Symeon/Simon, son of Clopas, cousin of Jesus (Hegesippus, in Eusebius, *Hist. eccl.* 3.11; 3.32.6; 4.22.4; Symeon/Simon is mentioned second, behind James, in the Jerusalem bishop lists of Eusebius, *Hist. eccl.* 4.5.3–4; 5.12.1–2, and Epiphanius, *Pan.* 66.21–22 [Bauckham 1990:16]).

J. Jesus.

K. James, brother of Jesus, "pillar of the Jerusalem church" (Mark 6 = Matt
13:55; Mark 15:40 = Matt 27:56; Gal 1:9 [cf. 1 Cor 5:9], 12; Acts 12:17;
15:13; 21:18; 1 Cor 15:7; see James 1:1; Jude 1; "his mother and his
brothers" stereotype: Mark 3:31 = Matt 12:46 = Luke 8:19; John 2:12;
Acts 1:14; *Gos. Naz.* 2; *Ep. Apos.* 5; see *Gos. Thom.* 99). (See Bauckham
1990:7; Meier 1992; 1997b.) James is mentioned first in the Jerusalem
bishop lists of Eusebius (*Hist. eccl.* 4.5.3–4; 5.12.1–2) and Epiphanius
(*Pan.* 66.21–22).

L. Judas/Jude (Mark 6:3 = Matt 13:35; Jude 1).

M. Joses/Joseph (Mark 6:3 [Joses] = Matt 13:55 [Joseph]; for spellings see
Mark 15:40 [Joses] = Matt 27:56 [Joseph]; Mark 15:47).

N. Simon (Mark 6:3 = Matt 13:35).

O. Sister 1 (Mary? Mark 6:3: "his sisters" = Matt 13:56 ["all his sisters"]; cf.
Mark 3:35). The names are in Epiphanius (*Pan.* 78.8.1; 78.9.6). Bauckham says, "[T]here is some degree of probability that these names are authentic" (1990:8).

P. Sister 2 (Salome?).

Q. Sister(s) 3 (+?).

In the New Testament there is nothing of Joseph's brothers and sisters, of
Mary's brothers, of the wives and children of Jesus' four brothers, or of the hus-
bands and children of at least two sisters. If such existed, there would have been
many nephews and nieces.

One could develop similar kinship charts for the Joseph/John family (Peter,
Andrew) and the Zebedee family (James, John) (see Duling 2000a). These
three families are linked by kinship, gender, village, activity fields, and association with Jesus, and they include multiplex relationships, unequal exchange,
and directional flow outward. One can image that they offered social support
to others in the network (network balancing). Three of the four were adjacent
to Jesus and, therefore, must have developed strong ties.

I have merely scratched the surface in this attempt to illustrate the potential
of network analysis for the Jesus movement. I do, however, try to construct the
network ties among Jesus, his core, Jesus' brother James, and Paul. which
might look like figure 16.10.

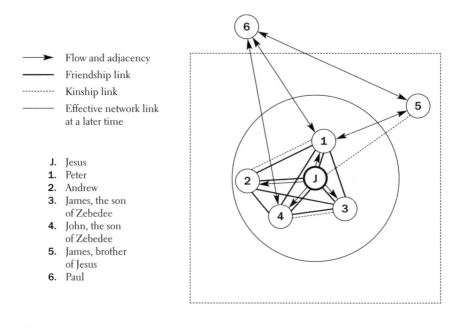

Flow and adjacency
Friendship link
Kinship link
Effective network link
at a later time

J. Jesus
1. Peter
2. Andrew
3. James, the son
   of Zebedee
4. John, the son
   of Zebedee
5. James, brother
   of Jesus
6. Paul

Figure 16.10: Jesus' network ties

Conclusion

Network analysis will not resolve current debates about the possible effect of urbanization and Greco-Roman cultural influence, including Cynicism, on a rural Galilean peasant artisan. Nonetheless, it might shed some light on these discussions.

Knowledge of roads and the lake, with its many towns and harbors, is suggestive for the physical environment in which Jesus' social network formed. One must imagine a great deal of travel and a lake full of fishing boats, especially with Galilee's relatively large population. Current population estimates are of two hundred thousand people, with an average of five hundred per village (Meyers 1997:59). Hanson's study of the fishing economy should be kept in view. It is important to give the Valley-Lake Region its due, along with Lower Galilee. Capernaum, as a minor central place, was strategically located for traveling both by roads and the lake. This observation may well have political implications—escape—with respect to the territories of Antipas and Philip. Thus, Capernaum is something of a *physical* "Ego," not more than a day's walk from Galilean villages to the west and south or a boat ride from the north, east, and south. Near Capernaum were Chorazin and Bethsaida. If Jesus condemned these three towns together, the condemnation is strong evidence that they were linked and that Jesus was active there. All this suggests that if the radical itinerants shook off the dust—or fish scales!—from their feet and moved on, they could return to either Peter's (or Jesus') house in Capernaum, from whence they could again depart in many directions.

If Jesus was a traveling artisan, he was no doubt exposed to at least some urban Hellenistic cultural influence in Galilee. Fiensy contends that as a traveling artisan Jesus would have had more status (1994). Edwards emphasizes Hellenistic influence (1992). Batey goes further. He suggests that a city like Sepphoris would have shaped Jesus' language and thought, indeed, his message of the kingdom; thus, Jesus was not hostile to cities (1991; 1992). Freyne admits to a certain degree of "urban overlay" (Strange's term) in Galilee, but he argues from his own experience of Irish peasants, from Redfield's great tradition and little tradition, from Carney's economic model, and, in general, from sources such as Josephus that peasants would not have held the values of urban elites. Rather, they would have opposed them (Freyne 1988; 1995; 1997). Horsley uses literary sources, coupled with a model of political economy, to suggest hostility between cities and villages (1994:122). This hostility was marked especially by Lower Galilean peasants' plunder of Sepphoris and the attack on Tiberias by Valley-Lake residents in 66–70 C.E. (Josephus, *Life* 30, 39, 373–80; 66, 99, 177, 381–92). Oakman, joined by Hanson, has made a similar point with respect to the temple economy and the plight of peasants straining under the burden of rents and debts: Jesus' core values were those of the peasant strata (Hanson and Oakman 1998:131–59). Even the regionalist Meyers recently admitted that Jesus avoided Sepphoris, at least relatively, because Jesus would not have received a sympathetic hearing among the elite Herodian and priestly classes (Meyers 1997:64). These latter views are much more likely.

How do these issues relate to the Jesus movement as an Ego-centered network? It is possible to hold together the more complicated picture of the physical connections, current among regionalists, and the model of a faction-, coalition-, or Ego-centered network. The latter functions in a conflict environment in which Jesus avoids the main urban centers. His most important central places were in the Valley-Lake Region. That was his primary physical network. One then needs to work out the many persons and relationships in the intimate, effective, and extended social networks, and to graph the nodes and lines. The above illustrations are only a beginning.

Works Cited ━━━

Aharoni, Yohanan, et al. 1993. *The Macmillan Bible Atlas*. 3d ed. New York: Macmillan.

Arav, Rami. 1997. "Bethsaida." In *OEANE* 1:302–5.

———. 1999. "New Testament Archeology and the Case of Bethsaida." In *Das Ende der Tage und die Gegenwart des Heils: Begegnungen mit dem Neuen Testament und seiner Umwelt. Festschrift für Heinz-Wolfgang Kuhn zum 65. Geburtstag*, edited by M. Becker and W. Fenske, 75–99. AGAJU 44. Leiden: Brill.

Arav, Rami, and Richard Freund, eds. 1995. *Bethsaida: A City by the North Shore of the Sea of Galilee: Bethsaida Excavations Project Reports and Contextual Studies*. Vol. 1. Kirksville, Mo.: Thomas Jefferson University Press.

Arav, Rami, Richard A. Freund, and John F. Schroder. 2000. "Bethsaida Rediscovered." *BAR* 26, no. 1:44–56.

Aviam, Mordechai. 1997. "Magdala." In *OEANE* 3:399–400.

Barnes, John A. 1954. "Class and Committees in a Norwegian Island Parish." *Human Relations* 7:39–58.

———. 1969. "Networks and Political Process." In *Social Networks in Urban Situations: Analyses of Personal Relationships in Central African Towns*, edited by J. C. Mitchell, 51–76. Manchester, England: Manchester University Press.

———. 1972. "Social Networks." In *An Addison-Wesley Module in Anthropology*, 1–29. Reading, Mass.: Addison-Wesley.

Batey, Richard. 1991. *Jesus and the Forgotten City: New Light on Sepphoris and the Urban World of Jesus*. Grand Rapids: Eerdmans.

———. 1992. "Sepphoris: An Urban Portrait of Jesus." *BAR* 18:50–62.

Bauckham, Richard. 1990. *Jude and the Relatives of Jesus in the Early Church*. Edinburgh: T. & T. Clark.

———. 2000. "All in the Family: Identifying Jesus' Relatives." *BR* 16, no. 2: 20–31.

Befu, Harumi. 1962. *Hamlet in a Nation: The Place of Three Japanese Rural Communities in Their Broader Social Context*. Ann Arbor, Mich.: University Microfilms.

Berkowitz, S. D. 1982. *An Introduction to Structural Analysis: The Network Approach to Social Research*. Toronto: Butterworths.

———. 1994. "Afterward: Toward a Formal Structural Sociology." In Wellman and Berkowitz 1994:477–97.

Boissevain, Jeremy. 1968. "The Place of Non-groups in the Social Sciences." *Man* 3:542–56.

———. 1973. "An Exploration of Two First-Order Zones." In Boissevain and Mitchell 1973:125–48.

———. 1974. *Friends of Friends: Networks, Manipulators, and Coalitions.* Pavilion Series. Oxford: Blackwell.

———. 1979. "Network Analysis: A Reappraisal." *Current Anthropology* 20:392–94.

———. 1985. "Networks." In *The Social Science Encyclopedia*, edited by A. Kuper and J. Kuper, 557–58. Boston and London: Routledge.

Boissevain, Jeremy, and J. Clyde Mitchell, eds. 1973. *Network Analysis: Studies in Human Interaction.* The Hague: Mouton.

Bösen, Willibald. 1985. *Galiläa als Lebensraum und Wirkungsfeld Jesu.* Freiburg: Herder.

Carney, T. F. 1975. *The Shape of the Past: Models and Antiquity.* Lawrence, Kans.: Coronado.

Christaller, Walter. 1966. *Central Places in Southern Germany.* Translated by C. W. Baskin. Englewood Cliffs, N.J.: Prentice-Hall.

Corbo, Virgilio C. 1992. "Capernaum." In *IDB* 1:866–69.

———. 1993. "The Church of the House of St. Peter at Capernaum." In *Ancient Churches Revealed*, edited by Y. Tsafrir, 71–76. Washington, D.C.: Biblical Archaeology Society.

Dorsey, David. 1991. *The Roads and Highways of Ancient Israel.* Baltimore: Johns Hopkins University Press.

Duling, Dennis C. 1995. "Social-Scientific Small Group Research and Second Testament Study." *BTB* 24:179–93.

———. 1997. "Egalitarian Ideology, Leadership, and Factional Conflict within the Matthean Group." *BTB* 27:124–37.

———. 1999. "The Jesus Movement and Social Network Analysis (Part I: The Spatial Network)." *BTB* 29:156–75.

———. 2000a. "The Jesus Movement and Social Network Analysis (Part II: The Social Network)." *BTB* 30:1–12.

———. 2000b. "Recruitment to the Jesus Movement in Social Scientific Perspective." In *Social Scientific Models for Interpreting the Bible: Essays by the Context Group in Honor of Bruce J. Malina*, edited by J. J. Pilch, 132–75. BibIntSer 53. Leiden: Brill.

Edwards, Douglas R. 1992. "The Socio-Economic and Cultural Ethos of the Lower Galilee in the First Century: Implications for the Nascent Jesus Movement." In *The Galilee in Late Antiquity*, edited by L. I. Levine, 53–73. New York: Jewish Theological Seminary of America.

Edwards, Douglas R., and C. Thomas McCollough. 1997. *Archaeology and the Galilee: Texts and Context in the Graeco-Roman and Byzantine Periods.* South Florida Studies in the History of Judaism 143. Atlanta: Scholars.

Elliott, John H. 1995. "The Jewish Messianic Movement: From Faction to Sect." In Esler 1995:75–95.

Esler, Philip F., ed. 1995. *Modelling Early Christianity: Social-Scientific Studies of the New Testament in Its Context.* London: Routledge.

Fiensy, David A. 1994. "Craftsmen as Brokers." *Proceedings: Eastern Great Lakes and Midwest Biblical Societies* 14:57–68.

Freyne, Sean. 1980. *Galilee from Alexander the Great to Hadrian (323 B.C.E. to 135 C.E.): A Study of Second Temple Judaism.* Wilmington, Del.: Glazier; Notre Dame, Ind.: University of Notre Dame Press.

———. 1988. *Galilee, Jesus, and the Gospels.* Philadelphia: Fortress Press.

———. 1992. "Urban-Rural Relations in First-Century Galilee: Some Suggestions from Its Literary Sources." In *The Galilee in Late Antiquity*, edited by L. I. Levine, 75–94. New York: Jewish Theological Seminary of America.

———. 1995. "Herodian Economics in Galilee: Searching for a Suitable Model." In Esler 1995:23–46.

———. 1997. "Town and Country Once More: The Case of Roman Galilee." In Edwards and McCollough 1997:49–56.

Graf, David F., Benjamin Isaac, and Israel Roll. 1992. "Roads and Highways (Roman)." In *ABD* 5:782–87.

Granovetter, Mark S. 1982. "The Strength of Weak Ties: A Network Theory Revisited." In *Social Structure and Network Analysis*, edited by P. V. Marsden and N. Lin, 105–30. Beverly Hills, Calif.: Sage. Reprinted in *Sociological Theory 1983*, edited by R. Collins, 201–19. San Francisco: Jossey-Bass.

Hanson, K. C. 1997. "The Galilean Fishing Economy and the Jesus Tradition." *BTB* 27:99–111.

Hanson, K. C., and Douglas E. Oakman. 1998. *Palestine in the Time of Jesus: Social Structures and Social Conflicts.* Minneapolis: Fortress Press.

Horsley, Richard A. 1996. *Archeology, History, and Society in Galilee: The Social Context of Jesus and the Rabbis.* Valley Forge, Pa.: Trinity Press International.

Isaac, Benjamin. 1994. "The Historical Jesus and Archeology of the Galilee: Questions from Historical Jesus Research to Archaeologists." In SBLSP 1994, 91–135. Atlanta: Scholar Press.

———. 1992. "The Babatha Archive: A Review Article." *IEJ* 42:62–75.

Jay, Edward J. 1964. "The Concepts of 'Field' and 'Network' in Anthropological Research." *Man in India* 44, no. 177:137–39.

Lewis, Naphthali. 1994. "The Babatha Archive: A Response [to B. Isaac 1992]." *IEJ* 44:243–46.

Malina, Bruce J. 1986. *Christian Origins and Cultural Anthropology: Practical Models for Biblical Interpretation.* Atlanta: John Knox.

————. 1988a. "Patron and Client: The Analogy behind Synoptic Theology." *Forum* 4, no. 1:2–32.

————. 1988b. "A Conflict Approach to Mark 7." *Forum* 4, no. 3: 2–30.

Malina, Bruce J., and Jerome H. Neyrey. 1991. "First-Century Personality: Dyadic, Not Individual." In Neyrey 1991:68–96.

Marsden, Peter V. 1992 . "Social Network Theory." In *Encyclopedia of Sociology*, edited by E. F. Borgatta and M. L. Borgatta, 4:1887–94. New York: Macmillan.

McRay, John. 1992. "Gerasenes." In *ABD* 2:991–92.

Meier, John P. 1992. "The Brothers and Sisters of Jesus in Ecumenical Perspective." *CBQ* 54:1–28.

————. 1997a. "The Circle of the Twelve: Did It Exist During Jesus' Ministry?" *JBL* 116:635–72.

————. 1997b. "On Retrojecting Later Questions from Later Texts: A Reply to Richard Bauckham." *CBQ* 59:511–27.

Meyers, Eric M. 1976. "Galilean Regionalism as a Factor in Historical Reconstruction." *BASOR* 220/221:93–103.

————. 1979. "The Cultural Setting of Galilee: The Case of Regionalism and Early Judaism." In *ANRW* II.19.1:686–702. Berlin: de Gruyter.

————. 1985. "Galilean Regionalism: A Reappraisal." In *Approaches to Ancient Judaism*, vol. 5: *Studies in Judaism and Its Greco-Roman Context*, edited by W. S. Green, 115–31. Atlanta: Scholars Press.

————. 1997. "Jesus and His Galilean Context." In Edwards and McCollough 1997:57–66.

Meyers, Eric M., ed. 1997. *Oxford Encyclopedia of Archaeology in the Near East.* 5 vols. New York: Oxford University Press.

Meyers, Eric M., and James F. Strange. 1981. *Archaeology, the Rabbis, and Early Christianity.* Nashville: Abingdon.

Mitchell, J. Clyde. 1969. "The Concept and Use of Social Networks." In *Social Networks in Urban Situations: Analyses of Personal Relationships in Central African Towns*, edited by J. C. Mitchell, 1–50. Manchester, England: Manchester University Press.

————. 1973. "Network Analysis: Studies in Human Interaction." In Boissevain and Mitchell 1973:14–38.

————. 1974. "Social Networks." *ARA* 3:279–99.

Morris, Aldon D., and Carol McClurg Mueller, eds. 1992. *Frontiers in Social Movement Theory.* New Haven: Yale University Press.

Neyrey, Jerome H., ed. 1991. *The Social World of Luke-Acts: Models for Interpretation.* Peabody, Mass.: Hendrickson.

Nun, Mendel. 1988. *Ancient Anchorages and Harbors around the Sea of Galilee.* Kibbutz Ein Gev, Israel: Kinnereth Sailing.

———. 1999. "Ports of Galilee: Modern Drought Reveals Harbors from Jesus' Time." *BAR* 25, no. 4:18–31, 64.

Oakman, Douglas E. 1986. *Jesus and the Economic Questions of His Day.* SBEC 8. Lewiston, N.Y.: Edwin Mellen.

———. 1992. "Was Jesus a Peasant? Implications for Reading the Samaritan Story." *BTB* 22:117–25.

———. 1994. "The Archaeology of First-Century Galilee and the Social Interpretation of the Historical Jesus." In *SBLSP 1994*, 220–51. Atlanta: Scholars.

Ore, Øystein. 1990. *Graphs and Their Uses.* Revised and updated by Robin J. Wilson. Washington, D.C.: Mathematical Association of America.

Peregrine, Peter. 1991. "A Graph-Theoretic Approach to the Evolution of Cahokia." *American Antiquity* 56:66–75.

Pospisil, Leopold. 1964. *The Kapauku Papuans of West New Guinea.* New York: Holt, Rinehart & Winston.

Reed, Jonathan. 1992. *The Population of Capernaum.* Occasional Papers of the Institute for Antiquity and Christianity 23. Claremont, Calif.: Institute for Antiquity and Christianity.

Rohrbaugh, Richard L. 1991. "The Pre-industrial City in Luke-Acts." In Neyrey 1991:125–49.

Rousseau, John J., and Rami Arav. 1995. *Jesus and His World: An Archaeological and Cultural Dictionary.* Minneapolis: Fortress Press.

Safrai, Ze'ev. 1994. *The Economy of Roman Palestine.* London: Routledge.

Saldarini, Anthony J. 1998. "The Social World of Christian Jews and Jewish Christians." In *Religious and Ethnic Communities in Later Roman Palestine*, edited by H. Lapin, 87–127. Studies and Texts in Jewish History and Culture 5. Bethesda, Md.: University Press of America.

Sawicki, Marianne. 2000. "Magdalenes and Tiberiennes: City Women in the Entourage of Jesus." In *Transformative Encounters: Jesus and Women Re-viewed*, edited by Ingrid Rosa Kitzberger, 181–202. BibIntSer 43. Leiden: Brill. [Rewritten in Sawicki, "Israel as Little Italy," *Crossing Galilee: Architectures of Contact in the Occupied Land of Jesus.* Harrisburg, Pa.: Trinity Press International.]

Scrinivas, M. N., and A. Béteille. 1964. "Networks in Indian Social Structure." *Man* 64:165–68.

Seland, Torrey. 1987. "Jesus as a Faction Leader. On the Exit of the Category 'Sect.'" In *Context*, edited by P. W. Bøckman and R. E. Kristiansen, 197–211. Trondheim, Norway: TAPIR.

Shroder, John F., Jr., and Moshe Inbar. 1995. "Geologic and Geographic Background to the Bethsaida Excavations." In Arav and Freund 1995:65–98.

Snow, David A., Louis A. Zurcher, and Sheldon Ekland-Olson. 1980. "Social Networks and Social Movements: A Microstructural Approach to Differential Recruitment." *American Sociological Review* 45:787–801.

Stansell, Gary. 1999. "Gift-Giving in the First Testament." *Semeia* 87:65–90.

Stark, Rodney, 1996. *The Rise of Christianity: A Sociologist Reconsiders History.* Princeton: Princeton University Press.

Stark, Rodney, and William Sims Bainbridge. 1980. "Networks of Faith: Interpersonal Bonds and Recruitment to Cults and Sects." *AJJ* 85:1376–95.

Stegemann, Ekkehard W., and Wolfgang Stegemann. 1999. *The Jesus Movement: A Social History of Its First Century.* Translated by O. C. Dean Jr. Minneapolis: Fortress Press.

Stegemann, Wolfgang. 1984. "Vagabond Radicalism in Early Christianity?: A Historical and Theological Discussion of a Thesis Proposed by Gerd Theissen." In *God of the Lowly: Socio-Historical Interpretations of the Bible,* edited by W. Schottroff and W. Stegemann, 148–68. Translated by M. J. O'Connell. Maryknoll, N.Y.: Orbis.

Strange, James F. 1992. "Magdala." In *ABD* 4.463.

———. 1997. "First-Century Galilee from Archaeology and from the Texts." In Edwards and McCollough 1997:39–48.

Strickert, Fred. 1998. *Bethsaida: Home of the Apostles.* Collegeville, Minn.: Liturgical Press.

Theissen, Gerd. 1978. *Sociology of Early Palestinian Christianity.* Translated by J. Bowden. Philadelphia: Fortress Press.

Theissen, Gerd, and Annette Merz. 1998. *The Historical Jesus: A Comprehensive Guide.* Translated by J. Bowden. Minneapolis: Fortress Press.

Tsafrir, Y., L. Di Segni, and J. Green. 1993. *Tabula Imperii Romani: Iudea, Palestina—Eretz Israel in the Hellenistic, Roman, and Byzantine Periods.* Maps and Gazetteer. Jerusalem: Israel Academy of Sciences and Humanities.

Tzaferis, Vasillios. 1983. "New Archaeological Evidence on Ancient Capernaum." *BA* 46:198–204.

———. 1989. "A Pilgrimage to the Site of the Swine Miracle." *BAR* 15:45–51.

Vogeler, Ingolf. 1996. http://uwec.edu/Academic/Geography/Ivogeler/w111/urban.htm.

Wachsmann, Shelley. 1995. *The Sea of Galilee Boat: An Extraordinary Two-Thousand-Year-Old Discovery.* New York: Plenum.

Walker, Michael E., Stanley Wasserman, and Barry Wellman. 1994. "Statistical Models for Social Support Networks." In *Advances in Social Network Analysis,* edited by S. Wasserman and J. Galaskiewicz, 53–78. Research in the Social and Behavioral Sciences. Thousand Oaks, Calif.: Sage.

Wasserman, Stanley, and Katherine Faust. 1994. *Social Network Analysis: Methods and Applications*. Cambridge: Cambridge University Press.

Wellman, Barry. 1983. "Network Analysis: Some Basic Principles." In *Sociological Theory 1983*, edited by R. Collins, 219–50. San Francisco: Jossey-Bass.

———. 1988. "Structural Analysis: From Method and Metaphor to Theory and Substance." In Wellman and Berkowitz 1988:19–61.

Wellman, Barry, and S. D. Berkowitz. 1988. *Social Structures: A Network Approach*. Cambridge: Cambridge University Press.

Wellman, Barry, Peter J. Carrington, and Alan Hall. 1988. "Networks and Personal Communities." In Wellman and Berkowitz 1988:130–84.

Whitten, N., Jr., and A. Wolfe. 1973. "Network Analysis." In *Handbook of Social and Cultural Anthropology*, edited by J. Honigmann, 717–46. Chicago: Rand McNally.

Yeivin, Ze'ev. 1987. "Ancient Chorazin Comes Back to Life." *BAR* 13:22–36.

Politics and Political Economy

Money in the Moral Universe
of the New Testament

Douglas E. Oakman

You cannot serve God and mammon.
—Luke 16:13

For the love of silver [money] is the root of all evil.
—1 Tim 6:10

Standard treatments of biblical numismatics are limited in shedding light on the social significance of ancient money.[1] The usual attention to art motifs and denominations is useful from a historical and metrological point of view, but does very little as far as illuminating money's social place. This essay proposes an alternative approach that produces insights on a number of fronts: in relating numismatics to social-world questions, in assessing the social character of the Jesus movement, in developing social indices for decisions about redactional settings in life, and, generally, in shedding light on the origins and composition of the New Testament Gospels.

The discussion is organized through four theses and two excursuses. It is first suggested that standard treatments of biblical numismatics do not attain sufficient social insight. Part of the reason for this is that numismatic treatments related to the Bible have not been sufficiently in dialogue with the larger field of numismatics, as Richard Oster pointed out more than a decade ago. Moreover, there is palpable need for conceptual approaches informed by broader social questions and controlled through theory-informed models. For this reason, the discussion turns to the elaboration of a model regarding ancient money's social functions. This impels an analysis of descript money in the Jesus traditions, with an eye to the historical Jesus' views on the institution of money, and concluding comments about nondescript money in the New Testament outside the Gospels—indicative of increasing elite control over the early Jesus traditions.

Thesis 1: *Standard treatments of biblical numismatics either do not provide sufficient social insight or are misleading as to the social insight tendered.* Four recent publications are considered as representative of "biblical numismatics," and I wish first to acknowledge my appreciation for and debt to them before I turn to critique. It is not that the publications are of poor quality, or do not present viable methodologies or results, but that they perhaps construe the work of numismatics too narrowly.

The work of Yaakov Meshorer is justifiably respected within biblical numismatics. One may reasonably take issue, however, with his assertion in a summary article that "the dispute over the chronology of the Hasmonean coins is still the major issue in the field of Jewish (sic!) numismatics" (1986:212). Further, when he speaks of symbols on the coins of Herod the Great, he comments merely on the debate about whether they represent Israelite or non-Israelite motifs. The chronology and symbolism of coins are important, but focusing on them without reference to the role of coinage within agrarian social relations or the politics of aristocratic empires is too constrictive.

A second recent numismatic treatment, in the dictionary of John Rousseau and Rami Arav (1995), also illustrates the issue under consideration. The authors claim that money originated for the sake of convenience in exchange and that "the old barter system was relegated to minor local transactions" (55). They show awareness of functions of money as well as the political importance of money. However, in remarks about the parable of the talents (59), they speak of the "lack of logic in both stories," without awareness of Richard Rohrbaugh's excellent treatment (1993a) of these "texts of terror" from the standpoint of Palestinian peasantry. Moreover, their article assumes that the exchange utility of money was widespread and keeps the usual emphases on art motifs, weights, and denominational relationships.

Fred Strickert reaches a more helpful outcome (in Rousseau and Arav 1995:61) and achieves a clearer statement of the relationship between interests of power and purposes of money. Strickert illustrates this social fact with reference to the images on coins, which serve typically as propaganda for the powerful. In the most interesting section, a discussion of a series of coins minted by the tetrarch Philip in northern Transjordan, Strickert traces the correlation between new coins and a series of important events in Roman Palestine. He reaches the following conclusion: "It seems that issuing coins served to publicize the legitimacy of Philip's own authority in the face of foreign domination"

(62). While it is possible that Philip felt challenged by the prefects to the south (as Strickert suggests; cf. Luke 23:12), it seems more likely that the coin series was intended to show Philip's loyalty to Rome as a faithful client ruler (see Bethsaida/Iulias, Caesarea Philippi). The prefects would have been in a position to report this fidelity upon its "publication" through coinage. Strickert at least is appreciative of the political significance of coinage, in contrast to views that might see a "free market" or freely circulating money economy in the area.

A third example of the point under consideration is provided in *The Anchor Bible Dictionary* article on coinage, by John W. Betlyon (1992). When Betlyon examines coinage in the Hellenistic and Herodian periods of Palestine, he observes that major mints were located in Acco and Tyre, and states that "coinage and the right to produce it were the perquisites of political and military supremacy" (1084). No further inferences are made from this important statement, either about the role and function of money or about implications for social interpretation.

Most of Betlyon's comments deal with the dating of coins, brief descriptions, or historical notes. These observations are, again, important. Information that could be of use for social understanding, however, is obscured because the writer has no sense for what "political and military supremacy" really meant for social institutions.

A few brief illustrations: Again and again, Betlyon observes that Hasmoneans and Herodians struck bronze coins. He says, "No Hasmonean silver is known" (1085). Apparently he thinks this is because silver and gold were in short supply. Rather than appeal to natural scarcity, why does he not suspect social constraints, particularly political constraints? Tyre and Acco were privileged by both Syrian and Roman interests in the minting of silver. Commerce, as well as taxation, had to do with power. Bronze coinage likewise served particular political functions within client realms, but Betlyon does not help us to understand these dimensions.

He thinks Hasmonean coins "functioned as supplemental currency with the larger coins circulating from the major mints" (1084–85); or Herod's coins "are meant to support silver from regional mints" (1085); or "the procuratorial coinage was secondary to imperial and Herodian issues, and was used to fill out the denominational system" (1086); or Herodian-period coins "were the pocket change supplementing silver coins from imperial mints" (1086).

Betlyon's statements might hold true in peculiar social contexts (cities within commercial networks like Tiberias, Sepphoris, Jerusalem, or Tyre, or farther-away Pompeii), but mislead us, I would argue, about the experience of most people. He assumes that commerce back then was like commerce now, that common folks back then had ready access to money of all denominations as now, and that money functioned then as now. These deceptive social assumptions are what social theory and models compensate for; conversely, contemporary biblical numismatics would do well to take social theory and societal models more seriously.

A final example derives from the recently published book of Larry J. Kreitzer (1996). This is a very fine study, with copious drawings of coins and excellent annotated bibliography, and should be of enduring value for students of the New Testament. While many of Kreitzer's chapters are devoted to studying the relationship between coin images and particular New Testament motifs (for instance, deification, triumph imagery in Paul, or Jesus' parousia), the first part on Julio-Claudian propaganda overlaps with our concerns. The political function of money (propaganda for the empire) is clearly in view. However, since Kreitzer is concerned with the standard art-history approach, coins are understood as illuminating history or textual motifs rather than as phenomena carrying significant social information.

The limitations of standard treatments urge a search for alternative methods.

Thesis 2: *Numismatic approaches informed by broader social questions and controlled through theory-informed models can lead to important social insights.* The model in figure 17.1 was suggested initially by the work of Michael Crawford (1970), and developed in conversation with views of T. F. Carney (1975), Karl Polanyi (1977), Marshall Sahlins (1966), Herman Daly and John Cobb (1994), Richard Rohrbaugh (1993a:34), and William J. Booth (1993). In the background are considerations about agrarian societies (Lenski), the politics of aristocratic empires (Kautsky), and systems sociology such as I employed in an SBL Seminar Paper a few years ago. The model permits a functional analysis of money in the New Testament and raises the broader question of the function of money within societies whose key social institutions were structured through kinship and political relations.

Economic historians have long recognized the functions. Function 3 (F3) was probably the originating intent of money in seventh-century B.C.E. Lydia. However, the model does not outline historical-genetic relations; rather, money's political-functional logic is displayed. The model in one sense extends downward from the elite household through the elite-controlled mechanisms of taxation and debt to the preferred barter exchange within peasant villages. I find it striking therefore that the Babatha Archives, containing the personal records of a wealthy woman of En Gedi from the early second century C.E., consist substantially of deposit receipts and debt contracts. These important archaeological records indicate the prevalence of the first and third functions of the model, a pattern repeated in the Jesus traditions. These are precisely the

An Analytical Model and Database
for Studying Money Functions in the New Testament

Metal Basis	Function (F)
Gold, silver	**F1.** Storage (hoards, bullion)

Mark 6:8 (Bronze as?); Matt 10:9/Luke 9:3 (Q, "Gold, silver, *bronze"/"Argurion"*); Matt 13:44/*Gos. Thom.* 109 (M or Q? "hidden treasure"); Matt 25:18/Luke 19:20 (Q, talent/mina); Luke 15:8–9 (L, drachma); Matt 2:11 (M? gold); 23:16–17 (M, gold); *P. Yadin* 5 (mina), 17 (denarius), 18 (denarius), 27 (denarius)

Silver	**F2.** Measurement

Mark 6:37/John 6:7 (denarius); Mark 14:5/John 12:5 (denarius); Rev 6:6 (denarius)

F3. Standard of payment

a. Taxation (nonelite or elite retainers > elite)

Mark 12:41 (Bronze as?); Mark 12:15/Matt 22:19/Luke 20:24 (denarius); *Mark 12:42/Luke 21:2 (Lepton)*; Matt 17:24 (M, Tyrian didrachma); Matt 17:27 (M, stater [Tyrian tetradrachma]); *P. Yadin* 16 (mina)

b. Debt (nonelite > elite)

Matt 5:26/Luke 12:59 (Q, Quadrans/Lepton); Luke 6:34–35/*Gos. Thom.* 95 (L or Q? "money"); Luke 12:15–21/*Gos. Thom.* 63 (L or Q? *Chremata*); Luke 7:41 (L, denarius); Matt 18:23–25 (M, talent); Matt 18:28 (M, denarius); *P. Yadin* 11 (denarius), 21 (denarius, mina)

    c. Elite or estate payment (elite > nonelite)

      Mark 14:11/Matt 26:15/Luke 22:5 (silver [stater?]); Matt 20:2–13 (M, denarius); Matt 28:12 (M, soldiers' pay)

F4. Exchange-value orientation: M-C-M'

      Matt 25:27/Luke 19:23 (Q, talent/mina, "bankers")

| Bronze | F5. | Use-value orientation, or money barter: C-M-C |

      Mark 6:37/John 6:7 (denarius); Mark 14:5/John 12:5 (*denarius*); Matt 10:29/Luke 12:6 (Q, bronze as); Matt 13:45–46/*Gos. Thom.* 76 (M or Q? "went and sold"); Matt 22:1–14/Luke 14:16–24/*Gos. Thom.* 64 (Q, buying fields, oxen); Luke 10:35 (*L, denarius*); Matt 27:6–7 (M, *shekel?*); Rev 6:6 (*denarius*)

In kind   Barter: C-C

      Luke 11:5? (with intimations of F3?)

C = Commodity, M = Money medium, M' = Money increase or profit, > direction of transaction; *italicizing* indicates database exceptions to the metal classification system (left column).

Figure 17.1: An analytical model and database for studying money functions in the New Testament

functions one would expect in societies whose key institutions were structured by family or power: F1 (storage) represents the need for household security and F3 (standard of payment) the need to control others, especially those outside the family.

If F1 and F3 were prevalent in antiquity, F4 (exchange-value orientation) is surprisingly rare in the database I have accumulated so far. This function would indicate a universal utility of money: money buying everything (including land, labor, capital), anywhere, for anyone. But such utility is not much in evidence in the material I am focusing on; function 5 (use-value orientation) looks more like an extension of barter than an expression of some "economic rationality" with which we would be familiar. This general picture suggests that money functioned differently in ancient agrarian societies, which follows from a very different institutional configuration.

The database of money references in the Jesus traditions, when classified, permits the following summary observations: Mark provides one instance of F1, two of F2—each perhaps implying F5 (John and Revelation similarly attest F2/F5 in terms of money equivalencies for bread)—and four instances of F3. Q contains two instances of F1, one certain instance of F3, one of F4, and one certain instance of F5. L represents one instance of F1, three of F3, and one probable instance of F5. M represents three instances of F1, six of F3, and one of F5. Overall, the Gospels represent seven instances of F1, two of F2, fourteen of F3 (five of F3a, six of F3b, three of F3c), one instance of F4, and three explicit instances of F5.

This picture compels more nuanced social conclusions. F1 is securely attested, though the instances of gold and silver are only in elite connections. Mark 6:8 provides perhaps the only nonelite instance. F2 appears directly only in Mark, John, and Revelation. This fact, and the sizable sums involved in Mark and John (200, 300 denarii), leaves an unclear picture of the social significance to be inferred. I return to this matter in a moment in the excursus.

F3 is most frequently attested. The many examples of money involved with taxation or in debt transactions show the reality of power behind money and the political significance of money.

F4 is rarely attested. Money changing is the only explicit context, with nothing in the Jesus traditions to show increase of money through commercial transactions. Only three instances of use-value operation (F5) are clearly discernible (Q/Luke 12:6/Matt 10:29; L/Luke 10:35; M/Matt 27:10). Of these, L and M demonstrate use-value in operation for the elite, while the Q passage alone shows the everyday use-value of bronze coins. The rarity of F4 (only in Q/Luke 19:23/Matt 25:27), taken with the less rare F5, should persuade us that money did not function in the social world of the Gospels as it does in the modern world (where F4 and F5 are major dimensions). How many of the instances of F2 should be understood as implying F5 is unclear. The rare appearance of money with "general utility," and the heavy use of money for value storage (hoarding) and payment standards (taxes and debts), imply a monetary functionality in Jesus' day notably different from our experience.

F5 especially shows what is at stake politically even with bronze coinage: peasants ordinarily want to see something for barter exchange. The interposition of money means that the peasant family holds a token in place of some real good; but a token cannot be eaten, so a peasant will prefer barter. Holding a token is a form of indebtedness (Daly and Cobb 1994:420). But if political pressures impose a bronze currency and enforce its use (especially through legal debt instruments or by requiring taxes to be paid in money), then peasant exchanges based upon generalized reciprocity can be "converted" by political alchemy into exchanges of balanced reciprocity accountable in money. Thus, the political authority can better assess full agrarian production and maximize the taxation take.

Careful consideration of the functions of money in Jesus' social environment underscores how money was a crucial element in a *political* economy (Rohrbaugh 1993a:35). As evident through the analysis guided by the model, F1, F3, and F4 essentially are available for gold or silver coinage only to the elites or their agents. F2 is nominally available to the common person, but its utility (F5) seems rare and only appears in terms of "small change." In other words, people might estimate value in terms of hundreds of denarii, but few would actually command such sums at one time. Conversely, nonelites are primarily familiar with bronze provincial coinage, but unfamiliar with silver coinage. This sheds an interesting light on a text like Mark 12:16.

Overall, the analysis confirms Crawford's conclusions (1970:43) that the rural empire knew little of money as a universal medium of exchange. Finley's three ordinary elite uses for money—in strongbox, in land, or on loan (1973:116)—are also clearly evident in the Gospels.

Excursus 1. One way to specify these insights further is in terms of "market." What was the extent or depth of ancient market relations? What was their essential social character? While a complete answer cannot be given here, a perusal of Gospel passages related to *agora* or to relations of buying and selling offers some hints.

Instances of the use of *agora* in a Jerusalem setting need to be bracketed out as unrepresentative because they are characteristic of a city of pilgrimage (Mark 12:38 and par.; include here Luke 11:43). Generally, "market" in our sense was developed somewhat in Roman-period cities and perhaps in towns.

This leaves several passages of interest regarding the *marketplace*. Q/Luke 7:32/Matt 11:16 shows children sitting in the marketplace; however, no moneyed relations are indicated, children were not subject to the same social constraints as adults, and the Q tradents would have been familiar with town and city markets. Mark 6:56 likewise shows a place for the sick to be laid, but no moneyed relations are in view. Only M/Matt 20:3 depicts idle laborers, with the estate owner having access to hire them. This suggests privilege on the part of the landlord, and the vulnerability of labor is surmised. The canonical Gospels do not depict widespread market relations, in the sense we understand them, in Roman Palestine.

As far as *agorazō* or *pōleō* are concerned, or the monetary relations concomitant with markets, Jerusalem passages are again bracketed. John 4:8 also shows the possibility of food purchase at Sebaste. The most significant instances seem to be these: for *agorazō*, Q?/Luke 14:18–19 (buying field, 5 yoke of oxen); Q/Luke 17:28 (buying in Noah's day); M/Matt 13:44, 45 (buying field, pearl); and Mark 6:36–37 and par. (feeding). For *pōleō*, Q/Luke 12:6 (5 sparrows/2 *assaria* or 2/1); Q/Luke 17:28 (selling in Noah's day); M/Matt 13:44, 46 (selling all for hidden treasure, for pearl). Q/Luke 12:6 might reflect the experience of the average villager (but what were the sparrows for?); the reference to Noah is associated with the Q tradents' experiences, perhaps in Capernaum or Chorazin. The remaining instances indicate market functions that would have been accessible to the wealthy, for whom we are willing to concede access to both market and the exchange-value function of money.

The feeding of the multitudes also seems to presuppose the availability of bread in the market, but a comparison of Mark 6:36–37 and John 6:5, 7 suggests that irony, exasperation, and improbability may be as much the point as the presumption of widespread market relations.

I conclude this excursus by saying that the picture developed through the model is reflected also in a study of buying and selling: in Roman Palestine, *monetization* had proceeded apace in the service of controlling interests of debt and taxation, while *marketization* in terms of money was limited to towns and cities, with access controlled by the powerful, except for exchanges of political-economic insignificance.

Thesis 3: *Jesus mounted a radical critique of money and mammon.* Space permits only a statement of the broad outlines of this argument.

Money in Jesus' day was an elite political tool, not a universal economic medium. It benefited the powerful inordinately, but held captive values esteemed by common folk. Money for tax collection, in safety deposits, or on loan to the weak and powerless characterized money's general appearance.

Jesus called these security arrangements "mammon," from the Aramaic word that, at root, means *trust*. Taxes, deposits, and loan receipts were items trusted by the powerful to provide future security. To this, Jesus responded, "You cannot serve God and mammon" (Luke 16:13). A critique of such arrangements is still visible in Mark 10:29–31; Q/Luke 19:11–27; L/Luke 12:16–20; and L/Luke 16:1–8.

For Jesus, "God or mammon" specifies another social modality radically independent of money. In seeing this, Luke 11:5–13 is instructive. Luke 11:5–8 belongs to L; Luke 11:9–13 belongs to Q (Matt 7:7–11). The link seems forged by Luke. Notice that Luke's redactional framework is centered on prayer (11:1, 13). At the Lucan level, the subject matter has to do with patronage.

Despite redaction, the friend-at-midnight passage illumines the words of Jesus in Luke 11:9–13 in a peculiarly substantive way. The neighbor's importunity is often seen as the point of the similitude, but I take the second autos (his) of 11:8 to refer to the man in bed, not the man at the door. Besides, a truly shameless man would not be at the door at midnight out of sight of everyone. The meaning of the similitude does hinge upon the word anoudera (shamelessness). Egyptian papyri strongly urge the meaning "shameless desire for personal gain" (MM, s.v.). The point then is: The man in bed may not get up at midnight to provide for an embarrassed neighbor, but to keep the other in debt he certainly will. The "friend" will make a loan at midnight on this basis. In this vignette, relations of "balanced reciprocity," in which accounting for exchanges is noted and enforceable, are prominently in view.

In Luke 11:9–13, by contrast, another sort of relation comes into focus. The similitude in Luke 11:11–12 provides commentary, wittingly or unwittingly, on the friend-at-midnight story. The Jesus similitude asks whether fathers would try to meet their children's needs by offering them stones/serpents/scorpions. When the children ask for bread/fish/eggs, the natural course is to make these provisions. What does this similitude drive at?

Within a nonelite purview, Jesus asks whether money is of any use at all. Theissen's "local color" method (1991) may be of assistance here: to the villager the coins are worth no more than stones. Consideration of the images on Gratus or Pilate coins suggests derivation for Jesus' other metaphors. *Caduceus* or *Lituus*—emblems of numinous imperial power—were to villagers ironically suggestive of common scourges: the Galilee serpent ready to strike or the scorpion's stinger.

Strikingly, the juxtaposition of Luke 11:5–8 and 11:9–13 illuminates the role of money as exchange "cipher." The friend-at-midnight passage shows how debt works to control people in basic exchange relations. Money plays a pivotal role in facilitating such indebtedness. Money acquired through debt may be placed in deposit, become an object of trust and security. From the peasant villager's perspective, money barter is useless. What father would think of giving his children stones/serpents/scorpions to meet real needs? What peasant wants to hold money instead of bread? But money is now more necessary than bread.

The Lucan material reveals a connection between the critique of mammon and a more radical (nonelite) critique of money. Jesus rarely mentions money barter (only at Q/Luke 12:6/Matt 10:29). Most often, the Jesus tradition laments the problem of indebtedness, which, for the powerless, is the result of money transactions in preindustrial societies (Childe 1964:166–68, 202). Important elements of the Jesus tradition shed indirect light on Jesus' hostility to mammon, to money on deposit, or to commercial and money transactions generally (Luke 12:16–20; Mark 11:15–16).

Other elements of the Jesus tradition become intelligible in light of a radical critique of money. There is sense in injunctions like Q/Luke 6:30/Matt 5:42/*Gos. Thom.* 95. "God" in the dilemma "God or mammon" in part represents (not to be too reductionistic) relations of general reciprocity, wherein exchanges are gifts, accounting is forsworn, and the basic "currency" is trust itself—trust between God and humans, trust between humans (see Malina 1988). Mammon as an idolatrous trust-center apart from God represents a terminal disruption in the social-construction project that Jesus envisions.

The point of Luke 11:11–12 in the original setting of Jesus, therefore, had to do with a radical rejection of money in favor of the mutuality of the kingdom of God. Luke 16:13 likewise rejected trust in mammon in the interest of God's gracious benefactions worked out through human gift-giving (see L/Q?/Luke 6:34–36; Q/Luke 11:3; Q/Luke 12:29–31). We can understand why the one saying of Jesus preserved in the New Testament outside the Gospels was this: "It is more blessed to give than to receive" (Acts 20:35).

Excursus 2. Something has to be said about the glōssokomon ("money case" or "money box") of John 12:6 and 13:29 in relationship to what is claimed about Jesus' attitude to money. These passages, combined with the evidence of Acts 2:45, 4:32, or 4:37, might suggest less a radical rejection of the institution of money than a reconfiguration of the use of money (also in accord with Jesus' critique of mammon). A couple of things in my mind speak against this interpretation: (1) "A Qumran reading" of Jesus and money has likely crept into Acts and is to be understood both as a perspective conditioned by elites and as Lucan anachronism. (2) The picture of John 12 and 13, moreover, may not depict Judas so much as "treasurer" for Jesus' followers (Brown 1966:244) as a security arrangement adopted by Jerusalem pilgrims (redemption money to be spent in Jerusalem?), again indirect testimony to the political nature of money.

We might recall in this connection the coin hoard found on Mount Carmel in 1960. Containing 3,400 Tyrian tetradrachmas and 1,160 didrachmas, the hoard was perhaps on its way to Jerusalem (Rousseau and Arav 1995:56) but never reached its destination.

A striking fact about money in the New Testament outside the Gospels and Revelation is the generic nature of its designation. Money of any specific denomination (denarius, stater, etc.) appears only in the Gospels and Revelation. Paul of course refers to the collection for the poor of Jerusalem, but he refers to money only by indirection (2 Corinthians 8–9; 1 Cor 16:2). Later, "money" is designated either by *chrēmata* or simply under the generic labels "silver" or "gold."

Thesis 4: *The early Christian tradition softened Jesus' critique and focused on the moral dangers of "love of money," more apparent to those who had money than to those who did not.* Initially in Galilee, the scribes who shaped the original Q material (perhaps town accountants) reflected on the dangers of mammon (Luke 16:13) and preserved some of Jesus' basic concerns (Luke 11:9–13). Mark's scribal tradition also incorporates nonelite perspectives to a significant degree (Rohrbaugh 1993b; Theissen 1991:236–49). The views of people within the kinship networks of the empire's provincial urban elites shaped these early Jesus traditions.

While the social background of New Testament writers beyond the Gospels is obscure, it is reasonable to say that many of them evidence a commercial literacy reflective of freedmen interests (Meeks 1983; Rohrbaugh 1993b:115–17). The greatest preoccupation with love of money appears in Acts, the Catholic Epistles, Hebrews, and the Pastorals. These documents attest to the spread of the urbanizing Christian movement throughout the eastern empire. They show, as in James 5 or Acts 4–5, the need to reckon with moneyed interests. The interests displayed do not question the value or utility of money, only its moral place in the heart. Such sentiments primarily speak out of an elite consciousness: the views of people within the kinship networks of powerful urban-imperial elites now strike the dominant note in the movement. Not surprisingly, when Matthew had incorporated earlier traditions into what was to become the authoritative Gospel, elite views of money came to prevail (as the M material shows).

Conclusion

The Jesus traditions retain an echo of a vigorous critique of political economy and its exploitative monetary system in the interests of urging the alternative "network" of the kingdom of God, with exchanges of goods organized through principles of generalized reciprocity. Outside the Gospels, with the single exception of Revelation, which maintained this vigorous critique of the Roman imperial order, Jesus' negative view of money was dropped in favor of moralisms about "love of money." Such moral exhortation made sense to commercial types whose livelihoods depended on Roman currency, but whose fidelity to Jesus needed acknowledgment as well. For Jesus, money was at the heart of evil apart from God's rule. The compromise worked out in nascent Christian tradition—seeing love of money as the danger—has maintained its salience in Western culture ever since.

Notes

1. Earlier versions of this material were presented to the Social Sciences and New Testament Section at the Society of Biblical Literature meeting in 1996, and the Catholic Biblical Association in 1997. A preliminary form of the model and discussion also appears in Hanson and Oakman 1998:120–25.

Works Cited

Betlyon, John W. 1992. "Coinage." In *ABD* 1:1084–89.

Booth, William James. 1993. *Households: On the Moral Architecture of the Economy.* Ithaca, N.Y.: Cornell University Press.

Brown, Raymond E. 1966. *The Gospel According to John.* Anchor Bible 29. Garden City: Doubleday.

Carney, T. F. 1973. *The Economies of Antiquity: Controls, Gifts, and Trade.* Lawrence, Kans.: Coronado.

————. 1975. *The Shape of the Past: Models and Antiquity.* Lawrence, Kans.: Coronado.

Childe, Gordon V. 1964. *What Happened in History.* N.Y.: Penguin.

Crawford, Michael. 1970. "Money and Exchange in the Roman World." *JRS* 60:40–48.

Daly, Herman, and John B. Cobb Jr. 1994. *For the Common Good: Redirecting the Economy toward Community, the Environment, and a Sustainable Future.* 2d ed. Boston: Beacon.

Finley, Moses. 1973. *The Ancient Economy.* Berkeley: University of California Press.

Hanson, K. C., and Douglas E. Oakman. 1998. *Palestine in the Time of Jesus: Social Structures and Social Conflicts.* Minneapolis: Fortress Press.

Hauck, Friedrich. 1967. "*Mamōnas.*" In *TDNT* 4:388–90.

Kautsky, John H. 1982. *The Politics of Aristocratic Empires.* Chapel Hill: University of North Carolina Press.

Kreitzer, Larry J. 1996. *Striking New Images: Roman Imperial Coinage and the New Testament World.* JSNTSup 134. Sheffield: Sheffield Academic.

Lenski, Gerhard E. 1984. *Power and Privilege: A Theory of Social Stratification.* 2d ed. Chapel Hill: University of North Carolina Press.

Malina, Bruce J. 1988. "Patron and Client: The Analogy Behind Synoptic Theology." *Forum.* 4/1:2–32.

Meeks, Wayne A. 1983. *The First Urban Christians: The Social World of the Apostle Paul.* New Haven: Yale.

Meshorer, Yaakov. 1986. "Jewish Numismatics." In *Early Judaism and Its Modern Interpreters,* edited by R. A. Kraft and G. W. E. Nickelsburg, 211–20. The Bible and Its Modern Interpreters 3. Atlanta: Scholars.

Oakman, Douglas E. 1994. "The Archaeology of First-Century Galilee and the Social Interpretation of Jesus." In *SBLSP 1994,* 220–51. Atlanta: Scholars.

Oster, Richard. 1982. "Numismatic Windows into the Social World of Early Christianity." *JBL* 101:195–223.

Polanyi, Karl. 1977. *The Livelihood of Man.* Edited by H. W. Pearson. New York: Academic.

Rohrbaugh, Richard L. 1993a. "A Peasant Reading of the Parable of the Talents/Pounds: A Text of Terror?" *BTB* 23:32–39.

———. 1993b. "The Social Location of the Marcan Audience." *BTB* 23:114–27.

Rousseau, John J., and Rami Arav. 1995. *Jesus and His World: An Archaeological and Cultural Dictionary.* Minneapolis: Fortress Press.

Sahlins, Marshall. 1966. *Tribesmen.* Englewood Cliffs, N.J.: Prentice-Hall.

Theissen, Gerd. 1991. *The Gospels in Context: Social and Political History in the Synoptic Tradition.* Translated by L. Maloney. Minneapolis: Fortress Press. Originally published as *Lokalkolorit und Zeitgeschichte in den Evangelien.* NTOA 8. Göttingen: Vandenhoeck & Ruprecht, 1989.

Gifts, Tributes, and Offerings

Gary Stansell

> *The measure you give will be the measure you get.*
> —Mark 4:24

The exchange of gifts, with its accompanying rules about reciprocal activity between two parties, is now assumed to be a universal human phenomenon. All human societies exchange gifts, but the norms that govern exchange in a given society exhibit their own cultural adaptation and setting. Not much has been done to study gift exchange relative to the New Testament. At most, scholars interested in the social sciences have studied patterns of reciprocity (Malina 1986; Oakman 1986; Moxnes 1988), especially as the principle of reciprocity relates to the economy or to the socioeconomic relations of patron-client arrangements. I know of only two recent studies that focus on gift-giving in the Bible and that attempt an analysis with some help from anthropological models: Herman's *Tithe as Gift* (1991) and Peterman's *Paul's Gift from Philippi: Conventions of Gift-Exchange and Christian Giving* (1997).

I offer a provisional overview of gifts and gift exchange in the New Testament on the basis of selected passages of the Synoptic Gospels. Further, I hope to suggest several lines of interpretation as they emerge from a social-scientific perspective with the help of a cross-cultural model.

Historians and anthropologists have long noted the importance of gift exchange in the ancient world. The world of Homer attests to its significance in archaic Greece (Finley 1956). In the classical Greek world, Aristotle and others take up the notion of giving and receiving (*Nichomachean Ethics* 2.7.4). For the Greco-Roman world, Seneca (*De beneficiis* 56–62) is particularly significant, for he discusses the social conventions of giving and receiving. The "aim of *De beneficiis* is to give a definition of what binds human societies together" (Peterman 1997:53). Asserting that people in his day lack knowledge of how to give and how to receive benefits, Seneca wants to correct the errors of not choosing worthy recipients, not giving gifts in the proper manner, and not receiving gifts with proper gratitude. Giving and receiving is social exchange, and it puts the receiver under obligation. For Seneca, exchange constitutes the chief bond of human society (*De beneficiis* 1.4.2; see also Cicero, *De officiis* 2.55–60, who distinguishes between two kinds of men who give gifts: the "extravagant" man lavishes banquets, distributes meats, money, etc.; the "liberal" man ransoms captives, pays off a friend's debts, or gives assistance).

The Vocabulary of Gift-Giving

A thorough study of gift exchange in the New Testament would require an analysis of Greek terms for "gift," "to give," and related words. Here we may only sketch a few significant factors that bear on the present study. The following is indebted to the work of Benveniste (1997), who states: "In most Indo-European languages, 'to give' is expressed by a verb from the root *do*—which also has a large number of nominal derivatives" (34). The stability of this definition was disturbed by the discovery of the Hittite verb *da*, which meant the opposite, "to take." But *da* is not a different verb. Benveniste resolves the puzzle by showing that *do* does not mean either "give" or "take," but both "give" and "take," depending on the context (34). This curious semantic ambivalence has significance for the broader discussion of gift exchange and the social, material, and reciprocal connections that gift-giving creates. That is, to give and to receive are not two acts, but, in essence, one, for which there is ample anthropological data. The semantic facts support this conclusion.

If we turn to ancient Greek, we have the verb *nemō*, which has two values: to *give* legally as an allotment and to *have* legally as an allotment. It is significant that there is not one word for "gift," but many. Ancient Greek has no fewer than five distinct words, all typically rendered in standard dictionaries as "gift, present": *dōs, dōron, dōrea, doris, dōtinē*. Aristotle defines *dōrea* as a gift that does not impose obligations of a return gift (*Top.* 125a.18; Benveniste 1997:34). In Hesiod, *dosis* can be promised to someone as a recompense for a bold deed (*Works* 354; Benveniste 1997:35). In Homer, *dōtinē* is the gift given under obligation to honor the chief (*Iliad* 9.155, 297; Benveniste 1997:36), or the gift to a guest; this term always includes the idea of reciprocity. The *dōron* is the generous gift, given out of gratitude or homage (for further on gift exchange among the Greeks of antiquity, see Burkert 1996; Mitchell 1997).

In Latin, *hostis* "is properly one who compensates and enjoys compensation, one who obtains from Rome the counterpart of the advantages which he has in his own country and the equivalent of which he owes in his turn to the person he pays reciprocally" (Benveniste 1997:38). Later the word took on the meaning of "foreigner" and "public enemy." The related term "hospitality" came to mean "compensatory offering." *Munus* means in literary usage "function, office, obligation, task, or favor," and also takes on the sense of respects paid or service accomplished. In the community, "each member is compelled to give in the same proportion as he receives" (Benveniste 1997:39). Exchanging gifts is thus different from utilitarian commerce, for when one gives, he gives the most precious thing that he has. The term *daps*, "sacred banquet" (cf. Gk. *duponē*, "expense"), is a festive and sumptuous expense that has social and religious meanings and that is made for prestige and as a "pure loss." Ancient derivatives of *daps* show that the word implies largesse and "associate it with festive banquets of hospitality" (Benveniste 1997:40).

A Definition of "Gift"

In its simplest meaning, a gift (X) is an object, material property, or a service, which A transfers to B; thus A gives X to B; B accepts X. A and B may represent individuals or groups. An important difficulty arises with the definition of X. In modern societies, the narrower sense of the word "gift" connotes "presents," typically wrapped and offered on specific gift-giving occasions: anniversary, wedding, birthday, and the like. In Mauss's study of archaic societies, and in most ethnographic and anthropological studies, gift is understood in a much broader sense: the things exchanged are not simply "property and wealth, movable and immovable goods," but "banquets, rituals, military services, women, children, dances, festivals, and fairs," and the like (1990:5). The anthropological literature, however, appears to speak of gift exchange in both the narrow and broad senses, at times indiscriminately.

The Anthropology of Gift Exchange

The following features will help focus the issues encountered in selected biblical passages. The model (fig. 1), relying especially on the work of Mauss, Sahlins, Bourdieu, and Carrier, will also help minimize the ethnocentrism and anachronism of the modern reader, who naturally approaches gift exchange in the ancient world with the Western, industrial view of the gift, "that

(a) it is something voluntarily given, and that (b) there is no expectation of compensation" (Belk 1979:100, quoted in Carrier 1995:22). Following Carrier (1995:10), we may dub it a "Maussian model," because it incorporates the essential insights from Mauss with critical refinement and development by later students of the gift.

- There is a universal *obligation* to give, to receive, and to return gifts.
- Gifts are presented as though they are *voluntary*, thus masking the *obligatory* character of exchange and hiding economic self-interest.
- Gift-giving aims at *reciprocity*, but it is not always balanced or symmetrical.
- Gifts are not protected by *law*, yet public scrutiny and one's personal honor require that exchanges be reciprocal.
- Gift exchange is a *public act*. As such it may be ceremonial and also emphasize display of wealth and prestige.
- *Kinship* closeness or distance is related to objects exchanged, the function of the gift, and the accompanying reciprocity.
- Gift exchange is *not* the same as *commodity exchange*, which is impersonal. The former obligates, while the latter does not.[1]
- The object given is *inalienable*, that is, the giver participates in or is part of the object given away; hence, the giver has a lien on his gift.
- Gifts establish a *bond* between persons or groups, or strengthen an already existing social relationship. Thus the purpose is not simply the circulation of wealth.
- *Honor* accrues to the giver, who must be *generous*; it is shameful to be stingy. The size of the gift is correlated with the status/wealth of the giver and the needs of the receiver. But generosity may mask antagonism or competition, with the power to humiliate the receiver of the gift (the "poison" of the gift).
- The gift is a *challenge*, which does honor to the person addressed and at the same time tests his/her pride. To challenge someone who cannot riposte is a *dishonor* to the giver; likewise, to make a gift so great that it cannot be reciprocated dishonors the giver. The gift as challenge must be reasonable.
- A gift, like a challenge, is a *provocation* to reply. He who accepts a gift inescapably commits himself to a series of exchanges. The countergift is a fresh challenge.
- The *refusal* of a gift heaps scorn upon the challenger. The refusal to offer a countergift dishonors both the giver of the initial gift and the recipient of that gift.

- The gift must *please* the recipient and be valued by the giver. One cannot give just anything away.
- The *commensurate countergift* halts the exchange. Only outbidding someone continues the exchange. The absence of a countergift brings dishonor to the giver of the initial gift; it also brings dishonor to its recipient.
- The countergift must be *deferred and different*; an immediate return of a identical gift is tantamount to a refusal of the gift.

Figure 18.1. Cross-Cultural Model of Gift-Exchange in Antiquity

Gifts in the Synoptic Gospels

For a brief orientation, let us note a few familiar passages that incorporate the language of gift exchange:

1. "The measure you *give* will be the measure you get." (Mark 4:24; see Matt 7:2; Luke 6:38)
2. "Do not *give* to dogs what is holy." (Matt 7:6)
3. "Ask and it will be *given* to you. For everyone who asks receives." (Matt 7:7–8)
4. "What man of you, if his son asks him for bread, will *give* him a stone? You . . . know how to *give* good gifts to your children." (Matt 7:9, 11)
5. "You received without paying [i.e., a gift]; *give* without pay." (Matt 10:8)
6. "*Give* to the poor and you will have treasure in heaven." (Mark 10:21)
7. "I will *give* all this authority and glory to you if you will worship me." (Luke 4:6–7; Matt 4:9)
8. "Because of his importunity, he will rise up and *give* him whatever he needs." (Luke 11:8)
9. "What shall a man *give* in return for his life?" (Matt 16:26)
10. "To him who has even more will be *given*." (Matt 13:12)

These and similar passages raise a host of questions for the anthropologist: Who gives gifts in the biblical world of the first century c.e.? To whom and in which social contexts? What objects or commodities serve as gifts? What obligations are imposed? What is the material or symbolic value of the gifts? What things are *not* given, that is, held back for a specific reason? May one ask for a gift? Is there such a thing as a "pure gift," a gratuity that expects no return? A thorough study would have to deal with all these questions. The limits of the essay require only a partial consideration of such issues, although the significance of the questions will become apparent in the passages and discussion that follow. We commence with an example of "royal gifts."

Gifts to the King/Patron

a. "And when they had opened their treasures, they *presented* to him gifts" (*dōra*; Matt 2:11).

The significance of gift-giving at the beginning of the New Testament and at the beginning of the Gospel of Matthew cannot be overlooked. The action has been theologized, for the context of the presentation of gifts is an act of worship. Seen through the anthropologist's lens, other things come to light. Magi are offering gifts to a (Judean) king (v. 2). As 2:11 makes clear, the relationship is one of patron to client: foreign clients honor Jesus as patron (on patron-client, see Elliott 1996; Malina 1996). Their gifts (*dōra*, gifts of generosity and homage) and their posture confer honor; moreover, they are threshold gifts or gifts of passage (van Gennep 1960), common in ancient cultures and today, which mark beginnings, transitions, ends, and so on. Finally, the gifts come from their treasure (*thēsaurous*), where wealth is stored. Gift-giving scenes from Homer's *Odyssey* indicate that treasure (in Homer, *keimēlion*)—bronze, iron, gold, and so on—possessed not utilitarian wealth but had value as symbolic or prestige wealth.[2] "The twin uses of treasure were in possessing it and giving it away" (Finley 1956:65). But gifts require reciprocal action; what will be given in return to the foreign visitors? They will have to wait, for as Bourdieu (1990:105) argues, the length of time before a countergift is offered is significant: it cannot or should not be immediate (see Eph 4:8–13, in which Jesus' [counter]gifts to the world are not given until his ascension).

b. "All these I will *give* you, if you will fall down and worship me" (Matt 4:9; par. Luke 4:6–7).

The king worshiped and honored with gifts in Matt 2:11 is, with supreme irony, invited to worship Satan and receive even more wealth and treasure in 4:9. What are a few exotic spices compared to the "kingdoms of the world" (v. 8)? In Matt 4:9, Satan offers the gift on a conditional basis, deliverable when the condition has been fulfilled. The promised gift is a challenge,[3] inviting Jesus to a relationship of subordination: Jesus by obedience can become a client of Satan, who will reward him. The exchange is to be reciprocal: worship and subordination for *doxa* and "the kingdoms of this world." Luke's version expands the gift to include power: "I will give you all this authority (*exousian*) and their glory (*doxan*), for it has been delivered to me and I may give it to whom I will" (Luke 4:6). Satan is prepared to give further what he has received, presumably also a gift (*paradedotai*). The dialogue is presented in terms of challenge and riposte. Honor is offered to Jesus both by the invitation to become a client and by the promise of future honor itself. Jesus declines the offer of the gift (Matt 4:10); but it is bad form to refuse a gift, an act that heaps scorn on the challenger: no further exchange is possible. The refusal is grounded in a theological claim, made by citing Deut 6:13, which abruptly halts the dialogue and the temptation scene.

The Reciprocity of Gifts

> "Give *and it shall be* given *to you*. . . . *the measure you* give
> *will be the measure you* get."
>
> —Luke 6:38

Reciprocity of gifts means that a gift, at some later time and in some appropriate way, must evoke a (different) countergift (Bourdieu 1990:98–111). Sahlins speaks of "balanced reciprocity" to denote exchange between social equals within larger kinship groups, such as friends, who exchange gifts of approximately the same worth (1972a:194–95; see Malina 1986). Luke 6:38 is a remarkably succinct statement of a balanced exchange. In the peasant, advanced agrarian society of Jesus' time, would it not be the accepted custom, indeed, the general principle, that "the measure you give will be the measure you get"?[4] If so, we must ask why the statement is formulated as a command: "*Give* (imperative) and it shall be given . . ."?[5] To be sure, the saying (in Luke) is situated in a string of prohibitions and commands: judge not, condemn not, forgive, give. The imperative command corresponds with Mauss's notion of the obligatory nature of giving. But the Maussian model shows that, in ancient societies, gift-giving is outwardly conceived as a *voluntary* action that in reality is *obligatory*. This suggests that Jesus is stating directly what is kept unspoken, hidden below the surface: one is obligated to give. If so, Jesus' command "Give" is at one with what is a moral obligation; the act of giving is required, it is obligatory. The passage designates an audience: the disciples, a great multitude, the sick and troubled (6:17–18)—clearly the nonelite—while 7:1 suggests a mass of people. Thus the command to give is not directed to wealthy elites, called to share their worldly goods with the poor; there is even less necessity to think of wealthy generosity, which is a customary interpretation.

Curiously, the words about the countergift ("and you will receive") are expanded, unlike the preceding imperatives (v. 37) in the series, by an interpretive phrase that emphasizes and heightens the reciprocal action: "good measure, pressed down, shaken together, running over, will be put into your lap" (v. 38). The meaning appears simply to be that one will receive in abundance far more than one gives. Mark 4:24 expresses the idea less poetically: ". . . and still more will be given you." Behind these words lies, it would seem, the principle enunciated by Mauss: "[E]xchange of goods produces an abundance of riches" (1990:14). But the following words in Luke 6:38, "the measure you give will be the measure you get," make an ill fit, for they speak of a rather precise balance.

Jesus' command "give" leaves unspecified to whom his audience is to give. This is neither about "loans" (v. 34) nor about charity to the poor and destitute, for the larger context has already mentioned giving to those who beg (v. 30). Nor can Jesus be referring here to one's enemies, for the relationship to enemies has been treated in verses 27–30. The symmetry of the exchange ("the measure you give will be the measure you get") fits well with Sahlins's model of "balanced reciprocity," the exchange of gifts between members of the same tribe or clan or between friends and neighbors.[6] We conclude that, in Luke 6:38, Jesus speaks of a kinship or domestic economy[7] in which giving and reciprocity are customary and obligatory. Nor is the passage about disinterested giving, the gracious or "pure" gift. The principle is that one *must* give (the addressees named in 6:17–19 do not suggest at all that Luke intends his words for the elites). The result, however, is that such giving calls forth returns that are equal to, or exceed ("pressed down, shaken together, running over"), the initial gift. This is an economic view of abundance, largesse, a generous exchange of gifts among fictive kin who, hearing and obeying Jesus' words, can only be called "honorable" ("blessed") in light of Luke 6:20–23.

Banquets and Gifts

The giving of banquets is one form of gift-giving, according to Mauss's analysis of archaic societies. Of course, primitive and agrarian peasant societies give banquets, too, as do modern folk.

A banquet provides a setting for giving the gift of food, a commodity that due to its very nature cannot be given as a gift in customary ways (Sahlins 1972a:215–19). Many of the most famous gift systems we know of center on food and treat durable goods as if they were food. The potlatch of the American Indians of the Northwest Pacific was originally a "big feed" (Hyde 1983:9). The Chinook term "potlatch"[8] was translated by Mauss as "to nourish or to feed." In ancient societies, relatives have rights over food and thus relatives provide or eat the food of their kinsmen.

Anthropologists are interested in various aspects of banquets and meals, such as food, table manners, purity, social meaning, and the like. A distinction is made between ceremonial and ritual feasts, the former an occasion that "celebrates mutual solidarity," the latter marking "a transition or transformation" (Malina 1993:82; see Neyrey 1996:174). Banquets are, of course, a part of hospitality. In the New Testament, meals "function as boundary markers between groups . . . indicators of hierarchy. . . and as occasions for reciprocity" (Neyrey 1996:171). But at banquets, in addition to the gifts of food and drink, presents are also bestowed (see Gen 43:15–34; 1 Kings 10:13; Dan 5:1, 17; Esther 2:18).

A brief look at Herod's (infamous) banquet (Mark 6:14–29), at which food and gifts are offered, will take us a step further in understanding gift exchange in the New Testament. "Herod on his birthday *gave a banquet* (*deipnon epoiēsen*) for his courtiers and officers and the leading men of Galilee" (Mark 6:21).

As a "birthday banquet," Herod's feast qualifies as a "ritual" feast, marking a transition. The social relations of Herod's feast, clearly, are that of patron-client; the reciprocity is not symmetrical, but it is, Sahlins's terms, balanced. Herod's invited retainers and the elite will not likely invite him to a banquet. But the element of reciprocity is clear: Herod as patron provides food and festivities; his clients will give him the appropriate countergifts of honor, praise, and support.[9] The significance of honor-values attends the entire action: invitations are positive honor-challenges; acceptance and presence at the meal constitute a riposte, which is a countergift. Moreover, the seating arrangements signal honor and rank among the guests, so the symbolic exchange of honor is clear (cf. Mark 12:39; Luke 11:43; 20:46). But let us note the element most salient for our purposes, the *bestowal of gifts* within the banquet setting. Herod Antipas, pleased by Salome's [thus Josephus] dancing, said to her: "Ask me for whatever you wish and I will *give* (it) you" (*dōsō soi*, Mark 6:22). To emphasize the offer being made, Herod vows and says again, "I will *give* it to you" (the echoes of Esther 5:6ff. are unmistakable).

After consulting with her mother, Herod's wife, Salome said: "*Give* me (*dōs moi*) the head of John the Baptist" (v. 25). Later, the guard *gave* the head of John the Baptist to the girl and then she *gave* it to her mother, Herodias. It is a grisly story of gift-giving, with the act of passing along the gift-object emphasized by the multiple use of the root "to give." Herod not only *gives* a banquet, but he *gives* the head of a dead prophet, which is then passed from daughter to mother. It is indeed a gift given within the family—hence generalized reciprocity—which means the countergift can remain outstanding indefinitely. But it is the gift of death. A gift can be poison, as the double meaning of the Greek word *dosis*, or the German word *Gift* (gift, poison), suggest (cf. the ambiguity of *pharmakon* and *venenum*).[10] Herod's gift for Salome is poison for John the Baptist. The narrative exhibits a somewhat elaborate pattern of exchange and of gift-giving and transference: (1) Herod is pleased; (2) he offers a gift to Herodias's daughter, (3) requesting that she, with limitations, stipulate the gift; (4) she makes her request; (5) receiving the gift, she (6) transfers it to her mother. While some gifts may reconcile parties at odds with one another, Herod's gift removes Herodias's grudge by removing a prophet's head.

After this episode follows the story of Jesus' feeding of the multitudes (Mark 6:30–44). We note in passing only two elements significant for our question. (1) Just as Herod, the host, provides food (gifts) for his clients, so does Jesus; compare his words to the disciples: "You *give* them something to eat" (Mark 6:37); ". . . he broke the loaves and *gave* them to his disciples . . ." (v. 41). (2) The contrast between the two scenes, surely intended by their redactional juxtaposition in Mark 6, could not be stronger: the elites dining sumptuously and witnessing actions that lead to murder versus the ragtag group of peasants eating outside, with no festivities and a minimum of food, whose meal ends in "being satisfied" and with overflowing abundance (vv. 42–43), the mark of a generous gift-giver, who, in giving food, offers communion and life.

Requested Gifts

a. The story of Herod and Salome raises an important question: May one *request* a gift? The answer is, of course, that one may (see 1 Kings 10:13). And one can invite a guest to ask for a gift, as Herod does with Salome. But the anthropology of gifts requires closer definition. Thus, is it a *gift as gift* when the object bestowed merely corresponds to a request? Does not a "true" gift come from the heart, out of a desire to bestow a good thing upon someone? In our society, it is not unusual for parents to ask children: What would you like for Christmas this year? But a narrow definition of gift requires that gifts be understood to exclude petition and request. Yet in the realm of patron-client relations, the request for bestowal of some favor, object, or service is customary and is often designated as "gift" in the anthropological literature. Patronage and benefaction in general, however, are not, I mean to argue, about gift-giving in this narrow sense. Nevertheless, biblical passages make it plain that certain cultural-social contexts allow a request for gifts; further, requests are invited, as Herod invites Salome. Here, however, the exchange is within the kinship unit, father to wife's daughter, although the setting is a public ceremonial meal.

b. Other passages illustrate the issue, namely, the precise nature of gift exchange when a gift is requested. The Sermon on the Mount (Matt 7:7–11; cf. Luke 11:9–13) appears to be an exposition of the issue: "Ask, and it will be given to you. . . . Everyone who asks receives" (Matt 7:7–8).

A concrete illustration of the general principle is presented within the context of family: "What man of you, if his son *asks* for bread, will *give* him a stone?" (7:9). If there is doubt that the passage is about gift-giving, 7:11 dispels it by stating that fathers "know how to give *good gifts*" (*dormata agatha*; see Sir 18:17) to their children. The point is that when children ask for gifts, it is in the nature of parenting to bestow good gifts upon them. This is kinship economy, and it operates in the realm of generalized reciprocity. The words of the Lord's Prayer to the heavenly Father, "Give us this day our daily bread" (Matt 6:11), further illustrates the connection of gift and request by placing it in the realm of the divine economy and the metaphor of father-children or patron-client. This suggests a basic distinction between gifts offered in response to a specific request and those that "appear" to be given unmediated, or that are rooted in social contexts in which the giver initiates an exchange by a first gift.[11]

The Gift as Charity

Modern society speaks of charitable gifts. But does charity qualify as gift-giving in the premodern or nonindustrial economies? Put a different way, is the giving of alms a part of the gift-exchange system?

"Sell all that you have and *give* alms . . ." (Luke 12:33). These words were spoken by Jesus to his disciples, according to Luke 12:22.[12] The immediate literary context is an exhortation not to fear. How does the verse relate to the larger system of gift-giving? Significantly, the previous verse states that Jesus' followers will receive a gift, namely, "the kingdom." In view of this, they are to dispossess themselves of their goods and wealth and to "give alms."[13]

To give alms would undermine the normal standards of reciprocity, for if charity is gift, it is not gift exchange. Put another way, Jesus' command moves balanced reciprocity in the direction of generalized reciprocity or of one of its subforms, "chiefly redistribution" (see Moxnes 1988:117). But the keynote is the generosity implied. The command to give alms is in effect an attack on the mutuality that near-kin and friends practice in normalized gift exchange. If so, then the giving of alms in this verse has moved the notion of gift far away from Mauss's model and theory, for, to him, a "true" gift always entails mutuality and solidarity expressed by exchange. Mauss was therefore interested in Emerson's famous essay "Gifts," which speaks of the wound charity does to the one who accepts it. According to Mauss, "the unreciprocated gift still makes the person who has accepted it inferior" (1990:65). If this is true, then almsgiving cannot qualify as a genuine gift,[14] whose purpose always and everywhere means to establish positive human community and relationships. On the other hand, if almsgiving is not and cannot be reciprocated, the relationship between giver and receiver of alms can be understood in terms of fictive kinship. This means that the poor and destitute are not the Other, but family, who, in terms of generalized reciprocity, have received gifts from community or family members; the gift of alms, like other gifts, creates and at the same time establishes ties that bind human beings together.

Gift exchange in the New Testament is attested to much more richly than this brief sampling of passages indicates. Many aspects of the gift remain to be explored in light of the anthropology of the gift, to say nothing of a *theology* of the gift. The exchange of gifts is both an economic and a social activity: giving gifts transfers material goods from one party to another; giving gifts establishes or strengthens already existing interpersonal ties and relationships. Further study of the gift in the Bible would need to explore these twin aspects with much more precision than could be offered here. Nevertheless, what we have seen above may be summarized in a few brief statements.

In general, we have seen that our passages conform to many elements of the basic model set forth at the outset. The highlights may be summarized as follows:

1. There is an *obligation* to bestow gifts; gifts confer honor while at the same time they challenge the receiver both to accept and to respond. Jesus received gifts and was thereby honored and exalted, his claims to status confirmed; but he also refused the gift that had the power to undermine his authority and status. Jesus commanded that gifts be given. And Jesus himself bestowed gifts.

2. Gifts belong to domestic economy (kinship). Fathers/patrons act upon requests for gifts. Clients receive gifts, whether directly requested or not. Reciprocity moves between generalized and balanced.

3. Food and feasts bestow life, like gifts — indeed, they are gifts. Gifts given at feasts are a part of ceremony and the display of wealth, power, and honor. But the potential for gift exchange to bring death, even in commensality, is always a danger. Therefore the gift always possesses a certain ambivalence.

4. The principle of reciprocal exchange is upheld. One receives back what one gets. But the principle does not stand alone, for it is bound up with the imperative "Give."

5. The command to give alms (charity) appears to undermine the principle of exchange. The giving of alms allows no possibility for returning the gift. While this may appear to subvert the creation of a relationship between giver and receiver, it rather establishes a fictive kinship that operates according to generalized reciprocity, which means that the close family members do not need to return gifts, or may delay them indefinitely.

Notes

1. In gift exchange and in commodity exchange, an object or service is transferred from A to B and then in a countertransfer from B to A. It is not the use of money that distinguishes one from the other. Rather, what distinguishes a gift from a commodity exchange is that, in the former, a relationship links the transactors to one another and to the object they transact. "Put most simply, in commodity relations the objects are alienated from the transactors. . . . such objects are treated solely as bearers of abstract value or utility" (Carrier 1995:20).

2. Neyrey (1998:60) argues that the narrative intends to emphasize not the wealth that comes to Jesus but the honor/gifts that uphold his claims. Jesus is not a man of wealth—"his own honor is not tied to wealth as a display of worthiness" in Matthew.

3. On positive and negative challenges, see Malina 2001:34 and Malina and Neyrey 1991:49–52. Neyrey (1998:45–46) notes that "negative challenges explicitly seek to humiliate and shame the person challenged," and understands the temptation story as a negative honor challenge. But if one reads the challenge and response between Satan and Jesus *without* reference to the interpretive framework (Matt 4:1, ". . . tempted by the devil"), it would appear to be a *positive* challenge: it is an invitation to enter a relationship that provides honor and wealth if Jesus will be Satan's client. The hostility that belongs to a negative challenge is not present in the entire dialogue; to be sure, the story is interpreted and understood by the redactor as veiled hostility.

4. Cf. Mark 4:24; Matt 7:2. Neither Mark nor Matthew contains the imperative "give" preceding the phrase "the measure you give."

5. It is striking that Matthew has Jesus say, "*Ask*, and it shall be given you" (7:7), which is not about giving at all, but rather about receiving *because* one has made a request. See below for a consideration of the "request" for a gift.

6. Moxnes's study of the entire Gospel of Luke arrives at quite a different picture: "Luke argues for a system of generalized reciprocity and outright distribution" (1988:155). His claim is that Luke's Jesus is opposed to "negative reciprocity in the form of exploitation of the poor by the powerful, as well as against a balanced and even generalized reciprocity among the well-to-do in which the needy are excluded." Oakman (1986:169), by contrast, sees in Luke 6:38 a claim for generalized reciprocity.

7. The distinction between domestic or kinship economy and political economy is important for understanding the structure of ancient economics. According to Malina (1997:10), "[T]he Jesus tradition, like the pre- or anti-monarchic Israelite traditions, emphasizes reciprocal economic exchanges (kinship economy) and opposes or discourages redistributive economy (political economy)."

8. The literature on the potlatch, a founding concept in anthropology, is enormous. For a recent treatment, see Bracken 1997. On the "anti-potlatch laws," which

prohibited "any Indian festival, dance or other ceremony of which the giving away or paying or giving back of money, goods or article forms a part . . ." (sec. 114 of the Indian Act), see Bracken 1997:167–225.

9. Luke 14:12–14 provides a significant counterpoint to Herod's banquet. In terms of gift exchange and reciprocity, this narrative, which proposes a guest list of the poor, lame, blind, and so on, instead of friends, relatives, and the rich, breaks the norm of balanced reciprocity: "invite the poor and so forth because they cannot *repay* you." See Moxnes (1988:129ff.), who argues that the passage demonstrates a shift from balanced reciprocity to the redistribution model, in which rich give to poor.

10. See Mauss's brief article on the linguistic ambiguity of gift/poison (1997).

11. The Maussian model understands gift exchange to be voluntary while in fact standing under constraint and obligation. But the "first gift" offered in a beginning gift relationship stands outside the net of obligation, according to the sociologist Georg Simmel (1950:392). He asserts that the first gift "has a voluntary character which no return present can have. For to return the gift we are obliged ethically; we operate under coercion." But Mauss himself noted that the "first gift" (the *vaga*), a preliminary present, is given by the Trobrianders as an inducement to potential partners in the *kula* exchange relationship (1990:27).

12. Malina and Rohrbaugh understand Luke 12:33 to be addressed to the rich by virtue of Luke's placement of an earlier tradition after the warning to the rich in vv. 15, 16–21 (1992:359). But this does not solve the literary problem posed by v. 22 ("he said to his disciples") and v. 32 ("little flock"), the more immediate context.

13. See especially Moxnes for an extended discussion and pertinent bibliography (1988:113–23).

14. Mary Douglas begins her forward to Mauss's *Gift* by saying that "charity is meant to be a free gift, a voluntary, unrequited surrender of resources. Though we laud Christian virtue we know that it wounds" (Mauss 1990:vii). She comments that Mauss's book prevents the confusion of donations with gifts.

Works Cited

Bataille, George. 1985. *Visions of Excess: Selected Writings, 1927–1939*. Edited by A. Stoekl. Minneapolis: University of Minnesota Press.

Baudrillard, Jean. 1981. *For a Critique of the Political Economy of the Sign*. Translated by C. Levin. St. Louis: Telos.

———. 1987. "When Bataille Attacked the Metaphysical Principle of Economy." *Canadian Journal of Political and Social Theory* 11, no. 3:59–62.

Belk, Russell. 1979. "Gift-Giving Behavior." In *Research in Marketing*, vol 2, edited by J. E. Sheth, 95–126. Greenwich, Conn.: JAI.

Benveniste, Emil. 1997. "Gift and Exchange in Indo-European Vocabulary." In *The Logic of the Gift*, edited by A. D. Schrift, 33–44. New York: Routledge.

Bourdieu, Pierre. 1990. *The Logic of Practice*. Translated by R. Nice. Stanford, Calif.: Stanford University Press.

Bracken, Christopher. 1997. *The Potlatch Papers: A Colonial Case History*. Chicago: University of Chicago Press.

Burkert, Walter. 1996. "The Reciprocity of Giving." In *Creation of the Sacred: Tracks of Biology in Early Religion*, 32–55. Cambridge: Harvard University Press.

Carrier, James G. 1995. *Gifts and Commodities: Exchange and Western Capitalism since 1700*. New York: Routledge.

Cixous, Helene, and Catherine Clement. 1986. *The Newly Born Woman*. Minneapolis: University of Minnesota Press.

Derrida, Jacques. 1992. *Given Time: I. Counterfeit Money*. Translated by Peggy Kamuf. Chicago: University of Chicago Press.

Douglas, Mary. 1990. "Forward: No Free Gifts." In Mauss 1990:vi–xviii.

Elliott, John H. 1996. "Patronage and Clientage." In *The Social Sciences and the New Testament*, edited by R. L. Rohrbaugh, 144–58. Peabody, Mass.: Hendrickson.

Emerson, Ralph Waldo. 1997. "Gifts." In Schrift 1997:25–27.

Finley, M. I. 1956. *The World of Odysseus*. London: Chatto and Windus.

Godelier, Maurice. 1999. *The Enigma of the Gift*. Translated by Nora Scott. Chicago: University of Chicago Press.

Gregory, C. A. 1982. *Gifts and Commodities*. London: Academic.

Heidegger, Martin. 1962. *Being and Time*. Translated by J. Macquarrie and E. Robinson. New York: Harper & Row.

Herman, Menachem. 1991. *The Tithe as Gift: The Institution in the Pentateuch and in Light of Mauss's Prestation Theory*. Distinguished Dissertation Series 20. San Francisco: Mellen Research University Press.

Hyde, Lewis. 1983. *The Gift: Imagination and the Erotic Life of Property*. New York: Vintage.

Lévi-Strauss, Claude. [1950] 1987. *Introduction to the Work of Marcel Mauss*. Translated by F. Baker. London: Routledge & Kegan Paul.

———. 1969. *The Elementary Structures of Kinship*. Translated by J. H. Bell et al. Rev ed. Boston: Beacon.

Malina, Bruce J. 1986. *Christian Origins and Cultural Anthropology: Practical Models for Biblical Interpretation*. Atlanta: John Knox.

———. 1993. "Feast." In *Handbook of Biblical Social Values*, edited by J. Pilch and B. J. Malina, 81–83. Peabody, Mass.: Hendrickson.

———. 1996. "Patron and Client: The Analogy behind the Gospel." In *The Social World of Jesus and the Gospels*, 143–75. London and New York: Routledge.

———. 1997. "Embedded Economics: The Irrelevance of Christian Fictive Domestic Economy." *Forum for Social Economics* 26:1–20.

———. 2001. *The New Testament World: Insights from Cultural Anthropology.* 3rd ed. Louisville: Westminster/John Knox.

Malina, Bruce J., and Jerome H. Neyrey. 1991. "Honor and Shame in Luke-Acts: Pivotal Values of the Mediterranean World." In Neyrey, ed., 1991:25–65.

Malina, Bruce J., and Richard L. Rohrbaugh. 1992. *Social-Science Commentary on the Synoptic Gospels.* Minneapolis: Fortress Press.

Mauss, Marcel. 1990. *The Gift: The Form and Reason for Exchange in Archaic Societies.* Translated by W. D. Halls. New York: Norton. Originally published in *Année sociologique* 1 (1923–24):30–186.

———. 1997. "Gift, Gift." In Schrift 1997:28–32.

Mitchell, Lynette G. 1997. *Greeks Bearing Gifts: The Public Use of Private Relationships in the Greek World, 435–323 BC.* Cambridge: Cambridge University Press.

Moxnes, Halvor. 1988. *The Economy of the Kingdom: Social Conflict and Economic Relations in Luke's Gospel.* OBT. Philadelphia: Fortress Press.

Neyrey, Jerome H. 1991. "Ceremonies in Luke-Acts: The Case of Meals and Table Fellowship." In Neyrey, ed. 1991:361–87.

———. 1996. "Meals, Food, and Table Fellowship." In *The Social Sciences and New Testament Interpretation*, edited by R. L. Rohrbaugh, 159–82. Peabody, Mass.: Hendrickson.

———. 1998. *Honor and Shame in the Gospel of Matthew.* Louisville: Westminster John Knox.

———, ed. 1991. *The Social World of Luke-Acts: Models for Interpretation.* Peabody, Mass.: Hendrickson.

Oakman, Douglas E. 1986. *Jesus and the Economic Questions of His Day.* SBEC 8. Lewiston, N.Y.: Mellen.

Peterman, Gerald W. 1997. *Paul's Gift from Philippi: Conventions of Gift-Exchange and Christian Giving.* SNTSMS 92. Cambridge: Cambridge University Press.

Sahlins, Marshall. 1972a. "On the Sociology of Primitive Exchange." In Sahlins 1972c:185–230.

———. 1972b. "The Spirit of the Gift." In Sahlins 1972c:149–83.

———. 1972c. *Stone Age Economics.* Chicago: Alderline-Atherton.

Schrift, Alan D., ed. 1997. *The Logic of the Gift: Toward an Ethic of Generosity.* New York: Routledge.

Simmel, Georg. 1950. *The Sociology of Georg Simmel.* trans. ed. Kurt H. Wolff. Glencoe, IL: Free Press.

van Gennep, Arnold. 1960. *The Rites of Passage.* Translated by M. B. Vizedom and G. L. Caffe. Chicago: University of Chicago Press.

An Overview of the Task

19

The Gospels in Comparison
with the Pauline Letters:
What We Can Learn from Social-Scientific Models

Albert Verdoodt

> *Social-scientific criticism involves a process of logic that is
> neither exclusively deductive (from model to material) nor
> inductive (from material to hypothesis), but inclusive of
> both. . . . This requires consideration of realities that are not
> explicit in the material under analysis.* (Elliott 1993:48)

In this essay, I briefly consider the New Testament Gospel documents in comparison with the letters of Paul, in the light of perspectives deriving from the social sciences. Much of what follows has been inspired by the insightful work of Anton Mayer (1983, quoted from an English summary of the work [Malina, Kazmierski, and Hollenbach 1984]). I offer three salient points of comparison. The first deals with social setting and medium of communication. Jesus lived in a rural society; his usual language seems to have been Aramaic. Paul lived in an urban society; his usual language seems to have been Greek. The second point of comparison looks to social organization. Jesus' movement group operated as a faction embedded within the structures and norms of a broader corporate body, the house of Israel. Paul entered into conflict with the house of Israel over fundamental issues, and finally transformed the messianic faction he had entered into an Israelite sect. The final point of comparison has to do with institutional structure. Jesus proclaimed theocracy, a new political religion. In the interim he suggested that his following take the shape of fictive kinship groups, thereby undermining the authority of the blood-kin group and of the patriarchal family. Paul had no interest in a new theocracy for Israel, but adopted the fictive kinship group as a primary form of social bonding, and implanted it among urban Israelite families. He turned families into congregations, in which new members who needed a new primary group could find an alternative household.

1. *Jesus lived in a* rural *society; his usual language seems to have been Aramaic. Paul lived in an* urban *society; his usual language seems to have been Greek.*

If Jesus was a child, then the laws of childhood development applied to him as well. The fact is that Jesus did not belong to higher rural strata. "There are three pieces of data supporting this point: his penurious birth situation, the low status of his parents, and, most clearly, his low class language" (Malina, Kazmierski, and Hollenbach 1984:3). Jesus came to the city of Jerusalem only occasionally. While the vocational socialization of Jesus remains somewhat in the dark, such is not the case with his language.

Aramaic was the language of lower-class people, hence of Jesus as well. The only reason why the sayings of Jesus are found in Koine Greek is that they were presented in the civilized language of the upper classes (Malina, Kazmierski, and Hollenbach 1984:3). These classes were much more present in the cities. Consequently, the Semitisms and Aramaisms we find in the Gospels are an indication of low status and rural origins. Further, the syntax, vocabulary, and style of the presumably authentic sayings of Jesus all point in the same direction.

1. *Syntax:* most of the sentences consist of fewer than five words.
2. *Vocabulary:* only 450 words, one-tenth of the New Testament vocabulary, are found in these sayings.
3. *Style:* Jesus stays in the realm of the concrete.

With Paul, all this changes. According to Luke, Paul indeed was born in a city, was well educated and well treated by the Romans after his arrest in a way that contrasted with the way Jesus was treated at his trial. Paul invokes his Roman citizenship (but see Stegemann 1987). He was not interested in being considered as a peasant, a person without entitlement or rights in Roman law. Further, it would take a specialist in Koine Greek to compose the fine language of Paul's letters. In any case, let us consider:

1. *Syntax:* Paul provides many instances of the optative, of the genitive absolute, and various infinitive structures.
2. *Vocabulary:* Paul quotes pagan poets (1 Cor 15:32; cf. Acts 17:28). He speaks of "mystery" twenty times, while John "the mystic" never mentions the term;

3. *Style:* Paul distances himself from the concreteness of life in the essential concepts of his Christology. Paul's abstract style was duly noted by (pseudo-)Peter: "There are some things in them [i.e., Paul's letters] hard to understand, which the ignorant and unstable twist to their own destruction" (2 Pet 3:16).

In Col 2:14, Paul describes the crucified Jesus as a bill (*cheirographon*) nailed to the cross. He does away with the image of Jesus as a concrete, physical person (Malina, Kazmierski, and Hollenbach 1984:8). "The idea of sacrifice, so alien to Jesus, entails a devaluation of taste, of joy in eating and drinking (labeled 'serving the belly'). Thus the depreciation of elementary needs leads to quite unusual behavior-vegetarianism, avoidance of wine (see Phil 3:19; Rom 14:2 ; 1 Tim 5:23). Devaluation of taste leads to that of touch e.g. in marriage (1 Cor 7:1)" (Malina, Kazmierski, and Hollenbach 1984:11). "In Mark sexuality plays no role; the Pauline tradition (Pauline letters) is never free from concern over it: chastity (10x), adultery (20x), virginity (7x). How to account for this divergence? . . . The Jesus movement, as an uprising of exploited peasants, had no interest in sexuality. This interest was awakened when the wealthy upper class of the cities crushed the revolts. Not by chance does Paul introduce his maxim 'not to deny one another (sexually)' (1 Cor 7.5) in Corinth" (Malina, Kazmierski, and Hollenbach 1984:31).

Mayer treats Paul further in the sections of his book on sexism, anti-Semitism, and capitalism. In all these domains, Paul's texts are overrated. "Luther (a Paul devotee) considered disobedience to authorities a bigger crime than killing a peasant; Calvin required unconditional obedience even to a tyrannical regime" (Malina, Kazmierski, and Hollenbach 1984:13). Further, "if one defines capitalism as the power to turn everything into purchasable commodities, then in Christendom the idea can be traced back to Paul. God sells people into sin, buys them back for a cash payment, brands them as slaves, credits the debt, and so forth. He even sees the body of Christ capitalistically, (God) using his own son to cover the unpayable guilt of people" (Malina, Kazmierski, and Hollenbach 1984:35). As for Jesus, Oakman (1986:198) demonstrates that Jesus envisioned an "egalitarian" solution to the economic and social problems of his day.

2. *Jesus' movement operated as a faction embedded within the structures and norms of its corporate body, the house of Israel. Paul entered into conflict with the house of Israel over fundamental issues, and finally transformed a messianic faction into an Israelite sect.*

In the context of Jesus' lifetime, the Jesus movement is best understood as an Israelite faction interacting with other Israelite factions and coalitions. The concepts of coalition and faction have been adopted from the research of anthropologist Jeremy Boissevain. He defines a "coalition" as a temporary alliance of distinct parties for a limited purpose (Boissevain 1974:171). A "faction," in turn, is "a coalition of persons recruited personally according to structurally diverse principles by or on behalf of a person in conflict with (an)other person(s) with whom they were formerly united, over honor and/or control of resources" (192). The distinguishing feature of the faction is its central focus on the person who recruited its members. At times, some followers, in their turn, will also mobilize members of their own networks. "The nation of Israel, rooted in Torah and Temple, constituted the 'corporate group' within which various Israelite coalitions emerged: Herodians, Pharisees, Essenes/Qumranites, Jesus group and John the Baptist group" (Elliott 1995:76–77).

Neither Jesus nor the Jesus movement was interested in the Gentiles (see Malina 2000). "If we leave out of account quotations, summaries, and allegorical interpretations of parables, we find that (in) Matthew, the only solid evidence for Jesus' acting among the Gentiles consists of the accounts of two cases of healing at a distance (Matt 8:5–13 and parallels; Mark 7:24–30 and parallel), alongside of which the story of the Gadarene demoniac may perhaps be placed" (Jeremias 1958:19). Moreover, Jesus argues: "Go nowhere among the Gentiles, and enter no town of the Samaritans, but go rather to the lost sheep of the house of Israel" (Matt 10:5–6).

In order to recapture the dynamics of Jesus' career in Israel, it is necessary to remember that Mark 6:3 tells us that the people of Nazareth identified him by his trade: "the carpenter," *tekton.* "Admittedly, the word could have a broader sphere of meaning—artisan in general—but by Jesus' time the division of labor in Palestine (at least for carpentry) was sufficiently advanced, so that the specialized meaning could be expected to apply" (Oakman 1986:177). Moreover, "There is some reason to suspect that people who were acquainted with Jesus prior to events related in the gospels hold prominent positions in that tradition" (198). "With regard to the Jesus tradition, it seems to me that the role of Galilean fishing has been severely underrated. Because Jesus . . . took up residence in the fishing village of Capernaum and traveled up, down, and across the Sea of Galilee, the lives of these real fishing families became the fabric from which he wove many of his metaphors and stories [in the Synoptic as well as in the Johannine tradition]" (Hanson 1997:109). Finally, the resurrected Jesus appeared to his disciples on a beach (Luke 24:36–43; John 20:19–23), organized a wondrous catch of fish, and even ate broiled fish (John 21:1–14). All of this demonstrates how he remained within the structure and the norms of the corporate body in which he was socialized.

On the contrary, Paul initially engaged in arduous, physical labor (1 Thess 2:9; 2 Thess 3:7–8; 1 Cor 4:11–12; 9:6 ; 2 Cor 11:27) as tentmaker (Acts 18:3) or leather worker (Meggitt 1998:80). He shared the bitter experience of the urban poor (Stegemann 1987:200–209). Eventually he departed from his customary behavior and created economic relationships exhibiting the generalized reciprocity characteristic of kin groups. This sort of reciprocity has been called "mutualism."

> "Mutualism," as a term, might strike the modern reader as . . . anachronistic . . . it has been associated . . . either with the thought of anarchists . . . or the proponents of the co-operative movement . . . Nevertheless, it is an appropriate term to employ in our study, if it is defined as the implicit or explicit belief that *individual and collective well-being is attainable* above all *by mutual interdependence.*
>
> The "economic mutualism" of the early Christian communities is found principally in the so-called "collection," something which absorbed a great deal of Paul's attention . . . and appears in nearly all his major epistles.
>
> [The collection] was thoroughly *mutual* in its character. . . . *The material assistance given was understood as something that would, in time, be returned, when the situation was reversed* [2 Cor 8:14]. . . .
>
> 2 Thess 3:6–12 provides evidence that mutualism was a guiding assumption of economic relations, not only *between* but also *within* the communities.
>
> The poor who lived in the cities could take only very limited *direct* action in the face of subsistence risk. . . .
>
> Christian mutualism therefore emerged to meet a very real need.
>
> We could . . . look at the evidence for the collection. . . functioning in . . . the . . . general parenesis [especially in the apostle's use of the term "one another" (passim, e.g., Col 3:9, 13), which has been neglected in the study of early ecclesiology.]
>
> It is not the case . . . that I view economy as base and all other forms of social life . . . as superstructural. . . .
>
> But in this particular case [economic mutualism], . . . I believe it has a visible . . . role to play. (Meggitt 1998:157–78)

Meggitt stresses that he has no desire to deny the possibility of a "transcendental referent" nor to dismiss the validity of other explanations. He mentions literary innovations, special terms applied to insiders/outsiders, and perhaps fundamental metaphors. At this point, I find Elliott's contribution (1995:75–95) to be particularly well suited: following the death of Jesus and under changing social conditions, Jesus groups gradually adopted the features and strategies of an Israelite sect.

At the outset of his study, Elliott summarizes the features typical of sects by quoting the sociologist Bryan Wilson (1961:354): "A sect serves as a small and 'deviant' reference-group in which the individual may seek status and privilege and in terms of whose standards he may measure his own talents and accomplishments in more favorable terms than are generally available in the wider society. It alters the context of striving, puts a premium on attributes different from those counted significant in the world, and provides the reassurance of a stable, affective society, whose commitment and value-structure claim divine sanction and divine permanence. Its ideological orientation and its group cohesion provide a context of emotional security so vital to the adherent that its teaching necessarily becomes, for him, objectively true. It is for the individual an adjustment and an accommodation, offered even at the cost of institutional maladjustment." This conception pays much attention to preindustrial societies and offers insight for New Testament interpretation. Moreover, the typology of Wilson directs attention away from the relation between church and sect to the relation between world and sect. It is consequently adaptable to the conditions of early Christianity.

Here I concentrate on some typical sectarian strategies, both social and ideological. My considerations are based on Elliott's essay (1995), in which he presents eight features of the changing conditions that fostered the development of the Jesus-oriented group from messianic faction to Israelite sect, along with twenty-one characteristics of the resulting early Jesus groups. The following three points are characteristic of sects:

1. The establishment and promotion of group consciousness. Examples from the Pauline letters include metaphors for communal identity: holiness; brotherhood; family of God; *ekklēsia*; body of Christ; flock; and so forth. Further, sects entail communal assemblies and rituals, the "we" form of communication and appeal, personal contact via visits and communication through letters. See, for example, Col 1:21–22: "You who were once estranged . . . , he [Jesus] has now reconciled you . . . so as to present you holy and blameless and irreproachable."

2. The fostering of a distinctive identity. Examples include the replacement of the main institutions of the parent body, notably purity rules and calendar. Thus, for example, Col 2:20: "Why do you submit to regulations?"; Col 3:11: "There is no longer circumcised and uncircumcised"; Col 3:17: "Whatever you do, do everything in the name of the Lord Jesus."

   Moreover, Paul is accused before the governor Felix as "a ringleader of the sect of the Nazarenes" (Acts 24:5). Even Israelite leaders in Rome declared: "We would like to hear from you what you think, for with regard to this sect we know that everywhere it is spoken against" (Acts 28:22).

3. The establishment and enforcement of clear and nonporous social and ideological boundaries. Thus, for example, Col 3:9: "You have stripped off the old self with its practices"; Col 4:5: "Conduct yourself wisely toward outsiders."

The sectarian struggle with the parent body was intense precisely because it was an interethnic conflict. Eventually, members of this Israelite sect would be labeled pejoratively by outsiders as "partisans of the Christ," or "Christ-lackeys" (*Christianoi*), a label that could gradually supplant all others and preserve forever the group's common Israelite origin but distinctive identity (Elliott 1995:92).

Finally, viewing the emergence of the Jesus group through these lenses begins to provide social scenarios according to which early Jesus-group literature can be read perceptively and interpreted as expressions of factional or sectarian consciousness and purpose. As a result, modern interpreters can gain a clearer understanding of the pragmatic dimensions of these writings and of the factors determining their content, organization, and rhetorical aims and strategies (Elliott 1995:91).

3. *Among his following, Jesus created fictive kinship groups undermining the authority of the blood-kin group and of the patriarchal family. Paul accepted this alternative form of social bonding, but implanted it in urban families. He turned families into congregations, in which the Jesus-group members who needed a new primary group could find an alternative household.*

For the period prior to the advent of the new theocracy, Jesus redefined the role of the family for his following: "Whoever loves father or mother more than me is not worthy of me; and whoever loves son or daughter more than me is not worthy of me" (Matt 10:37). "As they were going along the road, someone said to him: 'I will follow you wherever you go.' And Jesus said to him: 'Foxes have holes, and birds of the air have nests; but the Son of Man has nowhere to lay his head.' To another he said: 'Follow me.' But he said: 'Lord, first let me go and bury my father.' But Jesus said to him: 'Let the dead bury their own dead; but as for you, go and proclaim the kingdom of God.' Another said: 'I will follow you, Lord; but let me first say farewell to those of my home.' Jesus said to him: 'No one who puts a hand to the plow and looks back is fit for the kingdom of God'" (Luke 9:57–62).

Similarly, "Jesus' mother and his brothers came, and standing outside, they sent to him and called him. A crowd was sitting around him; and they said to him: 'Your mother and your brothers and sisters are outside, asking for you.' And he replied: 'Who are my mother and my brothers?' And looking at those who sat around him, he said: 'Here are my mother and my brothers! Whoever does the will of God is my brother and sister and mother'" (Mark 3:31–35). This perspective is underscored in the parable of the judgment: "And the king will answer them: 'Truly I tell you, just as you did to one of the least of these who are members of my family, you did it to me'" (Matt 25:40).

The surrogate-family model has two exceptions: "Whoever gives his wife a certificate of divorce and marries another commits adultery" (Matt 19: 9); and "Anyone [who] tells father and mother: 'Whatever support you might have had from me is Qorban' (that is, an offering to God)—then you no longer permit doing anything for a father or mother [is] making void the word of God" (Mark 7:11–13). In the redefined kin group, "You are not to be called rabbi. . . . And call no one father. . . . Nor are you to be called instructors. . . . The greatest among you will be your servant" (Matt 23:8–11).

Paul, in turn, entertains a dialogue with the cultural forces of a patriarchal and rigidly stratified society. Thus, for example, the extent to which the Pauline writings favor slave owners over slaves is indicated by statistics. In all, 16 percent of his words of exhortation are directed to owners, but 84 percent to slaves. (The passages are Col 3:22; 4:1; Eph 6:5–9; 1 Tim 6:1–2; Titus 2:9–10). Of course, there is the personal and timely letter of Paul to his disciple Philemon, especially verse 16: "Do no longer consider [Onesimus] as a slave, but more than a slave, a beloved brother . . . both in the flesh and in the Lord." "But Paul is not so vocal when it comes to how he expects Philemon to put this into action. The only thing that comes through very clearly is that Paul expects him to practice hospitality to his slave. . . . Paul has no intention to overturn Philemon's position as host and benefactor. . . . Paul expects Onesimus to accept whatever decision Philemon will make" (Sandnes 1997:161–62).

The starting point of Paul's churches was normally the conversion of the paterfamilias, who embraced the "gospel of God" together with his whole household. This is witnessed in the book of Acts in particular. In telling about the conversion of households, Acts is reliable: the embryo of the community was a family. The household was turned into a congregation. In light of this fact, we have to imagine the circumstances caused by an individual embracing the Jesus-group ideology. Many converts needed a new primary group, and for them the Jesus-group fellowship that they joined took the role of an alternative family (see Sandnes 1997:153). But this alternative family was embedded in the structures and behaviors of the traditional Mediterranean family. In particular, the *household codes* represent not so much the institutionalization of early Jesus groups as the codes' injection into the stream of family tradition (e.g., Eph

6:4). "The *Pastorals* lay some stress on the bearing and raising of children and assume an ideal of 'obedient'/ 'believing' children as a key mechanism for the continuation of the Christian tradition into the (now indefinite) future. Christianity thus becomes a sustainable tradition which can begin to create its own 'familial' and ancestral 'customs'" (Barclay 1997:77).

As a case in point, let us consider Paul's rejection of desire in sex:

> The treatment of desire by ancient philosophers and even (medical) doctors has recently received new attention. Early Christians were, of course, also concerned about the control of desire. What is striking, and important for the placement of early Christianity in ancient culture, is the radical difference between the therapy of desire among the ancient (medical) doctors and philosophers, on the one hand, and early Christian writers, on the other. The apostle Paul in particular viewed sexual desire as a dangerous pollution that must be extirpated from the body entirely. . . . Paul viewed marriage not as the legitimate arena for controlled sexual expression of desire, but as a prophylaxis against desire. Sex within marriage for Paul was not the proper expression of desire but the means for the exclusion of desire entirely. Once desire is seen as an evil, foreign, polluting agent, it is clear why physicians' and most philosophers' solution to the problem of desire could not be entertained by Paul. Paul's views would have been viewed as "superstitious" by the professionally trained therapists of desire in his days. (Martin 1997:209).

In contrast, we have noted previously that, in Mark, sexuality played no role. Moreover, the *Gospel of Thomas*, in spite of its ascetic traits, never mentions marriage or sexual continence. A saying like Luke 20:35, "[T]hose who are considered worthy of that age . . . neither marry nor are given in marriage," cannot be found in *Thomas* (see Uro 1997:223).

Nevertheless, it is not possible simply to state that Paul replaced the assumed egalitarian community structures of the Gospels with patriarchal ascetic structures, especially when he states: "If any believer has a wife who is an unbeliever, and she consents to live with him, he should not divorce her. And if any woman has a husband who is an unbeliever, and he consents to live with her, she should not divorce him. . . . But if the unbelieving partner separates, let it be so; in such a case the brother or sister is not bound" (1 Cor 7:12–13, 15).

In the New Testament, Jesus groups conceived of themselves as forming "the household of God." To have a proper understanding of the family metaphors involved, it is necessary to bring together questions about what the documents say and questions of the historical and social contexts of these documents. Otherwise, family metaphors may easily be seen as referring solely to a spiritual relationship. Hence I adopt the perspective of Sandnes, who writes: "My thesis is that in the family terms of the New Testament old and new structures come together. There is a convergence of household and brotherhood structures. The New Testament bears evidence of the process by which new structures emerged from within the household structures. What we see in the New Testament is not an egalitarian community which is being replaced by patriarchal structures; the brotherhood-like nature of the Christian fellowship is in the making, embedded in household structures" (Sandnes 1997:156).

Works Cited

Barclay, J. M. 1997. "The Family as the Bearer of Religious Culture in Judaism and Early Christianity." In *Constructing Early Christian Families*, edited by H. Moxnes, 66–80. New York and London: Routledge.

Baumgarten, Albert F. 1997. *The Flourishing of Jewish Sects: An Interpretation*. Leiden: Brill.

Boissevain, J. 1974. *Friends of Friends: Networks, Manipulators, and Coalitions*. New York: St Martin's.

Elliot, John H. 1993. *What Is Social-Scientific Criticism?* GBS. Minneapolis: Fortress Press.

———. 1995. "The Jewish Messianic Movement: From Faction to Sect." In *Modeling Early Christianity*, edited by P. F. Esler, 75–95. New York and London: Routledge.

Hanson, K. C. 1997. "The Economy of Galilean Fishing and the Jesus Tradition." *BTB* 27:99–111.

Jeremias, Joachim. 1958. *Jesus' Promise to the Nations*. trans. S. H. Hooke. Studies in Biblical Theology 24. Naperville, IL: Allenson.

Malina, Bruce J. 2000. "Three Theses for a More Adequate Reading of the New Testament." In *Practical Theology: Perspectives from the Plains*, edited by M. G. Lawler and G. S. Risch, 33–60. Omaha: Creighton University Press.

Malina, Bruce J., Carl Kazmierski, and Paul W. Hollenbach. 1984. *Summary of Anton Mayer, "Der zensierte Jesus: Soziologie des Neuen Testaments."* Omaha, Neb.: Private printing.

Martin, Dale B. 1997. "Paul without Passion: On Paul's Rejection of Desire in Sex and Marriage." In *Constructing Early Christian Families*, edited by H. Moxnes, 201–15. New York and London: Routledge.

Mayer, Anton. 1983. *Der zensierte Jesus: Soziologie des Neuen Testaments*. Freiburg im Breisgau: Walter.

Meggitt, Justin J. 1998. *Paul, Poverty and Survival*. Edinburgh: T. & T. Clark.

Oakman, Douglas E. 1986. *Jesus and the Economic Questions of His Day*. SBEC 8. Lewiston, N.Y.: Mellen.

Sandnes, K. O. 1997. "Equality within Patriarchal Structures: Some New Testament Perspectives on the Christian Fellowship as a Brother- or Sisterhood and a Family." In *Constructing Early Christian Families*, edited by H. Moxnes, 150–65. New York and London: Routledge.

Stegemann, Wolfgang. 1987. "War der Apostel Paulus ein romischen Burger?" ZNW 78:200–229.

Uro, R. 1997. "Asceticism and Anti-familial Language in the *Gospel of Thomas*." In *Constructing Early Christian Families*, edited by H. Moxnes, 216–34. New York and London: Routledge.

Wilson, B. R. 1961. *Sects and Society: A Sociological Study of the Elim Tabernacle, Christian Science, and Christadelphians.* Berkeley: University of California Press.

———. 1973. *Magic and the Millennium: A Sociological Study of Religious Movements of Protest among Tribal and Third-World Peoples.* New York: Harper & Row.

Index of Ancient Sources

Index of Subjects

proverbs, 179
psychohistory, 65, 66, 84, 115
psychology, 15, 22, 23, 41, 43, 65, 66, 84, 100, 104, 105, 111, 113, 114, 121, 130, 155, 157, 186, 202–5
public, 10, 13, 20, 34, 35, 37–39, 89–93, 95, 99, 117, 122, 123, 125, 128, 139, 150, 162–65, 167–69, 171, 173, 175, 196, 226, 234, 238, 241, 246, 248, 249, 264, 270, 273, 299, 305, 321, 351, 352, 358, 364
purification, 91, 192
purity, 24, 48, 69, 77, 81, 86, 91–93, 95–97, 99–101, 181, 208, 209, 214–17, 219, 238, 356, 372
purity rules, 91, 372
reading, 3, 21, 23, 48, 85, 86, 154, 155, 162, 210, 217, 271, 299, 326, 330, 345, 348, 376
reciprocity, 58, 59, 176, 315, 347, 350, 352, 359, 361
redistribution, 289, 359, 362
relationships, 25, 37, 59, 76, 77, 87, 93, 105, 159, 169, 175, 181, 182, 185, 204, 218, 254, 257, 263, 266, 267, 273, 301, 302, 314–17, 323, 325, 326, 329, 336, 359, 360, 364, 371
reputation, 99, 167, 178, 260, 293, 295

resentment, 12
reversal, 47, 141, 175, 180, 182
righteousness, 67, 113, 181
riposte, 6, 69, 109, 167, 168, 352, 355, 357
ritual, 13, 66, 74, 85, 107, 109, 117, 123, 124, 127, 131, 133, 137, 138, 141, 146–51, 153–55, 192, 208, 273, 294, 356, 357
roads, 306, 307, 311, 324, 327, 328
rural, 36, 89, 92, 93, 98, 99, 166, 257, 285, 291, 296, 298, 299, 302, 324, 326, 328, 342, 367, 368
ruralized society, 7
sabbath, 48, 51, 53, 54
sacred, 92, 221, 293, 351, 363
sacrifice, 22, 192, 214, 349, 369
salvation, 97, 103, 227–29, 240, 273, 320
Samaritan, 69, 185, 187, 188, 191–202, 204, 238, 299, 330
satan, 88, 161, 162, 168, 169, 172, 232, 246, 247, 354, 361
science, ix, 17, 19, 21, 23, 45, 60, 86, 99–101, 119, 130, 179, 183, 214, 254, 255, 266, 326, 364, 377
scientific method, 3
scribes, 165, 166, 172, 178, 264, 312, 346
self-consciousness, 27, 40–42
shame, 6, 23, 24, 50, 115, 155, 163, 168, 173, 176,

178, 180, 183, 189, 361, 364
sharing, 11, 32, 175, 195, 196
sin, 68–70, 79, 80, 160, 192, 369
slavery, 240, 257, 265, 276
slaves, 78, 240, 257, 265, 369, 374
social, vii-x, 3–5, 8, 10, 12, 15–25, 28, 29, 31–33, 35, 38, 41, 42, 47, 52–61, 65, 66, 71, 72, 74, 76, 77, 79, 81–93, 95–101, 104, 105, 108, 109, 112–15, 122–26, 128, 129, 131, 137, 138, 145, 148, 149, 151–56, 159, 161–66, 171–83, 185–88, 190, 193–95, 197–205, 207, 209, 210, 215–20, 226, 228, 236, 244, 245, 247, 250–53, 255, 260, 261, 263–68, 271, 273, 274, 276–81, 283–304, 306, 313–16, 318, 319, 321, 323–32, 335–38, 341–53, 355–60, 362–64, 367, 369, 371–73, 375, 376
social identity, 20, 72, 79, 90, 186, 187, 190, 193–95, 197, 199, 202, 205
social location, 42, 348
social network, 89, 301, 302, 306, 313, 318, 324, 327, 329, 331, 332
social psychology, 15, 22, 23, 65, 66, 84, 100, 105, 113, 114, 155, 186, 202–5

Index of Authors

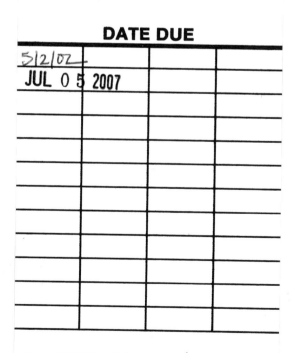

DATE DUE

5/2/02			
JUL 0 5 2007			